dams and other disasters

a century of the army corps of engineers in civil works

dams
and
other
disasters

a century of the army corps of engineers in civil works

by
arthur e. morgan

an extending horizons book

PORTER SARGENT PUBLISHER
11 Beacon Street • Boston, MA 02108

Porter Sargent Publisher, 11 Beacon St., Boston, MA 02108

Books by Arthur E. Morgan

Edward Bellamy—A Biography

Nowhere Was Somewhere

The Philosophy of Edward Bellamy

Search for Purpose

The Community of the Future and the Future of the Community

The Small Community, Foundation of a Democratic Life: What It Is and How to Achieve It

The Heritage of Community

Bottom Up Democracy: The Affiliation of Small Democratic Units for Common Service

Industries for Small Communities

A Business of My Own: Possibilities in Small Community Occupations and Industries

Design in Public Business

The Long Road

The Miami Conservancy District

Compendium of Antioch Notes

Books About Arthur E. Morgan

A Road to Creativity: Arthur Morgan, Engineer, Educator, Administrator
By Clarence J. Leuba

introduction

By Paul H. Douglas
Former Senator from Illinois, 1948-1966

This is a remarkable book by a remarkable man. Arthur Morgan at the age of 93 can look back on a career of great influence and public service. After working as a hydraulic engineer for the Department of Agriculture, with only a high school education, he was chosen in 1913 by the flood prevention committee of Dayton for devising and constructing an adequate system of water control and management, at first for the City of Dayton, and then for the entire Miami Valley.

The Valley had just experienced what, up to that time, was the most disastrous flood in American history. Two hundred people were drowned, and hundreds of millions of dollars worth of property destroyed.

Dayton was a center of innovation and invention. John H. Patterson had developed the cash register into a national institution, Wilbur and Orville Wright had given birth to the "flying machine," which soon became the airplane, and Kettering was at work on his inventions culminating in the self-starter. Morgan was of the same breed.

Dayton turned to its first citizen, John H. Patterson, who with his great industrial plant above the flood level, had served an heroic part in flood relief, and caused the public to forget and forgive earlier criticism of corporation policy. He became the self-appointed chairman of the Flood Prevention Committee, but he shortly delegated that function to his vice president, Edward A. Deeds, who acted, first as chairman of the Flood Prevention Committee, and then as chairman of the later organized Conservancy District, for thirty years.

The Flood Prevention Committee, backed by the scientific and innovative bent of Mr. Deeds, tolerated an innovative and creative program by Morgan which might not have been tolerated by more conservative engineers, and certainly not by the U.S. Corps of Engineers.

Morgan scoured the country for engineers of first-rank competence, skill and daring, who would not be afraid to depart from convention in a field which called for action beyond precedent. Some of their research results stand today as classics in their field.

He also pioneered in designing a "conservancy district" and a board which would treat the system as a whole, instead of subjecting it to the anarchy of conflicting local and county governments. The program was helped by Governor James M. Cox of Ohio, the innovative newspaperman and governor, who in 1920 was the Democratic candidate for President, with Franklin Roosevelt as his running mate.

Nearly sixty years have passed since these new ventures were begun, with major features in direct disagreement with the "sacred" code of the Corps of Engineers, and of their Bible, *The Physics and Hydraulics of the Mississippi River.* During that time the Miami Valley has been immune from flood destruction. Morgan's program has met the test of time and experience.

Morgan had earlier formed an engineering company which gave conspicuously good advice and service to communities located on tributaries of the Mississippi. The United States Corps of Engineers, putting its trust in higher and higher levees, felt itself threatened. It launched an offensive which has continued for many years.

When Morgan has been proved right, as he has been in reservoirs and upstream control, the Corps has executed a strategic retreat, only to emerge after a time with a rewriting of history, by which the Corps could be represented as the sponsor and originator of the programs they had originally opposed.

Morgan has continued as a consulting engineer, but during the last half-century his chief efforts have been in other fields. In 1920 he took over the presidency of nearby Antioch College, founded by Horace Mann. Antioch had been allowed to decline almost to its death. By a series of experimental educational reforms, including the adoption of the cooperative plan of alternate semesters, or quarters, of study and work in an outside job, and the recruitment of a keen young faculty, Morgan so built up Antioch that it became and has remained a pioneer type of American college.

Then in 1933, when Morgan was in his middle fifties, came his appointment by Franklin Roosevelt as chairman of the Tennessee Valley Authority. Here he designed and built the model dams which originally generated the power, and he laid out the communities which, like Norris, grew up in their wake.

During the 40's, 50's, and 60's, Morgan busied himself with his private engineering firm and with a variety of good causes. He indulged in a variety of cultural interests. A fascinating one was his discovery that the great prehistoric empire of Peru was the basis of Sir Thomas More's *Utopia*. In his *Nowhere Was Somewhere* Morgan argued that Sir Thomas More's *Utopia* (Nowhere), instead of being a fictionalized cover for More's romance, was based on the actual story as narrated by a Portuguese sailor of the pre-conquest Inca empire he had found in Peru.

I was convinced by this book alone when the correspondence columns of the London *Times* showed that Professor H. Stanley Jevons of the University of Singapore (and son of the great Stanley Jevons) had independently come to the same conclusion. I have waited for years for a further discussion of this most interesting literary hypothesis, but have not found it. It has reminded me of how Morgan discovered much earlier in his life the closest living relatives of Abraham Lincoln in the mountain lands of rural Missouri and Arkansas.

But this is perhaps enough about Arthur Morgan, the man. In this book, he reviews the whole history of the civil works of the Army Engineers. He correctly traces it as being based on the West Point tradition first enunciated by its founder and first Superintendent, Sylvanus Thayer.

Thayer was a passionate admirer of Napoleon and studied the essentials of his system. Unity and esprit de corps have always been emphasized at West Point. Unfortunately, this hardened into a strong resistance to change and a deep-rooted dislike for civilian initiative and authority. In education, it has led to an emphasis upon memory and recitation and a shunting aside of originality and the critical appraisal of alternatives. It is this tradition, combined with its spiritual attributes, which Morgan holds as being responsible for the Corps' many failures.

After some general considerations, the historical scene opens on the Corps' efforts to defeat and disgrace the brilliant engineer James Buchanan Eads in building the great steel arch bridge across the Mississippi at St. Louis. As Morgan shows, the Corps opposed and ridiculed Eads' insistence upon the steel arch, which put all foundations on the underlying bedrock, and limited the height of the arches. Fortunately, Eads finally prevailed. The St. Louis bridge has now stood for a century and has been proved an engineering marvel.

But the Corps did not learn. It opposed with equal vigor Eads' plan for jetties at the outlet of the Mississippi below New Orleans. These would narrow the effective width of the river, cause a faster flow of the water, and hence lead to the reduction of sedimentation and the deepening of the river. This of course would greatly improve navigation. The Corps favored, instead, a ship canal from New Orleans to the Gulf.

Again, Congress stood behind Eads and he was again vindicated by experience. Having failed, and with experience against them, the Corps attempted to rewrite history by claiming that they had originated the idea of using jetties.

The scene now shifts to the national hydraulic laboratory. Building on European experience, Morgan had initiated this for the Miami Conservancy District as early as 1915. Senator Randell of Louisiana sponsored this in 1922, backed by the able engineer, John R. Freeman. For fifty years the Corps had fought the very idea; then they supported it, provided it could be under their direction. With the aid of President Hoover—himself an engineer—such a laboratory was finally authorized in 1930. Along with the great floods of 1927 and 1936, this disproved some of the essential shibboleths upon which the Corps had always based their work, namely: (1) opposition to reservoirs, (2) the policy of levees only, (3) the opposition to cutoffs across bends in the river.

The last direct conflict which Morgan had with the Corps was over the Kinzua dam and reservoir on the upper Allegheny River. This was pushed by the Corps, but required the displacement of about 2000 members of the Seneca tribe of Indians, whose rights to the land which was to be inundated were guaranteed by a treaty that the federal government had signed in 1794.

The Senecas did not want to agree, but the Corps was determined to ride roughshod over them. The Quakers and the tribe asked Morgan to serve as a consultant. He devised an alternative plan. This was to utilize the Conewango reservoir site. This would have stored far more water, and protected the Indians. The excess floodwater also would have ultimately flowed into Lake Erie and not the Ohio. I was then a member of the Senate, and after some study of the alternatives, concluded that Morgan was right. The Corps, however, prevailed and we have been saddled with the Kinzua dam and reservoir.

Morgan makes his history clear and definitive by an incredibly voluminous documentation of the correspondence, newspaper and periodical stories, and Congressional hearings and reports. To me, he has made out an airtight case, and the Corps in justification to itself will have to prepare an answer.

What should their answer be? If they continue their former policy of abusing their critics, they will only meet with intensified disapproval. For the American public has become convinced by Arthur Morgan's long life of combining high technical competence with a devotion to public service. Those who feel this way will believe that Arthur Morgan should be honored and not run down.

If the Corps is wise, they will take this book to heart and study the author's criticisms. Then it is hoped that in a manly fashion they will admit their errors and the correctness of Morgan's criticism. It will be interesting to see what the Corps does. I am not an absolute cynic, and I still have hope. But the time is short.

Senator Paul H. Douglas
Washington, D.C.
August 1971

who wrote this book?

Commonly an author gathers and presents significant data concerning his subject. Here the situation is different. The value of this book depends not only on skillful presentation, but upon judgment concerning a wide range of the activities of the Corps, including the general character of engineering, ecology and fundamental human relations. That being the case, the public has a right to know who wrote the book. Its worth will depend in no small degree on answers to that question. Arthur E. Morgan is 93 years old. Few of his contemporaries are living. Among those few have been found a number of persons who have worked intimately with him, and who can speak with authority. Their expressions are included in the following biographical statements.

From J. Dudley Dawson, Vice-President and Dean of Students, Emeritus, Antioch College, Yellow Springs, Ohio

Arthur Morgan has combined the utilitarian concern for preventing flood damage with human values, aesthetic consideration, economic use of resources and the needs of ecology.

In the Miami River Valley in Ohio, through his leadership a system of dams was designed and built which not only have continuously protected the lives and property of the citizens of Dayton and the Miami Valley but have provided recreational areas and conservation of agricultural values as well.

The economic, political and social foundation for launching this Dayton flood control project grew out of the ingenious invention of the Miami Conservancy District, a product of Morgan's vision and efforts. In fact in the development of the new form of regional organization, Morgan wrote the flood control laws for Ohio which are now found on the statute books of several states. The Dayton project stands as an early demonstration of city, county and state coordination and organization; local financing and management; engineering planning and competence; resolution of varied interests; and satisfying environmental and human benefits.

Through the years Arthur Morgan's name has been identified with flood control and land reclamation in many states: Alabama, Arkansas, Colorado, Florida, Louisiana, Minnesota, Missouri, New Mexico, Ohio and Texas. He has served as consultant on river development projects in this country and abroad, among them for the Damadar River in India and the Volta River Dam project in Ghana.

In 1933 President Franklin D. Roosevelt appointed Arthur Morgan Chairman of the Tennessee Valley Authority. In the T.V.A. undertaking, Morgan's knowledge of engineering and flood control and his commitment to human welfare were given expression. His creative leadership was largely responsible for setting the T.V.A. pattern for total regional development, which has become an international model of economic, physical and social planning for a river valley. Morgan's later break of relations with President Roosevelt and his subsequent removal from the T.V.A. Board of Directors arose out of differences of philosophy and personalities within the Board. His overall concept was in contrast to ideas of the other directors, who were concerned with power and fertilizer interests. The controversy over the ethical phases of the execution of the power program does not detract from his enormous contribution and responsibility for the concept and initiation of the total T.V.A. program. The quality and economy in the design and construction of the T.V.A. dams reflect the high caliber of Morgan's engineering staff, many of whom had worked with him over a period of years.

It is out of this lifetime background of experience, wisdom and public service that Arthur Morgan writes his critique of the Army Corps of Engineers. He has had an almost unique opportunity to observe the functioning of the Army Engineers over a period of years in a variety of situations, and to evaluate the far-reaching effects of much of their work on the ecology and environment in several areas of the country, and on its engineering effectiveness.

My forty-six years of personal and working association with Arthur Morgan, including two years (1933-35) as Director of Training for the T.V.A., have provided an intimate acquaintance with the range of his concerns, experience and wisdom as an engineer, an educator and a public servant. I know the depth of his concern for the shortcomings he has observed first hand in the work of the Corps of Army Engineers. Others have made similar observations which have been recently publicized. Arthur Morgan's carefully documented treatise will shed light on many of what he perceives as mistakes of the Corps and why they were made.

This enlightening revelation of the working style and some of the ill effects of a powerful agency, which have heretofore been largely unchecked, comes at a time when public interest and attention is focused on the many adverse factors affecting the quality of our environment. In his usual lucid style Arthur Morgan illuminates basic ideological and operational faults in the practice of the U.S. Corps of Army Engineers, for which correction seems to be far overdue. November 27, 1970.

About Arthur E. Morgan
By Harry Wiersema, Assistant to Chief Engineer of the Tennessee Valley Authority.

My first acquaintance with Dr. Morgan was in 1914. I was an engineer on the construction of the Mississippi River Bridge at Memphis for several years. I had already heard of him through Mr. Albert Fry, who was working for the Morgan Engineering Company of which Dr. Morgan was President. One Sunday I dropped in to the Unitarian Church in Memphis and to my surprise heard him give an interesting and inspiring sermon as a lay reader.

This led me to want to know him better, and I was impressed to find that he carried out his ethical and moral principles in conducting his engineering organization, bearing out the philosophy he had expressed in his sermon. I also became familiar with the work of his company in drainage and flood control throughout the South, which appealed to me as a very commendable public service—an engineering company guided by the highest ethical and humanitarian principles.

It was appealing to me, therefore, after finishing a world war assignment in 1919, to accept employment with his company. By that time he himself had left Memphis to become Chief Engineer of the Miami Conservancy in Ohio and to found the Dayton Morgan Engineering Company in Dayton, Ohio, of which he became President. However, he maintained his interest in the Memphis company, and contributed to the success of both companies for more than a decade. During this period I came in frequent contact with him during his visits to the Memphis office, or occasionally when I visited the Dayton project, the Miami Conservancy District, which turned out to be perhaps the most successful flood control project in history.

This was due entirely to Dr. Morgan's genius and inventiveness in using automatically controlled storage dams to retain flood waters in five reservoirs during flood crests, and releasing them at pre-determined rates, thus preventing major damage to the cities of Dayton and Hamilton, as well as to agricultural land. The successful construction of this outstanding project, during the stress of World War One, and the assembly of a superb engineering and construction organization, was also proof of his management ability, and the soundness of his engineering and management ideas.

My contacts with Dr. Morgan became much more intimate when he was appointed Chairman of the Board of Directors of the Tennessee Valley Authority in 1933, and I became an assistant engineer with T.V.A. at its headquarters in Knoxville. During the early years of T.V.A. I was assigned to assist the Chairman in preparing budgets and defending them before the Congressional Appropriations Committee in Washington. This experience led me to greatly admire his genius in developing the engineering plan, his grasp of the essentials and purposes of the entire T.V.A. program, and his effectiveness in the presentation to Congress.

It was during these years that I also became aware of his breadth of knowledge of social and economic problems, and his resourcefulness and foresight in proposing solutions to many of these problems. Reviewing these years, it is amazing to realize how many of his ideas turned out to be eminently successful, in spite of insistent opposition to such innovations.

As Chairman of the Board as well as in his capacity of Chief Engineer his insistence on thoroughness in engineering analysis greatly influenced the work of his engineering staff in developing the most efficient and economical engineering plan. Not only was he mainly responsible for this engineering plan which was in his own field, but also he was the leader in many other fields; in forestry, ceramics, cooperatives, and the economics of power, to mention only a few.

In all of the activities carried out by the T.V.A. Board, Dr. Morgan could always be counted on to consider the ethics and human problems involved. In fact, it was his insistence on honesty and integrity in all T.V.A. dealings, including those involving political situations, that led to his severance before the expiration of his term. By this time he had made an impressive impact on the plans and policies of T.V.A. development, so that much of the success of this project must be credited to the foundation he laid.

The friendship with him made during these formative years of T.V.A. has lasted after he left in 1937. During all these years I have never failed to admire his consistency in advocating ethical and humanitarian principles in all his activities, in his consulting and community work. One instance of this is the cooperative project at Celo, in the Blue Ridge Mountains of North Carolina, a community preserving simple living in a setting of rare beauty; and the Arthur Morgan School there dedicated to developing the basic virtues of work and education for learning to live together. He has maintained his interest in this project throughout the years, contributing his knowledge and skills to its benefit.

Another is Community Service, Inc., of Yellow Springs, Ohio, which he founded and headed during many years of service to small communities, and which has contributed much to the development of important aspects of life, such as his booklet on *Education for Engineers*.

It is as an engineer and educator that he has made his finest contribution, to movements of national and international importance—in Ghana, India, Finland and Mexico. His influence on the development of our civilization during his long life has had and will continue to have a profound effect.

Service Record of Harry Wiersema, Knoxville, Tennessee

I. *Engineering Record*

1914-17   Assistant Construction Engineer with Ralph Modjeski, Consulting Engineer, Chicago, Illinois, on Mississippi River Bridge at Memphis, Eads Bridge at St. Louis, etc.

1917-19   Assistant Supervising Engineer, U.S. Navy Yards, Norfolk, Virginia, construction of buildings and naval yard facilities.

1919-33   Supervising Engineer, Morgan Engineering Company of Memphis, Tennessee. Planning, design, and construction of drainage, levee, flood protection, highway, and irrigation projects.

1933-60   Tennessee Valley Authority, Knoxville, Tennessee. From 1938 to date, Assistant to the Chief Engineer.

II. *Non-Engineering Organizations (presently a Board Member)*

East Tennessee Civil Liberties Union (past president)
American Civil Liberties Union of Tennessee (vice president)
Knoxville Community Action Committee
Knoxville United Nations Association (president)
Knoxville Human Relations Council
Knoxville Symphony Society (Honorary)

III. *Consulting Assignments*

U.S. Study Commission for Southeast River Basin
Development and Resources Corporation—New York and Iran
R. W. Beck and Associates, Seattle
International Power and Engineering Consultants, Vancouver, B.C.
October 3, 1970

About Arthur E. Morgan

By Albert S. Fry, former director, hydraulic laboratory, Tennessee Valley Authority.

I first came to know Arthur E. Morgan in 1913 when I went to work for the Morgan Engineering firm in Memphis, Tennessee, which had been formed a few years earlier by Mr. Morgan and a fellow engineer, Leroy Hidinger. Both had been working in the Division of Drainage Investigations in the U.S. Department of Agriculture, which meant reclamation of thousands of acres of overflowed swamp land in the Mid-South. The Morgan Company's chief work was in this field, in which they had a reputation for competence and integrity. Arthur Morgan was also helping several Mid-South States in writing drainage laws.

The Company's drainage projects were also virtually flood protection works. When the great flood came to the Miami Valley in 1913, they were called in as Chief Engineer of the Miami Conservancy District. Later, when he was Chief Engineer for that district, Arthur Morgan with his great creative and imaginative planning worked out the pioneer use of large flood detention reservoirs, at a time when these were not generally accepted in America.

During the later years of the Miami project, Arthur Morgan and his Memphis partner established the Dayton Morgan Engineering Company, with himself as President.

In 1919, Arthur Morgan became President of Antioch College, which he rehabilitated into one of the leading educational institutions in the United States.

In 1933, summoned by President Roosevelt to be Chairman of the Board of the newly created Tennessee Valley Authority, his creative imagination was responsible for the major features of the T.V.A. program and other resources of the T.V.A. territory.

Foremost in my recollections of the first occasion I met Arthur Morgan comes a sense of being in the presence of greatness, much as I have when I have visited the Lincoln Memorial in Washington, D.C. Now, looking back over the more than half a century that I have known Dr. Morgan, the qualities that stand out to me in his greatness are creative imagination, integrity and honesty, sincerity of purpose, resolve and thorough analysis to find the best solution to every problem. Always intermixed with these is a sincere interest in people to the end that, whatever the project, they will always receive the maximum benefits and the highest measure of fair treatment. These are the essence of his greatness. Here truly is a man possessed with the qualities of greatness that only a few can claim.

September 29, 1970

*Bryce Browning's Biographical Sketch of Arthur Morgan,

My acquaintanceship with Dr. Arthur E. Morgan covers a period of over forty years. As the nation's foremost authority in the flood control field, we of the Zanesville Chamber of Commerce turned to him for direction in developing flood protection for our city. This was followed by a broadening of our objectives and his employment in the making of a comprehensive flood control and water conservation study for the entire Muskingum Watershed.

The District involves 11 lake dams, 360 miles of publicly owned shorelines, and 60,000 acres of land. Annually, these attract several million visitors.

Thanks in large measure to his broad vision and encouragement we were able to secure both federal and state assistance in the construction of our nation's first flood control project to provide permanent lakes with both water conservation and recreation as vital parts of its program.

September 21, 1970

---

*Bryce Browning is head and most active member of the Muskingum Conservancy District, Ohio.

acknowledgements

During more than ten years many persons have contributed to the preparation of this book. In the early period Ralph Keyes searched the National Archives and other sources for significant letters and other first-hand expressions of members of the Corps and of others. He interviewed men who at one time had been members of the Corps of Engineers and then had separated from it. He located much data and assembled it in good order. It would be much less of a book without the search he made. In the early years of the undertaking, before many others had given their help, I had thought of naming him as associate author.

The late Barton M. Jones at one time was Chief Engineer of the Miami Conservancy District, and for about the first five years of the Tennessee Valley Authority was Chief Designing Engineer, especially for dam and power plant design. He worked both in the field and office on hydraulic factors of the Upper Allegheny-Kinzua and on the Conewango Projects.

Ross Riegel had been Chief Designing Engineer of the Miami Conservancy District and a member of the design staff of the TVA. He worked with me on hydraulic factors and on elements of design for the Upper Allegheny project. Earlier he had been a member of the staff of the Pittsburgh Flood Commission, and was one of the two authors of the last report on the Pittsburgh Flood Commission.

Albert Fry, Honorary Member of the American Society of Civil Engineers and an early associate of Sherman Woodward on the TVA, was for 28 years the director of the TVA hydraulic laboratory. He carefully and critically read almost every chapter of the book and was extremely helpful.

Harry Wiersema was for many years assistant to a series of Chief Engineers of the TVA. He read most of the chapters of the book and was critical and helpful.

Charles Okey for many years was in charge of drainage problems of the TVA. Albert Fry, Harry Wiersema and Charles Okey in recent years have been consultants on water control problems in this or other countries. Mr. Okey did field work and hydraulic studies with me on the Upper Allegheny project.

Members of the present engineering staff of the Miami Conservancy District have been helpful on special problems.

George J. Schmidt of Peoria, Illinois, was a specialist in estimating the cost of large earthwork in relation to the Upper Allegheny project. His work was of great value to me in my efforts to make dependable estimates. I have his estimates in the same careful detail he would use in serving large earthwork contractors. Most of the uncritical and irresponsible criticisms of my estimates by headquarters officers of the Corps were criticisms of estimates carefully made or checked by Mr. Schmidt.

Henry Case of Bismarck, North Dakota, who has for forty years worked intimately with the Allied Tribes on the Upper Missouri, has supplied a wide range of data and records. He critically read all of the manuscript relating to that area, and introduced me to the wide range of persons I visited.

Walter Taylor, who spent some years for the Philadelphia Friends Meeting in an effort to help the Senecas, was helpful in making contacts in the Upper Allegheny project. Also, he went ahead of me to the Upper Missouri, where he gathered data and arranged for me to meet informed persons. He accumulated a large amount of pertinent material, which he has placed with the Historical Society of Wisconsin.

Victor Jacobs, lawyer of Dayton, Ohio, critically read the entire manuscript, some of it repeatedly. Also he advised on legal and constitutional matters with reference to the Upper Allegheny project.

Mrs. Constance Sontag of Yellow Springs, Ohio, was particularly helpful in reading and assisting with the editing of the entire manuscript.

Along the way, there were many persons who were helpful through direct contact, or through correspondence, but who are not mentioned.

The staff of Community Service, Inc., has also been helpful. Following the work of Jane Gordon Keyes, Mrs.

Margot Ensign did much work in finding records and in checking data. The staff has helped in gathering material selected from government publications and handled typing and editing. Especially Mary Jane Brown was a genius in looking up sources and in arrangement of data. Seldom does it fall to the lot of a person to have the help with secretarial work of such sustained intelligence, competence, interest and indefatigable, orderly persistence in dealing with large quantities of material, in following up elusive quotations and in improving sequence. This has greatly lightened what otherwise would be onerous drudgery.

Arthur E. Morgan
Yellow Springs, Ohio
September 1971

preface

For generations, the men controlling the U.S. Corps of Engineers have been trained at the U.S. Military Academy at West Point. Their basic and psychologic orientation has been for war not peace. This training in the "profession of war" has not prepared them to direct the management of public works. Yet in the past and increasingly in the present, the Corps has been and is exerting constant and extreme pressure for extension of function and power in the fields of civil engineering.

It is my purpose in this book to show (1) that the training of the Corps of Engineers is of a kind unsuited for civil engineering needs; (2) and more importantly, that there have been over the past 100 years consistent and disastrous failures by the Corps in public works areas. These failures have resulted in enormous and unnecessary costs to ecology, the tax payer and the people whose culture, homes and lands have suffered under the control of the Corps. Furthermore, throughout its career the Corps has persistently avoided or prevented objective appraisal of its projects while, at the same time, presenting itself to the public as unequalled in its field. The public has remained ignorant of the quality of its work.*

Even the fairly wide range of this book does not permit adequate exploration of many very important issues and activities of the Corps of Engineers such as their misuse of the cost-benefit ratio to justify projects; their misuse of "pork-barreling"; their dominance of governmental agencies; their policy in water transportation; and their practice in secondary harbor improvement.

I have not made the record. I merely record it.

Arthur E. Morgan

Yellow Springs, Ohio

September 1971

*There are, of course, creative engineers with integrity who, despite their training, have remained unmarred and have produced excellent work. The criticism of this book is not directed toward these men.

contents

part i

chapter 1

the
lingula
on the
hudson

The Corps of Engineers is a product of the West Point Military Academy. Most of the members of the Corps who had their initial training at West Point have displayed the permanent mark of the Academy in their approach to engineering problems, as is described in the succeeding chapters. The limitations of West Point education are reflected again and again in the extreme inadequacy of the civilian works of the Corps of Engineers. An examination of the West Point system is necessary for an understanding of the persistence of the inadequacy of the Corps of Engineers, as they were a century ago and as they are today.

West Point has a pattern which is old and highly resistant to change. Its pattern might be compared to a rare but persistent type of organism in the biological world. This is a mollusk-like creature called the lingula. In striking contrast to the nearly universal course of evolutionary change, the lingula has remained unchanged for half a billion years. But for well established fossil records, such an instance of exception to the general course of evolutionary change would be dismissed as impossible.

Some very unusual habits or conditions of the lingula which seem to account for that long lasting uniformity will not be discussed here. The lingula has a striking counterpoint in a human institution—the U.S. Military Academy at West Point.

In 1815 Sylvanus Thayer, an ardent admirer of Napoleon, was sent by the American government to Europe to seek a pattern for military training for the United States. His institutional visiting seems to have been limited largely to the Parisian École Polytechnique. He reached France just as Napoleon was being taken to St. Helena. Two years later Thayer, with two or three ex-Napoleonic generals, returned to America and to West Point. He was appointed Superintendent, and retained that position for sixteen years. There he and his Napoleonic ex-generals created what came to be known as the Thayer system, and Thayer became known as the Father of the West Point Academy. One of his first graduates, Dennis Hart Mahan, like Thayer a great admirer of Napoleon, also went to France and returned to West Point to found the Napoleon Club there.

It seemed to many Americans that the spirit of West Point was not the spirit of America. Criticism began almost as soon as the character of West Point became evident. The U.S. Military Academy conflicted with Jeffersonian America. West Point was viewed by many with disapproval as undemocratic. Jackson clashed frequently with Thayer, reportedly thundering at one time, "Sylvanus Thayer is a tyrant. The autocrat of all the Russias couldn't exercise more power."[1] There was opposition in Congress to the spirit and methods of West Point.

The Lingula and West Point

After an existence of more than a hundred and fifty years, what is the outcome? To get a hint of what West Point would have its future cadets think about the institution, we quote from the current West Point catalog:

The academic and military training program is a vital, everchanging one that is continuously examined and adjusted to the changing times, and yet the Academy builds always on the cornerstone of the Thayer system: leadership integrated by excellence of character and excellence of knowledge.[2]

Taking this compact and impressive statement, let us compare it with what well informed persons and groups have reported from direct, personal knowledge. The first of the major points in this quotation is that the Academy program is an "everchanging one . . . adjusted to the changing times." That statement is apparently an effort to refute persistent charges of failure to change.

Just as the lingula has gone through vast periods of time with only slight traces of change, so to a large degree has it been with West Point. The Academy has been criticised for more than a century because of resistance to change. "The great charm of West Point," wrote a biographer of the Academy in 1917, "is that so many things never change. Some of the cadets, sons of graduates, are doing exactly as their fathers did at their age, and again a few cadets are reenacting the youth of their grandfathers."[3]

In 1919, General Peyton C. March, Chief of Staff, sounded out Douglas MacArthur about MacArthur's going to West Point as Superintendent. When March entered West Point in 1883 he was already a graduate of Lafayette College, and he found much of the course at the Academy elementary.[4] "West Point is 40 years behind the times," March told MacArthur.[5] The younger General, a graduate of the institution, agreed and began his attempt to rebuild a more modern Academy. He said:

> I am convinced now of what I had opined all along. The Academy has come to the end of an epoch. We are training these cadets for the past, not the future. We are adhering to certain customs because they are customs. Conceits, sentiment, blind worship have sustained outmoded offshoots of tradition too long.[6]

Colonel T. Bentley Mott, graduate and former instructor at West Point said in 1937:

> Of course there have been changes since my day as cadet or instructor, and I have taken the greatest pains during all of twenty years in an effort to estimate correctly their depth and their effect. I have repeatedly interviewed

young instructors, recent graduates, general staff men,
officers whose sons are at the Academy. From this
examination there comes out the uncomfortable fact that
West Point has not adapted its conception of military
discipline to the conditions which existed in our country
since the Spanish War Period. In the next great conflict
its graduates of today will have to unlearn much of what
they are now absorbing, just as those of yesterday had to
discard the same baggage when training and commanding
the conscripts of 1917, 1918 . . .[7]

In a 1951 study of West Point's academic history, Professor
and future Superintendent Benjamin E. Tillman showed that
the Academy's curriculum remained essentially static, except
for minor additions and adjustments, between 1820 and
1900.[8]

In 1962, a visitor to the Academy reported:

. . . I was startled at the pre-nuclear consciousness of both
officers and cadets. There seemed to be a striking failure
to recognize that warfare has entered a radically new
phase with the introduction of nuclear weapons. It was
hardly reassuring to hear again and again that nuclear
weapons are simply 'another member of the weapons
family' or that 'people were also disturbed when the
crossbow was introduced.'[9]

Scholarship at West Point

The West Point catalog characterizes its work as "leadership
integrated by excellence of character and excellence of
knowledge." Note what men who knew West Point well
through more than half a century have to say about
"excellence of knowledge."

A group of West Point graduates in 1895 held a rare public
discussion on the West Point educational system. They
commented on the recitation method:

A recitation may be perfect but parrot-like, and may find
no permanent registry in the higher thought centers for
subsequent use . . . it is well known that cadets often
study only or mainly those parts of the lesson upon

which they have calculated that they will be called upon to recite.[10]

By 1917, a biographer of and former Assistant Professor at the Academy complained:

I think that the cadets give entirely too much thought to attaining a good grade rather than to the thorough mastering of the subject; that is, they have a tendency to develop the memory at the expense of the thinking functions.[11]

In 1924 Professor Lucius H. Holt commented,

The textbook is openly or tacitly assumed to be the last word on the subject under consideration. Time seldom allows extended classroom discussion of opposing theories or of further developments;—time presses; we must cover the material in today's lesson and go on to the next.[12]

In 1932 a former Professor said of the West Point student, ". . . he cannot be encouraged to question the accuracy of the statements in the text; still less to question their philosophy."[13]

A former teacher at West Point lamented in 1934:

The work of an instructor is reduced to the sole function of listening to recitations, marking the students, transferring them to higher or lower sections, passing on their examination papers. It can hardly be said that he is a teacher: he is a machine for grading cadets upon their knowledge of prescribed texts, and he operates with conscientious precision. He never sees his pupils outside of the classroom, except on very rare occasions.[14]

In 1945 a board appointed to study the Academy invited ". . . continuing attention to the problem of 'spec' memorization rather than understanding."[15]

In 1950 a former instructor concluded, "Student indifference to exploring bypaths is understandable when no recognition is made of achievements beyond the level of the text."[16] In that same year a panel on Social Sciences reported that the intellectual mission of the Service Academies seemed to be to

> ... impart to each cadet or midshipman a minimum amount of information as efficiently as possible. Assignments are short, frequent and tend to be uniform among students. While a critical approach is not wholly avoided, the accent is on the positive. Teaching methods and the selection of teachers is often not such as to stimulate original inquiry either among teachers or students.[17]

A Science and Engineering Panel in 1950, made up of distinguished educators in the field from Pennsylvania State University, Harvard, Massachusetts Institute of Technology, Michigan, Yale and Detroit, with General Eisenhower as vice chairman, gave what might be the definitive critique of West Point's scientific and engineering education (though it has application for all other fields as well). The panel reported:

> The danger of the academy system of instruction, however, is that it may lead to organization of classwork as a matter of specific routine to too high a degree. This does, indeed, appear to exist. Even though instructors give opportunity to students to ask for help in understanding an assignment and systematically give explanations in the classroom, in their undergraduate work cadets and midshipmen alike appear not to develop an attitude of critical inquiry or to have acquired habits of resourceful thinking in their scientific and engineering studies. This is a serious and basic fault of the system of instruction pursued at the Academies.

> Far from doing any such injury, we believe that the development of originality and resourcefulness in technical and scientific matters will enhance the fundamental qualifications of Academy graduates as military officers.[18]

In 1957 a student of the Military Academy stated:

> Rare is the textbook that inspires a student to creative

thought or that quickens the curiosity necessary to
sustain the habit of self-study in later life.[19]

John Phillip Lovell, West Point scholar and graduate of
West Point, pointed out in 1962, "Great stress in the Thayer
System is placed on memorization, which through repetition
guided the mind to the truth."[20]
In 1964 a first classman reported that things have not
changed significantly.

There's no doubt that most of the courses here are
'spoon-fed.' If you want to you can get through your
four years with hardly a thought of your own. Just
follow the course and read the text-book.[21]

Obedience and the Process of Molding

The most important element that the Academy expresses in
its catalog, in its wish to encourage prospective cadets, is
"leadership integrated by excellence of character." Let us
take note of the character and program of the school and see
what quality of character is instilled in its students.

The regime set up by Sylvanus Thayer was designed to take
in young Americans and to subject them to a rigid program
of brainwashing, reconditioning and remaking of personality
such as probably never has existed otherwise in America,
even in the most orthodox of religious orders. This design
was generally successful in achieving its intended goal.

The West Point cadet's life is under a strict set of
regulations and is under constant scrutiny. From the moment
the cadet is awakened by the cannon blast at 5:50 AM almost
every hour of the day is directed. In the past, regulations
forbade leaving the Post except in emergency. They strictly
limited the number of books which could be taken from the
library, forbade the possession of magazines, newspapers or
other literature, precluded the use of money, and imposed
many more curbs on cadet life. Today, passes may be
obtained to leave the Post, the library is more open, one
magazine subscription is allowed, and cadets are permitted to
have money.

Obedience at West Point is part of the overall process of molding. This process utilizes the principles of conditioning. A former instructor at the Academy referred to an objective of West Point's system as being "the creation of attitudes and habitual patterns of response. . . . satisfactory reactions are continually demanded until their forthcoming is habitual."[2] [2]

In 1963 Azoy and Banning wrote in *West Point Today*,

> It is a part of the system to instill the fundamental principle of obedience. Obedience is so prompt and so unquestioning as to become automatic.[2] [3]

Fellow students are one of the main influences on college or university students. This fact has been effectively utilized by West Point in the molding process. The coercion of young cadets by upperclass cadets, known as the hazing system, was and continues to be a method of eliminating an existing cultural spirit, and of replacing it by the West Point pattern. With the legal prohibition of hazing but with the actual and active approval of nearly all the faculty, this factor of hazing came to be intensively exploited.[2] [4]

Especially for the first century and a quarter, the official routine was heavily loaded with rules and restrictions, many of which were offensive to reasonable personal standards. The enforcement of penalties for non-observance were set by the upperclass cadets, requiring a first year cadet to surrender the personality he had brought with him. In only a few rare cases were the penalties carried to the point of causing death. If a young man would not submit to that process, usually he would leave. He was not "West Point material."

In 1879, when the hazing practice had become particularly troublesome, Major General J. M. Schofield, Superintendent, felt compelled in an address to the Corps of Cadets to "lay down the law." Said Schofield:

> . . . the poison seems to have spread and become more and more virulent, until now insulting and opprobrious names and epithets are applied to new cadets, and they are subjected to degrading treatment, such as no gentle-

men can possibly justify or defend. Better, far better, that West Point be destroyed and its greatness exist hereafter only in history than such a standard of gentlemanly honor become the established standard of the corps of cadets.[2 5]

Thirty years later in 1908, an article was printed in the *New York Post* concerning the hazing of cadets at West Point which indicates a continuity of pattern:

> Every regulation was brought into play as an aid to the upper classman's tyranny. If we refused to 'brace' to a point of torture at every order, additional punishment was provided. The word was passed that a certain plebe was refractory. After that, every cadet officer made life as hard as possible for him. There have been many cadets driven from the academy, I assure you, by this apparently lawful system of persecution.[2 6]

Passing another decade, we have a glimpse of the hazing system from General MacArthur. After World War I, when MacArthur loosened up the Book of Regulations, the reaction of the old graduates was fierce. With regard to hazing MacArthur's assistant, Ganoe, recalls:

> There were cries of: "I could take it. If they can't they're not worthy of being cadets." There was also a little of the sadistic: "I got hell. Why shouldn't he?"[2 7]

MacArthur was very much opposed to hazing as a form of leadership training. He once said in criticizing the West Point system:

> . . . I am sure there were officers overseas shot in the back by their own men simply because they had been brought up with the mistaken idea that bullying was leadership.[2 8]

After his first meeting with a group of cadets, the then newly-appointed Superintendent MacArthur remarked, "Their actions bore witness to their habit of just going along by rote, of being withdrawn in their formative years from society."[2 9] He was afraid of the conditioned uniformity and narrowness of vision: "Too long have we fostered this inbreeding which is no better for us than for a royal family."[30]

But, according to Ganoe, MacArthur had little tangible effect on the academic side of West Point. Though he was unable to move mountains, he did achieve some departmental revision. He was able to make some detailed changes in the curriculum, and initiated today's extensive athletic program. During his tenure, however, the Old Guard was largely successful in thwarting him and MacArthur was removed as Superintendent after three years.

The molding process, with or without the extreme form of hazing, produces a uniformity among the cadets. As reported by Ganoe in 1962, MacArthur pointed out this flaw when he commented on cadets who are:

> . . . immured as they are here normally for four years, conversing in their own language of cadet slang with a vocabulary of about a hundred words, talking occasionally in puerile phrases with young women at the hop, doing their chores in the classrooms with only a parade and study period at night to look forward to? And this regime keeps up for months and even years without a break. At one end, we boast about a cadet's truth and honesty; and at the other, we don't trust him to go out the gates of this medieval keep. I have been unable to discover the need for this combination of a cloistered monastery and walled penitentiary.[31]

Robert E. Lee found a way to avoid the indignity of the regimenting process. He meticulously learned all rules and obeyed them punctiliously, so that he never became subject to the indignities of hazing. In discussing the matter of discipline with one of his professors, while President of Washington College, Lee stated, "But as a general principle you should not force young men to do their duty, but let them do it voluntarily and thereby develop their characters." The professor noted later, "I must have showed some surprise, for, making some remark that showed he had read my thoughts, he added these exact words: 'The great mistake of my life was taking military education.' "[32]

After the Civil War, when Robert E. Lee became President of Washington College, there was some thought that he would introduce the West Point system of discipline.[33] To the contrary, he administered the college with few explicit standards. The former General told a new student, "Young gentleman, we have no printed rules. We have but one rule here, and it is that every student must be a gentleman."[34]

In recent years, as West Point physical hazing has become more and more abhorrent to the country, physical forms of hazing have been replaced by various forms of mental coercion, which have been no less effective. The problem of hazing has not been one of just a period, early or late, but has persisted for more than a century and a half. Up to a generation ago the physical hazing practice continued though publicly denied in spite of its being specifically outlawed by Congress. John P. Lovell gives the picture in 1962. He describes West Point's Beast Barracks as a "mortification process," the function served by this experience being one of integration into the "system." He describes the process in this way:

The self, deprived of previous sources of emotional support, becomes increasingly dependent upon the satisfactions provided by responding to the rewards and deprivations of the system.[35]

Up to and including 1968, hazing has been West Point's informal method of instilling the value of obedience in cadets. The concept of obedience is implicit in Sylvanus Thayer's military philosophy. Through nearly two centuries the Corps of Engineers has emphasized the importance of obedience and of subordination to authority. Obedience has been authoritatively taught at West Point far more than self direction, independence of thought and freedom to explore for one's self.

However, according to an article in the July 5, 1970, *New York Times* magazine by Thomas Fleming, a historic experiment was tried out on the plebes in 1969:

They were the first newcomers in over 100 years who

have not had to endure the 8-week introduction to the Academy known as Beast Barracks, or the nine months of plebe hazing. . . .a majority of the cadets seem to agree that it has finally become an anachronism, and the current plebes are better West Pointers for having missed it.

As the proportion of still active hazing-conditioned West Point graduates reduces through the passage of time, we can expect that by about 1990 this long-time source of human insensibility will gradually disappear. A century of brainwashing will not disappear overnight. It remains to be seen whether upperclassmen will continue to have authority and to define demerits.

In recent years the allowable age of entrance has been lowered to 17 years and the applicant must not have reached the age of 22. Beyond 22 years, a young man's personality may be far along in the maturing process. There is usually less resistance to the process at 17. A study in 1949 of fifteen classes at West Point showed that with three exceptions, the "outstanding" group studied (in this case meaning conforming to the West Point role) was the one which entered prior to their 18th birthday. They found that a group entering after their 19th birthday never achieved first rank, and that almost invariably groups entering after their 20th birthday made the poorest showing.[36]

The Outcome

Perhaps the best summary of this system and its effects was made by Hugh Mullan, M.D. in the *American Sociological Review* of March 1946:

The Academy insidiously molds. The cadet enters at a malleable age. Many happenings encourage this rapid mutation; isolation from almost all civilian contact and activities, physical restriction to a relatively small campus, constricted and specialized curriculums, regimentation, the development of marked dependence upon the will of superiors.

This mutation is accelerated by immediate awareness of
class distinction. ... He begins as a 'plebe' and is not
allowed to forget it for a year. He is constantly,
physically and mentally, mortified by hazing. ...The
hazing of course is unlawful but, by giving upperclassmen
the authority to assign demerits, which may and often do
terminate the plebe's career, hazing is not only permitted
but in a sense supported by the regular service group.

Under this regime the embryonic regular...develops
false values which mold his personality into a sameness
devoid of individuality. The plebe must first submit to
severe punishment—he has no alternative. When his time
comes, a year later, all his pent-up sadism is vented upon
the lower class.[3 7]

The denial of the existence of hazing has not changed in
character since the practice was outlawed by Congress in
1910. On September 3, 1970, a letter was written to Senator
Charles Goodell of New York by Major-General William
Knowlton, Superintendent of West Point, in which there is a
total denial of hazing, not only at present, but for the entire
period since 1910. The letter follows:

3 September 1970

Honorable Charles E. Goodell
United States Senate
Washington, D.C. 20510

Dear Senator Goodell:

The letter sent to you by Mr. Arthur E. Morgan, which
discussed the subject of hazing and its possible existence
at the Military Academy, has been referred to me by the
Office of the Chief of Legislative Liaison.

Under the provisions of an Act of Congress approved 19
April 1910, the responsibility for defining hazing was
placed upon the Superintendent of the Military Academy. The following definition has been in effect since it
was published in *Regulations for the United States
Military Academy* subsequent to the passage of the 1910
Act:

"Hazing is defined as any unauthorized assumption of authority by one cadet over another cadet whereby the latter shall or may suffer or be exposed to suffer any cruelty, indignity, humiliation, hardship, or oppression, or the deprivation or abridgment of any right, privilege, or advantage to which he shall be legally entitled."

It is important to distinguish between hazing, and proper administration of the Fourth Class System which serves two purposes. First, it develops in the young man the attributes of discipline, poise, self-confidence, sense of duty, physical and mental toughness, and pride in himself, his unit, and his profession. Secondly, the Fourth Class System is a vehicle for the upperclass to practice leadership by wisdom, interpersonal skill, and example. It is dynamic and constantly under review to keep pace with the changing conditions.

The Fourth Class System does not permit hazing in any form, physical or mental. On the other hand, the cadet is placed in conditions of stress as part of his training to perform under pressure. The same amount of "stress" affects each cadet differently depending upon his development. This is by no means the mental dictation and coercion to which Mr. Morgan makes reference.

All cadets pursue courses which teach them an understanding of human development, adjustment, emotion, personality, motivation and social relations. They learn the basic principles and concepts of leadership derived from the behavioral sciences. In essence, the cadets learn and apply the human aspects of command as opposed to "indoctrination in insensitiveness to human relations" to which Mr. Morgan referred.

Hazing has not been permitted in any form at the Military Academy since it was prohibited by law. Violators will continue to be appropriately punished.

If I may be of further assistance in replying to Mr. Morgan, please do not hesitate to contact me.

> Sincerely,
> William A. Knowlton
> Major-General, USA, Superintendent

General Knowlton a few weeks previously succeeded to the office of superintendent a man who resigned because of his alleged involvement with other graduates of West Point in suppression of the facts concerning massacres in Viet Nam. Did West Point provide a half century of training for such a course?

A former instructor at West Point objected in 1934 to the "impersonality" of the disciplinary system. "The play of personal relations is almost entirely absent," said this graduate of the Academy in 1937,

> and ...[this] removes the element of education in applying that law and gives to the impressionable young cadet a false notion as to how he must exercise the function of discipline when he becomes an officer and is dealing, not with other cadets, but with various kinds of human beings he is going to find in a company of soldiers.[38]

This is an important aspect of West Point training as it relates to the Army Engineer Corps. Again and again we see the Corps of Engineers dictating their will to the people involved in their projects.

The character of the more than a century long regime of the U.S. Military Academy at West Point, known as the "Thayer system," as referred to in this chapter help to explain the tragically long record of the generally low quality public works of the Corps, as documented in the succeeding chapters. The unlimited praise of that régime in the catalogs of the West Point Academy is typical of the century-long presentation by the Corps to the Congress and the public of its extremely inadequate public works program as being the best in all the world.

West Point has demanded rigid adherence to certain ancient ways of behavior. It has been relatively isolated from the American temper, and relatively uninfluenced by neighbors or critics. The ability of graduates to react creatively and with appreciation of the common needs and spirit of man, is thereby diminished. West Point to a large degree has followed the pattern of the lingula.

All of these characteristics of West Point: the sheltered and isolated atmosphere, the rigid regulations, the antiquated curriculum, the rote method of learning, compulsory obedience without question and the psychological conditioning of hazing commonly have produced graduates who are not independent or creative thinkers. These habits of dictatorship would naturally lead to coercion of subordinates by their superiors.

An instance of the unsatisfactory relationships within the Corps will illustrate. Under General Humphreys as Superintendent and generally recognized authority, the survey of the Great Lakes was undertaken in 1868 under the direct supervision of Lieut.-General Raynolds, a member of the Corps. (He was instructed by Humphreys to use methods of measuring current flow which Humphreys had established.) The actual work of flow measurements was in the hands of Daniel Farrand Henry, a graduate of the Yale Scientific School. In conducting his measurements, Henry undertook to follow the methods Humphreys had laid down. He found these to be very inaccurate, although he used great diligence in applying them. He wrote:

> I still had great faith in the Mississippi Report, (of Humphreys and Abbot) and thought the failure must be due to my methods of reduction. I therefore more carefully examined that portion of the report, describing these methods. I do not think there can be found, at least in any scientific work, a more mystifying description; and yet it is so skillfully written as to seem to the casual reader perfectly straightforward and simple.[39]

He therefore explored for superior methods and developed the electric current meter, which with slight improvements came to be the standard of America.

Humphreys' associate, General Abbot, corresponded with Henry on the merits of his meter, as one technician to another, in normal relations. When General Humphreys found that his instructions were not followed, he dismissed General Raynolds under whose direction Henry had worked, and practically ended his career. General Abbot changed abruptly from matter-of-fact correspondence with Henry to bitter denunciation of him.

General Abbot wrote Humphreys concerning Henry, with whom he had recently been carrying on a friendly correspondence. He said concerning the principles of Henry's current meter:

> These are the imaginary difficulties of a theorist, well known as such by any hydraulic engineer of experience who has practically used a double float of the pattern, and in the manner, recommended in the Mississippi Report.
>
> In my opinion, founded on a somewhat close study of the subject, *instruments of this class are pretty toys, which have contributed more to retard the progress of discovery in the science of river hydraulics than any other cause.* (Emphasis added.)[40]

Eventually, the most telling vindication received by Raynolds and Henry was the imitation and use of the telegraphic current meter by officers of the Army Engineers soon after the initial controversy had died down.

In their report for 1875, Warren and Ellis, members of the Corps, showed themselves to be painfully aware of the potential difficulties that could be caused by proclaiming the superiority of the meter method over Humphreys' float method of measurements. While they were using the recently invented current meter, they were careful to reassure Humphreys that *The method adopted was substantially that described in the report of the survey of the Mississippi River by Humphreys and Abbot.* (Emphasis added.)[41] Carefully eschewing the dangerous straightforwardness of Raynolds and Henry, Warren opened his introduction to his and Ellis' progress report for 1875 by comprehensively reviewing and supporting every advantage ever mentioned by Humphreys and Abbot for the use of double floats. He assured the Chief that double floats, all things considered, have proved to be the most reliable means of measuring surface velocities, where a sufficiently uniform channel can be found to use them.

That Ellis and Warren had chosen the correct method to attain favor with the Chief was made clear when General Humphreys commented proudly:

> The most accurate observations made since (the Mississippi survey) in this country, on a river the character of which admitted of the most refined mechanisms being used—that is, the observations made by General Ellis' party on the Connecticut River—confirm the laws deduced from the Mississippi observations.[42]

This was written in 1875, yet only five years earlier Humphreys had endorsed the opinion of Abbot that current meters were little more than "pretty toys,"[43] that they had retarded the progress of the science of river hydraulics, and that double floats were "by far the superior instrument."[44] Ellis and Warren were adept at military etiquette and received enthusiastic praise from the Chief. Raynolds and Henry reported their results unadorned, and paid the penalty.

Can it be that Corps officers and employees jeopardize their professional careers, when they fail to follow orders and question correctness of work done by their superiors, regardless of justification? The experience of General Raynolds and Daniel Henry point in that direction.

An interesting sequel to the Humphreys and Abbot versus Raynolds and Henry chapter in this history of the Corps of Engineers is given by General Lewis Pick, former Chief of Engineers. In 1949, he wrote a long, glowing tribute to the Corps' glorious history, attributing all manner of technical and creative genius to his distinguished organization. In referring to the accomplishments and pioneering inventions of the U.S. Lake Survey, he included among the Corps' notable achievements, "It designed and built the first electric recording current-meter."[45] Belatedly the Corps gathered unto itself the credit for an important invention by one of its civilian engineers, although at the time of the Survey this course was scorned, rejected and punished as a flagrant violation of Corps discipline!

In conclusion, West Point Academy is training men for war. It seems that if a person has internalized the basic precepts of battle theory, such as "think quickly and act without hesitation," that person would scarcely be qualified for the intensive and thorough theoretical and practical thinking necessary for the highly complex job of civil engineering projects. Complex civil engineering calls for a high degree of independent, critical and creative thought. That subject is dealt with in the next chapter. The succeeding chapters will illustrate the human and financial cost to the nation of the civil works of the Corps of Engineers.

notes

The Lingula on the Hudson

1. Morris Janewitz, "The Professional Soldier" (Glencoe, Ill.: The Free Press of Glencoe, 1960), p. 15.

2. United States Military Academy 1968-1969 *Catalogue*, West Point, New York, p. 11.

3. Captain Robert Carlwood Richardson (late Asst. Prof. of English, U.S.M.A.), *West Point* (New York: G. P. Putnam's Sons, 1917), p. 73.

4. Frazier Hunt, *The Untold Story of Douglas MacArthur* (New York: The Devin-Adair Co., 1954), pp. 98-99.

5. Ralph Keyes, "West Point, The United States Military Academy," Community Service Research Paper, Community Service, Inc., Yellow Springs, Ohio, 1965, p. 29.

6. William Addleman Ganoe, *MacArthur Close Up* (New York: Vantage Press, 1962), p. 30.

7. T. Bentley Mott, *Twenty Years as Military Attaché* (New York: Oxford University Press, 1937), pp. 29-30.

8. Cecil Henry Wood, "The General Education Movement and the West Point Curriculum," unpublished Doctor of Education thesis, Teachers' College, Columbia University, 1951, p. 33.

9. David Boroff, "West Point: Ancient Incubator for a New Breed," *Harper's*, December 1962, pp. 61-69.

10. First Lieut. Elmer W. Hubbard, "The Military Academy and the Education of Officers," *Journal of the Military Service Institution of the United States*, January 1895, pp. 329, 320.

11. Richardson, *op. cit.*, p. 183.

12. *Infantry Journal*, May, 1924, p. 557.

13. C. L. Hall, "West Point System of Education," *School and Society*, Vol. 35, June 11, 1932, pp. 783-9.

14. Col. T. Bentley Mott, "West Point: A Criticism," *Harper's*, March, 1934, p. 470.

15. Board of Consultants, Report of a Board of Army Officers and Distinguished Civilian Educators appointed to study the Curriculum of the U.S.M.A., Nov. 7, 1945.

16. Dwight P. Flanders, "The West Point Educational System and the Proposed Air Force Academy," University of Illinois, April, 1950, p. 238.

17. Service Academy Board, U.S.M.A., *A Report and Recommendation to the Secretary of Defense*, January, 1950, p. 61. (Known as the Stearns-Eisenhower Report.)

18. Service Academy Board, *op cit.*, p. 46.

19. John W. Masland and Laurence I. Radway, *Soldiers and Scholars* (Princeton University Press, 1957), p. 242.

20. John Philip Lovell, Ph.D., "The Cadet Phase of the Professional Socialization of the West Pointer: Description, Analysis and Theoretical Refinement," Doctoral Dissertation, University of Wisconsin, 1962, p. 35.

21. Ralph Keyes, *op cit.*, p. 70.

22. Flanders, *op. cit.*, pp. 229, 240.

23. A. C. Azoy and Kendall Banning, *West Point Today* (New York: Coward-McCann, Inc., 1963), pp. 37-38.

24. Mott, *Twenty Years as a Military Attaché, op. cit.*, pp. 29-30.

25. An Address delivered by Maj. Gen. J. M. Schofield to the Corps of Cadets at USMA, Aug. 11, 1879, "On Hazing At The Academy," pp. 3, 4.

26. "Hazing of Cadets: Old Ways and New," *New York Post,* Aug. 1, 1908, p. 1.

27. Ganoe, *op. cit.,* p. 124.

28. Ganoe, *op. cit.,* p. 104.

29. Ganoe, *op. cit.,* p. 112.

30. Ganoe, *op. cit.,* p. 97.

31. Ganoe, *op. cit.,* p. 113.

32. Franklin L. Riley, editor, *General Robert E. Lee After Appomattox* (New York: MacMillan, 1922), p. 38.

33. Arthur A. Ekirch, *The Civilian and the Military* (New York: Oxford University Press, 1936), p. 121.

34. Riley, *op. cit.,* p. 121.

34. Lovell, *op. cit.,* pp. 7-8.

35. Lovell, *op. cit.,* pp. 7-8. ???

36. UMSA Committee on Service Associates, Report to the Superintendent, West Point, New York, May 1949, p. 39. (Committee composed of four senior members of the West Point faculty.)

37. Hugh Mullan, M.D., *American Sociological Review,* March, 1946.

38. Mott, "West Point: A Criticism," *op. cit.,* p. 468.

39. D. Farrand Henry, "Flow of Water in Rivers and Canals," Appendix, p. 52; Detroit, 1873.

40. Report of the Chief of Engineers to the Secretary of War, 1870, p. 70. Appendix BB, pp. 616, 620, 621.

41. Report of the Chief of Engineers: Appendix B, "Survey of the Connecticut River," Part I (1878), p. 308.

42. D. Farrand Henry, "The Gaging of Rivers," *Scientific American Supplement,* no. 31 (July 29, 1876), p. 486.

43. Report of the Chief of Engineers to the Secretary of War, 1870, p. 70. Appendix BB, p. 626.

44. *Ibid.* ???

45. Lewis Andrew Pick, 1949. Report, p. 12.

chapter 2

inclusive
engineering
analysis

It is essential on important engineering projects, in order to insure that the best design will be achieved, to have thorough investigation, study and analysis of all the factors involved. Only by so doing will conclusive results be assured as to what is best. Unfortunately, this process is not always followed. It has rarely been followed by the U.S. Corps of Engineers that is charged with the responsibility for a major part of the Nation's public works concerned with water control.

No expression comes more easily to the Corps than the declaration concerning a project under consideration that "all feasible alternatives have been examined and compared, and the best under the circumstances have been selected." Yet throughout the course of a century no characteristic of the work of the Corps of Engineers has been more common than the absence of overall, conclusive examination of its undertakings. The following nine chapters are evidence of the century-long failure of the Corps to practice objective and conclusive analysis.

In contrast to the Corps' policy and practices is the characteristic of engineering practice known as inclusive engineering analysis. This concept was long ago set forth in my report on the Miami Conservancy District Project in Ohio in 1913 in which I stated the following policy of inquiry— one that I have observed for more than fifty years—as I used it then in exploring for the best solution to the Miami problem:

The principle in essence is that, to whatever extent the importance of the work justifies, every possibility for solution of the problem, whether promising or not, should be explored, with effort to become aware of unrealized and unexpected ways of approach; and that each such possibility be explored to a point where, in comparison with other methods of solution, it either is proved to be inferior or finally emerges as the best possible solution.

In a number of cases in my engineering practice I have brought about radical changes of design on important projects on which plans were supposed to have been completed. In most cases the plans had been prepared by men with far greater technical ability than I possessed. Their limitation lay in the fact that, having found a good solution to a problem, they had not relentlessly explored every other approach, with the possibility that some still better solution might emerge.[1]

One of my own early experiences with conclusive engineering analysis had unexpectedly favorable results. The largest drainage engineering project in the United States during the early twentieth century was the Little River Drainage District of Southeast Missouri. In ancient times the Gulf of Mexico extended north to the hilly and mountainous land of what is now southern Missouri. There was a sharply defined shore line along the margins of the hills. As the ocean bottom gradually rose above sea level that sharp border line remained. The mountain and hill land ended abruptly at what had been ocean bottom, but which had become what is called the Mississippi delta. At some points along that old shore line the sand dunes of the ancient ocean shore are as sharply defined as though they had been formed only yesterday.

In the extreme southeast corner of Missouri the Little River came down from the rugged hill and mountain land to the north and poured out over half a million acres of this extremely flat ancient sea bottom or "delta" land, in

Missouri, and a similar area in Arkansas had become very fertile, and would be exceptionally valuable farm land but for the fact that adequate stream channels had not developed. The natural rainful of the area and the occasional torrential outflow of Little River from the north turned it into largely useless swamp land.

The Little River Drainage District was a project for reclaiming half a million acres of this extremely fertile land in Missouri, both from the excess of local rainfall and from the water of Little River from the hills, which had not yet had time to dig a channel for itself. To provide drainage from excess of local rainfall was difficult enough. To take care of the flow of Little River, especially the rush of water during exceptional floods, was a real problem.

The owners of this half million acres of fertile land, largely residents of Cape Girardeau, Missouri, determined to undertake its reclamation. It would be a serious problem, but the winning of one or two hundred million dollars worth of fertile land would be worth the effort. They assembled an engineering staff with a long experienced man as chief engineer, and took a brilliant young man who then was chief engineer of one of the smaller railroad systems as his assistant. They also secured competent legal services to deal with legislative problems. The first ten years of the present century was spent in working out that project, always in accord with standard, recognized engineering methods. Finally in about 1910 they were ready, and submitted the plans to the two foremost hydraulic engineers of the Midwest, Anson Marsden, Dean of Engineering of Iowa State College, and Isom Randolph, who had been Chief Engineer of the Chicago Drainage Canal. They approved the plans.

The plans were not fully satisfactory, but were considered the best under the circumstances. The local drainage was not difficult, but the control of flood waters from the Little River was a baffling problem. The decision was to carry the water of moderate floods south between levees for a hundred miles to the Arkansas state line, and there leave it to Arkansas interests to carry the water another hundred miles to the first opening in the Mississippi levees at the mouth of the Saint Francis River. To carry the flow of great fifty-year or hundred-year floods to the line between Missouri and Arkansas would cost ten or twenty million dollars, and there was available only five million dollars for the entire project, including hundreds of miles of local drainage channels.

The Mississippi River was flowing by, less than twenty miles away. But the Mississippi also was subject to floods, which were held back from the land by levees fifteen feet high. Sometimes the water in the Mississippi River stood ten feet higher than the surface on the land side of the levees. So the nearby Mississippi did not seem to be a feasible outlet for floods on the Little River.

As "practical men" the promoters of the project and the engineers decided to go as far as they could. They could afford a channel for the Little River to carry about 12,000 cubic feet per second. When a great flood of 50,000 cubic feet or more should come down the Little River and onto this flat land that problem would be left to the farmers who would buy and settle on the land. That "practical, business-like course" had been decided on by the owners of the land, and by the engineers and lawyers, and had been approved by the consulting engineers.

In ten years of effort a program had been developed which had been approved by leading consultants. It remained to finance the project and to proceed with construction. A purchaser was found for the bonds which would be issued. It was customary for financial firms in announcing the sale of bonds to state that the firm had employed an independent engineer to examine the project to assure its soundness. Since I was engineer for a large drainage project in the adjoining state of Arkansas I was asked by the bond firm to examine the plans of the Little River Drainage District.

Already I had adopted the policy of trying to see all the possibilities of an undertaking, whether or not they seemed especially favorable. The plans for the Little River District troubled me. In ordinary years they would be satisfactory. But when a great flood should occur, especially if the land were generally occupied and developed, such a flood might cause a disaster. Instead of the 12,000 cubic feet per second prepared for by the plan, a flood of 50- or 75,000 cubic feet per second might drown the livestock, flood and destroy buildings, and perhaps cause extensive loss of life. A once-in-a-century great flood is as likely to come tomorrow as a hundred years from now. The solution was not adequate, but larger investment was not feasible. Was there no way out of this dilemma? Had any possibility been overlooked?

The Mississippi was less than twenty miles away. Why not tie the Mississippi levees to the mountains? Simply dig a fairly large channel, using the excavated earth to build parallel levees several hundred feet apart and twenty feet high, creating a channel between levees large enough to carry even 150,000 cubic feet per second, far more than any Little River flood in recorded history.

What about turning this much more water into the Mississippi River? There were three reasons why that was not a serious concern. While 100,000 cubic feet per second would exceed the historic limit for the Little River, it would be a minor fraction of one per cent of the vast flood flow for the mile-wide Mississippi River. Second, nearly all great rain storms move north from the Gulf. To catch a Little River flood quickly and get it out of the way might be better Mississippi River flood control than to let its flood waters take a longer and slower course to the Mississippi, and then to coincide with the great flood from the North. Third, great floods are very rare, both for the Little River and for the Mississippi River. The prospects of their peaks coinciding in the same week and year is very, very remote.

Another possibility was for one or more flood control reservoirs on Little River in the hills to hold back the flood. For more than forty years the Corps of Engineers had been strongly and positively opposed to flood control reservoirs. (See Chapter IX.) It was not until three years later that, in spite of long Corps of Engineers' opposition to the idea, I became Chief Engineer on the design and construction of the first large flood control reservoirs in the United States, those on the Miami River in Ohio.

Taking all conditions into consideration I recommended tying parallel leveees to the hills to capture Little River floods, and taking a course directly to the Mississippi River. My proposal was presented to the engineers and to the consulting engineers and was adopted. The entire job was done by that plan. The half million acres of the Little River Drainage District was made safe from all Little River floods. And yet the entire cost of the project as a whole was reduced by half a million dollars.

Moreover, this plan also removed the necessity of carrying flood waters of Little River for a hundred miles in Arkansas to the first outlet to the Mississippi River, at the mouth of the St. Francis River, at an additional cost in Arkansas of ten or fifteen million dollars. Had it not been for the longtime Corps dogma against flood control reservoirs, perhaps even better results might have been secured. Thus this case of inclusive engineering analysis was highly profitable. A few years later our company, the Morgan Engineering Company, was made the Chief Engineering firm of the Little River Drainage District.

About two years after the Little River incident, in 1912, I had my first official relations with the U.S. Corps of Engineers. The Morgan Engineering Company had been retained to plan the reclamation of that part of the drainage area of the Black River in Missouri which is in the flat lands of the Mississippi Delta, about fifty miles west of the Little River Area. During about a year of time and with the expenditure of several thousand dollars, a plan was prepared.

The Black River rises in the mountain and hill region of south Missouri and flows with a fall of several feet per mile to the extremely flat land which once was the ocean floor. There it spread out over the old sea bottom, with a fall of only about one foot per mile. At very long intervals a flood from the hills might have a discharge of 100,000 cubic feet per second. During most of the time, especially in growing seasons, the low season flow was served by a crooked and roundabout channel with a bank-full capacity of only perhaps 3,000 cubic feet per second.

The problem was both to reclaim this flat "delta" land so that it could safely raise crops and provide residence, and also to protect the flat land in case of the greatest flood, even if it should occur only once in a century. If the area should be thickly settled an extreme flood, if not protected against, might cause a great disaster.

One method for protection would be by providing for storage in the hills. Such a method not only would protect the land in Missouri, but also down stream in Arkansas where a much larger area would be subject to flood. However, as already mentioned, the U.S. Engineer Corps had been firmly opposed to flood control reservoirs. Since the Black River is an interstate stream, under Corps supervision, that course was not feasible.

The method I had adopted was to catch the water of large or small floods as they came out of the hills, and to carry the water between two dykes about a quarter of a mile apart to the Arkansas state line. As to the natural channel, formed by low water flow of one to three thousand cubic feet per second, that was an excessively crooked and winding channel, which at bankfull stage would not carry five percent of the extreme flood flow.

It was this situation and my solution which I took to the engineer officer in charge of the large Memphis District of the Corps. He looked at my map and plan for about five or ten minutes. Then, pointing to the winding and roundabout course of the low water stream, he said, "Are you not leveeing the river?" When I started to explain the situation, the engineer officer interrupted me and said, "In the past flood control has been by means of levees, and I anticipate it will be so in the future. Good day." He turned and walked out of the room. This was the Corps' traditional "levees only" doctrine in authoritative action. So ended my relations with the U.S. Corps of Engineers with reference to the Black River.

The principle of conclusive and inclusive engineering analysis applies both to the solution of a problem as a whole, and to the recognition, understanding and best treatment of every significant element. It is important to note that if there are several possible alternatives for a project, some fairly good solutions may be strikingly inferior to the best.

As one example of the Corps' persistent failure to make adequate inclusive engineering analysis, I shall mention one case which involves inadequate examinations and planning of the Corps.

When the Tennessee Valley Authority had been organized in 1933 and replaced the Corps of Engineers in charge of water project developments in that area, an early need was to locate reservoir sites on the Tennessee River. The Corps of Engineers already had located some dam sites, primarily for navigation and power but not for flood control. At this time the Corps was opposed to the use of reservoirs for flood control as they had been for fifty years past.

The location the Corps had selected for a reservoir site lowest down on the Tennessee River—the Aurora site—was more than twenty miles in a direct line from the mouth of the Tennessee in the Ohio River. By conclusive engineering analysis the Aurora site was found to be inferior to a location much nearer the mouth of the Tennessee River. The Aurora site had major disadvantages.

First, to locate the dam farther upstream than necessary would waste valuable storage space. Second, an unusual advantage of a site near the mouth of the Tennessee River was the possibility of getting interchangeable use of two reservoirs. In its lower reaches, the Cumberland River, which is under the control of the Corps of Engineers, somewhat paralleled the course of the Tennessee River. Near the Ohio River, and nowhere else, the two rivers were very close, separated by relatively low land through which a canal could readily be excavated, uniting the two reservoirs. There would almost certainly be a dam built by the Corps across the Cumberland River near its mouth in the Ohio, where physical conditions were favorable. If each river had a dam and reservoir near its mouth, then a canal connecting the two would make them act as one. On whichever river the greatest flood should occur, the excess would flow over into the other reservoir. This would be equivalent to a substantial increase of the total reservoir capacity and protection provided by the two reservoirs. With the Aurora site, chosen by the Corps, that connection of the reservoirs would not be feasible and, in view of the fact that the Corps could not even see the value of reservoirs for flood control, this plan would be far beyond their imagination. The validity of this reasoning is shown by the fact that, as of this writing, the dam on the Cumberland, Barkley Dam, has been built and the two reservoirs have been connected by a canal just as I had envisioned.

The Tennessee River dam was placed nearer to the Ohio River and several million dollars was saved which otherwise would be required to excavate and to maintain a twenty-mile navigation channel to connect the reservoir with the Ohio River. Such an excavated canal would be far less desirable for present-day passing of large scale barge-trains than the open waters of the reservoir. Thus a dam site near the mouth of the Tennessee River was greatly preferable to the Aurora site with an excavated transportation channel, as chosen by the Corps.

To locate the lowest dam near the mouth of the Tennessee River was not easy. Near the mouth of the river, above the solid rock bottom of the river bed and valley, was ninety feet of mud and sand, which made explorations for a dam foundation difficult. As Chief Engineer of the TVA, I decided that there should be an inclusive engineering analysis of this situation. One research party spent more than six months in search of a safe downstream location for the dam but finally surrendered without finding a suitable one. I decided that the search had not been conclusive, and set up another exploration team headed by a persistent and resourceful engineer, Eugene Prokop. Core drillings were not sufficient to examine the rock foundation under ninety feet of mud and sand. To be sure of a good foundation, the rock had to be examined in place. By the use of a combination of steel pilings and of refrigeration pipes ninety feet below the surface, an area of this overlying material was frozen, and then excavated, and the foundation rock was examined in place. The rock proved to be of excellent quality, and a safe structure, Kentucky Dam, was located and built near the mouth of the river.

This example of conclusive engineering analysis is paying good returns, and has insured greater values for centuries to come. It supplies much increased storage space. It provides a superior navigation course for the lower river, while the ability to unite Kentucky Reservoir with Barkley Reservoir on the Cumberland River adds perhaps ten to twenty per cent to the combined value of the two reservoirs.

Failure to find a suitable reservoir site lower down the river was not the greatest error of the Corps in this case. Had the Corps continued in charge of the Tennessee River, the failure to make the conclusive engineering analysis necessary to disclose the flood control and low water storage value of reservoirs throughout the length of the Tennessee River would not have been corrected and would have meant a loss of value of more than $200,000,000 to the country. The Aurora Dam, as planned, approved and recommended by the Corps, would have provided only one million acre feet of controlled, useful storage. The Kentucky Dam, twenty miles nearer the mouth of the river, and about fifteen feet higher, as actually built and in use by the T.V.A., has a capacity for controlled and useful storage of four million acre feet. This was by far the lowest cost storage along the channel of the Tennessee River, costing less than $30 per acre foot of storage. The Army Corps of Engineers never envisioned this enormous increase in storage capacity.

The policy of conclusive engineering analysis is an essential method of reaching optimum possible results. Persistent exploration often results in financial savings and increased values. Sometimes it does not, but it is essential to prevent oversight. Only by a policy of conclusive engineering analysis can such realities be dependably determined.

Lack of conclusive analysis is repeatedly revealed in the Corps' estimates of cost. While supervising water control projects in the T.V.A., I found it necessary to check the Corps' estimates of the T.V.A. Norris (Cove Creek) Dam. In order to get a judgement on the general dependableness of the Corps' estimates, I looked up the official estimates of cost of all the navigation dams on the Ohio River built by the Corps of Engineers during the preceding ten years, and compared these with the reports of the finished cost of those dams. I found that on the average the finished costs exceeded the official estimates by about fifty per cent.

In 1954 the T.V.A. published a comparison of estimates before construction with the actual cost of the finished work for major T.V.A. projects. During my period as Chief Engineer and for twenty years afterward, during which substantially the same policies and engineering staff prevailed, eighteen dams were constructed, at a total cost of $800,000,000. During that period the finished costs exceeded the estimated costs before construction as given to Congress by less than three quarters of one per cent.

The habit of the Corps of Engineers of making inadequate cost estimates has been chronic. This habit was referred to by Chairman Cannon of the Appropriation Committee of the House of Representatives in reviewing the annual request of the Corps for funds for public works in July, 1959. He stated to the House:

> The crowds of applicants for appropriations which came in such numbers that it was sometimes impossible to get them all in the committee room, was preceded by the Corps of Engineers, who were invariably in favor of the largest expenditures the committee could be prevailed upon to make. Much of their testimony was wholly unreliable. When they were consulted on the cost of a proposed project they invariably underestimated the cost. In no single instance in the last several years have they given us a true figure on estimated costs. In many instances when the committee had under consideration the advisability of undertaking a project we discovered after it was too late, that the cost of completion was a number of times the figures given to us by the Corps of Engineers. . . . It is impossible to escape the conclusion that they either were incompetent or deliberately misleading.[2]

Such underestimation of cost may be helpful to the Corps in their making the statement of relative cost and benefits appear favorable to Congress, and may induce Congress to commit itself to greater expenditures than it realizes.

In 1961 Chairman Cannon was as usual dealing with this problem and in particular with Colonel Renshaw of the Corps of Engineers. The following is a discussion from the Congressional Record concerning the inland waterway from the Delaware River to the Chesapeake Bay:

> Mr. Cannon. Colonel Renshaw, why are you asking for $1 million more for this project this year than you asked last year, and why are you asking $2 million more this year than you asked 2 years ago, and may we expect that by next year you will be asking $3 million more?

> Colonel Renshaw. First, let me say, sir, we believe that the estimate we now have will complete the project.

> Mr. Cannon. You made jumps of $1 million a year, and there is certainly a wide difference when you increase 2 years in succession at the rate of $1 million a year. There must be something wrong here.

> Off the record.

> (Discussion off the record.)

> Mr. Cannon. There is poor engineering to begin with, or there is some factor in it that is not at first apparent to the committee.

> Colonel Renshaw. Of the $1 million increase this year, over last year $375,000 of that is due to change in conditions in the foundations.

> Mr. Cannon. About one-third is due to changes in the foundation?

> Colonel Renshaw. Yes, sir.

> Mr. Cannon. Have those changes in the foundations taken place within the year, or were they unobserved a year ago?

> Colonel Renshaw. Our original estimates was based upon test piles driven by our architect engineering firm. When we actually went out to build the project, we

found that our foundation piling had to be much longer than we had previously anticipated.

Mr. Taber. Does that mean you did not do the job of locating your foundations correctly? It is just about that, is it not?

Colonel Renshaw. It meant that if we had driven more test piles we might have found the condition.

Mr. Cannon. Can you determine such important matters as this in advance in your original estimates, or your original designs, and specifications? Do we have to wait until we actually undertake it to discover we had made a mistake of $1 million?

Colonel Renshaw. Mr. Chairman, we hope to find this condition or these conditions in advance, and we think we take all engineering precautions that are normally taken.

Mr. Cannon. There seems to be a lot of loose engineering here.

We cannot depend upon hopes, Colonel Renshaw. We ought to know what we can depend on when the project is first presented, and your preliminary investigations ought to satisfy us on that point, so that we would not have to go back and readjust them.

Really, Colonel Renshaw, are we doing the corps an injustice in reaching the conclusion that it makes such mistakes as this, and that we cannot depend entirely upon the data you submit at the time the matter is first taken up?

Colonel Renshaw. I believe, Mr. Chairman, that the corps follows the usual practice among engineers. We drive what we feel are sufficient test piles and take such borings during the investigation stage to determine fairly accurately what we will find. We are wrong in some cases, but we think that we save money in the long run by not spending more on our engineering to determine down to the last degree—

Mr. Cannon. You mean that it would have been more expensive to have reached a determination of unquestioned accuracy?

Colonel Renshaw. Over the long run and taking all of our projects as a whole; yes, sir. I believe we carry our engineering to a reasonable point. I represent only one Division. Maybe General Person would like to comment on this.[3]

The following table of cost increases on Corps projects taken from the *Atlantic*, April, 1970, indicates typical inadequate cost estimation on the part of the Corps.

Cost Increases on Corps Projects[4]

Name of Project	Cost Estimate at Time Project was Authorized	Amount Spent Through Fiscal Year 1966	Percentage Overrun
Whitney (Tex.)	$ 8,350,000	$ 41,000,000	391%
John H. Kerr (N.C. & Va.)	30,900,000	87,733,000	185%
Blakely Mountain (Ark.)	11,080,000	31,500,000	184%
Oahe Reservoir (N. & S. Dak.)	72,800,000	334,000,000	359%
Jim Woodruff (Fla.)	24,139,000	46,400,000	92%
Chief Joseph (Wash.)	104,050,000	144,734,000	39%
Fort Peck (Mont.)	86,000,000	156,859,000	82%
Clark Hill (Ga. & S.C.)	28,000,000	79,695,000	185%
Bull Shoals (Ark.)	40,000,000	88,824,000	122%

Thus the total cost estimates for these projects amounted to $405,319,000, while the total amount spent on them through the Fiscal Year 1966 came to $1,010,745,000, which makes an excess of $605,426,000 of spending above estimating.

In the *Reader's Digest* for January, 1971, Robert H. Haveman, Professor of Economics at the University of Wisconsin, is quoted as having made a study of 147 Corps of Engineers projects with a total price tag of $2.6 *billion*. His conclusion is:

"There was a consistent and persistent overstatement of benefits and understatement of costs. On pure economic grounds—leaving the environmental aspects aside—about half the projects should never have been built."[5]

Thorough-going planning and investigations help to make accurate estimating of costs. Conclusive engineering analysis is not just an appealing idea. It has practical consequences.

In recent years the Corps' estimates of benefits include more and more indefinite factors of value. Many of these cannot well be quantitatively measured, such as dilution of pollution and added facilities for recreation. These benefits are included as counting toward justification of a project.

Engineering and the Military

In an important project, military engineering, as long taught and practiced in the West Point tradition, differs markedly from what I have termed conclusive engineering analysis. A common characteristic of military engineering in practice has been action-in-crisis. Military action may not wait for deliberate reflection, or for searching our unexpected or unprecedented alternatives, or meticulous comparison of data. The philosophy of military action, as applied to civil works, as taught for more than a century at West Point, is expressed in an article, "The Civil Activities of the Corps of Engineers," by Gilbert Youngberg, in the *Military Engineer:*

> Now let us consider the mental qualities required in a successful commander. These are:
> First: The power of analysis so that the mind may reason to a logical conclusion; that is to say, the ability to weigh facts and figures, to detect and discard the false, the improbable and non-essential, to harmonize apparently divergent elements and to appraise each at its proper value; in brief form to perform quickly and accurately those mental processes we call "the estimate of the situation."
> Second: The power of synthetical decision, the ability to decide rapidly and unerringly upon measures, which though not necessarily the best, shall nevertheless be adequate to meet the situation as it has been determined to exist, with a ready resourcefulness in devising ways and means to that end; *the power to resist the temptation to temporize and delay while searching for the ideally perfect course.*

Third: Steadfastness of purpose, confidence in one's own judgment *and the determination to abide by decisions previously made: the adopted, though not ideal, is yet sufficient to the purpose in view;* the tenacity, the self-reliance, and the will "To fight it out along these lines if it takes all summer."

These qualities are in constant daily exercise by the engineer officer *engaged in civil works where the full responsibility for such work is placed upon his shoulders . . .*[6] (Emphasis added.)

The above quotation is but repetition of long established Corps doctrine. Masland and Radway, in *Soldiers and Scholars*, include in a summary of traits impressed on the cadet:

He is able to examine a situation, come to a quick decision, and stick to it.[7]

These traits, long and persistently drilled into West Point cadets, are those the academy considers necessary in war.

In many respects these West Point traits are almost diametrically opposite to those required in large-scale civil engineering. In such undertakings, which have far reaching consequences, the impulse to bring a quick end to inquiry may be fatal to good work. In the working out of a great civil works issue, the first requirement is not for quick decision, but for suspension of judgment until all major factors are considered, and selection is made by comparison of all significant possibilities. It also is important that judgment be kept open to take into account new and significant evidence.

The atmosphere of West Point is certainly not conducive to the development of a true understanding of the necessity of thorough conclusive analysis, particularly on important public works as contrasted with the indoctrinated principle of quick decision on military matters. Quick intuition and appraisal in accord with established military doctrine and refusal to change plans because of the emergence of theoretical or other untried possibilities may be the characteristics of a good commander, but they are not the characteristics of a good civilian engineer.

notes

1. Arthur E. Morgan, *The Miami Conservancy District* (New York: McGraw-Hill Book Company, Inc., 1951), p. 284.

2. Clarence Cannon, Chairman, Public Works Appropriations Committee, *Congressional Record*, Vol. 105, No. 92, July, 1959, p. 9049.

3. House Appropriations Committee, Part 4: Department of the Army, 1961, pp. 69-70.

4. Elizabeth B. Drew, "Dam Outrage: The Story of the Army Engineers," *Atlantic*, April, 1970, p. 57. Copyright 1970 by *The Atlantic Monthly*. Reprinted with permission.

5. Robert H. Haveman, Professor of Economics, University of Wisconsin, quoted in "Battle Tactics for Conservationists," by James Nathan Miller, in the *Readers' Digest*, January 1971, p. 177.

6. Gilbert Youngberg, "The Civil Activities of the Corps of Engineers," *Military Engineer*, Jan.-Feb. 1921.

7. John W. Masland and Laurence T. Radway, *Soldiers and Scholars*, Princeton University Press, 1957.

chapter 3

conclusive analysis for human wellbeing

There is another phase of conclusive engineering analysis which differs markedly from those we have described and which enters into the making of cost estimates and project justification. Results which actually increase hardships for individuals and communities affected by a project often are ignored by the Corps in estimating the cost of a project. Some of such costs and losses relate to entire cultures large and small, which may have existed for centuries and may sum up to massive hardship and unnecessary tragedy and injustice.

Conclusive analysis of a large public project may commonly make the difference between results which excellently serve their purpose and results which are irreparably disappointing. And this conclusive analysis should include not only a few of the major aims of the undertaking, but every element of vital human concern. In this respect the training of West Point and the long time tradition of the Corps of Engineers has been unfortunate not in a few particular cases, but habitually. This has been the case in many areas of human contact and especially in the taking of property for public works.

When a massive reservoir project is under way the public may see the large features, but may not clearly realize that, especially in the taking of property, the project is largely made up of many small economic and human relations, many of which may be major life issues to the persons directly involved. It has been characteristic of the Corps of Engineers to be deficient in human sensitivity in this class of relationships. The cases here mentioned are significant as representative of a type of attitude for which the typical patterns of West Point seem to be largely responsible.

The Fort Berthold Indians

In March, 1945, the Corps of Engineers began preliminary work on building the Garrison Dam. This dam was to flood the lands of the Three Tribes of the Fort Berthold Reservation in North Dakota. I do not have a clear judgment as to whether the Garrison Dam should have been built. It is my unconfirmed opinion that an adequately conclusive analysis might have disclosed very superior opportunities without the many losses which resulted from the building of the Garrison Dam. However, we shall assume here that the dam should have been built.

The Arikara Indians migrated about a thousand years ago from Asia across the Behring Strait, down to the tip of South America, and up the Mississippi and Missouri Rivers. They were searching for a place to settle where the environment would be hospitable and where they would be free from invasion by hostile tribes. Winding among the treeless, semi-arid and windswept prairies of North Dakota, the deep wooded valley of the Missouri River offered an almost ideal situation. Below the prairies and in the woods the driving, sub-zero winter winds of the prairies were tamed and more gentle. Free from tropical diseases and parasites, from which the Arikaras must have previously suffered, on their long, long search and remote from other human settlements, the valley abounded in game and provided shelter in the substantial forests that grew along the river margin. Along the lower slopes of that deep valley were perennial springs. The valley had fertile land for agriculture, wild fruits, and good rivers for fishing. The hillsides provided lignite for fuel. There was grass, water and shelter for cattle. The values of this location seemed to justify the long, long pilgrimage around two continents.

Just beyond the Missouri River bottoms were the bare prairies, without water except for wells 100 to 300 feet deep which were too alkaline to be used for drinking water. There was no fuel and no timber for building. The Missouri River bottom was a garden spot in a forbidding country and it was here that the Arikaras joined the Mandan and Hidatsa Indians. At their North Dakota home, the Three Tribes set up an unusual culture marked by considerable fellowship and good will and skill in agriculture and other arts.

The tribes had a remarkable variety of vegetables, apparently accumulated from Asia and both continents of the Western Hemisphere. They had potatoes, varieties of beans, numerous varieties of squash, flint corn, dent corn, sweet corn, pop corn, and many other garden crops. Over the centuries they bred these vegetable species to survive the cold springs and short summers of the north and of the high altitude.

Their social relations were, in general, intimate and humane. The family pattern was extended to include grandparents, uncles and aunts. To a large extent the rearing of children was a community project.

The Three Tribes were largely a self-sufficient people. In their economy, money did not play a large part. The people exchanged their products and their labor and their interest with each other as neighbors.

> Their way of life rested upon a "gardening-gathering-hunting economy," made possible by the resources of the Missouri River and Lowlands. . . .Annual cash income was low because there was little need for it; "Grandmother River" provided the necessities of life. . . .before the flooding, the Ft. Berthold people had one of the lowest rates of Welfare in the United States.[1]

On September 17, 1851 the U.S. Government approached the Three Tribes with the Treaty of Fort Laramie. In exchange for surrendering vast areas of their traditional domain, the Government made a solemn promise that their choice home tract—the river valley, as well as additional uplands, in all 12,500,000 acres—should be theirs in perpetuity. This treaty was not a generous gift from the federal government, but the purchase price for a vast ancestral domain. However, by successive executive orders and Acts of Congress the Three Tribes' 12.5 million acres were reduced to 643,368 acres, and often without the knowledge and consent of the Indians.[2]

In the late 1940s and the 1950s the life and harmony of the Three Tribes were disrupted by the U.S. Corps of Engineers. The Corps sought flood control legislation calling for the construction of the Garrison Dam, which would flood the best lands of the Ft. Berthold Indians. And it was the Corps which was to be in charge of the Dam's construction. When built, the dam would be the largest earth dam in the world.

The Garrison Dam would uproot and destroy the economy and social organization of the Ft. Berthold Indians. The flooding of this valley would break up the existing balance between range, shelter, water and shade and disrupt the agricultural and livestock enterprises of the Indians which had come to provide 70% of their earned net income.

The Business Council of the Three Affiliated Tribes of the Fort Berthold Reservation adopted a resolution opposing the building of the Garrison Dam. Part of the introduction to this resolution sums up the effects of the Garrison Dam on the Indians:

> The construction of the Garrison Dam will have the following results to the Indian people of Fort Berthold Reservation:
>
> 1. All of the bottom lands, and all of the bench lands on this Reservation will be flooded, most of it will be under water to a depth of 100 feet or more.
>
> 2. The homes and lands of 349 families, comprising 1544 individuals will be covered with deep water.
>
> 3. The lands which will be flooded are practically all the lands on our Reservation which are of any use or value to produce feed for stock or winter shelter.
>
> 4. We are stockmen and our living depends on our production of cattle.

5. All of the area of this Reservation which will not be flooded will be of little or no value to us if the bottom and bench lands are lost.

6. There are over 2,000 individual members of the Three Affiliated Tribes of this Reservation and it is now proposed by Acts of Congress to remove 1544 of us to some other unknown location, leaving at least 456 of our people permanently separated from the others of the Tribes by the proposed removal.

7. All of our people have lived where we now are for more than 100 years. Our people have lived on and cultivated the bottom lands along the Missouri River for many hundreds of years. We were here before the first white men stepped foot on this land. We have always kept the peace. We have kept our side of all treaties. We have been, and now are, as nearly self-supporting as the average white community.

8. We recognize the value to our white neighbors, and to the people down stream, of the plan to control the River and to make use of the great surplus of flood waters; but we cannot agree that we should be destroyed, drowned out, removed and divided for the public benefit while all other white communities are protected and safe-guarded by the same River development plan which now threatens us with destruction.

9. We see on the plans and maps of the proposed Missouri River development, that five great dams are to be built across the River. Four of those dams are carefully located above the white communities of Yankton, Chamberlain and Pierre in South Dakota, and Bismarck in North Dakota. We also know that the Garrison Dam was first planned to hold water at the level of 1,850 feet above sea level but when it was shown to the Congress that water at that height would flood some of the streets of Williston, North Dakota, that plan was promptly changed to 1,830 feet to save Williston.

10. Our Indian community of 2,000 individuals is larger than some of the cities which have been so carefully safeguarded by the original plan but we are as much entitled to protection and consideration as is anyone or all of the cities along the River.[3]

When it was decided to build the dam and to take away the river valley land they had prized through the centuries, the Three Tribes faced their desperate loss, and sought peaceful and friendly settlement. In such circumstances a decent course would have been to help them meet these difficult circumstances and to do all that would be reasonably possible to reduce their loss and tragedy. The effort would have been worthwhile even if chiefly to preserve this rare small culture as one would preserve a precious work of art or an outstanding work of nature such as the Everglades. As might be expected after West Point conditioning, this sensitivity was not in evidence in the Corps.

Negotiations with the Corps were formally initiated by the Tribes in accordance with law. A meeting was arranged and negotiations were begun in a spirit of friendly examination. The Indians requested that from the electric power generated by the dam, they be given a small amount—20,000 kilowatt hours per year—in order to light their houses and to pump their water when they were removed from the ready sources of water and were relocated on the dry prairies. They asked for the privilege of pasturing their cattle along the margin of the reservoir where grass would be available during the dryer season. They asked for the privilege of using the timber, which grew only in the narrow valley of the river, for building houses, fences, and so forth. They asked for a bridge across a narrow part of the reservoir, so that the different sections of the tribe could have communication with each other, without going 500 miles around the border of the reservoir. They also wanted access to the water of the reservoir for their cattle.

wanted access to the water of the reservoir for their cattle.

Since the U.S. Government, by formally enacted treaty, had unreservedly affirmed the full and perpetual ownership of this land to the Three Tribes, some of whom had owned and occupied this choice land for up to 900 years, it seems that the requests of the Indians were very moderate.

The negotiations were proceeding in apparently a friendly spirit, with acceptance by the Three Tribes of very moderate terms, when an incident occurred which ended the entire program of negotiation. This had the effect of putting the Indians again under arbitrary servitude to the Corps.

A small group of Indians, led by a man called Crow Flies High who had long considered themselves enemies of the Tribes and of the government, were opposed to negotiations and endeavored to get support for this position. They were able to get a petition signed by about 10% of the membership of the Three Tribes. When the negotiations were underway a few members of the Crow Flies High group appeared at the negotiations, dressed in ceremonial feathers. The leader of the Crow Flies High group pointed at General Pick, who was in charge of the negotiations for the Corps of Engineers, referred to Pick disrespectfully and condemned the negotiations. General Pick became enraged and said that he would remember that insult as long as he lived.

Without attempting to understand the situation, General Pick abruptly interrupted the negotiation, and despite the desire of the Three Tribes to continue, stated that he would have nothing to do with the negotiations. He and his staff went to Washington and refused to visit the reservation for further negotiations. As stated by several of the Indians who were active at the time and were present at the negotiations: "He threw the negotiations into the waste basket" and repudiated all the elements of agreement which had been reached. On a recent visit to North Dakota I talked with members of the Tribes. I found a nearly unanimous opinion that the Corps welcomed the attack of the Crow Flies High group because it provided a semblance of justification for ignoring the clear terms of the law passed by Congress and for interrupting the negotiations, on the ground that negotiation was impossible with the Three Tribes. The Indians believed that the Corps did not want to negotiate as the law required, but wanted an excuse to negate the law in order to dictate. Rev. H. W. Case, a Congregationalist who worked with the Indians for 40 years, said:

> . . .My own observation was that the Govt. had sent a man out, who knew so little of Indian History and

people. One could see this when he said in his approach "I want to *show you* where we will place you people."[4]

The Garrison Dam had been authorized by the Flood Control Act of 1944. The Bureau of Reclamation had disapproved of the Garrison Dam as unnecessary and as an undesirable waste of fertile land. General Lewis Pick of the Corps of Engineers was responsible for having the Garrison Dam included in this Act, which was part of the compromise with the Sloan plan of the Bureau of Reclamation known as the Pick-Sloan plan. It became the duty of the Secretary of the Interior to approve alternative land sites providing they were "comparable in quality and sufficient in area to compensate the said tribes for the land on the Fort Berthold Reservation."[5] The lieu lands offered by the War Department were rejected by the Secretary of the Interior, J. A. Krug, as they did not meet these requirements.

Because of the need to conclude settlement with the Indians, and because there was no land comparable in quality to the valley that had not already been settled by white men, a campaign culminated with passage of a bill providing for a payment to the Indians of $5,105,625 in exchange for the entire value of the taken lands—both above and below the surface.

The first bill drafted for the taking of the Indian lands seemed to have been carefully and fairly designed by the Bureau of Indian Affairs, and to give evidence of sensitiveness to the desperate adjustment presented to the Three Tribes. This bill left the administration of the change in the hands of the Bureau of Indian Affairs in the Department of the Interior.

Then, when the control of the proceedings was transferred from the Indian Bureau to the U.S. Engineer Corps, the bill was largely rewritten by the Committee on Interior and Insular Affairs to suit the Corps. The terms of the bill were greatly changed, probably by General Pick. Various provisions for protecting the rights and interests of the Three Affiliated Tribes were eliminated and the administration was put into the hands of the Corps of Engineers. It was adopted

George Gillette (left foreground), chairman of the Fort Berthold Indian Tribal Business Council, covers his face as he weeps in the office of the Secretary of the Interior, J. A. Krug. On May 20, 1948, Krug signed a contract whereby the tribe sold 155,000 acres of its best reservational land in North Dakota for the Garrison Lake and reservoir project. Gillette said of the agreement, "The members of the tribal council sign this contract with heavy hearts . . . Right now the future does not look good to us." (Wide World Photos)

as Public Law 437 on October 29, 1949. The following extracts from the earlier law illustrate elements of protection which were included in the Indian Bureau draft *but were eliminated* from the final draft as desired by the Corps:

Section 1. The tribes and the members thereof may salvage, remove, reuse, sell, or otherwise dispose of all or any part of their improvements within the Taking Area . . .

Section 2. The tribes and the members thereof shall have the privilege of cutting timber and all forest products and removing sand and gravel, and may use, sell, or otherwise dispose of the same until at least October 1, 1950 . . .

Section 3. The tribes and the members thereof may remove, sell, or otherwise dispose of lignite until such date as the District Engineer, Garrison District, fixes for the impoundment of waters.

If, in the future, sub surface values are discovered within the Taking Area, which if known at this time would increase the value of said area, and said values are reduced to money, then the tribes shall be entitled to have paid to them a royalty of one-eighth of the money received for the oil and gas extracted after the ratification of this agreement.[6]

According to the Act passed by Congress, the Indians were not allowed the privilege to fish or to graze their cattle along the river, nor could they bring their cattle to drink at the river. Their mineral rights were denied. Their hunting and trapping rights were denied. Their right to some royalty in case oil or gas should be discovered was denied. Non-taxation of future land purchases within the boundaries of the remaining reservation was denied them. Twenty thousand KWH of electricity from the dam, at cost, was also refused. The irrigation facilities of the dam and reservoir were not made available to the Indians. As it was finally drafted, the Act forbade the Indians to use the funds provided in it to hire attorneys or agents to represent them. There was no assurance that the road system would be ·built, nor that schools would be moved or rebuilt, or that the Indian Agency would be reestablished. It was provided that the Tribes should receive interest from the date the Act is accepted, thus pressuring the Indians toward acceptance. A more reasonable provision would have the interest begin on the date of Presidential approval. Furthermore, their money was "placed to their credit" but remained under the absolute control of Congress.

Except in one case the Indians were not allowed to cut the timber before flooding. In this case when the Indians were permitted to cut timber, they were refused permission to take it away. Now the trees are dead and half submerged in water where they are useless, unsightly and a barrier to navigation and recreation.

The Indians were ordered to come to Washington, where, under pressure and in a strange environment and under threat that the alternatives were to sign or be entirely without protection, some of them were brought unwillingly to sign the agreement, which left decisions in the hands of the Engineer Corps. The Indians apparently did not understand its terms at the time it was being drawn up. This legislation was forced on the Indians and whether they understood it or not, they did not at any time favor it.[7] Later Congress approved an additional $7,500,000 which gave the Indians approximately $12.5 million. There is a photograph of the signing of the agreement in Washington. The official head of the Three Affiliated Tribes is holding his hands over his face, showing his grief and despair over the course of the proceeding. After signing the agreement the Tribes were largely at the mercy of the Corps.

According to law, construction of the dam proper had to wait until agreement was reached with the Indians. Yet preliminary work on the project was done during 1945 and 1946. Representative D'Ewart said "The wrong in this method is that negotiations with the Indians were not started until after construction was actually begun on this project."[8] Representative Lemke said "I do not consider it a just or moral settlement."[9] And according to Representative Francis

Case of South Dakota, there was $60,000,000 already invested in the Garrison project and a money solution was the only solution to be considered at this late stage.[10]

Without even token concessions, the Affiliated Tribes had to leave their precious river bottom land and home for the treeless, waterless, relatively barren prairie, where temperatures ranged from 40 below zero to more than 100 above. The Tribes left behind them the natural values and their centuries of development, living and culture. Families were largely scattered across the prairie on patches of land which were assigned them. Almost no attempt was made to maintain their high degree of community life, and the fundamental basis of their culture was destroyed. All of this added much to the emotional injury over and above the economic.

Here is a statement from the U.S. Indian Service in 1946.

> . . .It is evident . . .that the secondary effects of the Garrison Reservoir taking breaks up the residual reservation lands into five separate tracts, which will render utilization and intercommunication difficult, costly, and time-consuming to their Indian owners.

> These remaining tracts will lose much of their value when disassociated from the homes, hay lands, shelter, and water of the valley lands, to be inundated by the reservoir.

> The existing Indian cattle economy—dependent upon the proximity and balance of range, shelter, water, and feed—will be completely disrupted by the Garrison reservoir taking. The types of land to be lost cannot be duplicated on the residual lands.[11]

The Rev. Austin Engel, Special Worker for the Ft. Berthold Council on the Fort Berthold Reservation, wrote on the "principle of just compensation:"

> The flooding forced them out of the River Valley into the white man's town, or out to some lonely piece of

land on the Prairie, where a combined 'Plains Cash'
economy soon drove them into a nearby small town. For
the past ten years the Ft. Berthold people have been
struggling to 'find themselves,' to learn the ways of a
'Cash economy,' to adopt the white man's nuclear
pattern of family life, to develop habits of steady work,
to live by the clock, instead of the sun and moon, to find
meaning for their lives in the midst of white communities
that look down on them and often make fun of them.
Many have found a new way of life. Many have
floundered and wandered aimlessly, wasting what resources they had. All have suffered, if not physically,
then emotionally and psychologically.[12]

On my visit in the fall of 1968 I talked with a number of
persons who had been active in the conditions of that time.
The degree of their general agreement on what had occurred
was very marked. There were differences in detail but on the
whole there was consistent agreement.

I feel particularly justified in quoting the statements of
Mrs. Ina B. Hall of Parshall, North Dakota. She has been a
leading citizen for many years. She is vigorous, intelligent and
speaks excellent English. Mrs. Hall had been principal of a
high school of white and Indian children. She had been active
in organizing and directing young people's clubs and in
general was active in the affairs of the community. She had
been chosen by the Women's Organization of North Dakota
as the "Woman of the Year" for the state for the entire
population both white and Indian. In quoting her I feel that I
am giving a representative impression.

Mrs. Hall said:

It was a terrible thing which happened to us. We were
working along to get our children educated—then wham!
This happened to us. I was supporting my children by
teaching. When the Government took our land, they gave
us $13 an acre. We had 800 acres. Sixty acres were
unreachable. We had an excellent spring. When our land
was taken away, we had to go out of the river-bottom up
on to dry land. Our fine spring was replaced by a well
300' deep with undrinkable water. We had to pump by

hand. Our old land was fenced. We had to move our own wire. We were not paid for this. There was no payment for the difference in water. "If you want a fence, you must go pick up your old wire." The Corps of Engineers contracted moving of houses but did a miserable job of it.[13]

The Halls were promised cheaper electricity—but even these promises were forgotten.

Prior to their uprooting, the Halls' community—"Lucky Mound Community"—was well-organized and self-sufficient. As Mrs. Hall noted:

This dam separated families and broke up communities. It destroyed neighborhood and church groups. It broke up 4-H groups, Gold Star Mothers, Homemakers groups. All ethnic groups were disrupted.[14]

Reverend Case, elaborating on the Corps of Engineers, said:

The engineers, as I recall, made no personal approach to the people and their problems. On our reservation, if a man owned a strip of land, they cut it right in half and the man couldn't make a living on the rest. Even though they had paid the bill for relocating the houses, the contracts were with unreliable movers. There was a loud complaint about that. It is my own opinion that some other department than the Army engineers should make an approach to the people who are being affected.[15]

Robert Fox of Ross Glen, North Dakota, who was former head of the Tribal Council, said:

At that time we would have had to relocate ourselves. Actually, we did relocate ourselves. We had this land up above and we just moved out of the valley and relocated ourselves.

They (Corps of Engineers) just paid you off in money. . . .I had some land in the taken area, well—all I got was $2,000. . . . I couldn't buy a piece of land for $2,000. Maybe I could've, but it wouldn't have been half as good as the land I lost in the taking area.[16]

Robert Lincoln from the Charging Eagle District said:

> Have known that plans were under way for the Govern-
> ment to construct Garrison Dam but never did they come
> to consult us until its own plans were completed before
> informing us as to what they proposed to do. We are
> much like the hen and her young fighting off the hawk
> that is swooping down to attack.[17]

The U. S. Army Engineers' inability to deal on a human
basis with the Indians is further examined in a letter from
Rev. Case to me on September 2, 1968:

> ... It is sufficient to help folks to realize what havoc the
> U.S. Army Engineers have brought about thru their
> inability to deal in human relations. The chief of the U.S.
> Army Engineers down thru the personnel, on the Ft.
> Berthold situation, showed their inability to accept the
> American Indian as people too. I was in the midst of the
> fight for justice among these people on Ft. Berthold
> where the largest displacement of people took place in
> the Missouri Basin development, and saw and heard so
> much discrimination.
>   It is a blessing that you have tackled this job for the
> U.S. Engineers should never have the responsibility of
> dealing in human relations in making ready for a
> project.[18]

The post-reservoir conditions were as disastrous as had been
anticipated. The well informed Indian, D'Arcy McNickle,
wrote:

> ... When families were taken out of the sheltering river
> valley and caused to make home selections on the
> exposed prairie above the river, they were called up in
> alphabetical order, and the kinship groups that had lived
> in close association for countless generations were scatter-
> ed everywhere. The people are still dazed by this
> experience after a dozen years and search vainly for
> leadership. They were compensated for the land, and for
> certain "intangibles," but of course no one even attempt-
> ed to put a price on the worth of a society which had
> been built out of man's creativity through centuries of

time. Obviously, it can have value and meaning only to those who live in it.

The case is worth detailed study, because it represents the first major taking under eminent domain of Indian lands guaranteed by treaty. The earlier procedure for quieting Indian title was the treaty process: when Indian lands became desirable for settlement or for public purposes, a treaty, or a revised treaty, was negotiated. The Indians always yielded, but at least a show of respect for tribal sovereignty was maintained. Under the new procedure, the Indian tribe was put in the category of a private land owner, against whom the state could proceed; compensation in money was made the equivalent of ethnic and cultural identity. The process, in time, can only lead to the extinction of the Indian people as a separate and identifiable thread in American life.[19]

What occurred as to the Three Tribes in the upper Missouri was not the accident of circumstance. It was the working out of a philosophy of life. An organization, such as the Corps of Engineers, should be especially concerned that not only in its chief functions, but in all functions which concern the life of the people, it should conduct itself in such a manner that it is an asset and not a blight. Great power should carry great responsibility.

The Sioux Tribe of the Standing Rock Reservation

We do not have to go far afield to find another case of Corps insensitivity to the human condition. Down the river from the Fort Berthold Reservation was the Sioux Tribe of the Oahe Dam, which the Corps of Engineers had constructed.

With the certainty that the Federal Government would be taking some of their land for the Oahe Dam, the Standing Rock Sioux had to negotiate for the damages to be paid. The Corps of Engineers assured the tribal leaders that they would have money for relocation by September, 1959. It was not until January, 1960, however, that any money was actually delivered. Furthermore, it was at this time, January, 1960, that the Indians received a notice of eviction and were told to be moved from their homes by the end of February, 1960. The Sioux Indians, therefore, had to move in bitter winter weather, with temperatures as low as 30° below zero. Because of the short notice, they had to live in trailers until relocation housing could be prepared. Living in trailers was an additional expense for the Indians, but, according to tribal leaders, they were told that this was their problem, not the Corps'. In order to meet the deadline imposed by the Corps of Engineers, they had to move twice. Sadly enough, this harsh inconvenience was unnecessary and seemingly arbitrary. The Corps of Engineers could have let them remain in their own homes for many more months without delay to the construction of the dam.[20]

Another experience of the Standing Rock Sioux will illustrate how the Corps of Engineers works. The Corps of Engineers established with the Standing Rock Sioux a certain date for taking possession of the lands to be flooded. Until that date the tribe retained the right to have its timber sawed for lumber. The tribal council arranged with the Hart Brothers, a small lumber company, to saw timber on condemned tribal lands and to sell the rough lumber back to the tribe. There followed a long period of interference by the Corps, with litigation too complicated to report in detail, in which the Corps was defeated in the Courts.

Even though the Corps eventually lost the decisions in court, the salvaging of timber was effectively stopped by the legal action of the Corps. The hearings took so long that the tribe lost practically all further possibilities of salvaging timber. The government did not salvage the timber, either, apparently deciding that it was cheaper to leave an unsightly forest of drowned trees standing in the reservoir. The wood which could have been an important asset to the tribe was simply wasted.

I drove along most of the length of the Oahe Reservoir and observed the condition of the timber. It is located on the narrow valley bottom, where the trees could get ground water for growing. Mile after mile after mile stands this strip of dead forest in 5 to 15 feet of water, a monument to the fact that the Corps would neither allow the Indians to cut the timber for their needs, nor would they harvest it themselves. The timber is a vast obstruction to navigation, which the Corps has indicated as one of the purposes of the improvement. The timber also interferes with recreation, which was another of the purposes of the improvement. An ordinary, human, friendly attitude would have set up conditions in which the Indians could legally get timber for their houses and barns and fences, and for fuel for their home fires, and could sell what otherwise would be worse than wasted. A century of unimaginativeness and inhumanness as characterized by West Point hazing was being expressed in a new setting.

The Papagos of Sil Murk Village

The Painted Rock Reservoir, authorized in 1950 as part of the comprehensive plan for the Colorado River Basin, necessitated the complete removal of about twenty Papago Indian families in the village of Sil Murk, Arizona. However, it was not until six years (March 25, 1956) after Congress authorized the project that the Corps actually met with the Indian people whose land and homes would be flooded by it.

The Corps of Engineers promised to construct suitable homes for this village in a new location and was to provide 40 substitute non-taxable acres with a well. This proposal was accepted by a resolution of the Papago Tribal Council on March 16, 1959. Resolution #1036 stated that the new village would be constructed "at the expense of the Corps of Engineers," in accordance with construction plans submitted by the Engineers, which had been examined and approved by the Indians.[21] On the same day the Agency Superintendent wrote to the Area Director of the Bureau of Indian Affairs that "The Corps of Engineers has assumed responsibility for the entire transaction."[22]

The situation was well summarized by the Papago Tribal Chairman in his letter of March 28, 1961, to the office of Senator Carl Hayden:

After the Senator has satisfied himself that the title objection of the Corps of Engineers has been met, it is our hope that he will urge the Corps of Engineers to proceed with their original plans of moving Sil Murk Village to another location out of danger of flooding. We understand the money is available out of the existing appropriation for the dam construction, and all that is necessary is the administrative decision by the Chief of Engineers to carry out the original plan. We understand that such action is still the recommendation at all subordinate department levels.

The Papago Tribe will be happy to cooperate in every way and will deed the present site of Sil Murk to the United States whenever the Corps of Engineers agree to go ahead with the relocation they originally proposed, thus avoiding any need for the United States Engineers to acquire the land by condemnation. . . .

We understand some question has been raised about the amount of money necessary to make this relocation. The United States Engineers set the figure, not the Tribe, and the Tribe is not insisting on any particular amount of money, but feels that the United States Engineers are under a moral, if not legal obligation to go through with the plan that they themselves presented to the villagers.

It might also be mentioned that most of the Gila Bend Reservation is in the flood area from the reservoir and a flowage easement was agreed upon as part of the entire settlement which included the relocation of Sil Murk Village. When the Chief of Engineers refused to carry out the agreement to relocate the village, the Tribal Council withdrew its approval for the flowage easement, because it was part of the same settlement. The Engineers have now begun the legal steps to condemn the land for a flowage easement, but the Tribe will be glad to reapprove the earlier settlement if the Engineers' promises to relocate the village are fulfilled.[23]

On July 14, 1961, the Tribal Council resolved to offer 40 acres of land without charge in exchange for the 40 acres for relocation, "so that there will be no cost to the government in acquiring the land."[24]

Legislation "to provide for the relocation and reestablishment of the village of Sil Murk" was introduced in both houses of Congress in March, 1961, and finally enacted into law in August, 1964.[25] The Painted Rock Dam was by then already completed.

The attitude of the Corps of Engineers and the Department of the Army is clear in the letter of March 12, 1964, from the Secretary of the Army to the Senate Committee on Interior and Insular Affairs, asking for a less expensive reparations bill than S. 90 which was being considered. The existing law, S. 90, provided for compensation for all losses and damages as part of the cost of the project. The Corps opposed this and held that such full costs should not be met unless the government should be inclined to make a gift for that purpose. The Corps wrote to the Congressional Committee:

. . . this bill [S. 90] directs the Chief of Engineers to take such action as will assure, to the extent feasible, that the economic, social, religious, and community life of the members of the Papago Indian Tribe shall be restored to a condition not less advantageous than that which they enjoyed as inhabitants of the Village of Sil Murk . . .

Subject legislation would provide payments and/or benefits over and above normal just compensation. [Just compensation is defined by the courts as the market value, the amount that would pass from a willing buyer to a willing seller.] This Department has consistently, as a matter of policy, opposed the utilization of project funds for these additional benefits. However, it is recognized that Congress has in the past, in connection with other civil works projects, enacted legislation designed to provide for the Indians benefits in addition to payments they would receive in accordance with a conventional determination of just compensation. In such acts the costs to the projects were confined to payments for direct and indirect damages, and the relocation of townsites, roads, utilities, and community facilities; reestablishment and rehabilitation features were provided as a function of the Department of the Interior and funded from other than project appropriations. For this reason, the Department of the Army is reluctant to concur in S. 90 in its present form as such could create a new precedent in cases of this kind of further increasing the costs to the project to include extensive rehabilitation features. [26]

While the Corps of Engineers often states positively that it only does the will of Congress, the opposite is the case. It opposes "consistently" and "as a matter of policy" the concept of restoring members of a community damaged by one of its projects "to a condition not less advantageous than that which they enjoyed" previously. The Department of the Army continues its letter on the Village of Sil Murk:

> However, it is also recognized that extenuating circumstances may exist in the present case stemming from a misunderstanding during initial discussions between representatives of the Corps of Engineers and the tribal council for the acquisition of a flowage easement in the lands of the Sil Murk Village. These discussions were premised on the erroneous conclusions that the Government, under existing law, and as a project expense, relocate the village facilities and the dwellings of the inhabitants. . . .

> The Department of the Army considers that the relocation and reestablishment of the inhabitants of the village of Sil Murk is more appropriately within the purview of the functions of the Department of the Interior. To this end, recent discussions between this Department and the Bureau of Indian Affairs resulted in a mutually acceptable proposed substitute draft bill more in keeping with previous similar Indian legislation, which proposal is being submitted to this committee by report of the Department of the Interior on subject bill. . . .[27]

The truth which the above paragraphs are so carefully designed to obscure is that the Corps of Engineers made an offer to the Papago Tribe in order to get what it wanted and then the Corps withdrew the offer. After calling this sequence of events a "misunderstanding," the Corps then collaborated with the Bureau of Indian Affairs to arrange for

Congress to smooth the whole matter over with minimum cost to the project.

As indicated by the Corps in its letter quoted above, there was a continuing habit of misrepresenting the cost of a project by shifting the cost of legitimate adjustments from the official estimated cost of the project. Where the Corps is establishing a reservoir, a reasonable estimate of cost should include all factors of legitimate cost of every nature. The Corps has habitually avoided this responsibility. The agency carrying through such projects should not only endeavor to avoid meeting the costs, but should be concerned that all elements of cost should be its concern, and should not be left to casual gift appropriations. In that respect the Corps has continuously shown its disregard for elements of cost which were of vital concern to those involved. While undertaking to shift the legitimate cost of payment for losses and damages from the estimate of the cost of the project to general government expenditure, this constitutes a clear case of evading actual and legitimate costs of Corps of Engineers projects. Also the Corps habitually states that it is not a law-making body but is only an executive agency to carry out the dictates of Congress, with which it has had nothing to do. The actual seeking of a change of federal law through the influence of the Corps, and the Corps' admission that this was in accord with its conventional practice, illustrates the falsity of the Corps' frequently repeated declaration that its concern is not with law-making.

It seems likely that any family or community which has ever experienced a significant loss of land to the Corps of Engineers could relate at least one such case of "a misunderstanding during initial discussions."

The Corps of Engineers' insensitivity to humanity is not limited to Indians. While I was President of Antioch College, I had as secretary a young woman who with other members of her family were owners of two farms, large parts of which were taken by the Corps for a Toronto, Kansas project. As the project advanced I was kept informed of the conditions. A striking characteristic of the proceedings was the almost

complete disregard of the Corps for the human and circum-
stantial conditions of the landowners involved. My secretary's
brother had a stock farm with quite a large number of cattle.
He could not buy another farm until he had been paid for the
large part of their farm, which was being taken. They needed
to know how much of their farm would be taken, when it
probably would be paid for, and about how long the cattle
might be kept before the land would be taken. In these and
other respects they could not get ordinary business courtesy
and information about their farm, when they asked for
somewhat routine information or consideration. He finally
was pressed to sell his stock and gave up farming in that area,
as he could not indefinitely hold an option on a farm he
wished to buy. The parents had a similar experience, as did
most of the land owners who had to deal with the Corps.

As Chairman of the Tennessee Valley Authority I developed and put into active operation policies by which the T.V.A.
staff was consistently concerned with the personal circumstances of persons whose land was being taken. Each case of
home taking was treated without favors on its individual
merits as an issue of human concern, for which the
Government had responsibility. This policy was effective to
such an extent that in a majority of cases, the information,
counsel and consideration given to land owners resulted in
more desirable situations after the taking than had existed
before. The lack of human consideration of the Corps is not
one of the hard facts of life which are unavoidable. It is
largely the consequence of their West Point training and
military background as well as the century long heritage of
Corps insensitivity to the human condition. Anyone who has
not actually lived through such an experience may tend to
doubt that an agency of the United States government could
possibly be guilty of such practice.

Landowners are sometimes kept in ignorance of the
appraised value. Large and experienced landowners are
informed, or inform themselves. It is reported that often the
small landowner can be argued or coerced into selling his land

for materially less than the government appraisal. But it seems that the effort to acquire land in this way has sometimes been a habit with the Corps.

> . . . for public use, I had been of the firm conviction that the Government would observe the constitutional mandate that private property shall not be taken for public use without just compensation.

> However, I soon learned that the Government, and especially the real estate division of the Army Engineer Corps, did not understand what was meant by just compensation. In place of decency and justice, I discovered that they used the bulldozing and threat methods. Until I had some experience with the real estate division of the Army Engineer Corps, I felt that the Government would be fair and honest with its people as it expected them to be with it. Up to that time, I thought the constitutional provision "just compensation," protected the home owners, but to my amazement, I discovered that that was not the case. I discovered that the Government is out to take and take by threats and by using its great power in the courts if necessary.[2 8]

If it is possible for the Corps of Engineers to conceal its tactics so successfully from Congressman William Lemke, imagine the ease with which the Corps might deceive other citizens far less experienced in such matters than their representative in Washington.

As can be seen from the cases of the Upper Missouri, the Standing Rock Sioux, the Papagos and later the Senecas, there has been insensitive exploitation of individuals, families, committees and cultures. This aspect of human relations may seem petty in relation to a multi-million dollar project but it can be extremely important to the individuals involved. When broken promises, big and small, accumulate to the point where they form a regular pattern of unwritten procedure, it is time for public concern.

notes

1. Rev. Austin Engel, "Just Compensation was Unjust at Fort Berthold." (Bismarck, N.D., Fort Berthold Council—Congregational Christian Churches.)
2. Ray H. Mattison, ed., *North Dakota History: Journal of the Northern Plains*, Vol. 35, Nos. 3 & 4 (North Dakota: State Historical Society of North Dakota, 1968), pp. 229-232.
3. The Business Council of the Three Affiliated Tribes of Fort Berthold Reservation, North Dakota; Chairman—Martin T. Cross, "Resolution as the Act of this Council" (May 25, 1946).
4. Letter from Rev. H. W. Case, Ft. Berthold Council of Congregational Christian Churches, to Arthur E. Morgan, March 19, 1970.
5. Public Law 374, 78th Congress, 2nd Session, May 2, 1946, Section 6.
6. H. J. Res. 33, Report No. 605, 81st Congress, 1st Session, July 1st, 1949, pp. 70-72.
7. Mattison, *op. cit.*, p. 258.
8. *Ibid.*, p. 263.
9. *Ibid.*
10. *Ibid.*, pp. 263-264.
11. "Report and Recommendations to the Commissioner of Indian Affairs on the Offer of Lieu Lands to the Indians of the Fort Berthold Reservation, North Dakota" by the Honorable the Secretary of War, Nov. 21, 1946. Prepared under the direction of District Office No. 2, U.S. Indian Service, Billings, Montana, December 10, 1946, Chapter 3, Section 2, pp. 26-29.
12. Engel, *op. cit.*
13. Ina B. Hall, Parshall, North Dakota, Statement by tape, Oct., 1968.

14. *Ibid.*

15. Rev. H. W. Case, conversation between Arthur Morgan, Gillette and Case at Newton, North Dakota, Oct. 18, 1968.

16. Robert Fox, from Conversation between Arthur Morgan, Robert Fox, Jefferson Smith and others at the Arikara Congregational Church on the evening of October 18, 1968.

17. Robert Lincoln, Charging Eagle District, Statement, December 6, 1946.

18. Rev. H. W. Case to Arthur E. Morgan, letter, Sept. 2, 1968.

19. D'Arcy McNickle, American Indian Development, Inc., to Arthur E. Morgan, Letter, Dec. 12, 1964.

20. Notes prepared by Walter Taylor, Friends Representative to the Seneca nation of Indians, on his visit in July, 1965 with some leaders of the Standing Rock Sioux at Fort Yates, N.D., including Aljoe Agard, Tribal Chairman, Theodore Jamerson and J. Dan Howard.

21. Resolution No. 1036 of the Papago Tribal Council, March 16, 1959. Files of the Bureau of Indian Affairs, Washington, D.C.

22. Letter from Harry Gilmore, Agency Superintendent to F. M. Haverland, Area Director, Bureau of Indian Affairs, March 16, 1959. Files of the Bureau of Indian Affairs.

23. Letter from the Chairman, Papago Tribe of Arizona, to the Administrative Assistant to Senator Carl Hayden, March 28, 1961. Files of the Bureau of Indian Affairs.

24. Resolution of the Papago Tribal Council, July 14, 1961. Files of the Bureau of Indian Affairs.

25. Public Law 88-462, 88th Congress, H.R. 11329, August 20, 1964, "An Act to Provide for the relocation and re-establishment of the village of Sil Murk and of the members of the Papago Indian Tribe inhabiting the

village of Sil Murk, and for other purposes." 78 Stat. 559.

26. Letter to Hon. Henry M. Jackson, Chairman, Senate Committee on Interior and Insular Affairs, from Stephen Ailes, Secretary of the Army, March 12, 1964.

27. *Ibid.*

28. Statement by Hon. William Lemke before the House of Representatives on July 5, 1949.

chapter 4

esprit
de
corps

The graduates of West Point, including the Corps of Engineers and the officer corps of the Army, have a strong spirit of solidarity. This is an essential precondition for military effectiveness. But this quality can be turned against the interests of society, as well as for it, as the organization of the Mafia so well illustrates. It is a universal need of society, to attain a strong group spirit among persons who live and work together as in the family, but society must take care that such group spirit shall not be at odds with and injurious to the welfare of the larger society, of which families and groups are parts.

The military academy at West Point was organized after the pattern of the French Army under Napoleon. The evils that developed from the in-group loyalties of French officers were disclosed in Emile Zola's famous *Dreyfus Affair*, which opened up a festering sore of injustice. Leo Sauvage has summarized the issue in France over that affair:

"If Dreyfus is innocent, then our generals are guilty," cried Paul Déroulède, a French "Birchite" of the day, on the eve of the trial at Rennes in 1899.

On September 21, 1899, two days after Captain Dreyfus—pardoned but not rehabilitated—had been given his freedom, General Gallifet, the Minister of War, issued an order of the day:

"The incident is closed. The military judges, respected by all, have pronounced their verdict with complete independence. We bowed to their decision without hesitation, just as we bow now to the act of mercy performed by the President of the Republic. There should be no further question of reprisals against anyone. I repeat: The affair is ended."

L'Affaire did not end until July 12, 1906, when the judicial error was officially recognized and the innocence of Dreyfus solemnly proclaimed. If it *had* ended seven years earlier, as General Gallifet wished, the stain on the honor of France would never have been erased.[1]

The injustices from American officer in-group loyalty today are far more serious than the Dreyfus affair that aroused the French nation. Esprit de corps or "Honor" as it is called by West Point and the Mafia and some other organizations, does not necessarily imply mutual respect and goodwill on the part of those involved. With the Mafia it implies the prospect of the murder of any member who does not protect fellow members. In the Engineer Corps, as we will show in the case of the Current Meter, a breach of discipline by a fellow member of the Engineer Corps was punished by the wreck of a man's life-hopes and plans, even though the disobedience was for the sake of an important technical advance.

The explicit falsehoods that are resorted to by vested interests in political power—and that we have documented with regard to the U.S. Corps of Engineers—are tacitly assumed to be necessary conditions of political life. Any one who attacks the employment of such falsehoods is regarded as a political enemy or as a naive, politically unrealistic simpleton. This is deepseated in American political life, and it is the more serious as the groups and political interests that wield such power are firmly entrenched and growing stronger behind their barricades of power and standing. I personally experienced such intrigue in the Tennessee Valley Authority, where criticism of dishonest reports was interpreted as treason to the project.

If America has no contrary standards of truth, justice, and

public interest it would be assumed that all exercise of power was for selfish and factional ends, and such ends would prevail completely. But a higher ethics is still expected of public officials, and when these higher standards are used as facades for unethical conduct the entire social order is corroded as a result. There are organizations in and out of the government, or partly in and partly out, the interests of which conflict with those of open, responsible democratic government. One of these is the Congress of Rivers and Harbors, which is officially associated with and works very closely with the Corps of Engineers.

All officers in the Corps are ex-officio members of the Rivers and Harbors Congress. Its semi-secret membership list includes a powerful alliance of contractors and their suppliers, who do the work on Army Engineer Corps projects, representatives of other water resource development lobbies, utility, oil, and coal interests, big farmers, shippers, a galaxy of local and state officials, and members of Congress. Inquiry from the Corps of Engineers as to its membership list brought the reply that the list would be as long as the dictionary. The Rivers and Harbors Congress is a major source of the Corps of Engineers' political support. Like most government departments, the Corps has a vested interest in maintaining its existing structure, policies, and programs. And the Congress of Rivers and Harbors has supported the Corps' fight to retain its civilian functions, authority, and administrative autonomy seemingly regardless of the quality of its work. The following resolution passed at the 1947 annual convention of the Congress of Rivers and Harbors is typical of its assertions:

> We affirm our conviction that all planning and execution of public improvements of our water resources for navigation, flood control, and allied purposes, including beach and shore protection, continue as in the past to be under the jurisdiction of the War Department as a function of the Corps of Engineers. We affirm our faith and confidence in the Corps of Engineers whose devotion to this nation and loyalty to the Chief Executive have

made possible the orderly and efficient development of the greatest waterway and flood control projects on earth. In their many years of experience, during peace and war, they have met many emergencies and have never failed to accomplish the greatest good for the greatest number of people in a manner most advantageous to the Government and to the people. Furthermore we believe that only through the plans developed by the Corps of Engineers can we obtain a consistent and coordinated improvement of our water resources.[2]

This is a typical illustration of the false representation by the Rivers and Harbors Congress and the Corps, and its extravagant self-praise as consistently misstated realities. For instance, as to their claim of loyalty to the Chief Executive, this statement is completely and grossly false. The Corps with the help of the Rivers and Harbors Congress has made sustained effort for a long period of time to thwart and nullify the policies of presidents, especially Herbert Hoover and Franklin D. Roosevelt, in their effort to control gross privilege and exploitation of public water interests for private profit, as was the case in Kings River and Central Valley, California. There electric power, generated at public expense, was kept out of public hands and placed in the hands of a large private corporation. That organization also makes unlimited assertions of loyalty to the government, the Congress and the executive. No record of the Corps of Engineers can be adequate without consideration of its relation to the Congress of Rivers and Harbors.*

*Our government, including the Congress and the Executive, had established a national policy with reference to the Central Valley. Very large areas of semi-desert land were held in a few large ownerships. In its unimproved condition that land had very little value. The federal government had major elements of policy with reference to the improvement of these large tracts of land. One principle was that it would be reclaimed by irrigation on condition that the improvement be paid for by those benefiting. Another was that such reclamation should be carried through on condition that the large ownerships should be broken down into family sized farm tracts of 160 acres. The work was being done by these principles under the direction of the U.S.

With the influence which comes with largely controlling the expenditure of large amounts of money in the districts of congressmen, through its actual power to grant or to deny the requests of individual Congressmen for expenditures in their districts, and with the power of being members of one of the most powerful lobbies in the country, (The Congress of Rivers and Harbors), and being in intimate relations with the several powerful special interest groups, the Corps in some respects dominates Congress. Thus largely independent both of the executive and of the free judgment of Congress, the Corps of Engineers has some of the characteristics of an independent factor in government.

The reasonable limit of the Corps is to do work which is beyond local resources, not to relieve individual communities of local burdens. The Corps is more and more tending to carry out local projects at national expense. If the general government is to carry the whole cost, local communities may ask for vastly greater expenditures than would be justified if they were required to carry even a half or a third of the cost. Here is a field of political influence and manipulation which is not wholesome. The Corps is ready and eager to be the national authority for various types of public expenditure where definite estimates of cost and benefits are difficult. Here it is important that the agencies of government which are responsible have a tradition of freedom from political manipulation.

Reclamation Service. The Corps of Engineers determined to be the agent for much of that work. The recognized, constitutional government process would be for the Corps to present its proposals to the executive, and for him to present it to Congress, with his own statement of national policy. President Franklin D. Roosevelt made very clear that he wished to have continued the policy of earlier administrations. The Corps took the course of bypassing the President and of sending its proposals directly to a committee of Congress, which committee, apparently with the help of the Rivers and Harbors Congress, had exceptional influence. Through this evasion of responsibility to the executive the Corps was an active agent in reversing established national policy.

The Corps of Engineers is on the way to vast enlargement of its function. Its members were trained, not for public works, but for war. Our government might well consider an overall department of public works which will draw on the highest capacities in every related field. With the training at West Point for war, it is by no means suitable for effective directing of public works on such a scale.

Today the foreign policy of the United States has been significantly taken over by the graduates of West Point. Those who go from the West Point training and conditioning into the Corps of Engineers are applying the traditions and the indoctrination and the spirit of West Point to civilian fields. In the catalog of West Point there is hardly a suggestion that it is training for civil works. It is part of the complex of which President Eisenhower warned the country in his farewell address:

> Now this conjunction of an immense military establishment and a large arms industry is new in the American experience. The total influence—economic, political, even spiritual—is felt in every city, every state house, every office of the Federal government. We recognize the imperative need for this development. Yet we must not fail to comprehend its grave implications. Our toil, resources and livelihood are all involved; it is the very structure of our society.
>
> In the councils of Government, we must guard against the acquisition of unwarranted influence, whether sought or unsought, by the military-industrial complex. The potential for the disastrous rise of misplaced power exists and will persist.
>
> We must never let the weight of this combination endanger our liberties or democratic processes. We should take nothing for granted. Only an alert and knowledgeable citizenry can impel the proper meshing of the huge industrial and military machinery of defense with our peaceful methods and goals, so that security and liberty may prosper together.[3]

The members of the Corps, being public officials and

concerned with public works, can infest the Senate and House office buildings, and need not register as lobbyists. Hundreds of contractors, working under the Corps, are also members of the Rivers and Harbors Congress. Thus the members of the Corps have two relations with these contractors. First, they are the officers of government whose duty is to insure that the work of the contractors is properly done. Second, they are fellow members of the Rivers and Harbors Congress lobby. When I suggested to the principal financial organization of Pittsburgh that they employ their own engineers to make a comparison of two plans for work vital to the welfare of Pittsburgh, a major opposition to that proposal which I met was by one of the chief contractors under the Corps, and almost certainly a member of the Rivers and Harbors Congress.

When a congressman dares to oppose a proposal of the Corps he may find himself, as some of them have made public, bombarded by protesting letters from members of the Rivers and Harbors Congress.

Fortunately there are members of the Corps, who through inborn quality and early life, have had definition of character and personality which has survived West Point without serious damage. Through the years, I have become acquainted with West Point men whom I have admired and respected. I have felt that this book must not bring harm or embarrassment to such men. My old friend, General Hiram Chittenden, one time Chief of Engineers, though the Corps failed to stir in him the development of original, creative thinking, for which I believe he had native capacity, maintained his deeply imbedded honesty of purpose and behavior.

From time to time young men have enrolled at West Point whose character and quality prevented them from surrendering to the system of isolation, coercion, and indoctrination known as the "Thayer system" and who retained their character and independence of judgment. Let us refer to two of these men at the beginning and the end of a century.

In the eighteen-sixties a major issue arose in the Corps of Engineers, perhaps the most important in its history up to that time. This concerned improvement in the outlet to the Mississippi River. A commission of the Corps of Engineers, presumably of the ablest members of the Corps, was appointed to deal with that important subject.

The Chairman of that Commission was General J. H. Barnard, one time Superintendent of West Point and during the Civil War General Grant's chief engineer and most relied-upon assistant. He was strikingly objective and independent. In his earlier years he had expressed the conventional appraisal concerning the Corps: "They have commanded the entire confidence of the Government and the communities which they have served."[4]

Then, working in the field with a number of the highest ranking of these men, and observing them at first hand in action, he reached a different conclusion. His opinion is expressed at length in the chapter on the Mississippi Jetties. He wrote:

> The incompetence from first to last with which the thing has been managed by the E.D. [Engineer Department] has thrown it irrevocably into the hands of politicians . . . To talk about the inadequacy of the study . . . is nonsense . . . The utter superficiality of the views of the members of the "board" . . . were so evident to me that it was perfectly immaterial to me which way they voted . . .
>
> I am in an impossible situation to criticize . . . they don't know their own deficiency. Each one finds he knows as much as the rest . . . and the conventional word "engineer" which they unhesitatingly assume, supplies all the rest. And they are kept in that delusion by a large outside world which, having no means of judging, consistently conceded to "government engineers" a profound deference . . .
>
> It is no longer a pride nor a satisfaction to be an "engineer" . . . I can never feel as I used to towards the Corps of Engineers.[5]

Now for a case of independence and responsibility which brings us up to date. Among the engineers now actively involved professionally, few are better qualified to appraise

the Corps of Engineers than Charles D. Curran. Mr. Curran
got his start as a West Point-graduated Corps Engineer who
subsequently took special training in hydraulics. In the
course of time he worked in the office of the Chief of
Engineers of the Corps and he was chosen to review Engineer
Corps projects for the Legislative Reference Service of the
Library of Congress. Curran was responsible for review of
government engineering work for the Bureau of the Budget,
and was chosen to study the role of the Engineer Corps for
the Second Hoover Commission on reorganization of the
government. He was also chosen by the Congressional Jones
Committee to study the Corps. Mr. Curran's views could be
paralleled by those of others in comparable positions of
oversight.

In a taped interview Mr. Curran asserted in 1965, and
approved in 1970:

> The Corps is not different in having its eye on
> organizational aggrandizement. Most organizations of
> government want to get more money to spend—human
> vanity—power. The financial rewards are low, it is status
> and power they are after. The Corps is more successful
> because it works as an organization—it is a body, not a
> person.

Charles Curran emphasizes that unless politically proficient
an officer

> won't succeed in his handling of civilian works. Because
> no matter what you call it, it's still a big pork barrel. It
> isn't the biggest one any more. We've got much bigger
> ones with AID, defense procurement, space and other
> things, but unfortunately the waterways development is a
> pork barrel operation and so you get a separation of
> people who are commissioned within the Corps, those
> who are most astute politically and able to get along in
> that realm, who get into the river and harbor work.

The Corps' seeking more and more dams and projects for it
to keep working on, often largely regardless of their value in
relation to other needs and their economic justification, is

necessary to its existence as a political power-wielding organization. With this basic political orientation so dominant all of the quality, competence and involvement of other persons, resources and assets of American society that the Corps can buy tend to be colored and involved.

For example, the increasing participation of the Corps in the American Society of Civil Engineers brings this characteristic to those of the committees the Corps dominates. In his interview already referred to Mr. Curran asserts:

> Some technical society committees are recently tending to be dominated by the Corps. Like most people the Corps does not like opposition, and they look for people of their own group since we all know that the only people who are competent are people who agree with us.
>
> There was conscious effort to participate in the A.S.C.E. after they (the Corps) were criticized for not being competent, and the easiest way to eliminate a criticism was to have the people who are criticizing join their number. And that soon shifted the criticism.

The basically political and feudal character of the Corps that is thus brought to bear on American society is not on the wane. Charles Curran observes that before the Second World War

> The Corps was in my opinion in many respects a much less political organization than it is today. (1965) Up to the start of the Second World War there were only three general officers, they were the only ones whose rank was really subject to political control. The division officers were colonels and at that time a colonel was a man of considerable stature in the military establishment . . . The attitude as I've understood and seen it was in those days that they should not be rigid in opposing a survey but then be pretty hardboiled in looking at the economics of whether a project should be built . . . But since World War II the division engineer has been a brigadier or major-general. We're got more generals in the Corps and it means that an . . . officer has greater opportunity of becoming a general officer if he watches his P's and Q's so

that he will be confirmed if nominated. So there you get into a vulnerability to political control. Whether they want it or not, it is true that they are aware of political pressure . . . In recent years we see it in a number of these projects being recommended, particularly those for navigation, in which the "economics" are just fantastic.

Gilbert White has observed that great improvement has been planned for the Corps. He said, "I disagree with Arthur Morgan on the ability of the Corps of Engineers. The recent self-examination done by the Corps officers shows that great modifications are proposed."[6] But the fundamental character of the Corps is not just a matter of *ability*. Gilbert White made the distinction in saying, "To expect the Corps of Engineers or Bureau of Reclamation to adopt a new *approach* as opposed to a new technique, is like trying to set fire to soggy newspapers."[7]

In reference to this kind of weakness of the Corps Charles Curran commented:

> There are no degrees of integrity; either you have integrity or you have not. And I must say that I'm not impressed with a number of my colleagues in that they consider themselves honest if they don't accept any personal material gain. The fact that they come up with an unsound report that will help someone politically means that they do not recognize intellectual dishonesty.

The effect of this kind of organization on the management of the nation's resources should be obvious. It is summarized by Charles Curran as follows:

> Our present setup with the Corps is not leading to balanced planning. It is still trying to carry leadership and with the leadership the control.
> To what extent can the Corps be considered responsible for the haphazard development of water resources? Oh, quite responsible, because it's their recommendations the Congress acts on. Congress does not write engineering reports.

The general attitude is to justify projects. A project has to be pretty poor before they will turn it down. And part of this is due to competition—if one agency won't do the job another will ... The Corps is unsound, but the Bureau of Reclamation is worse, which is not much merit.

I have made numerous criticisms both of the ethical character and of the engineering competence of the Corps of Engineers. I have described those characteristics as not being occasional lapses from a generally high level of character and achievement, but as fundamentally characteristic of the Corps. I have shown that this characteristic of the Corps resulted from the fundamental character and structure of the U.S. Military Academy which in turn grew out of and was characteristic of the little group including Sylvanus Thayer, a great admirer of Napoleon.

I can picture the vitriolic contempt and the indignation or severe disregard with which this record will be treated by the Corps, and by the persons of dignity and position whom they will choose to tell of the long standing honor and competence of this great organization.

In view of this probable reception by the Corps, it seems desirable to lift out from this record and to present at this time a few typical cases, extending over a century, one from its beginning, one from the middle of a hundred year period, and also from more recent occasions, which are representative of the characteristics to which I have brought attention in the book.

Let us begin with a century ago, during the administration of General A. A. Humphreys as Chief of Engineers of the Corps. His is the most honored and revered name in the history of the Corps. For more than half a century his book, *The Physics and Hydraulics of the Mississippi River* was the "Bible" of the Corps. Important engineering decisions were made, not by critical and objective analysis, but by reference to that book. Humphreys intended that it should be so. In presenting that book to the Corps and to the world he stated in the introduction:

The problem of protection against overflow solved.
Thus every important fact connected with the various
physical conditions of the river [the Mississippi] and the
laws uniting them being ascertained; the great problem of
protection against inundation was solved.[8]

It was only after sixty years of worshipful, uncritical
observance of Humphreys' dogmas by the Corps, covering
vital elements of Mississippi River control, that Herbert
Hoover, engineer President, brushed aside the long time
control of the Corps on the Mississippi River, and brought
about a revolution. Among the most revolutionary changes,
each of which had been repudiated by Humphreys, and
vigorously repudiated for sixty years by the Corps, were
reliance on the use of the hydraulic laboratory, the adoption
of which profoundly changed and improved engineering
practice; the acceptance of cutoffs on the Mississippi River
by which high water levels are lowered ten or fifteen feet;
and the use of reservoirs in Mississippi River system flood
control.

It was not only in technical engineering methods that
Humphreys acted by the doctrine of Napoleon, as completely
accepted by Thayer and by the Napoleonic generals who had
lived under that doctrine. A fundamental doctrine of
Napoleon, which was incorporated into the West Point code,
though commonly kept from the public eye, was set up as a
greeting to incoming members of the armed forces at Fort
Leonard Wood, which read:

> No war was ever
> Won with compassion
> Or conscience- ———kill.

Under the American home conditions physical assassination
is not feasible. The alternative is assassination of character
and reputation. At this General Humphreys was adept. This is
clearly disclosed in the chapter on the Mississippi Jetties. It
was not a personal trait of Humphreys alone, but was
characteristic of the typical members of the Corps of
Engineers who participated in an intensive effort to discredit

both the competence and the character of James Eads, one of the greatest civil engineers America or the world has produced.*

In the attempt to remove James Eads as competitor to the Corps, every type of lying, make-believe, misrepresentation, and effort were made to embarrass him and frighten those who were financing him. Through ex-Corps members in public life, scarcely any kind of threat, abuse and warning of danger was omitted. In this, the Chief of Engineers and patron saint of the Corps united with his staff all along the line. When Humphreys took official action leading to the prevention of the building of the Eads Bridge, President Grant expressed great indignation and countermanded that action, thereby saving the building of the Bridge.** On a visit to St. Louis, he personally took occasion to visit Eads and express his admiration. A reading of the chapter on the Mississippi Jetties and the Eads Bridge will confirm this statement. The dogma that compassion and conscience do not win was observed.

At the close of President Grant's term of office, when on board ship for his trip around the world, his last government directed action was to write a letter to his friend, Samuel Sherman, asking him to try to stop the cabal of Humphreys' organization conspiring against James Eads.

Other cases are described. In the chapter on the Hydraulic Laboratory a foremost hydraulic engineer, who had been president of the American Society of Civil Engineers and also of the American Society of Mechanical Engineers, who had received gold medals from each of them, and who had a world wide practice, on retiring from practice in his sixties, determined to give the remainder of his active life to trying to reduce what he believed was the vast incompetence and waste of the Corps of Engineers on the Mississippi.

*In a canvass of the deans of American engineering schools to name the greatest engineers of all time, James Eads was fifth in the list.
**Humphreys was under General Grant during the Civil War, and when Grant became president he showed unequivocally that he did not trust or respect the character of this most influential of Corps engineers.

At first this engineer sought to improve the management of the Corps on the Mississippi as friends, cooperating in search for more suitable methods, but he met with rebuff. When the Secretary of War asked the Chief of Engineers, Major-General Jadwin, for information about this man, John R. Freeman, the reply the Secretary received gave Freeman's name and a statement that it was understood that there had been criticism of some engineering he had done in China. That was all the significant information the Secretary was given in response to his inquiry. That, of itself, was deceit or extreme misrepresentation.

For eight years Mr. Freeman sought to change the situation. He was ignored, rebuffed or contradicted, as the Corps saw fit. During this period of Freeman's effort, while he was being rebuffed or ignored, the Chief of Engineers summed up his view of the situation as follows. Addressing the House Committee of Rivers and Harbors, he said:

> The science of river hydraulics in America, both in theoretical and practical, as a whole is more advanced than that of any other nation in the world, and this advance is due almost exclusively to the activities of the Army Engineers.[9]

This was less than five years before President Hoover's revolution which showed that almost every major policy of the Corps was basically and totally in error, including opposition to cutoffs, reservoirs and hydraulic laboratories. Hoover's action for a few years entirely changed the management of the Corps in controlling policies on the Mississippi, disclosing the Corps for the past sixty years to have been greatly in error concerning the major principles for control of the Mississippi River. The correction of those vast and fundamental errors in Mississippi River policy brought a new day of promise for this River.

At about the same time, in 1927-1928, at the Symposium of the American Society of Civil Engineers on Mississippi River improvement, I criticized the Corps for its long time failure to adequately study possibilities for reservoirs to help control the Mississippi, and also questioned the adequacy of the Study of the subject by an Engineer Corps Board created in 1927 for that purpose. The withering repudiation of my criticisms by the Chief Officer of the Corps on that study was worded with finality. He reported:

> Considerable criticism has been launched against those studies on the grounds that they are inadequate and based on incomplete data . . . The studies were efficiently and honestly made in such a way that the probable errors favor the reservoirs. Had they showed any reservoirs that offered even a remote chance . . . accurate and complete studies thereof would have been recommended. There is no reasonable hope that undiscovered reservoirs might overcome difference in cost.

> In regard to the second criticism, during thirty years of experience in the Corps of Engineers, the writer has never encountered a case where pride of Corps has affected the professional judgment of its members. On the other hand, such pride as the Corps has, is in its success in upholding its professional integrity and proficiency. The officers of the Corps are no different from other engineers. They are trained to seek facts and to form independent judgment therefrom and are never backward about expressing differences of opinion with each other. The fact that heretofore they have independently but uniformly reached a conclusion against reservoirs as a cure for Mississippi floods is a fairly good guaranty that under the conditions that have existed up to the present, reservoirs could not be economically used to relieve the Mississippi Valley.[10]

This published statement that the "studies were efficiently and honestly made" could be checked twenty years later when the correspondence of the Corps' office was transferred to the National Archives. There we found and examined them. The correspondence between the head office and the field showed that the studies were hastily and entirely inadequately made. This character was recognized and repeatedly commented on by the very field men who made the studies. The Task Force of the Second Hoover Commission, appointed by President Roosevelt and under the direction of ex-President Hoover, reported what had occurred under Chief of Engineers Lytle Brown, and showed that under him and his successors hundreds of reservoirs were being created. By the time of the Second Hoover Commission Report, more than a hundred were wholly or in part charged to the control of the Mississippi River. A dozen of these are fairly major reservoirs. Further details are given in the chapter on reservoirs.

In the late 1950's, twenty-five years after the incident just mentioned I was trying to persuade the Corps that on the Upper Allegheny River the Corps was making a very great mistake in adopting the Kinzua Reservoir rather than the Conewango Reservoir, violating America's oldest treaty signed by President Washington with the Seneca Nation of Indians. The Corps seemingly had overlooked the possibility of the Conewango Reservoir for the storage of water for low water control, and wanted to avoid acknowledging its oversight. The Conewango basin, because it was a glacial excavation and not a river valley, had been overlooked by the Corps. The Conewango reservoir would have four times as much capacity for storage for low water regulation as would Kinzua. If the larger storage were substantially needed, then the Conewango Reservoir would be incomparably superior.

The Appropriations Committee of the House demanded of the Corps that it make a comparison of the two plans. The only way out for the Corps was to make a flat mis-statement. Kinzua had a capacity of storage for low water control of a half million acre feet. Conewango Reservoir would have a total storage for low water river control of two and a half million acre feet, and a net storage for that purpose of two million acre feet.

The Corps of Engineers in its comparison of the two plans required by the Appropriations Committee, directly held that additional storage for low water river control was not feasible. The wording of the statement is:

> It is not practicable under present authorities to assess benefits for conjectural, possible future water supply needs as a basis for justifying additional water supply

storage . . . The additional investment [for Conewango] could not be justified on the basis of additional benefits that can now be evaluated.[11]

This pronouncement by the Corps to the Subcommittee on Public Works Appropriations was a mis-statement of facts. During this same period the same Chief of Engineers was going about the Ohio Valley telling of the extreme importance for just such storage for low water river control . . . Several quotations to that effect are included in the chapter on the Upper Allegheny. A single one of these quotes will be repeated:

Studies indicate that the future water demand-supply relationship in the Ohio basin to be one of the most critical in the most humid east . . .[12]

We face a critical problem of reservoir sites. Good locations for major impoundments are already being lost at an alarming rate as improvements of one kind or another . . . are built in the very places reservoirs should be located.[13]

The Conewango Basin is so ample that both it and the very inadequate Kinzua site were not needed. To build Kinzua first and Conewango afterward would be a waste and loss of more than $100,000,000. To "save face" for the Corps and to maintain the "principle" that outsiders must not critically look into Corps affairs, a gross, palpable lie must be presented to the Appropriations Committee.

On another occasion the Corps presented its view to a highly respected senator and then brought him to a committee meeting where the project would be discussed. A high official of the Corps then stood by this senator while the senator told the committee that no substantial plan had been presented, that I was an adventurer, and that the plan I presented was only a means by which an irresponsible adventurer could gain cheap publicity. There really was no serious plan calling for examination. When I inquired of the senator as to the basis of his expression his reply was that he knew nothing about the situation personally, but that his opinion came directly and also through another person, entirely from the Corps of Engineers. When I inquired from the "other person," he told me he knew nothing of the situation, and his opinion came from the Engineer Corps. At another meeting, attended by General Cassidy, later Chief of the Corps of Engineers, when the Conewango Reservoir possibility was being discussed, in contemptuously dismissing the subject he said: "If the Ladies' Society wishes to raise money to fight this case, that is their privilege." The clear inference was that there was no real problem to examine. The chapter on the Upper Allegheny deals with this subject.

By these extracts, mostly from the chapters of the book, we have illustrated the lack of integrity and the methods of the Corps through a full century. It is not primarily the individuals of the Corps who are responsible, but the entire Corsican, Napoleonic pattern, so completely embraced by Thayer and his Napoleonic generals, and so vigorously maintained by America's most striking case of isolating its young men, coercing, regimenting and indoctrinating them, as described in the first chapter of the book, that a pattern has been fixed and held for more than a century and a half. As the current catalog of West Point states: "The Academy builds always on the cornerstone of the Thayer system."

A final comment relates to the influence of the long time tradition of the Thayer system of the Corps of Engineers on the several governmental agencies with which it has had longtime intimate relations. Public agencies which have constant and important interrelations tend to develop similar patterns and standards. The Corps of Engineers is almost the oldest such agency in the United States. Its patterns of action became deeply established. As other agencies with similar functions developed, especially where there is intimate interrelation, the standards of the older and larger organization tend to be taken on by the newer and smaller agency.

Charles Curran and Gilbert White have asserted that in some respects the standards and patterns of the Reclamation Service are even worse than those of the Corps. That is not surprising, for the Bureau of Reclamation was much younger than the Corps. If West Point, instead of taking for its pattern the Corsica-bred Napoleon, had gone perhaps to Switzerland, whose democratically-minded soldiers, man to man in battle were more effective than those of the Empire, West Point might have developed a freedom loving, democratically spirited, very effective and humanly sensitive pattern and spirit. A spirit of good will and mutual helpfulness might have ruled, rather than a spirit which could lead a cadet, finally through his first year, to say with reference to hazing, "They gave us hell. Now it is our turn."

Such a change of spirit and attitude, if it is to emerge and prevail in public service in America, probably will not be an outgrowth of West Point, but a new beginning. The Tennessee Valley Authority, in spite of some tragic experiences in its course, has elements of promise and of human achievement. In the T.V.A. we have an alternative tradition which is in striking contrast to the Engineer Corps both in technical competence and in respect for human values.

Fifty years ago, in testimony before congressional committees, an expression from ranking members of the Corps was: "If it concerns water it is the function of the Corps." Little by little the fields of water control which the Corps of Engineers is inclined to see as exclusively its own, have increased, and today continue to increase, at first by participation, and then increasingly moving toward full control. Also, in old fields new functions appear. This volume deals with some of the functions which the U.S. Corps of Engineers now exercises. But many activities, relations and attitudes which are of great importance I have dealt with only tentatively, if at all. One relationship which may deeply affect the course of our national lives, but of which we have only touched the margins, is the Congress of Rivers and Harbors. The semi-secret relations of this organization calls for substantial, objective inquiry, which we were unable to make. The problems of cost-benefit relationships, recently made the study of scholarly books, deal both with inherently difficult and complex relationships and also with log rolling, and the rewarding of friends and the punishment of opposition. The entire field of harbor improvement, with the possibility of spending public funds for deep harbors where approaches are inadequate, needs also to be investigated. The undertaking to carry ocean harbors hundreds of miles inland, as in Oklahoma and Texas, at the expense of billions of dollars would not have been carried through without the Corps of Engineers' approval. The gradual increase of carrying through local public works as gifts of the federal government, without requiring the sharing of the burdens by those directly interested, is another product of Corps work.

The matter of pollution looms large. Since 1901 the Corps has had power from Congress to control pollution in navigable rivers. It is only by permission of the Corps that such pollution is legally possible. From being an agency in some cases largely responsible for pollution, the Corps is warming up to the attitude that it should be the agency primarily responsible for controlling it.

The habit of the U.S. Corps of Engineers to increase its functions and to enlarge the area in which it will be dominant, "built always on the cornerstone of the Thayer system," should be ended.

notes

1. Leo Sauvage, "The Oswald Affair," World Publishing Company, 2231 West 100th St., Cleveland, Ohio 44102. Published in France, 1965; in the U.S., 1966. Pp. 330,331.

2. Resolution at the Annual Convention of the Congress of Rivers and Harbors, 1947. 1028 Connecticut Avenue N.W., Washington, D.C.

3. Dwight D. Eisenhower, farewell address to the nation as President of the United States, Jan. 17, 1961. From Norman's Reference Book, "Vital Speeches of the Day," 1961.

4. Major J. G. Barnard, letter to the editors of the *National Intelligencer* (pamphlet), 1862, pp. 5, 10. (Also quoted in the chapter on the *Mississippi Jetties*, p. 12, source 34.)

5. General J. G. Barnard, letters to General C. B. Comstock, April-July, 1874. National Archives and Library of Congress Manuscripts. (Also quoted in the chapter on the *Mississippi Jetties*, pp. 12-13-14-15, Sources 35, 36, 37, 43, 48.)

6. Gilbert White, Professor, Department of Geography, University of Chicago, 1101 E. 58th St., Chicago, Ill. 60637.

7. *Ibid.*

8. Humphreys and Abbot, "The Physics and Hydraulics of the Mississippi River," Introduction, p. 11 (1861).

9. Major-General Jadwin, Statement before the House Committee on Rivers and Harbors, May 15, 1928, National Archives. (Also quoted in the chapter on the *Hydraulics Laboratory*, p. 14, source 10.)

10. Col. Kelly, *Transactions*, American Society of Civil Engineers, pp. 954-955, 1929. (Also quoted in the *Reservoirs* chapter, p. 55A, source 97.)

11. General E. C. Itschner, Analysis of Allegheny Reservoir and Alternate Proposal of Dr. Arthur E. Morgan, to the Sub-committee on Public Works of the House Appropriations Committee, 1958. (Also quoted in the *Upper Allegheny* chapter, p. 26, source 14.)

12. General E. C. Itschner, Address to the Ohio Valley Improvement Association, Cincinnati, Ohio, Oct. 26, 1959, pp. 6, 7, 8. (Also quoted in the *Upper Allegheny* chapter, p. 27, source 15.)

13. General E. C. Itschner, article in the *Saturday Evening Post*, June 5, 1959. (Also quoted in the *Upper Allegheny* chapter, p. 27, source 16.)

part ii

As of the year 1970, the U.S. Corps of Engineers have underway 275 projects, with 452 approved and awaiting construction. In the preceding few chapters we see the human effect of the Corps and the effect on the human environment. It would seem that characteristically the Corps does mass work, rather than good work, that characteristically most of the projects described were prepared without the thorough, inclusive engineering study necessary to insure competence, that they have characteristically lacked sensitivity to environmental values, and last but not least, that they have lacked sensitivity to human welfare.

The succeeding chapters, covering the course of a century case by case, from the 1860's to the 1960's, describe the work of that long period, including some of the major undertakings in the life of the Corps, as well as relations of the Corps with some of the more important achievements of the century, and indicate the errors of the Corps in relation to the work of competent men. We see in actual life the results of the kinds of training to which the members of the Corps have been subjected.

Trained at West Point, under the Thayer system, which they considered desirable for military training, West Point men are peculiarly unfitted for the execution of public works. The following chapters will make that evident as to the American public works program.

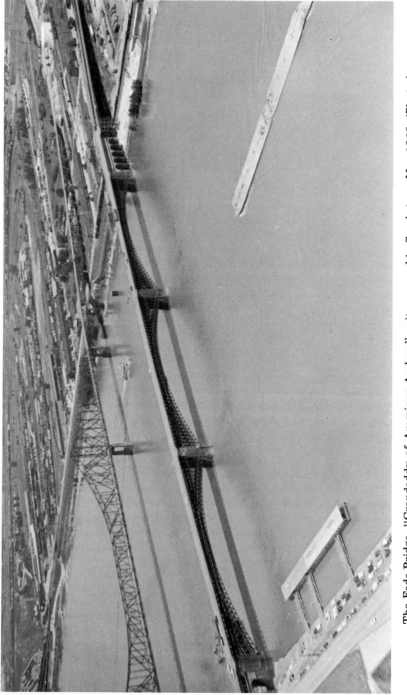

The Eads Bridge, "Grandaddy of American Arches," as it appeared in flood stage, May 1968. (Photo by Richard Horn)

chapter 5

james b. eads
and the
st. louis
bridge

In 1930 the deans of American engineering schools selected as the first five in a list of thirteen of the greatest engineers of all time, Leonardo da Vinci, James Watt, Ferdinand de Lesseps, Thomas A. Edison and James B. Eads.[1] Later Eads was the first engineer to be honored with a place in the American Hall of Fame.

Who was Eads? His two most noted accomplishments were the construction of a bridge across the Mississippi River at St. Louis, and the Jetties at the mouth of the Mississippi. His reputation and his services were international. His advice was sought by cities around the country and by numerous foreign governments. He made plans for improving the harbor of Toronto; advised on improving the harbors of Vera Cruz and Tampico; was an advisor to the Mersey Docks and Harbor Board of Liverpool and many others. In 1882, Eads was elected a vice-president of the American Society of Civil Engineers. In 1884, the British Society for the Encouragement of Art, Manufacture, and Commerce, awarded him their Albert Medal for his contribution to the science of engineering, the only American to be so honored up to that time. He had the very rare honor of an American being made a member of the British Institute of Civil Engineers and of the British Association.[2]

James B. Eads was born in Lawrenceburg, Indiana on May

23, 1820. He very early showed that his exceptional mentality included mechanical aptitude. By the age of ten, in a little workshop his father had provided him he was building his own miniature models of saw-mills, fire engines, steam engines and the like, including a tiny steamboat that would actually cross a pond. The boy's father was not very successful in his business pursuits, and at the age of thirteen young Eads had to leave school to work his own way. There his formal education ended. Shortly afterwards the whole family moved to St. Louis, where James took to selling apples.[3]

Soon, he found better work as a clerk for a dry goods firm. His employer, recognizing the boy's thirst for knowledge, let James use his unusually fine library, much of it treating of scientific subjects. In his five years with the dry goods firm, by his own almost wholly unassisted effort in this library, he achieved a range, clarity and penetration of scientific thinking, which, along with his marvelously creative mind, and his further incessant reading and experience, made it possible for him to become one of the world's foremost engineers.

For three years after leaving the dry goods firm he worked as a purser on a Mississippi River steamer. For such a mind and with such preparation, this period was very first hand introduction to river hydraulics. In 1842, when he was only 22, he applied this experience and his inventiveness to the construction of a diving-bell made of a watertight "hogs-head" barrel with weights. Beginning with this diving-bell, with air pumped down from a boat, he made about three hundred underwater exploratory trips, from above St. Louis to New Orleans, sometimes in 70 feet or more of water, searching for sunken vessels. Later, he developed diving equipment with a boat of larger tonnage, with machinery for pumping the sand out of sunken wrecks, thus making it possible to recover a large number of valuable steamers and their cargoes. Prior to this it had been deemed "impossible" to raise these ships due to the shifting sand and swift current of the Mississippi which soon buried any wreck.[4] With the exception of three years in which he owned and operated an unsuccessful glass plant, Eads pursued this salvaging work for fourteen years until 1856.

By this unique occupation, which he originated through a combination of active imagination, sound, tested practical judgment and well considered daring, by the time he was 26 he had accumulated a fortune, and had become one of St. Louis' distinguished citizens and river captains. His remarkable practical competence is evidenced by the fact that in more than three hundred trips on the bottom of the river, among logs and sunken trees, his self-invented outfit never failed him.[5]

The most valuable result of Eads' long years of experience below the surface of the Mississippi was the unparalleled, first-hand knowledge he gained of that temperamental river and its bed. Years afterwards he said that there wasn't a stretch in its bed fifty miles long, between St. Louis and New Orleans, in which he had not stood on the bottom of the stream beneath the shelter of the diving bell.[6]

Later, when Chief of Engineers Humphreys, relying on theoretical hypothesis, expressed disdain for Eads' statements as to how sand and gravel was moved along the Mississippi River, Eads frequently referred to his many first-hand, personal observations while walking on the river bottom under a diving bell. In these deep water explorations, the pressure of up to seventy feet of water damaged his health and finally shortened his life.

In 1861, shortly after the firing on Fort Sumter, which opened the War Between the States, Eads emerged from a retirement forced by ill health to write Edward Bates, Lincoln's Attorney General, of the critical necessity for iron-clad gun-boats on the Mississippi. He was called to Washington to present his ideas for such a river navy to the Cabinet. Despite some ridicule of the idea there, Eads was assigned a naval officer, a Captain Rodgers, to get the construction of his gun-boats started.

It was from this point that Eads' troubles with the military began. All ready to leave the capital, he was forced to waste several precious days while Army and Navy ironed out a jurisdictional dispute over the proposed fleet. That settled, he and Captain Rodgers departed for Cairo, Illinois. Once there, Rodgers brushed aside Eads' enthusiasm for metal-clad boats and went himself to Cincinnati to purchase three ships of the type he was more accustomed to—sidewheel packets with oak timbers.

Eads, the civilian, was hamstrung and his plan languished. Realizing the further division of the country that could result from Confederate control of the Mississippi River, he chafed to be able to commence building a fleet of protected gun-boats. Going once more to Washington, he found any plans for an iron-clad navy lost in the shuffle. In July, the three wooden gun-boats purchased and re-vamped by Captain Rodgers were grounded in the Ohio on their way to the Mississippi, just as Eads had warned they might be.

Eads then learned that the Quartermaster General of the Union Army had advertised for bids for seven modified ironclad gunboats. He made out a bid pared to the bone and promised to complete this fleet in the incredible time of 65 days. His bid was accepted and on August 7, Eads signed a contract with the government. The boats he was to build were utterly unconventional warships. To construct seven of these in slightly over two months would be a fantastic feat in peacetime, but with the crucial labor shortage, material shortage and utter confusion of a brand-new war, the feat seemed impossible. Eads was tremendously hampered by the necessity for getting approval of vital changes in the War Department's designs, by the aforementioned shortages of labor and materials and particularly by the government's refusal to pay him according to its contract. As a result he spent his own fortune on building the gun-boats and was in severe financial straits until the government finally paid him some of the money it owed him. Due to these and other problems, the ships were not completed until a hundred days had passed, but this in itself was a remarkable feat. In addition, he built eight boats, instead of the required seven. Of this feat, Boynton, the historian of the Navy, said:

Thus one individual put into construction and pushed to completion within a hundred days a powerful squadron of eight steamers aggregating five thousand tons, capable of steaming at nine knots per hour, large, heavily armed, fully equipped, and all ready for their armament of one hundred and seven large guns. The fact that such a work was done is nobler praise than any that can be bestowed by words.

Thus was commenced the squadron on the Western waters which became afterward such an important and even indispensable arm of defensive and offensive operations. Without it the rebellion could not have been overcome, for the Mississippi could not have been opened, and the lines of the rebels could not have broken through. . . . Mr. Eads was the efficient and successful pioneer, and by him, almost unaided, the Government was enabled to put the first fleet of ironclads on the Mississippi and its tributaries.[7]

Background

At the close of the Civil War there was no bridge across the middle or lower Mississippi. The tide of western migration had set in, and all traffic was increasing. Railroad, wagon, and foot traffic and the transferring of livestock across the river was by ferry or other boats. St. Louis, as the largest city on the river, was the logical place for a bridge.

The people of the city had long thought of a bridge. As early as 1839 the City Council employed a distinguished civil engineer, Mr. Charles Ellet, to outline a proposal. He presented a plan for a suspension bridge with a central span of 1200 feet, half again as long as any suspension bridge span built to that time. The city fathers could not tolerate any such disregard for traditional limits, and dispensed with his services. Ellet later engineered some of the world's large suspension bridges.*

---

*A pioneer, somewhat ahead of his times, before the Civil War, he recommended reservoirs for flood control and navigation, and thereby incurred the disapproval of the Army Engineers.

In 1855 and again in 1865 plans for a St. Louis bridge were presented which did not make headway. In 1865 the City Council of St. Louis resolved that it "had become indispensably necessary to erect a bridge across the Mississippi River at St. Louis, for the accommodation of citizens of Illinois and St. Louis, and the great railroad traffic now centering there." Already James Eads and his associates were planning to that end.[8]

At the time the Eads Bridge was planned and built, the laws of the United States with respect to the construction of bridges over navigable streams had not yet evolved to a point where the approval of plans by the Secretary of War and the Chief of Engineers was a required prerequisite to construction. That came later, several years after the construction of the Eads Bridge.

Plans and specifications for that Bridge were reviewed and reported upon favorably by a committee of the St. Louis Merchants Exchange of over a thousand members, some of whom were directly interested in navigation. The plans were unanimously approved by the Exchange for presentation to the U.S. Congress and were published in the papers and were put on display at the Exchange.

Following such approval by the Exchange, that body followed through and secured Congress' approval for the bridge and incorporation of the bridge plans in a charter granted by Congress to the Company formed to build the bridge. The approval of the Secretary of War at that time also was assured. In addition, legislation to authorize the bridge was secured from the legislatures of Missouri and Illinois.

In order to build the bridge under the charters which had been secured from Congress, a bridge company had been organized. Its charter in Missouri was secured on February 5, 1864, with about 25 prominent men as incorporators. The original name of the company was "The Saint Louis and Illinois Bridge Company."[9] Under this company Eads began the construction of the bridge in August, 1867.

There had been much talk of bridge building for more than

twenty years. So long as it was chiefly talk, people were not much disturbed. However, with construction actually under way, a confused scramble of conflicting interests began to find expression. Navigation interests opposed the bridge in fear that their business would be hurt. The same was true of ferry interests at St. Louis. Chicago interests sought to kill the project for fear that St. Louis might get some of their business. The northern railroads, going west through Chicago, did not like the prospect of a cross country route further south.

A ferry company which did not want the competition of a bridge secured legislation requiring the Eads Bridge to be built at a point which seemed impossible because of interference with other developments. Eads met this obstacle by providing entrance to St. Louis through a tunnel which did not interfere with these developments. A convention of engineers was arranged by Chicago and navigation interests, with the aim of discrediting Eads. Since Eads was a creative person, repeatedly finding unprecedented ways of achieving his ends, it was not difficult for conventional minds to find something to criticize.

A man named Boomer incorporated a competing bridge company and, rearranging the order of the words, called it the Illinois and Saint Louis Bridge Company. Relying on long-lasting delay through litigation, he finally secured a payment of $150,000 in money and $25,000 in stock of Eads company as a price of withdrawing. In the complexity of negotiation and bargaining, Eads came to take over the name of the other company, and thereafter his company was known, not as the Saint Louis and Illinois Bridge Company, but as the Illinois and Saint Louis Bridge Company.

In the maze of negotiations and bargaining and reorganization in the effort to be free from handicaps, there were some changes of officers of the two companies. As the storm settled, James Eads was the Chief Engineer of the surviving company and William Taussig was Chairman of the Executive Committee.

Two Major Hurdles

In carrying out his plans Eads faced two major hurdles: one consisting of the technical problems to be solved; the other, the human, social and political problems which accompany almost any large, pioneering venture in the field of engineering. We have mentioned some of his human problems.

In the years since the St. Louis Bridge was built in 1867-74, the methods involved in dealing with the numerous technical obstacles have become common. At that time, it required a man of much creative vision to reach the solutions and their application, as did Eads.

A major decision was to sink the four massive piers to bedrock, one of them going 136 feet below high water, through 90 feet of sand and gravel. Another pier was carried to solid rock 130 feet below high water, through 80 feet of sediment.[10] Eads felt this was necessary because he had been sixty-five feet below the Mississippi's surface at Cairo and found the river's bottom to be an unstable, moving mass. In the winter he saw that ice on the top forced water lower, eating away the bed. In addition, the fact that the surface of the bed-rock was smooth and worn underneath indicated that the sediment above this bed rock had probably all been moved many times in the river's long history.[11]

To sink his piers lower than any had ever gone before, Eads had to develop caissons in which the workers could go far below the surface. Pneumatic caissons had been invented in Europe but had to be adapted by Eads to the conditions of the Mississippi. When confronted with an unsolved obstacle in this effort, he would devise a means of meeting the problem. In this fashion he invented the "Eads sand pump," for removing material from under the caissons. In addition, he devised many of the peculiar arrangements of the air-locks.[12]

While Eads had the imagination of a dreamer, in the creation of his many unprecedented practical devices for carrying through his projects, he exercised great skills and practical ability in mechanical details of construction and operation, which proved him to be a person of discipline and genius. In 1881, the historian of the St. Louis Bridge, Professor C. M. Woodward,* commented: "The construction of the east abutment was a signal triumph in engineering. It was quite unparalleled both in size and in the depth to which it was sunk and it stands today the deepest subaqueous foundation ever built."[1][3]

In his Preface to his history of the St. Louis Bridge, Woodward stated:

> An eye-witness of many of the important operations attending the construction of the Bridge, and a frequent interpreter to those less familiar with the rationale of the work, I nevertheless feel as though I did not properly appreciate the magnitude, strength and beauty of the structure itself, nor the skill, courage, and energy displayed in its construction, until I had read the mass of correspondence and unpublished reports preserved in the office of the Company, and studied with the utmost fidelity every detail of both foundations and arches. I cannot expect to communicate to others the enthusiasm and admiration I myself feel. . . .[1][4]

The second notable aspect of Eads' plan was that this was to be a steel arch bridge. There were to be two decks, the lower to carry a double track railway and the other to accommodate all other traffic with three spans. Since the piers had to be so big and sunk so deep, it was obvious that the fewer of these spans called for the better. In addition, arches required much less material than trusses. Therefore, with an eye both to aesthetic possibilities and to economy, he designed three arches of 502, 520, and 502 feet, respectively.[1][5] These exceeded in length the span of any previous arched structure.[1][6]

*Professor C. M. Woodward taught engineering at Washington University in St. Louis. He was uncle as well as teaching guide and "guru" of Samuel M. Woodward, long on the staff of the author of this book and whom I consider to be the ablest and intellectually most penetrating man I ever knew in the field of hydraulic engineering. Samuel Woodward respected Prof. Woodward as a man whose character, insight and judgment were exceptional.

To build these arches, Eads determined that it would be necessary to take the unprecedented step of using steel, produced to exacting standards. Steel had seldom if ever before been used as a major factor in bridge construction.[17] Eads found that no manufacturers were adequately equipped or experienced to produce steel in the quantities he wanted with the high standards he set. Andrew Carnegie's Keystone Bridge Company took a contract to produce what Eads called for, and to erect the bridge.

In February, 1870 a contract was entered into between Eads Company, the Illinois and St. Louis Bridge Company, and Carnegie's Keystone Bridge Company. They would be responsible for buying the necessary steel in accord with Eads' specifications. Eads had presented his specifications in exceptional thoroughness and detail. He knew that he was working on the frontiers of engineering and metallurgic technology, and tried to leave as little as possible to indefinite general impression. He wanted definite assurance of the quality of the steel, and some idea as to characteristics of each piece which were not generally taken into account in bridge building.

For instance, he required of the steel he used that it be uniform in modulus of elasticity, a quality not then commonly tested. Not only did he prescribe the limits of this characteristic, but, since steel makers might not always be schooled in mechanics, he endeavored to make explicitly clear just what he meant by his terms. To make certain that this term, "modulus of elasticity," should be clear to the steel makers, he introduced a fairly full discussion in the specifications. The following are a few lines from that description:

> Suppose we test an oak post by compression. A length of 30 feet would be shortened one-fourth of an inch by a load of 2000 pounds per square inch. The original length being 1440 times the contraction, the modulus of elasticity is 1441 times the load, or 2,880,000 pounds. . . . It is easily seen that, in order that the strains

be equally distributed over the six staves of a tube,* for instance, and through the tubes to the upper and lower members of the bridge under different loads, the modulus of elasticity must be constantly the same in all the steel of the arch. Should some of the staves of a tube when under compression yield more than others, it is obvious that those others would be forced to bear more than their share of the load.[18]

Throughout the whole of this vast structure the needs of the materials were meticulously described and specified. The staff of able engineers that Eads assembled for the many phases of the job served their purposes well. It took such a man as Eads to find such associates, to appraise them and to work with them to guard against error. Commonly he had two staff members to independently calculate each particular step and to compare their results. For types of work which have been constructed many times, the engineer usually works by precedent. Eads worked largely by sheer original design and test. The convention of engineers which during this process of construction met to appraise Eads' plans and to declare them impracticable may never have experienced his quality of mastery.

There was something of a dilemma. Eads could not reduce the specified quality of his steel, for the success of his bridge depended on it. Either out of the need for more money for his product than he had named in his contract, or from a habit of striking hard bargains, Carnegie kept stalling and delaying delivery of promised material. Eads was stubborn, of necessity, and would not accept poorer quality. Carnegie kept failing deliveries until he could get larger and larger cash bonuses. When the bridge was on the verge of completion and a celebration was planned, Carnegie seized possession of the bridge and took up part of the flooring so that people could not go onto the bridge, until some of his money demands had been met. Fortunately a downpour of rain kept people away,

*The steel arches were made up of steel tubes, each tube being made of staves as a wooden barrel is made up of staves.

and the stopping of the celebration did not have embarrassing results.

When the Keystone Bridge Company called for bids for steel by Eads' exacting specifications, of all the steel making firms in Europe and America, only two decided to bid, and one of those was not prepared to meet the specifications. The contract was given by the Keystone Bridge works to the Butcher Steel Works of Philadelphia. The production of the steel of various qualities and for various uses was an extremely difficult and complex process. Eads and his associates spent much time at the steel works. Eads, a mechanical genius, sometimes helped the steel men out of difficult situations. These extra demands on his time and energy sometimes brought him near to the point of complete fatigue. The complications involved in getting the quality of steel Eads demanded seemed to be endless. Eads' specifications had been exceptionally clear and definite, but custom did not quickly rise to his unusual demands. Eads wrote to Carnegie:

> The interests of your company will, in my opinion, be promoted by its moving promptly forward to the execution of the contract it has made, without raising the question of extra pay for every deviation from "custom" in the execution of a work which it knew at the time the contract was made was so totally out of the line of ordinary bridge work as to constitute a novelty not only here but abroad in bridge construction.[19]

Carnegie wrote to Manager Taussig about Eads:

> Captain Eads must only require the custom of the trade. Everything beyond that must be allowed for in time and money. . . . This bridge is one of a hundred to the Keystone Company—to Eads it is the grand work of a distinguished life. . . . Nothing that would please and that does please other engineers is good enough for this work. . . . Meanwhile Keystone is experiencing the fact that of all men your man of real decided genius is the most difficult to deal with practically. . . . You must keep

Eads up to requiring only what is reasonable *and in accordance with custom.*[20]

The underscoring of "and in accordance with custom" is as in Carnegie's letter. In preparing specifications for the bridge, Eads and his exceptionally able staff had not wanted to take advantage of the contractor. So far as was possible every point concerning material and methods of its treatment was specified with great clarity and in detail. (Fortunately, C. M. Woodward, in his "History of the St. Louis Bridge," reproduced these specifications, so we can see just what they were.) Eads and his staff had tried to clarify every detail as to steel and its use, and to leave as little as possible to uncertain judgment. Then they had carefully and thoroughly gone over every detail, with representatives of the Keystone Bridge Company, in various cases making changes which would make the work more convenient or economical to the Keystone Company's methods. Agreements had been reached on every point.

Eads was not inconsiderate in his demands. He was constantly on the watch for ways of simplifying the methods and work of the contractor. Woodward comments:

Most of the real difficulties were actually overcome; and through the influence of Mr. Eads' specifications, the standard of good workmanship was raised throughout the world.[21]

In making its bid, apparently the little matter of specifications did not trouble Carnegie very much. The great Keystone firm had built a hundred bridges. A routine part of the job was handling engineers who had their own notions. Generally the Keystone Bridge Company, out of its vast experience, knew better. Here seemed to be just another case, and Carnegie would handle it in the course of business. So Keystone took the job, not troubling too much about the carefully drawn specifications. Size and economic power generally prevail. What was this unschooled engineer against the greatest bridge-building firm in America?

The difference in this case was that Eads and his very

The erection of the west and center arches of the Eads Bridge in 1861. (Photo courtesy of C. M. Woodward's *History of the St. Louis Bridge,* 1881).

exceptional staff had planned with masterly skill and relentless thoroughness to produce something beyond engineering experience. The quality of every part was necessary to the balanced excellence of the whole. Engineers' detailed specifications
adoption of the most appropriate current usages. The quality of each part was necessary to superlative excellence of the whole.

Carnegie doubtless in many cases had brushed aside unusual demands of engineers, and had held to profit-making custom. Eads had a vision of a great bridge, to stand through the centuries, and he would not easily surrender. It was a classical case of "an irresistible force meeting an immovable object."

Just before the completion of the bridge, the London magazine *Engineering* wrote:

> Our present requirement being to select some example of the most highly developed type of bridge-building of the present day, we have no difficulty in passing before ourselves in mental review the different works now in progress throughout the world, and we have still less difficulty in selecting as our example the magnificent arched bridge now almost completed by Captain Eads at St. Louis. In that work, the alliance between the theorist and the practical man is complete. The highest powers of modern analysis have been called into requisition for the determination of the strains; the resources of the manufacturer have been taxed to the utmost in production of material and perfection of workmanship, and the ingenuity of the builder has been alike taxed to put the unprecedented mass into place. In short, brain power has been called into action in every department. . . . One long-sighed-for result—the welding of the theoretical and practical man into one homogeneous mass, without which no truly great undertaking could possibly be carried out, has at last been attained.[22]

Dr. J. A. L. Waddell, noted American bridge engineer, paid tribute to the bridge when he wrote in 1916, "The first really important arch bridge in this country was the Eads Bridge.

. . . it has cast chrome-steel hingeless ribs, the first application of this metal to bridgework in America. . . . It ranks today as one of the finest bridges in the country."[23]

In addition to being the largest arch bridge of its day, Eads' structure was a pioneering venture in other respects. It made the first use of hollow tubular chord members. Eads built the cantilever arches toward each other, finally connecting them with telescoping tubes of his own invention. The arches were made of the hingeless, fixed-end type, involving problems of stress analysis and erection adjustment which would challenge modern-day engineers.[24]

Eads' early years, when he spent his "leisure" time alone in the technical library of his employer, must have represented some highly disciplined and sustained intellectual effort. He had been amassing knowledge that he continuously added to by his voracious reading, all without the support or encouragement of teachers or student companions.

"Impossible" was the comment frequently applied to his engineering designs where Eads' plans were really only *unprecedented*. He was severely taken to task for what some considered the unnecessary precaution of going to bed-rock. Others thought the arches were too long and could never stand up. His standards were far too exacting, particularly for the steel, commented a third group. Eads, an articulate man of much energy, was able to fight and usually to win these technical debates.

Opposition to the Bridge

Now a new and serious trouble appeared. In 1873, fully six years after Eads first made his plans public, and when he was approaching completion of the bridge, a new threat suddenly arose, brought about by steamboat and ferry interests, who saw the nearly completed bridge as a threat to their business. At that time navigation interests were powerful both along the river and in Congress.

Despite the fact that much publicity had been given to the plans for the bridge, steamboat men began to express concern over the seeming lack of height of the arches. A span so unusually long might create an illusion of being much lower than it really was. The arches were fifty-five feet above the river at high water. Mainly for competitive publicity purposes, the smokestacks of some of the new steamboats were almost twice that high.[25]

Some of the steamboat interests concerned, especially the Keokuk Steamboat Line, made formal protest to the Secretary of War, William Belknap. As a result, on August 20, 1873, the Secretary issued an order creating a Board of Engineers, "To examine the construction of the St. Louis and Illinois Bridge across the Mississippi River at St. Louis and report whether the bridge will prove a serious obstruction to the navigation of said river, and if so, in what manner its construction can be modified."[26] The board, all members of the Corps of Engineers, consisted of Major G. K. Warren, Chairman, Major G. Weitzel, Major William E. Merrill, Major Charles R. Suter, and Colonel J. H. Simpson.

The order convening this Board was issued on the same day that James Eads sailed for England for reasons of health. The Illinois and St. Louis Bridge Company, though only after asking for it, was given a copy of the convening order, but was not informed of the nature of the complaints made against the bridge. On September 4, 1873, the date the Board first met, the president of the Bridge Company, Gerard B. Allen, sent the Board a letter pointing out that the Bridge Company had been at work for over five years, had spent or had become liable for about $9,000,000, had published and circulated its plans widely, and had affected the commerce of the city by the anticipated completion of the bridge. The letter stated:

> During the whole of this long period no complaints have been made by either the government or the people. The citizens of St. Louis, all of whom are, directly or indirectly, largely interested in the commerce of both river and railroads, looked on with the utmost favor and approval, giving every aid and encouragement that would hasten the final completion of this great undertaking; whilst it is safe to say that its size, location and

importance render this structure one of national concern. If, therefore, under these circumstances, this Company learns for the first time that, just as its work is on the eve of completion, your honorable board is convened for the purpose of examining the construction of a Bridge the plans of which were well known all over the country, it cannot but be somewhat startled at the intelligence.[27]

The Bridge Company asked to be allowed to be represented before the Board by its officers and counsel, to have all proceedings recorded and to have meetings arranged so that company officials could attend.[28]

The Board members replied that, though company officials could attend, no matters of law were to be considered, thus making counsel unnecessary, though they themselves had lawyers present; and that since they were not authorized to take sworn testimony, a recording of the proceedings was unnecessary.

The Board met on September 4, 1873, for a two day session. Until 2 p.m. of the second day, all time was taken up by testimony of complaints from the steamboat interests. They pleaded the necessity for high pilot-houses and tall smokestacks, the impracticability of lowering or hinging these, and the difficulty of piloting boats under the wide arches of the bridge. When it became obvious that these witnesses all agreed, Major Warren of the Corps of Engineers said it would save time if he drew up a document which the opponents of the bridge could sign. This read:

TO THE BOARD: The river interests, represented by those present, hold that the lowering of the pipes and pilot-houses is impracticable, and any bridge requiring it to be done for any considerable portion of the season is a serious obstruction to navigation.[29]

The Board subsequently tore up this paper.

Witnesses brought by the Bridge Company were not given a chance to testify until late in the afternoon of the second and last day of the hearing. Though the Company had many experienced steamboatmen ready to refute the charges presented, at this late time of day only two of them were present. These two testified that, in their opinion, steamboat smokestacks were often one-third higher than was necessary, and even when reduced in size could easily be hinged to get beneath the bridge. In addition, they testified that any complaint about the difficulty of steering a boat between the piers was fanciful.

The Bridge Company officials wanted more time to present witnesses ("as many *hours* as the complainants had had *weeks* within which to prepare their testimony," said the vice president),[30] and asked that the Board adjourn to the following day, Saturday, or the next Monday in order to hear these. The request was denied emphatically by the Board of U. S. Corps of Engineers, Major Warren stating, "If a thousand steamboatmen should come and say that this bridge was no obstruction, it could not change my opinion."[31] Though the Board had not yet deliberated on the testimony taken, Major Warren had obviously reached his own conclusions.

Later, after this remark of his was given relatively wide publicity, Major Warren felt it necessary to offer some elaborating remarks. Pointing out that he had already dealt with similar cases, Major Warren contended, ". . . I really believe I know all that could be said on the questions involved." He maintained that his statement was only made in order to show that ". . . higher considerations than the statement of irresponsible river-men controlled my mind."[32]

Not having been given sufficient opportunity to present their case to an apparently prejudiced Board of members of the U.S. Corps of Engineers, the Bridge Company officials protested that the investigation was unfair, and withdrew. Later, Dr. William Taussig, vice-president and chairman of the executive committee of the Board of Directors of the Bridge Company, and John W. Noble, counsel to the Company, filed sworn statements with the Secretary of War protesting the manner in which the Board of Army Engineers conducted its hearing. Concluded Dr. Taussig:

Affiant (Taussig) says that the bridge company would have been prepared, if sufficient and reasonable time had been granted, to disprove, by a large number of experienced and expert persons, by statistics, by measurements, and by adducing of facts, all of the grounds of complaint which had been heard and considered by said board, but by the arbitrary and summary action of said board they were prevented therefrom.[33]

On September 12, 1873, the Board of U.S. Corps of Engineers presented their written report to General A.A. Humphreys, Chief of Engineers. Humphreys transmitted this report to the Secretary of War, commenting, "The views and recommendations of the Board are *concurred in by me.*"[34]

The conclusions of the Board were that it concurred in the steamboatmen's objections to the bridge, these being: first, the necessity for lowering smokestacks; second, the fact that maximum height is afforded only at the center of the arch, making navigation through them difficult; and third, that these difficulties would deter most boats from ever passing the bridge, thus, practically cutting "the Mississippi in two at St. Louis."[35]

In a more extensive analysis, the Board supported its findings. "The apparently unreasonable height and size of the chimneys in general use on these steamboats are really essential to secure a good draught to the furnaces and economical combustion of fuel."[36] The Board contended that lowering large smokestacks was expensive, complex and dangerous.

With regard to the difficulty of navigating through the wide arches, the arguments began to sound contrived. Essentially, what they reported was that the arches were so wide as to put the piers too far apart to be of service as guides. In other words, there was so much room between the piers as to make getting through them a chore. Lights on the piers would not work so well in such a crowded harbor, especially in foggy weather. Wind might send a boat into the bridge.[37] The Board's third conclusion, that the bridge would cut the Mississippi in two, would be correct only *if* the Board's hypothesis was accepted that the bridge would be impassable for a large number of boats.[38]

The Board concluded:

> The Board are, therefore, unanimously of the opinion that the bridge, as at present designed, will prove a very serious obstruction to the free navigation of the Mississippi River.[39]

But the most striking action of the Board of U.S. Corps of Engineers members was its action in ordering that all future bridges across the Mississippi at St. Louis must be of the (conventional) truss type. The Board was most presumptuous in this because it then had no legal authority to specify the type of bridge that could be built, and even today the Corps of Engineers has no such board power even though it does control building of bridges over the nation's navigable waterways.

As a solution to the problem at hand, the Board proposed a canal around the east abutment of the bridge. This was to be eight hundred feet long and spanned by a drawbridge. The Bridge Company was expected to build this canal and absorb the expense.

It is interesting to note that in the Report, as originally recorded and approved by all members of the Board, the following sentence appeared: "They [the Board of Engineers] think, moreover, that *it will only be in exceptional cases that boats will desire to pass through this draw*, so that delays to trains from this cause will not be excessive."[40] (Emphasis added.) The Report was handed to the press in this form and it was only after it was pointed out that this one phrase contradicted and largely invalidated all the rest of the Report that it was changed to read, "The use of this draw by the boats will be only in cases of necessity, and the inconvenience which this use may occasion to travel on the Bridge there seems no course but to submit to."[41]

The Chief of Engineers Humphreys began spreading the word around Washington that Secretary of War Belknap agreed with him in endorsing the findings and conclusion of this Board.[42] The Bridge Company, which heretofore had regarded the Board of Engineers and its report as little more than an irritating case of spite, now began to worry that it might have received such high official sanction. The effect on the Company's credit and public standing could be considerable.

Captain Eads returned from Europe in the last week of October, 1873, seven weeks after the hearing by the Board of the U.S. Corps of Engineers. He found the bridge virtually completed, but the Bridge Company officials dejected, the workmen depressed and the public displeased over the action of the Board of the Corps of Engineers, reportedly with the approval of the Secretary of War. Eads immediately departed for Washington with Dr. William Taussig, vice president and general manager of the Bridge Company. They saw General Humphreys who told them that Secretary of War Belknap did not really stand behind him, and that the intimation that he had done so was a mere inadvertence on the part of the Chief of Engineers. Actually, he said, Secretary Belknap had taken no stand.[43]

Then Taussig and Eads discovered that the Report had gone to Congress with Belknap's written approval. Disgusted by the apparent trickery, Eads and Taussig debated what to do. They decided to go to President Grant, though Eads had supported his opponent in the last election and Dr. Taussig had been the county judge who, before the Civil War, cast the deciding vote which refused the then destitute Captain Grant a post of county surveyor.

President Grant greeted Eads warmly, being somewhat less cordial to Taussig though he assured him that he had no hard feelings at being refused the job of county surveyor since he found his present job more attractive. The President was surprised at the story he heard, for the report of Belknap's Board of Engineers never had come to his attention. Grant, although a West Point graduate, never quite fit the West Point mold. He had known the traits of the Military Academy in peace and in war and he made his own appraisal of the situation. He called in the Secretary of War and questioned him. Belknap admitted that the bridge conformed to the demands of Congress and that his predecessor in the War Department had approved the structure. But, he declared, he was within his jurisdiction, having even the right to tear down the bridge, if he felt it obstructed navigation.

Grant grew livid with anger at this. "You cannot remove this structure on your own judgment," he replied. "And if Congress were to order its removal it would have to pay for it. It would hardly do that to save high smokestacks from being lowered when passing under the Bridge. If your Keokuk friends feel aggrieved, let them sue the Bridge for damages. (The Keokuk Steamboat line was the main complainant.) I think, General, you had better drop the case."[44]

Grant later showed his approval of Eads and his bridge by stopping to see Eads on a visit to St. Louis.

Although Grant's strong repudiation of the Secretary, the Chief of Engineers and the Corps of Engineers' Board forced Belknap from the scene, the Corps of Engineers lived to fight another day, for the Board would meet again in January, 1874.

Even before leaving for Washington to see President Grant, Captain Eads had begun a detailed reply to the Board of the U.S. Corps of Engineers. This soon was released, dated October, 1873. He first referred to letters attached to his report. These were from qualified steamboatmen, and disputed the findings of the Board. The first letter was from Joseph Brown, the Mayor of St. Louis and former Captain of several of the largest steamers on the river. Mayor Brown, while admitting that there would be some unavoidable obstruction from the bridge and admitting also that higher arches would have been better for navigation, pointed out that the arches had to conform to the height of the railroad tunnel leading to the bridge under the streets of St. Louis, and therefore could not be any higher. Concerning the possibility of a canal, he said:

> In regard to making a canal around the east abutment of the bridge on the East Saint Louis side, I should think it a poor commentary on the good sense of our lawmakers at

Washington to authorize the damming-up of the Mississippi to such an extent as to render it necessary to construct a canal in place of it. Indeed, I think it would be a poor way of remedying the evil, for it would create another by destroying the East Saint Louis levee; and even if constructed, I do not believe enough steamers would pass through it to pay toll sufficient to maintain it, saying nothing of the original cost.[45]

He concluded by pointing to the amount of time and money that had been put into the bridge, calling its completion of vital interest both to St. Louis and the country. Though regretting any disadvantages to large steamers in extremely high water, he contended that the advantages to business and commerce as a whole were such as to far outweigh these. "I consider the time for fault-finding or urging its removal as having more than elapsed. . . ." concluded the Mayor.[46]

In a second letter, Eads presented the comments of thirteen "well known, highly respected, and skillful commanders, who have also navigated some of the largest steamers afloat." He said that several of them were still deeply interested in the largest ones and would be financially injured should the Bridge really prove an obstruction, and adding that not one of them had any financial interest in the Bridge. In this letter, the thirteen contended that smokestacks and pilot-houses were often much too high, that it would require neither great labor nor danger and only $1000 to $1500 to hinge high smokestacks. They called the canal proposed by the U.S. Corps of Engineers "impracticable." Wider, lower arches were not detrimental in their opinion.[47]

Eads himself criticized the Report of the Board of Engineers with vigor and sarcasm. On the difficulty of navigating wide spans he waxed caustic, commenting, ". . . if piers 520 feet apart are too wide to serve as guides, there would be no means left the bewildered navigator, in approaching an opening 520 by 75 feet, but to run it by the compass, or by buoys placed in the channel."[48] About the proposed canal he wrote:

First, it is absolutely unnecessary; second, it would delay the completion of the bridge; third, it would be enormously expensive; fourth, it would destroy all the wharf of East St. Louis along the canal, by causing a deposit along the shore; fifth, it would ruin the landing for several hundred feet below the canal, by causing a deposit along the shore; sixth, it would involve a drawbridge, which would be inconvenient and dangerous, if ever opened; and, seventh, it would mutilate the Bridge.[49]

In addition, Eads pointed out that his bridge was fully in accord with specifications reported by a committee of fifteen members of the St. Louis Merchants Exchange, ten of whom were directly interested in river navigation. Specifications for the Bridge were *unanimously* adopted by the Exchange for presentation to Congress. "This Exchange," said Eads, "is composed of more than one thousand members, a large number of whom are owners and captains of steamboats, while almost every one in it is more or less directly interested in preserving the navigation of the river. On such questions it can speak more intelligently than any other body in this valley."[50]

Captain Eads concluded his statement:

The remarkable decision rendered against your Bridge, [by the Board of U.S. Corps of Engineers officers and as accepted and approved] and the remedial canal proposed, will constitute one of the notable incidents connected with its history. If there be any who still think the structure will prove a very serious obstruction to navigation, the indulgence of a little patience from them must be asked until the completion of the work, and then the Bridge will vindicate the judgment of the St. Louis Merchants' Exchange, which officially fixed its dimensions in 1866, and secured from Congress an incorporation of them in the charter of the company, in strict conformity to which the Bridge is now being constructed.[51]

The Board of the U.S. Corps of Engineers, unconvinced by Eads' refutation of its first Report, undauntedly convened a second time in January, 1874, both to consider and report upon the survey and estimates for the canal, and to reply to Eads and to Taussig and Noble.

The Board's second Report was issued on January 31, 1874. Detailed estimates of the cost of the canal totaled $1,172,436.12, this sum to be paid for by the Bridge Company. However, the Corps of Engineers' Board members decided at this meeting to abandon its proposal for a canal, recognizing that, "This plan does not give promise of all the accommodation to navigation that the steamboatmen and our own judgment deem necessary . . ." so the Board proposed other means of dealing with the threatening bridge.[52] Concluded the Board, "This bridge, though admirable in some engineering features, is so faulty in its relations to navigation that, if no acceptable modification can be made, then, in our opinion, it should be entirely reconstructed."[53] And how might this be accomplished? The simplest plan of doing this, commented the Board, "would be to remove all three arches and substitute for them horizontal trusses. . . ."[54]

Major Warren, who presented himself as the technical authority of the Corps of Engineers, referred to the bridge as "a monster."[55]

After reaching these considered remedies for the "improvement" of the almost completed bridge, the Board of the U.S. Corps of Engineers then turned its attention to questions raised about its previous Report. In this, the Board's attention was directed chiefly toward proving the value of tall smoke-stacks and the difficulty of lowering them with hinges if there is a strong wind. Then, instead of continuing a technical debate, the Board elaborately questioned the competence of the "thirteen experienced steamboat captains." (Cited by Eads in his letter.)[56]

The important point, ignored by the Board but stressed by these thirteen rivermen and by the Mayor of St. Louis, himself substantially interested in river transportation, was that commerce as a whole would be greatly benefited, with a minimum of obstruction to steamers. But the Board sided with the steamboatmen who opposed this viewpoint and who seemed to be using apparently specious arguments, particularly with regard to the necessity for high smoke-stacks and higher arches, to support their case against the bridge. To refute these arguments, it was logical for Eads to secure qualified observers, men who had worked the Mississippi and knew steamers, yet who did not have a direct interest whether or not a large packet-boat would have to make adjustments for the bridge. But the Board elected not to listen to the steamboatmen who were on Eads' side of the controversy.

The matter of the qualifications or lack of them by Eads' witnesses still begged the question. The Board of the U.S. Corps of Engineers members persisted in their original complaints about the obstruction of the bridge, excusing themselves from considering possible changes in the boats themselves by saying, "The board do not think it their province to enter on the question of possible changes in the character of river-vessels."[57]

Ignoring the human weakness of the boat operators for emphasis on *style*, the U.S. Corps of Engineers Board reached the conclusion that:

> Taking the navigation as it is and as it was before the late bridges were built, it seems reasonable to suppose that the character of construction, which is the result of fifty years' experience, is that which best meets the requirements of the trade which it accommodates. They therefore take for granted that there are sound, practical reasons for having elevated pilot-houses and high chimneys.[58]

In its opinion, the only trade to consider was that of the steamboats. That the bridge might best meet the *total* trade, railroad, passenger, wagon and other land commerce, failed to merit their consideration. Concluded the Board: ". . . some change ought in justice to be made. The cost of making the change is something for which the board are in no way responsible. It is the inevitable result of a badly-designed bridge."[59] The Board as a whole was at least somewhat less arbitrary than one of its members, Major G. K. Warren, who stated emphatically:

> There can be no doubt that this bridge is an obstruction to navigation. . . . If it should prove that no change can be devised and carried out that will satisfy the interests of navigation, without destroying the usefulness of the bridge, then justice demands *the bridge must come down* and a suitable one take its place. [Emphasis added.][60]

What emerges is not a picture of trained, open-minded investigators trying to reach a solution on the basis of all scientific and social evidence, but rather a group of U.S. Corps of Engineers members, including Chief of Engineers, starting their investigation with a pre-conceived notion and pushing this notion against all comers and the evidence.

Fortunately, after the Board of U.S. Corps of Engineers met the second time and made its recommendations regarding drastic revisions in the bridge to meet the objections of the steamboatmen who opposed the bridge, these recommendations were ignored and the bridge was completed according to the original plans. It was formerly open to traffic June 3, 1874.

On July 4, 1874 the city of St. Louis held a celebration for the completion of the Bridge. Quite naturally James Eads was the principal speaker of the occasion, and also quite naturally, in view of the many and extreme difficulties he had surmounted, he spoke with some elation. Had a critical and responsible editor been commenting on the occasion in the next day's paper, he might naturally have felt a considerable restraint in his exuberance.

However, viewing the situation across more than ninety intervening years during which every claim of James Eads has been sustained by the course of events, it may appear that there was greater justification for Eads' expression of assurance than could be realized by any but an unusually well qualified observer at the time. The following are extracted from Eads' remarks on that occasion:

> Everything which prudence, judgment and the present

state of science could suggest to me and my assistants, has been carefully observed, in its design and construction. Every computation involving its safety has been made by different individuals thoroughly competent to make them, and they have been thoroughly revised time and again, and verified and reexamined until the possibility of error nowhere exists. When the first deep pier reached bed rock 110 feet below the surface, those who knew nothing about the care that was used in insuring success, expressed their gladness that my mind was relieved by the occasion. I felt no relief, however, for I *knew* that it must go there safely.

[In testing] I could get no more engines or I should have imposed still greater loads upon it; for I knew that if thrice fourteen locomotives were to be put on each span, and the densest crowd of humanity which was ever packed together stood upon the upper roadway above them, I should feel no anxiety whatever for the safety of the structure, for I know it is capable of bearing up vastly more than that.

I am justified in declaring that the bridge will exist just as long as it continues to be useful to the people who come after us, even if its years should number those of the pyramids. That its piers will thus endure, few will doubt, while the peculiar construction of its superstructure is such that any piece in it can be easily taken out and examined, and replaced or renewed, without interrupting the traffic of the bridge. The effect of temperature upon the arches is such that in cold weather the lower central tubes, and the upper abutment tubes composing the spans, are so relieved of strain that any one of them may be uncoupled from the others and easily moved. In completing the western span two of the lower tubes of the inside ribs near the middle of the span were injured during erection, and were actually uncoupled and taken out without any difficulty whatever, after the span was completed, and two new ones put in their place in a few hours.

This is a feature of construction possessed by no other similar structure in the world, and it justified me in saying that this bridge will endure as long as it is useful to man. He alone will destroy it, for the earthquakes may rock its piers and shake its elastic arches in vain.[6 1]

One is fairly well justified in concluding that the chief danger to the indefinite life of the bridge lies not in its design and construction, but from the possibility that those who through the years are responsible for its care may not be aware of the full possibilities for indefinite continuity which were built into it. With the advances which have been made in steel during the past 90 years, could not the bridge be renewed piece by piece with these new and stronger steels and the bridge be made even stronger than when it was built?

When the U.S. Corps of Engineers has finally lost a battle against engineering progress, and, with all the grace with which a cat is led across a carpet by the tail, has been brought into line with engineering reality, there still is a way to recover its status and its public image. By rewriting its own history it may bury its mistakes and weave for itself a crown of synthetic laurels. This process is quite effective, for few of the public and few members of Congress or, perhaps most important, few of the young members of the Corps, have time or facilities to check such statements, which naturally they take at face value.

For instance, in *The Infantry Journal* in 1924, Major James R. Weave, in listing *the most important achievements of the Corps*, includes THE EADS BRIDGE!! and states:

> These works were conducted principally, or in most important executive or advisory capacity, by [West Point] graduates.[6 2]

How literally accurate is this statement! It was "in most important executive or advisory capacity" that an august board of Corps of Engineers officers, supported by their head, the Chief of Engineers, deliberately and unanimously, not only disapproved of the bridge, but decreed that all such arch trusses should be prohibited on navigable streams. Other instances of rewriting Corps of Engineers history will be given in subsequent chapters.

After its completion, there is no record of any significant

obstruction provided by the bridge. Professor Woodward of Washington University, one of the ablest of American engineers, quoted Major Warren's comments at the hearing, and added:

> After the lapse of seven years, those words (of the U.S. Corps of Engineers board) sound strange enough. It is scarcely credible that an army engineer could be found who would call the St. Louis Bridge a 'monster.' The verdict of time is that the Bridge is but a very slight obstruction to navigation; that instead of contriving apparatus for lowering chimneys, the better plan is to cut them down, and in new boats to build lower pilot-houses and shorter chimneys. The result is—as the old boatmen who formerly regarded the Bridge as a serious obstacle freely admit—a perfectly satisfactory draught, and boats safer in a gale in consequence of less exposure to the wind.
>
> Formerly, the display of tall, ornamented chimneys and tower-like pilot-houses added to the attractions and reputation of a boat. So long as there were no serious objections to these features, they developed freely and often immoderately. No concessions were asked, because none were needed until the development of railway interests, rivalling if not surpassing those on the river, demanded bridges, and even then the concessions required involved nothing beyond a few modifications of unessential points.[63]

To illustrate his conclusion, Professor Woodward quoted from a letter he received in 1881 from Mr. Joseph F. Wangler, an experienced maker of steamboat boilers and smoke-stacks in the city of St. Louis. Mr. Wangler wrote:

> In reference to steamboat chimneys, there has been quite a revolution within the last seven years. I will cite as an example the steamer Lake Superior. She used to have chimneys 56 inches in diameter and 50 feet high above the hurricane deck. Her chimneys were changed to 28 inches in diameter and shortened to 20 feet, with a decided improvement in the draught. All the chimneys of the Northern Line have been reduced in size and

height. . . . The new styles gives general satisfaction in various ways: they give better draught; weight less by fifty per cent; catch less wind; and, I think, look better.[6 4]

As to this letter from Wangler, Professor Woodward added the following comments:

> In estimating the value of this candid opinion, it should be remembered that a maker of chimneys is not of a class to be "pecuniarily benefited" by the building of the Bridge. This note furnished, perhaps, the best commentary on the reports of the board of United States Army Engineers.[6 5]

Repeatedly throughout a century, when engineering progress has brushed aside or has taken along with it a reluctant Corps of Engineers, there has been a rear guard which does not surrender. In 1892, eighteen years after the Eads Bridge was opened, Lieutenant Colonel W. R. King, U.S. Army Corps of Engineers, in an article in *Engineering Magazine*, entitled, "Government Engineering Defended," in describing what he considered to be non-government *engineering failures*, wrote: ". . . is it not a fact that the great St. Louis Bridge cost two or three times as much as a suitable bridge would have cost, besides being a great and unwarranted obstruction to navigation."

What is the verdict of history concerning the Eads Bridge at St. Louis? Let us follow it through the years.

Twelve years after completion of Eads' Bridge, the Encyclopedia Britannica referred to it as "one of the most remarkable structures in the world in character and magnitude."[6 6] In this century it has been called "the greatest engineering feat of that sort" up to its time.[6 7]

In 1916, a detailed inspection of the Eads Bridge was made by a competent consulting bridge engineering firm that required three months. This disclosed no evidence of overstressing of members despite the much heavier traffic loads than prevailed when the bridge was built. The inspecting engineers noted the complete absence of vibration under traffic that was present on more recently built bridges at St. Louis, which further attests to the ability of the Eads Bridge to carry the heavy modern traffic loads.

In 1960, an engineering historian reported that, "The Eads Bridge is still one of the great long-span railroad bridges in the United States. . . ." "The Eads Bridge is still referred to as 'The Grandaddy of American Arches.'"[6][8]

This bridge has been noted for its architectural beauty, for having the first pneumatic foundations in America and the deepest in the world; it was the first bridge anywhere to use steel extensively, the first to use tubular chord members, and the first to depend on the use of cantilever in building the superstructure.[6][9] Perhaps most important and most noteworthy, after more than ninety years of continuous service the Eads Bridge still stands, carrying the enormously increased load of automobile traffic (the automobile was not developed until the Eads bridge had stood for a quarter of a century) and carries the several times heavier and more heavily loaded railroad cars in trains several times as long.

Concerning the bridge's economic value to the city of St. Louis and the country as a whole, a recent history of bridges and their builders had this to say:

> The Eads Bridge was of tremendous importance to the development of St. Louis, establishing it as a focal railroad crossing and as the most important city on the Mississippi. The Bridge was also an important factor in the development of the transcontinental railroad systems. Its significance in 'the winning of the West' was recognized when the Eads Bridge was pictured on a U.S. stamp of the 'Trans-Mississippi Issue' in 1898—the first bridge to receive such philatelic recognition.

> But the magnificence of the bridge, great as it is, is not so wonderful as the genius and spirit of its builder. The penetrating vision and courageous will of Captain James B. Eads received worthy recognition when he was elected in 1920 to the American Hall of Fame, the first engineer to be so honored. His achievement marks a monumental milestone in the progress of bridge building.

The justification of the deans of American engineering schools in including James B. Eads among the first five of the thirteen greatest engineers of all time was not primarily because of the size of his undertakings, but because of a union of great qualities to a single end. High among these qualities was a creative capacity which very seldom occurs for meeting apparently insuperable obstacles by the invention of new, and often unprecedented means. This quality was supported by an integrity of purpose and a refusal to accept present success at the cost of possible, even far future, failure. This quality is illustrated by Eads' insistence on carrying the great piers to bedrock at a depth never before reached, and a depth which most engineers thought to be unnecessary. The noted English engineer, W. C. Unwin, called the construction of these piers, "a feat unprecedented in the annals of engineering."[70] His design, which made it feasible at any time in the future to remove any single piece of steel of the bridge, probably was unprecedented in the history of great bridges. Throughout the bridge at many points and in many respects this creativeness and integrity were incorporated. There was the strength of purpose which faced the powerful Andrew Carnegie in unrelentingly refusing to accept any compromise in the quality of any piece of steel provided. And so on with every element and every detail of the great structure. *All these qualities had been fully disclosed, all the construction difficulties had been overcome, and the great structure was nearing completion when the U. S. Corps of Engineers undertook to turn the clock back, to prevent its completion,* and to indulge the boat owners in their desire to monopolize traffic and to attract passengers by high ornamental stacks and elevated pilot houses. Fortunate it was that Captain Eads won his fight against his adversaries who were supported by the U. S. Corps of Engineers.

notes

1. *Journal of Engineering Education*, Vol. XXI, No. 3, November 1930, p. 256.
2. *Dictionary of American Biography* on James B. Eads, pp. 588-89.
3. *Popular Science Monthly*, "Sketch of James B. Eads," February, 1886, p. 545.
4. *Ibid.*
5. Estill McHenry, editor, biographical sketch in *Papers and Addresses of James B. Eads*, 1884.
6. *Popular Science Monthly, op. cit.*, p. 545.
7. Proceedings, from the March Proceedings, *Transactions*, of the ASCE, Vol. 17, 1887, "Memoir on James B. Eads."
8. C. M. Woodward, *History of the St. Louis Bridge*, St. Louis, 1881, p. 10.*
9. *Ibid.*, p. 12.
10. *Popular Science Monthly, op. cit.*, p. 549.

*Woodward's book, *The St. Louis Bridge*, is no ordinary volume. No one but a man of exceptional quality could have written an adequate account of the building of this bridge, which, all things considered, was among the great achievements of the world in engineering. C. M. Woodward, himself Dean of the Polytechnic School of Washington University, was probably, next to James Eads, the foremost engineer of St. Louis. In the theory of mechanics and mechanical engineering there probably was no superior in America in his day.

Here was a great engineer and man of quality, conscientiously and thoroughly recording, with much well selected detail, the principles, processes and personal circumstances of a great achievement. Would it not be wise for the American engineering profession to arrange for the republication of this unusual work, and for making it readily available in the libraries of all American engineering schools to stir the aspiration and increase the outlook of engineering students?

11. Louis How, *James B. Eads*, Houghton Mifflin, 1900, p. 64.*

12. Proceedings, *op. cit.*, p. 52.

13. *Ibid.*

14. Woodward, *op. cit.*, p. vii.

15. How, *op. cit.*, p. 62.

16. *Ibid.*, p. 91.

17. David Anderson, *Encyclopedia Britannica*, 1952, Vol. 4, 125-126.

18. Woodward, *op. cit.*, Chap. VII.

19. *Ibid.*, p. 71.

20. *Ibid.*

21. *Ibid.*, p. 70.

22. Proceedings, *op. cit.*, pp. 53-54.

23. J. A. L. Waddell, "Bridge Engineering," 1916, p. 27.

24. Anderson, *op. cit.*, p. 126.

25. Woodward, *op. cit.*, p. 263. *Executive Document No. 194*, House of Representatives, 43rd Congress, 1st Session, "Letter from the Secretary of War Transmitting Reports on the Construction of the St. Louis and Illinois Bridge Across the Mississippi River," p. 14.**

26. Woodward, *op. cit.*, p. 263.

27. *Ibid.*, p. 264.

28. *Ibid.*, p. 265.

29. *Ibid.*, p. 266.

30. *Executive Document No. 194*, *op. cit.*, p. 41.

31. *Ibid.*

*How is Eads' grandson.

**These two works carry some of the same documents concerning communications between the Corps of Engineers and the Bridge Company. Most of the references concerning communication between the Corps on the one hand and Eads or the Bridge Company on the other are from one or both of these sources.

32. *Ibid.*, p. 44.
33. *Ibid.*, p. 41.
34. *Ibid.*, p. 2.
35. *Ibid.*, p. 4.
36. *Ibid.*, p. 5.
37. *Ibid.*, p. 6.
38. *Ibid.*
39. *Ibid.*
40. Woodward, *op. cit.*, p. 270.
41. *Ibid.*
42. Florence Dorsey, *Road to the Sea*, Rinehart, 1947, p. 149.
43. *Journal of Engineering Education*, *op. cit.*, p. 151.
44. Dorsey, *op. cit.*, p. 152.
45. *Executive Document No. 194*, *op. cit.*, p. 37.
46. *Ibid.*, pp. 36, 37.
47. *Ibid.*, pp. 37-38.
48. *Ibid.*, p. 33.
49. *Ibid.*, p. 235.
50. *Ibid.*, p. 34.
51. *Ibid.*, p. 36.
52. *Ibid.*, p. 17.
53. *Ibid.*, p. 18.
54. *Ibid.*
55. *Ibid.*, p. 45.
56. *Ibid.*, p. 25.
57. *Ibid.*, p. 26.
58. *Ibid.*
59. *Ibid.*, p. 28.
60. *Ibid.*, p. 44.
61. McHenry, *op. cit.*

62. Major James R. N. Weave (Infantry), Article on U.S. Military Academy, *Infantry Journal,* Vol. 24, May 1924, p. 543.

63. Woodward, *op. cit.,* p. 282.

64. *Ibid.,* p. 283.

65. *Ibid.*

66. Dorsey, *op. cit.,* p. 165.

67. *Ibid.,* p. 164.

68. James Kip Finch, *The Story of Engineering,* Anchor Books, Doubleday, 1960, pp. 291, 292.

69. Anderson, *op. cit.*

70. William C. Unwin, *Encyclopedia Britannica,* 11th edition, Vol. 8, p. 542.

chapter 6

james b. eads
and the
mississippi
river jetties

Today, New Orleans ranks second among United States' ports in tons of goods shipped and received. Formerly it was not second but eighth among American ports. The jump from eighth to second place was not a slow process through decades. It came suddenly in five years as the direct result of the construction by James B. Eads of the jetties for the South Pass of the Mississippi River.

Before 1878, the South Pass was only 9 feet deep and the Southwest Pass had a depth which sometimes reached 20 feet through constant dredging. More often its depth was far below 18 feet. In the 1870's, though the Mississippi channel was an ideal national transport for the vast region from the Allegheny Mountains to the Rockies, to Latin America and Europe, the mud choking its passes kept most ships away. Smaller vessels could get in and out after some delay. A fairly large ship might even be taken through if enough dredging were being done. There was much public concern over this blockage to commerce.

As early as 1726, attempts had been made to deepen the channel by dragging iron harrows over the bars.[1] It was not until 1837 that the United States government took an interest in the problem, Congress appropriating money for a survey and for the dredging which had been recommended by a Board of Army Engineers.[2]

Not much came of this and in 1852, $75,000 was appropriated for improving the channel at the mouth of the river by contract.[3] A board of Army and Navy officers studied the question and recommended the following procedure: 1) stir up the bottom by suitable machinery; 2) if this failed, dredge with buckets; 3) if both these failed, construct parallel jetties; 4) if necessary, shut off the useless passes (there were three passes altogether). If all of this failed, the board recommended that a ship canal might be built as a last resort.[4]

In the light of results, the most significant of their suggestions was that of parallel jetties. The term jetties as used in this case referred to parallel artificial banks built along each shore of one of the mouths of the river. As the channel along which they are built is narrowed, the effect is that the water, confined to a lesser width, flows faster, and the more rapid flow will cause a significant deepening of the river.

Under the 1852 appropriation a contract was made with the New Orleans Towboat Association for deepening Southwest Pass to 18 feet. This depth was obtained in 1853 but no funds were provided by Congress for maintenance and the results of the dredging were soon obliterated. In 1856, "Congress appropriated $330,000 to open and maintain by contract ship channels through the bars at the mouths of Southwest Pass and Pass à l'Outre." A contract was let and, by dredging, a channel 18 feet in depth was obtained. The contractor failed to complete the job and the Federal Government took over and continued the work. During part of 1859 and 1860 channels through both Passes were maintained to the 18-foot depth. Then the War Between the States intervened and work was discontinued.[5] There was no significant permanent effect.

In 1859, a group of New Orleans businessmen visited the delta at the mouth of the Mississippi and were distressed by the existing conditions. There were thirty-five ships waiting outside to get in; three vessels were grounded on the bar. Meanwhile, merchandise was rotting in warehouses and commerce was a trickle.[6]

The War prevented any work being done until 1867 when dredging was resumed. But this was no solution for the channel problem. Slowly, an idea for a solution began to gain acceptance. Everything which had been tried had failed, so why not try a canal? The thought was appealing. It was not a new idea. Mississippi canals had been proposed on and off since 1832.[7]

Promoted by the U.S. Engineer Corps, which had charge of the River, sentiment in favor of a canal increased in New Orleans and was soon heard in Congress. In 1871, the House of Representatives requested the Secretary of War to have surveys made for a ship canal to connect the Mississippi River with Breton Sound, in the Gulf of Mexico.[8] The job of making a survey and plan was assigned to Major C. W. Howell, the Engineer Corps District Engineer at New Orleans.[9]

Major Howell was an ambitious young man of 29. He had been working for some years scraping and dredging the bed of the Mississippi mouth. It was an unparalleled opportunity for him.

It was also an opportunity for the Army Engineers as a whole. There was very strong demand for an open river mouth. There had been much criticism of the Corps of Engineers that had been working at the mouth of the river for forty years without much noticeable effect. Here the Army Engineers saw the ideal solution. A canal leading from New Orleans to the sea would greatly improve commerce at New Orleans, and it would also be the greatest engineering work ever undertaken by the government.

James B. Eads and His Jetties Plan

James B. Eads was still working on his bridge at St. Louis and had not even begun to spar with the Army Engineers there. On May 13, 1873, a convention of U. S. Congressmen, Governors and other interested parties was convened in St. Louis to discuss the improvement of the Mississippi River. Eads was there, and on the second day he offered a series of resolutions giving a strong case for improving the Mississippi channel. The delegates soon left on an excursion to New Orleans and the delta, James Eads with them. Enthusiasm was high for a canal, but Eads, a creative engineer, had his own plan.

He was one of the few men who had intelligent, first-hand knowledge of the bed of the Mississippi River. The average salvage operator who worked on the bottom of the Mississippi, preparing to raise sunken steamboats, was not too intelligent or technically knowledgeable. On the other hand, no members of the Corps of Engineers studying the Mississippi had similar advantage of having seen the river bottom they talked about. They were more generally limited to theories. James Eads was intelligent and had rigorously trained himself as an engineer. He had spent hundreds of hours and had covered many miles of the bed of the Mississippi in his diving bell. He had personal, first-hand knowledge. He had the disciplined intelligence to think and to speak with authority concerning the bed of the Mississippi.

While in Europe, he had become acquainted with the jetty method of deepening sluggish river channels and speeding their flow. He now argued strongly for the application of that method to one of the delta channels at the mouth of the Mississippi. This jetty plan, he judged from his experience on the Mississippi and from his knowledge of engineering, made sense both theoretically and practically. A 30-foot deep ship-canal, he contended, simply could not be quickly built and maintained through the seven miles of marsh and salt water, and not for the thirteen million dollars estimated. Jetties, he argued, would be cheaper and more effective, and could be built more quickly.[10]

His listeners were dubious. On that trip down river, almost no one was won over to Eads' plan. True, jetties had been successful on some European rivers, but were these streams comparable to the mighty Mississippi? In addition, the Army Engineers favored a canal and would build it at the Federal government's expense. By the end of 1873, the plan for a canal at Fort St. Phillip, proposed by Major Howell of the

Engineer Corps, was favored nearly unanimously by the people of the Mississippi Valley, since the Corps of Engineers was the official authority.

But Eads' views had not changed, and, ready to face human as well as physical difficulties, he began an almost single-handed effort in opposition to a canal and in favor of jetties. By lectures, pamphlets and personal persuasion Eads broadcast his message. So clear were his explanations of the misunderstood jetty system that experts round the world acclaimed them "unsurpassed as engineering exposition."[1][1]

In the meantime, a Board of seven Army Engineers had been convened by Engineer Corps orders of June 30, 1873 to "consider and report upon" the plan for a ship canal which had been submitted by Major C. W. Howell on February 14, 1873.[1][2]

Beginning at the end of July, 1873, this Board held sporadic deliberations in New York and New Orleans, and finally submitted a report on January 9, 1874. Since the deliberations and report of the Board have so much significance for the history of the jetties, they will be dealt with here at some length.

General J. G. Barnard, a distinguished civil engineer and a member of the Corps, was designated to be President of this Board. He had been General Grant's Chief Engineer during the Civil War. His high reputation was both national and international.

Realizing that the Board's expressed duty was unduly limited to studying the canal plans of Major Howell, General Barnard sought and received permission for the Board to consider alternative means of improving the New Orleans port in a separate report. After a few meetings in New York, in November, the Board went to New Orleans, where it spent about four days as a whole in inspection of sites and taking of testimony.[1][3] This Board of Army Engineers rejected the possibility of jetty improvement at the mouth of the Mississippi.[1][4]

General Barnard, President of the Board, did not share the conviction of his fellow Army officers that a canal was the answer. He had served on the Board of 1852 which had recommended stirring, dredging, or jetties, and he still wished to give further consideration to these means of serving shipping needs. He was not dogmatic on this point, for, as he later wrote the Chief of Engineers:

> . . . from first to last, I felt myself charged with a gravely responsible duty; that I approached the questions presented to the Board perfectly unprejudiced—if in any way biased it was in favor, not against the Canal as a great engineering structure, outdoing in magnitude and interest the remarkable work I had recently visited in Holland,— and moreover with the most conscientious desire not only to arrive at the true and best solution; but to do so in harmony and co-operation with the other members of the board.[15]

Barnard was unable to achieve such harmony and cooperation.

In a report dated January 9, 1874, six members of the Board, all except Barnard, endorsed the idea of a Fort St. Phillip Canal, remarking, ". . .the Board is of the opinion that no extraordinary difficulties in the construction and maintenance of the canal need be apprehended."[16] In a second report dated four days later the Board considered alternative methods, confining themselves to dredging and/or jetties.

In the light of the monumental Humphreys and Abbot report on the Mississippi and of the almost reverent respect in which it was held by the Army Engineers, it is interesting to note their comment here, that "the principle upon which a reply to these questions depends have been exhaustively treated in Chapter VIII of Humphreys and Abbot's Report upon the Physics and Hydraulics of the Mississippi River; and there is nothing more to add, except the conclusions which follow from that report."[17]

This attitude was entirely at one with the wishes of the Chief of Engineers, General A. A. Humphreys, who was the chief co-author of the Report on the Mississippi referred to above. He had already battled with Eads over the St. Louis Bridge, and had lost. He was certainly not now prepared to accept the theories of this "meddler."

Even at this date, nearly a century ago, the attitude of the Corps of being sole proprietor of the Mississippi made it natural to view as a "meddler" any civilian who would presume to challenge the conclusions of the Corps. As early as October 11, 1873, when asked his opinion on jetties, Humphreys' reply (it seemed almost reflexive) was to refer his correspondent to a specific section of his Report on the Physics and Hydraulics on the Mississippi River, written twelve years earlier.[1 8]

In this work, he had maintained that, "the development of the laws which govern the formation of the bars *has removed all uncertainty* as to the principles which should guide an attempt to deepen the channels over them."[1 9] (Emphasis added.) He viewed jetties as "correct in theory" but felt their use should be governed by economic considerations.[2 0]

The Chief of Engineers was opposed to the use of jetties at any pass of the Mississippi delta, largely because, according to his book, in the Mississippi sand and gravel was pushed along the bottom rather than carried by long leaps in suspension,* and that by this process the sand and gravel would create rapidly advancing bars beyond the jetties, requiring their extension every year. Assuming that such would be the case, Humphreys asserted that: "The depth of 21 feet thus obtained must be maintained by the annual extension of the jetties 700 feet into the Gulf...."[2 1]

The Board took its cue from this dictum of its Chief, and rejected the possibilities of jetties, the sure failure of which they held would be due to "... rapid extension of the bar, (which would) compel the works of improvement to con-

---

*Eads' three hundred trips, walking on the bottom of the river under a diving bell, had given him first hand knowledge that the contrary was true. In raising sunken vessels he had found that they had been filled with sand and gravel, which they had moved by leaps and bounds through the water, and not only along the bottom. Also he had vivid memories of being pelted by sand and gravel which, thrown up from the bottom by irregularities of the bottom, travelled by long leaps through the water. He had knowledge, not theoretical, as in the case of the Corps of Engineers officers, but by direct physical observation, that the theoretical conclusion of General Humphreys and his associates was mistaken.

tinue at a heavy annual cost until their entire abandon-
ment."[2 2] They felt that the yielding nature of the Mississippi
banks would make construction and maintenance of jetties
difficult or hopelessly expensive.

General Barnard, the President of the Board, found himself
unable to concur in either the report for the canal or the one
against the jetties, and appended lengthy dissents to each.

With regard to the Canal plan, Barnard first contended that,
assuming a canal was to be made, "more protracted and more
comprehensive study is required."[2 3] ". . . I think," he
maintained, "that the phraseology used in the report of the
majority, that 'no extraordinary engineering difficulties need
be apprehended,' rather underrates the real difficulties to be
anticipated."[2 4] His second contention was simply that,
before commencing on any canal plan, "a more attentive
consideration of the superior advantages of the natural
mouths, and of the fair possiblity of utilizing them, is
needed."[2 5]

In dissenting from the Board's second report, Barnard gave
a long and obviously well researched discussion on the
promise of jetties. In this, he took the risky step of
cautiously criticizing Humphreys and Abbot's Report, saying
"this theory is founded upon a theory of bar formation
which is doubtless true, and yet does not contain the whole
truth . . . the stretching of any theory of so complicated
phenomena to *numerical* results is generally putting upon it
more than it will bear."[2 6] He contended that, if successful,
the jetties would be cheaper and serve future needs much
better than a canal. "It would be a rash confidence which
would contemplate a realized 'Fort St. Phillip Ship Canal'
earlier than A.D. 1884," he felt.[2 7] Throughout his discussion, Barnard emphasized that his purpose was ". . . not so
much 'to recommend its trial' (of the jetee system) [an older
spelling of jetty] as to recommend its consideration and that
scrutiny and survey on which alone estimates can be
based."[2 8]

The reactions of Corps of Engineers' officers to this
moderate call by its own distinguished "president" for a

thorough study of the engineering questions bordered on the incredible. The Corps did not heed his questions or offer to re-examine the proposition and did not show concern for the weaknesses Barnard felt existed in the Corps' plan. In fact, the Corps did not deal with the engineering question at all. Below are examples of reactions by Barnard's fellow officers.

One officer wrote, "I wish to keep out of the discussion which General Barnard is going to force on us on that subject and which will be inconclusive because so much has to be assumed."[29] Another wrote, ". . . when we have so many external and active enemies, internal dissensions and criticism are greatly to be deprecated."[30] General Humphreys, in one of his milder references to Barnard's heresy, wrote that it "would necessarily lead to interminable controversy conducive to no good."[31]

Reactions based on the questions of good engineering raised by Barnard were few and far between. One view was advanced by a colonel, who commented, "Having made up my own mind that the Canal was the proper way of reaching the ocean, and never having any occasion officially to express or elicit opinions, I regarded that subject as a foregone conclusion and I am truly sorry to see any objections thrown in the way."[32]

Obviously, the rest of the Corps officers involved were not interested in considering the questions raised by Barnard. They seemed far more concerned with maintaining the united front and good name of the Corps.

As Captain Eads recognized, General Barnard had a ". . . reputation among both civil and military engineers . . . acknowledged in Europe and America to be equal to that of any other one living. . . ."[33] He was once slated to become Chief of Engineers but, unfortunately for the country's sake, was passed over. He had been Superintendent of West Point, and considered that institution as the "best *organizer* of our national strength." [Emphasis added.] He had once said at an earlier date about the Corps of Engineers: "They have commanded the entire confidence of the Government and the communities which they have served."[34]

Now, understandably hurt by the adverse reactions to his minority report, he chose a fellow officer, General Comstock, as being most likely to grasp the engineering details involved and at the same time to be sympathetic to his case. The following, compiled from a series of private letters written by Barnard to Comstock, constitute a striking tale of a regular, loyal officer trying to conscientiously serve his country's best interest against the petty opposition of the Corps as a whole. (These letters were dashed off in longhand and are therefore clumsy and ungrammatical in many instances.)

The incompetence from first to last with which the thing has been managed by the E.D. [Engineer Department] has thrown it irrevocably into the hands of politicians. (They had a pretty strong hand in starting it in order to make political capital.) Congress called on the Engineers for a survey and plan. To make survey by an inexperienced young officer was well enough—to leave him to be the sole *planner* and to come before the public with such a *plan* was a performance of the duty such as only those who don't know what the engineering of such a question is are capable of—as for "Boards"—our senior [Humphreys] has not developed engineering into such a state that even a sense of what is incumbent upon engineers *thus appealed to by the Government to decide grave questions* is to be found in "Boards!" not one who appreciates the mere "opinion"!!! of any man who writes "Engineer" or "Corps of Engineers" after his name is practically *useless* unless first his own long and hard-earned experience has enabled him to speak authoritatively, or second, he (for want of personal knowledge) has carefully gone over the *whole recorded experience.* (What engineer have we who on any subject outside his immediate official engagements, has or even conceived what and where is the recorded experiences? In place of this he generally picks up the first book he meets with and makes a show of wisdom by quoting it *apropos to* nothing at all—e.g., the report of the "Majority" on jetties, in which without credit they have quoted without any pertinence whole pages. Even *this* they had never met with in the very last days and after a reconvention—when they found it in this office.

Now the *plan* submitted to the Chief Engineer by Howell and by him to the Board simply ignored the engineering science of the present....[35] To talk about the "adequacy" of the study, either on the part of Howell, or the Board is nonsense. Previous experience was completely ignored. And it was very apparent we had no plans—no adequate study....[36] The utter superficiality of the views of the members of the "Board"—these engineers of the history and the merits of the work (you will scarcely believe that until the morning after our organization, they saw in my hands a copy of Abert's report—not one had seen or looked for it and the same of many important papers) were so evident to me that it was perfectly immaterial to me which way they voted....[37]

But it passed through this officer [Humphreys] to a "Board of Engineers" as a plan; and the Board resolutely shut their eyes to its engineering absurdity. Twenty-two years ago I was a member of a Board ... [the 1852 Board] had a less important question submitted, (sic) every member of which was familiar with the Mississippi and Louisiana engineers. *That* Board spent one whole week *on the bars.* The present Board all except Howell and myself—absolutely inexperienced and unfamiliar went as far as Howell's dredging steamer (one rainy day)—did not even go over the bar of Pass à l'Outre—did not go around to outer terminus.[38]

They then made a report so inadequate (but recommending in the extremest way an immediate appropriation of $1,000,000) the object being to get the government committed, as if not a moment's time was to be lost.[39]

And what could I do? I did not absolutely oppose the canal—I simply maintained that there was not a single essential element about it determined; that a Board could not pass any [handwriting unintelligible] opinion upon it.[40] ... All I *demanded* was a study and *candid consideration* of the *river mouths*—and that a Canal should not be *forced* upon us as the solution until the fundamental elements of its existence and cost be determined.[41]

No, nothing of this kind could be listened to a moment; and immediate irrevocable *committal* of the [unintelligible] *by an appropriation* was that the majority was set on—to talk of an investigation of an intelligent examining and discussion of this grave matter in our New Orleans visit is to me a mockery.[42]

I am in an impossible situation to criticize . . .[43] I did not ask the engineers should plunge blindly into the jetty system—I *did* ask that it should not do so in the canal, and I *did* ask, setting forth dispassionate and unprejudiced reasons for belief that jetties would succeed—and at least should be thoroughly studied.[44]

Now had the Chief of Engineers sustained me, even to a moderate extent, the matter would not be in its present hopeless muddle. But he virtually endorsed the "majority" to the last. . . .[45]

And against such influence is the importance of having, to direct and pass judgment, a head of the government and Engineering who can see from a higher Engineering standpoint. In all that I have seen lately, Humphreys has not done it.[46]

Firmly convinced, then as now, that the Canal Project was in [unintelligible] that it would be a national misfortune to commit the government—that at best it would prove a very *inadequate* outlet to the navigation of the great western river—believing that an "open mouth" *could be had* at moderate expense—that it would not only be immeasurably superior to any canal but would eventually be demanded at whatever expense—and felt it my duty to be plain and explicit—the interest of my country in this matter was far beyond that of supporting the incapabilities of the "Engineers"—and indeed if my action has any one effect, it will be to ensure hereafter more adequate engineering treatment.[47]

You speak of "able men"—more certainly "Able men", accomplished officers—but in a broad sense far from being "Engineers" except in a narrow executive capacity. They have not generally the wide induction of experience nor the wide observation of travel to see and judge other engineering works—nor that *indispensible* familiarity with *what engineering is* in its practical developments all over the world which alone can give any insight into an opinion on a great engineering question. Worse than that, *they don't know their own deficiency* in that respect. Each one finds he knows as much as the rest and mutual admiration and the conventional word "Engineer" which they unhesitatingly assume, supplies all the rest. And they are kept in that delusion by a large outside world which, having no means of judging, consistently conceded to "government engineers" a profound deference.[48]

Excuse this tirade, it is no longer a pride nor a satisfaction to be an "engineer". . . . I can never feel as I used towards the Corps of Engineers. . . .[49] [Emphasis in the original]

This expression is historically important. Only rarely is the public able to go below the surface to see what constitutes an Engineer Corps consulting Board and what makes up the "conclusive researches" so often referred to in succeeding years. Seldom, if ever, are conclusions later stated with greater finality and authority than were made concerning the findings of this board with only one man, General Barnard, in opposition.

General Barnard had served as "Chief Engineer" to General Grant. A brief quotation from Grant's Memoirs will illustrate Barnard's relationship to Grant:

Previous to ordering any troops from Butler I sent my Chief Engineer, General Barnard, from the Army of the Potomac to that of the James to inspect Butler's position and ascertain whether I could again safely make an order for General Butler's movement in cooperation with mine. . . . If I could not, whether his position was strong enough, etc. . . .

General Barnard reported the position very strong, but etc. . . . I then asked why Butler could not move out, etc. . . . He then replied that it was impracticable because. . . .[50]

It is evident that General Barnard had a position of significance in relation to General Grant.

It was in regard to this principled man, General Barnard, that one of the members of the Board had written Howell (who was conducting a personal dispute with Barnard), "You may get a better opening through which to strike or your antagonist (General Barnard) may kill himself off."[5 1]

What sort of official reception did General Barnard receive? Chief of Engineers Humphreys supported the majority of the Board. Their views concurred with his own Physics and Hydraulics Report. In transmitting the Board's report to the Secretary of War on April 15, 1874, in accord with administrative custom, Humphreys had reiterated his "ascertained fact" that sand, gravel and earthy matter in the Mississippi was pushed along the bed. He reiterated his other "ascertained fact" that the salt water in the Gulf of Mexico would force this sediment to extend the bar.[5 2] He had now raised his estimates and predicted that the attainment of a high water depth of 28 feet would mean an annual bar advance of "not less than 1,200 feet."[5 3] He estimated that jetties at the Southwest Pass would result in a total cost of $23,000,000. He maintained that a Canal would cost only $13,000,000.

Why was there such concern shown by the Corps of Engineers over the desirability of having a united front on this issue? Perhaps it was because, in January of that year, Captain James B. Eads had proposed to build jetties at the mouth of the Mississippi.

Captain Eads realized that the Corps would not look favorably on this threat to its undisputed dominance. He knew that some extraordinary inducement would have to be offered to get Congress to give him this most important work. He therefore proposed to secure a channel 28 feet deep and 350 feet wide in half the time it would take to build a canal with the agreement that, if he did not attain these dimensions, he would not be paid. His proposal called for $2,000,000 to be paid when he achieved a depth of 20 feet, and the remainder in proportion until 28 feet was attained.

$500,000 a year maintenance money was also to be paid for ten years. Thus, his ten million dollar total proposal would cost the government less than half the $23,000,000 General Humphreys had deemed necessary for jetties, and $3,000,000 less than Humphreys' estimate for a canal. Eads' plan would not necessarily eliminate the possibility of building a canal. If he failed he would not be paid and the government could then proceed with a canal. If he succeeded, the government would have an open river mouth at New Orleans much sooner and at a lower price than a less convenient canal.

Certainly this was an attractive offer. Perhaps, due to its attractiveness the Corps saw in it only a dangerous attack on its monopoly of river and harbor work.

Opposition to Eads' Plan

Opposition to Eads' offer was widespread. As early as May of 1873 Major Howell of the Corps had written a letter to the President of the New Orleans Chamber of Commerce pronouncing jetties on the Mississippi unfeasible. This letter largely rejected the engineering principles advanced by Eads. Among the reasons already stated by Humphreys he included the assertion that, "careful engineers have time and time again pronounced the application of jetties at these passes unworthy of trial at government expense."[54] This statement, so typical of the Corps, had little foundation in fact as the Board of 1852 had recommended jetties as a possible third choice and the Board of 1873 had not yet reported. As for individual civilian engineers' opinions, there were certainly at least as many favoring as opposing jetties.

This oft-expressed hostility of the Corps toward jetties, combined with its offer to build a canal, naturally resulted in much suspicion of Eads and his proposal for jetties. As Barnard pointed out, there was an aura of blind confidence granted to the opinions of "Government Engineers" regardless of the quality of their engineering.

As a result, editorials in New Orleans papers soon began to accuse James Eads of plotting to obstruct the city's outlet to the sea in order to increase the business of the railroad line using his St. Louis Bridge. Excited meetings were held to oppose the plan for jetties.[55] A group of New Orleans businessmen wrote Eads pleading that he drop his crazy scheme. Echoing the Corps arguments, they prophesied that jetties would sink, worms would eat them, and that they would cause the bar to move constantly forward, leaving New Orleans far inland.[56]

To help in the effort to save New Orleans from the monster jetties, the Chamber of Commerce sent Professor C. G. Forshey (West Point graduate), scientist, and ex-Governor of Louisiana, P. O. Hebert (West Point graduate, 1840) to lobby for the Canal and against Jetties. Appearing before House and Senate Committees, Hebert criticized Eads' plan on the basis of his own examination of jetties and deltas in Europe and Egypt[57]

Following these personal appearances, the two West Pointers addressed a joint appeal to Congress asking:

> Would you, can you, honorable Senators, at such a moment contemplate or tolerate the half-insane proposition of strangers, who can know nothing of the habits of our inexorable enemy, to dam up his waters at the mouth by jetties or wing dams, that must inevitably send back the flood waters like a tide to the very city of New Orleans, or beyond, and complete the impending destruction? . . . We have exhausted argument, and laid before you the results of science and experience. We come now with prayer.[58]

As a final shot, Hebert and Forshey distributed in the halls of Congress a leaflet reading terrifyingly, "MUD LUMP BLOCKADE, At Mouths of the Passes." This charged, in frightening type and tones that, "INEVITABLE MUD LUMPS . . . must destroy any jetties," and urged, "For Pity and Economy's sake, if not in the interest of the commerce of the Mississippi Valley, give us the FORT ST. PHILLIP CANAL."[59]

On the day the jetty proposal came up before the House of Representatives a letter written by Chief of Engineers

Humphreys was circulated among its members. Though he had previously contended that jetties would cost $23 million, General Humphreys now charged that Eads' $10 million proposal would mean a $6 or $7 million profit for him![60] The pressure from the Corps and its cohorts in New Orleans was strong, and the Canal bill was passed by the House in preference to the jetties proposal.

In the Senate, Eads had more allies. The Canal bill was referred to the Senate Select Committee on Transportation Routes to the Seaboard. This committee heard testimony from Eads and from the West Pointers, Forshey and Hebert.

Humphreys, of course, was continuing undiminished his efforts to defeat Eads. Early in May of 1874 he received a critique of the jetty plan which he had requested a civilian employee of the Corps to write. This employee, R. E. McMath, revealed something of the intent behind the critique in a covering letter:

> The accompanying discussion of Mr. Eads' project has for its chief object the presentation of an *argumentum ad hominem* which, if it does not aid in solving scientific questions does overthrow his assertion in an important matter of fact.
>
> The suggestions of what the bill should be, of course do not imply a desire that it should pass, even if perfected in detail, *but merely to suggest amendments, that would defeat the purpose of its projector and render it unacceptable to him.* (Emphasis added.)[61]

Humphreys immediately sent a copy of this report, fully endorsed, but without the covering letter which disclosed his purpose, to an ally in the House of Representatives. He then had copies printed for distribution.

The report concluded, ". . . to entertain this project would be to open the door to a flood of schemes that would swamp all proper business, foster competition, and put our highway in the hands of monopolists." It is interesting to note that the author of this tract, Robert E. McMath, became a leader of the movement in the later 1880's trying to strip the Corps of its civil functions.[62]

To the Chairman of the Senate Committee now considering both Eads' proposal and the Canal bill, Humphreys sent a letter in late May, objecting to part of a speech in favor of jetties delivered by another Senator. "I do not doubt," wrote the Chief of Engineers, "that Senator West was designedly misled by someone to make his statement."[6 3] The inference could only be that the Senator had been misled by Captain Eads.

Within forty-eight hours after the Canal bill was referred to the Committee, a member rose in the Senate and said he had been authorized to ask that the committee be excused from further consideration of the Canal bill, which would mean sending it to the Senate for action. Regarding this startling move, one observer wrote later:

> If Mr. Eads had failed before the Senate Committee to refute the arguments of Messrs. Forshey and Hebert, and to convince it of the soundness of his own views, there is no doubt but that the committee, under the great pressure brought to bear upon it, would have reported the Canal bill favorably to the Senate, and in that event it would have been as promptly passed by that body as it had been by the House, and there would have been an end to the attempt to deepen the mouth of the Mississippi by jetties.[6 4]

Eads had foreseen that a deadlock was likely between his jetty proposal and the Canal bill, and had drawn up a third alternative. This new plan, which the Senate Committee reported favorably, provided for a commission of seven engineers, three from the Army, three from civil life, and a seventh from the Coast Survey, to decide upon the proper method of opening the mouth of the Mississippi. The commission was to be appointed by the President.[6 5]

Eads had friends in the Senate. One strong ally, the German-American liberal, Carl Schurz, rose in the Senate and declared that he did not believe "all the talent in this country was buttoned up in blue and brass."[6 6] It would be no calamity for an "outsider" to demonstrate his ability to deal with the Mississippi channels, contended Schurz. Why, in the much more military-oriented European nations, all civil works were handled by civilians. Surely the Army had had their turn already. "For thirty-seven years," he reported, "they have been planning, and today the depth of water is no greater."[6] [7]

The proposal for a Commission passed the Senate. In the mind of Eads, this was the crucial moment for his proposition. Five years later he wrote his friend Schurz, "You did not know at that time probably how much depended on the constitution of that board, but I shall believe it was then more than at any other moment that the fate of the proposition to deepen the mouth of the River by the jetty system trembled in the balance."[6] [8]

The commission was appointed and its members were among the most distinguished of America's engineering talent civil and military. None of the Army members was a publicly identified opponent of the jetty system. The Commission decided that the question was so important and complex that a trip to Europe was necessary to study jetties in use there.

When Congress re-convened in December of 1874 it had been widely reported that the study commission favored the jetty system. A remarkable change in public opinion was taking place at this time and the popularity of Eads' proposal was high. His prospects had never looked brighter.[6] [9]

Eads' plan had been to construct jetties on the Southwest Pass of the Mississippi. This was the largest and deepest of the three passes, and the one he deemed most suited to the successful application of jetties.

As expected, when the Commission reported on January 13, 1875, it declared itself in favor of jetties, rather than a canal. They reported, "the results of these examinations abroad (while additional information has been gained on almost every point relating to the problem before them) has been to largely strengthen their estimate of the value of jetties . . . at the mouth of the Mississippi River. . . ."[7] [0] One of the Army Engineers dissented, still favoring a canal.

To Eads' distress, however, the Commission recommended the application of the jetty system to the South Pass. This was only one quarter as large as the Southwest Pass and much more obstructed. It was much shallower and had a serious shoal (elevation in the bed) at the head of the pass which would be dangerous to remove. Most serious was the fact that the narrow South Pass could not be increased in width and depth when the growth of commerce demanded it.[71]

There were advantages to the South Pass. The *main contention* of the Commission was that it was entirely adequate to the present and prospective needs of commerce. The Commission also suggested that it would be far cheaper to improve. There was much feeling that an experiment such as jetties should be first tried on an inferior pass. Eads did not regard the jetties as experimental and disagreed with this contention.

Eads changed his proposition. He now proposed to develop a channel of 30 feet at the Southwest Pass for $8,000,000. In addition, $150,000 would be paid for the first 20 years of maintenance. His offer was still on the basis of "no cure, no pay," and the first payment of $500,000 was to be made only when a channel of 22 feet in depth and 200 feet in width was obtained. $500,000 more was to be paid when these dimensions were maintained for a year. $1,000,000 was to be paid him each year when two feet of permanent depth were added to the channel, up to 30 feet. The remainder was to be retained by the government, one-half for ten years and the other half for twenty years, as a guarantee for the performance of the work. With this more attractive offer (2 feet more of depth, ten years more of maintenance), he felt confident that Congress would give him the preferable Southwest Pass.[72]

On February 8, 1875, a bill embodying this new proposal was introduced in the House. The response of General Humphreys was predictable and immediate. He sent four so-called "memoranda" to the Secretary of War, reiterating his views on jetties.[73] As usual, he expressed his conviction that bar advance would render the proposed jetties dangerous and impracticable. Humphreys seemed hurt that anyone should question his and Abbot's "Report upon the Physics and Hydraulics of the Mississippi River." He stated that the condition of the South Pass, which some said disproved his theory of bar-formation, to the contrary, "is, when carefully examined, found to be an additional proof of its completeness and of its power. . . . "[74] "Now the experimental theory of bar-formation," he went on, "presented in the Mississippi delta report, will explain completely the manner in which the crest of the bar may advance 24,000 feet into the sea."[75] In these memoranda, he not only attacked Eads' theories, but went so far as to criticize the Commission authorized by Congress to pass on jetties, which included members of his own Corps of Engineers.

By the middle of February, 1875, Eads' bill had passed the House with only two dissenting votes. However, the Senate's version was amended, incorporating all of Eads' second offer, but applying them to the inferior South Pass. This was not necessarily a poor decision, from Congress' standpoint. It kept them from flying in the face of its experts' (the Commission's) recommendations. The South Pass was cheaper. It was preferable to experiment on.

Eads however, was understandably upset at this turn of events. His proposal had been made with the larger, deeper Southwest Pass in mind. He held that to take a proposal based on the larger Southwest Pass and apply the provisions unchanged to the restricted South Pass was not sound procedure. He was certain that if jetties were successful at the South Pass the larger pass would also soon need improvement.

The Senate Committee refused to be moved. Eads must give the same guarantee and produce the same depth for the little pass as he had proposed for the big one, do it for $3,000,000 less than offered (much less than the Commission's annual estimate). He could either accept these harsh terms, or allow the work to be turned over to the Corps of Engineers.[76]

Eads tried to explain to the Committee that their terms

were not only unfair but also dangerous. He was advised by Senators in favor of the proposal to accept the terms, being assured that if he did not achieve even the lesser channel envisioned by the Board of 1874, he would have no trouble at all in convincing Congress to lower its requirements.[77]

So Captain Eads reluctantly accepted the offer. He later wrote an associate, "I got all I wanted except the *big pass*. That is a national misfortune, not a personal one to me, as I believe with you that, as a speculation, the South Pass is the better."[78]

The bill passed the Senate in that form, and the House accepted the Senate's amendments. On March 3, 1875, it was signed into law.[79] A member of the House of Representatives' Committee on Commerce later said that the Committee had framed the law to bind Eads, "as in a vise," to avoid the possibility of his drawing a dollar from the government that was not absolutely his due.[80] The law was extremely thorough in spelling out the exact specification to be met by Eads at every step of the way. If, for any number of reasons, the Secretary of War should conclude that construction was not proceeding according to the spirit and intent of the Act, the government could step into the work.[81] These were the conditions that any civilian engineer who dared to encroach upon the exclusive domain of the Corps of Engineers had to face, even if he received far less money than the Corps' Canal would have cost.

The Corps' Hostility Toward Eads Continues

After the passage of this bill, it might have been expected that the Corps of Engineers' hostility towards Eads and harassments of him would have ceased, but this was not the case. To better understand the Corps' subsequent dealings with Eads, it is perhaps well to pause and examine its opinion of him.

The Corps' initial and major reaction to Eads was that he was a "stranger," an "outsider," a non-West Pointer and not a member of the Corps of Engineers. His engineering skill and political perseverance made him a dangerous threat to their hitherto tightly protected domain. Barnard had pointed out that "this undertaking by Captain Eads is the greatest work of river engineering that has ever been attempted."[8][2] To have this job snatched from its grasp by a civilian must have seemed a catastrophe to the Corps. Eads had already won one battle with the Corps over the St. Louis Bridge, and its defeat there had been humiliating. Interestingly enough, in the case of the bridge, the Corps' objection to Eads' work did not arise until July of 1873, six years after the bridge was started. This was two months after Eads' initial proposal to build jetties. Perhaps the Corps' opposition to him in the case of the bridge may have been largely to help defeat him in the more serious threat to the Corps at the mouth of the Mississippi.

Finding that its criticism of Eads on the basis of his being an "outsider" was not well received outside the Corps, it tried other tactics. He was a bridge builder, and knew nothing about hydraulics. He was in favor of the railroad interests. He was trying to destroy sea commerce at New Orleans. But the most persistent attack on him consisted of the charge that he was a profiteer trying to get a fat contract and help "monopolists" take over the work which "rightfully" belonged to the Corps. General C. B. Comstock referred to putting work "into the hands of an individual who agrees to do it for a round sum," and continued, "it should be remembered that the government by this last method places itself at a certain disadvantage, inasmuch as, if the individual finds the work profitable he pockets the gain, while if it is unprofitable, he throws up the job, or comes to Congress for relief."[8][3] Professor Forshey, referring to Eads' contract states, "Before such a sum of money, Senators, statesmen, judges, philosophers, and even great engineers, may well pause and analyze their own hearts, and answer to themselves, whether its attractive seductions may not have colored their opinions."[8][4] Major Howell wrote, "There can be no success except of a United States Treasury raid until it is ascertained that the jetties are of a permanent character. . . . "[8][5]

There is here perhaps an element of sincere concern at having America's public works conducted on the basis of contracts and profits. However, in this case, the fact that Eads' appropriation was considerably *less* than that required for a canal, and the fact that he of necessity was working on the risky basis of "no cure, no pay," seems not to have had any effect on the arguments of Corps members.

The worst opinion of Eads was, of course, that of the man who most lost face by Eads' contract, the Chief of Engineers, General Humphreys. To one correspondent he wrote, "Of course Mr. Eads' statement of objects is a mere pretence." His real object, maintained Humphreys, was "to get pay from Congress for works of a temporary character which I think from what I learn he wishes to substitute for those of a permanent character which he is required to make."[86] To another he stated, "The effrontery of Mr. Eads is on a par with that of Tweed, Gould & Fiske."[87] (Notorious swindlers of the day.) To a third he wrote, "It has been my fortune in the course of my duty as well as that of many others, to hit some persons very hard," and, in an obvious reference to Eads, "Among those are men . . . whose schemes for depleting the Treasury or for some other personal aggrandizement I have been under the necessity of exposing. . . ."[88]

Among Corps officers, the only one who seemed to be able to allow his engineering judgment and preference for the good of the country to transcend his personal feelings (he didn't like Eads), was the beleaguered General Barnard, who later wrote:

> . . . though I had been *the* official expounder and advocate of the jetty trial, I had nothing whatever to do with the award of the contract or concession to him. [Eads] I never believed *that* was the way the government should take hold of it. And I should have been something more than neutral: I should have been pronounced in my opposition to the concession to an individual had I not clearly recognized that (unfortunately) *that* seemed to be the *only* way in which a great end was likely to be attained—the trial with more than "probable" chances of

success of making an open river mouth to this great
river—and the *saving* the government from committing
itself irretrievably to the most questionably adequate—
and most certainly money-engulfing "Ship Canal."[8][9]

With the perspective of this almost unanimous hostility and
suspicion of Eads' motives by Corps officers, led by their
Chief, it is easier to understand the Corps' subsequent actions
in hampering the successful completion of his work.

Eads Faces Numerous Obstacles

In May of 1875, Eads and his party started work on the
jetties. With characteristic imagination, he had devised a way
to build a section of the walls of the jetties from willow
mattresses in only two hours, as opposed to the two days
taken by European engineers. Problems arose. A gale destroyed some of the work in September and again in December.
Willows were hard to cut and deliver in the torrential rain.
But these were Eads' risks, not the government's. By
February of 1876, the channel was deepened five feet and
now measured 14 feet.[90]

Nevertheless pessimism about the ultimate success of the
jetties had again overtaken residents of the valley. General
Humpheys' four "memoranda" in opposition to the jetties,
had been excerpted from his official report to the Secretary
of War, illustrated with maps, and distributed as pamphlets
around the country.[91] More serious, a series of anonymous
statements showed up in newspapers, ominously reporting
the formation of a new shoal outside the South Pass. Their
source and the reason for their anonymity became more
apparent later on.

To try to offset these negative prophesies, Eads decided to
celebrate the first anniversary of the passage of the jetty act,
March 4, 1876, by having the schooner, "Mattie Atwood," go
through the South Pass on its way to Russia. This ship was
loaded to carry 13½ feet. However, the ship was delayed at
the head of the pass until the tide went out, and when she
finally got under way, the skipper grounded her, not being

able to keep her in deepest water in the irregular channel. She remained on the bar all night and finally sailed out at noon the following day.[9 2]

With this situation, Eads had great difficulty raising money and was forced to pay exhorbitant rates of interest. The stockholders of the company organized by Eads to build the jetties were being affected by the rampant doubts prevailing publicly. He challenged them to come see the addition of over four feet of depth to the South Pass. The stockholders from St. Louis agreed to this, but in order to make their investigation friendly, they chartered a magnificent steamer, the *Grand Republic*, and made the trip a combination pleasure-business cruise. Families and members of the press accompanied them, and more people got on at New Orleans.

Unable to stop Eads in Congress, the Corps of Engineers tried to make his project financially impossible by finding excuses for withholding payments due, and also by discrediting him in the eyes of his financial supporters. The trip of the stockholders from St. Louis provided such an opportunity. As E. L. Corthell, Eads' assistant, later historian of the jetties, described the setting:

> To appreciate it, one should have been connected with the jetties during those discouraging days, which, while they brought an improved channel, were gloomy with forebodings of financial disaster; to still better appreciate it, one should have been in the place of Mr. Eads, on whose shoulders rested the heavy burden and the responsibility of the success of the undertaking.[9 3]

The steamer left New Orleans for Port Eads (the workers' town) in a holiday mood on April 26, 1876. Eads and his party waited for its arrival with keen anticipation. They saw a dark speck approaching on the horizon. But it wasn't the *Grand Republic*. It was much smaller. A little boat skittered here and there, apparently examining the surrounding area. It was Major Howell's steam launch with his assistant, Captain Collins, inside. He had decided to take this day off from the Corps' work at the Southwest Pass thirty miles away and help to greet the visiting dignitaries. Inside the little craft, Howell's assistant worked at plotting the soundings he was taking in the channel.[94]

The *Grand Republic* from St. Louis soon followed, its passengers gay and cheering, expecting to have their doubts allayed. Captain Collins boarded the steamer, paid his fare, and then stood prominently in the saloon, ready to show the results of his soundings to anyone who might be interested.[95]

These findings, of course, had an aura of the official attached to them. Despite the fact that a representative of the Coast Survey was making an official survey at the time, Major Howell maintained that Collins' soundings were simply part of a series of surveys he had been conducting for two years. That he chose this day and time to do his work did not seem unusual. And, he later asserted, his assistant was in no way trying to create an unfavorable impression about the jetties. Howell explained, "Mr. Collins, having completed his field work, in accordance with his instructions to return to New Orleans as soon as possible, took passage on the Grand Republic, paid his fare, simply answered questions when courtesy required it, and was an interested observer of the solemn farce. . . ."[96]

And what were these "official" findings? In opposition to Captain Eads' soundings of 16 feet of depth, Captain Collins maintained he found only 12. In addition, as Howell later deduced from Collins' findings, the nucleus of a new bar had been discovered, a shoal had started, the velocity of the river had decreased, the volume of the discharge of the pass had gone down, and the extension of the bar was going to require the lengthening of the jetties by 7½ miles.[97] These were examples of the false reports of the Corps, made particularly to discourage investors in Eads' project, as was shown by later accurate measurements. Captain Eads vigorously disputed these contentions and showed his own charts and records to disprove them. But it was his word against the official "government engineers" whose invulnerability to reason Barnard had referred to. The once-gay excursion returned to New Orleans in a state of depression. Stock in the jetty company began to go on sale at half price.[98] It appeared that the Corps might yet win.

To try to offset these findings, Eads immediately asked the Coast Survey to instruct their representative to repeat and speed up his survey. The jetty builder made special arrangements to facilitate his work. At the same time, he addressed a letter to the New Orleans *Times*, disputing Captain Collins' findings as reported by the paper. Interestingly enough, he ended by affirming his faith in Major Howell's honor and his assurance that the Major did not authorize his assistant's actions. Shortly thereafter, an editorial appeared in the New Orleans *Democrat*, containing presumed data which would have been available only from Howell's office and sustaining the report of his assistant. With regard to these and similar reports, Eads still maintained, "I did not, however, even then charge Major Howell with being the author or prompter of them."[99]

Howell felt compelled to refute this expression of faith and wrote a harsh letter to the New Orleans *Democrat*, repeating the charges against Eads' jetties and commenting, "The results, when fully submitted to the public, will greatly interest hydraulic engineers, and go far toward refuting many of the absurd statements and theories advanced by Mr. Eads before commencing his jetties, and on which all his specious plans are based." He objected to what he termed Eads' "usual browbeating manner" and maintained that his surveys were necessary, "to aid in solving the great problem present at the mouth of the Mississippi." "If the results had been available before the passage of the jetty contract," he continued, "it is probable that the country would not have been saddled with the adventure." Absurdly, in the light of Humphreys' memoranda and his own actions, he piously contended, "no army engineer has thrown a straw in the way of Mr. Eads' jetty work."[100]

Eads communicated with the President who directed the Secretary of War to order the following interdiction to the Chief of Engineers. One can only wonder at his thoughts, when, on June 8, 1876, Humphreys signed the order to Howell which read:

> You will make no soundings, current or other measurements of any kind whatever in the South Pass or on the bars at its river and sea ends or in the sea and off its mouth, but will limit your observations to the other passes and the main stem of the river, should such observations be necessary in the execution of duties heretofore assigned you.[101]

Was Howell simply doing his official duty, as he maintained, and letting the facts have what effect they would? Or was his conduct unsuited to a representative of the United States Government?

In this case the evaluation of ex-President Grant seems significant. He had followed the relations of Eads and the Corps of Engineers since the building of the St. Louis Bridge.

As President, Grant on two occasions came in touch with General Humphreys in relation to James Eads. As to the St. Louis Bridge, Grant very strongly disapproved of the course of General Humphreys, then Chief of Engineers, and acted effectively to counteract his decision. In the case of the Mississippi Jetties, the project was being promoted just as Grant completed his second term as President. Especially through his protege, Major Howell, Humphreys had done his best to defeat James Eads' proposals. After Grant's term as President, on the night when he was starting his trip around the world, one of his last acts, in relation to the Presidency, was to write the following letter to his friend, General W. T. Sherman:

Steamer Twilight
[Was he writing at twilight?]
May 17, 1877.

Dear General,

It was my intention before leaving the country to have written you a letter to show to the Sec. of War, that I had had a letter addressed to him by Capt. Eades (sic) in relation to the opposition to his enterprise for deeping the S.W. Pass of the Mississippi River by Major Howell of the Engineer Corps. The opposition of Maj. H. has been unreasonable in my opinion and unofficer like. The plan was adopted by the legislative branch of the Govt. and is entitled to a fair trial at least from officers holding commissions from that Govt no matter what they think of the success of the enterprise. Maj. Howell has unquestionably endeavored to prejudice the public mind against Maj. Eads (sic) plan and, in my opinion has cost him much money by weakening public confidence in his success. I feel individually culpable in not having removed Major H. from his present duties while I was still an officer.

If you will state what I have said to the Sec. of War, and explain the circumstances under which this note was written I will be much obliged to you.

Yours truly

Gen. W. T. Sherman   U. S. Grant[102]

Eads still had the problem of refuting the "facts" widely circulated by Howell's office. About the time Major Howell's letter was published in the *Democrat*, the builder of the jetties received a letter from the office of the Coast Survey informing him that the type of survey he wanted would have to be made by the inspecting officer of the Corps of Engineers assigned to look after the South Pass jetty construction. Humphreys had assigned the head of the Corps' Detroit office, his loyal associate, General Comstock (who had taken over the Lake Survey after the current meter incident) to this duty. Thus the latest data on improvements to the South Pass had to go from Comstock's representative on the spot, to Comstock in far-away Detroit, to the Chief of Engineers in Washington, to the Secretary of War, to Congress, to the public printer and then back to Congress—by which time Eads could get a copy. By that time the data were so outdated as to be virtually worthless. This also left payments for work done far behind the date they were due. By such strategy the Chief of Engineers was able to delay payments, and to increase the prospect of Eads' financial bankruptcy.

Immediately after the steamer excursion had left New Orleans, General Comstock's representative, Captain Brown, started sounding the South Pass. When approached by Eads, Brown refused to divulge his findings, saying they could only go to Comstock. Comstock, in New Orleans briefly, also refused to give Eads any official findings, saying they had to go to Humphreys first. Eads frantically appealed to the Secretary of War who said he would get some data, as soon as it was received from Detroit, whenever that would be. Eads now turned again to the Coast Survey, whose soundings were being made chiefly at his own expense. Their head again refused to divulge official data, saying, "General Comstock will give all information required by law."[103]

Eads returned to the Secretary of War, asking him to request information from the Coast Survey this time. He did not realize that President Grant had seen his earlier communication to the Secretary of War and on May 15th had told the Secretary of War to order General Comstock to make soundings at the Mississippi Pass immediately and furnish an official certificate of these to Eads. It was not until June 28 that the Secretary of War ordered this and several more weeks before Comstock got started, as he consumed more time by asking for several clarifications of the order.[104]

In the meantime, the Secretary of War, on June 19th had requested the Coast Survey to furnish the War Department with a comparative chart of soundings at the South Pass from May of 1875 to 1876. Astoundingly, wishing to avoid a conflict with the Corps of Engineers (they had been feuding on another matter already), the Superintendent of the Coast Survey refused the War Department's request. Eads then appealed to the Secretary of the Treasury (which had jurisdiction over the Coast Survey) to order the release of the data. The Secretary refused, saying it was the War Department's jurisdiction. As a last resort, the jetty builder finally appealed to the House of Representatives to order the release of the official findings, the only thing which could settle the accuracy of Howell's contentions. This body unanimously passed a resolution ordering the release of the information and finally, three months after Eads first started his quest for official data, the Coast Survey released its survey reports.[105]

As Eads had expected, this indisputable report, when it finally was revealed, completely refuted Howell's contention that a bar was forming outside the jetties.[106]

A certification was still necessary from Comstock to prove that the depth had reached 19 feet. The Secretary of War on June 28th had written Eads informing him that reports were now to be made directly to the Secretary, by-passing the hostile Humphreys, that only Comstock was to control such surveys, and that he (Eads) was to be furnished with data directly from Comstock. After some stalling on Comstock's part this was done, though Eads was forced again later on February 7, 1877, to unsuccessfully try to get results directly from Captain Brown in New Orleans.

So, the situation was that Eads could get data from the Coast Survey to refute charges of shoaling and bar advance and could get certification of depth, but only at the pleasure of the hostile General Comstock in Detroit.

On May 12th, 1876, two weeks after the untimely cruise of the *Grand Republic*, the Captain of the steamship *Hudson*, with a draft of 14 feet 7 inches, decided to go through the jetties South Pass. She made it through successfully, giving Eads his first empirical proof, though still "unofficial," that more than Howell's 12 feet of depth existed. On May 27th, the steamer *New Orleans*, drawing 17 feet 3 inches, made it easily between the jetties.[107] Thereafter the Cromwell Steamship Line began using the South Pass twice a week. Though not offering the satisfaction of official vindication, this semi-weekly use of the South Pass by large steamers gave heart to the builders and restored confidence to financiers.[108]

Now, Eads was faced with a troublesome problem. His original plan had called for temporarily closing the Western channel which the Cromwell ships were using, to work on the shallower Eastern channel. Now, if he followed this plan, the only evidence of the success of his work would be lost. His enemies would, of course, give wide publicity to the fact that steamers no longer used the Pass and the effects on his financing could be disastrous. At the expense of a large $180,000 dike already built in the Eastern channel, Eads determined to abandon his original design and concentrate on deepening the Western channel. As Corthell lamented:

> Had he been promptly furnished as in common justice he should have been, with the official certification of the actual condition of the channel, as often as it was measured by the United States inspecting officer, this change would not have been made, and the channel into the pass would have been a straighter and better one . . . as it is, East Dyke and the altered plan must remain forever a monument of official jealousy and opposition.[109]

The Corps of Engineers had still more ways of subtly working against their tormentor Eads. Before he was interdicted from participating in the surveys, General Humphreys had requested a survey by Comstock with the following orders:

> . . . if the jetties and other works do not possess the degree of strength and durability specified in the act of Congress, you will please state to what degree the jetties and auxiliary works are less massive, less strong, less enduring and less costly than the works planned by the Board of Engineers constituted under the River and Harbor Act of June 23, 1874. . . .[110]

After Humphreys was eliminated from the operation, we can assume that orders became more objective and were issued for the purpose of seeking data rather than proving a thesis.

At some point in their tenure of duty, General Comstock and later his assistant, Captain Brown, began making comprehensive reports on how much the jetty works *would* have cost if an engineer officer had done them. Their estimates, of course, ran consistently lower than the amount Eads was spending and being paid. This extremely hypothetical proposition began to be given some publicity and Eads was forced to complain about them.[111]

On October 5, 1876, careful soundings by Eads' crew showed a channel 20 feet deep and 200 feet wide, through the Pass into the Gulf. By the terms of his contract, this entitled Eads to a first payment of $500,000 and he wrote requesting the Secretary of War to authorize this payment on October 25th. General Comstock's opinion was sought on the matter and he gave his opinion that, since the shoal at the head of the pass had not attained a depth of 20 feet, that the first payment was not yet due. Since the jetty bill made no specification as to whether the South Pass included the shoal at its head or not, a Board of Army Engineers was convened to decide on this point and others. It consisted of General Barnard, General H. G. Wright (the lone dissenter in favor of a Canal on the Board of 1874), and General B. S. Alexander, who had served on an advisory commission Congress had set up to pass on the jetty plans. The Board was also asked to consider general aspects of the building of the jetties.

After careful considerations, the Board reported on November 19th that, although the channel of the shoal was part of the South Pass, the shoal as a whole was common to the three passes and Eads' improvements could be considered exclusive of the shoal. With regard to Eads' construction methods, the Board noted that he had modified the European methods and that while Engineer Officers would have applied stone more freely, still Eads was in the "spirit" of the act. To this qualified endorsement, Eads wrote a letter to General Barnard, stating, in effect, that it seemed he was not to get a single payment without some humiliation on his part.[112]

Eads was yet to get his money. On November 24th, the Secretary of War submitted the Board's report to Attorney General Alonzo Taft, asking for *his* opinion on the question of the shoal. On January 19, 1877, the Attorney General replied that Eads' payment was to be determined by the depth and width of the pass, independent of the shoal. As

General Comstock had certified on January 9th that Eads had obtained 20 feet of depth and 200 feet of width over the length of the Pass, his payment was authorized.[113] After traveling to Washington and doing much personal prodding, Eads finally got the money in the middle of February,[114] four and a half months after conditions warranted his being paid. Due to this delay and the critical lack of funds, very important works at the head of the passes had to be postponed and built at a high stage of the river, at much more expense and loss of time.[115] A late December gale had demolished many parts of the unfinished work which would have to be done over. So the strategy of the Chief of Engineers did make some headway toward bankrupting Eads.

Other problems dogged the work. Key staff members died. A yellow fever plague halted work and killed off workmen. Financial difficulties consistently harassed the jetty company and during one critical period, Eads even had to ask his crew either to stay on for a promise of pay in the future or leave. All but two stayed.[116]

A survey made by Captain Brown on December 15th, 1877, showed that the jetties had created a depth of 22 feet in the channel with a width of over 200 feet. This was 13 feet of additional depth since Eads had begun. Upon receiving this report, the Secretary of War convened a Commission consisting of Generals Barnard and Wright to go to Port Eads and examine the construction of the jetties, determine their effect on the South Pass, and decide whether or not Eads was entitled to a second payment. These gentlemen visited Port Eads, and on January 5th, 1878, reported that the jetties were well-built, permanent, had the desired effect, and that Eads' work had acquired the depth and width authorizing a second payment.[117]

The dimensions of the channel proposed in Eads' offer to Congress were for the larger Southwest Pass. When the Corps was able to force Eads to work in the smaller South Pass, it did not modify the dimensions to suit the differing conditions. As General Barnard had observed, the House had passed a bill providing for improvement of the larger pass and then simply substituted the South Pass in compromise with the Senate, without an adjustment in the specifications.[118] Corthell pointed out that this failure to suit the specification to the differing conditions of the channel prescribed by Congress would be dangerous both to the pass and the jetties. The specifications were inappropriate and unnecessary in many respects.[119]

Due to this fact and the arbitrary financial hardships placed on him, Eads, on May 7, 1878, asked for a modification of the restrictions. He did not ask for a reduction in the dimensions required, as the Senators earlier had said he should, and he did not ask for a greater sum of money in payment. Pointing out the extreme, unforeseen financial burdens placed on him he asked only that, in the light of the fact that over 80% of the work was done and that the jetties were a universally acclaimed success, he be paid $1,773,000, a sum which would still not pay off his debts.[120]

This communication was turned over to Generals Barnard and Wright, who disputed Eads' contention that he had completed 80% of the work, but did agree that 85% of the world's shipping could now get through the pass and that pushing ahead the work with utmost vigor was essential. They tactfully removed themselves from a final recommendation.[121] Congress debated the subject, but was unwilling to change the terms of the contract without further investigation. Congress did show its confidence in Eads by voting an immediate appropriation of $1,000,000, half of which was to go directly for the work, and by authorizing the President to appoint a Commission to report on the jetties.[122]

During this discussion, Chief of Engineers Humphreys, whose complaints had been discredited by the overwhelming success of the jetties, tried to recover lost ground. In a May 1, 1878 letter to a Congressman, on the pretext of discussing a proposed Mississippi River Commission (rumor had it that Eads would be its head), General Humphreys launched an attack on Eads and his jetties. In this letter, he contended that, though bar advance had not occurred as fast as he had predicted, it was taking place. He felt that the powerful new dredge being used by Eads was also helping to upset his predictions. (Barnard and Wright had asserted that the effects of dredging were minimal compared to the actual effects of the jetties.)

In regard to costs, Humphreys now disregarded the *total* cost of $23 million he had estimated for Southwest Pass jetties and referred only to his estimate of $7 million for the *first* cost. This, of course, compared unfavorably with Eads' total cost of $10 million, though this was $13 million less than Humphreys' estimate for total cost.

Humphreys ended his diatribe with a profusion of italics and capital letters, asserting that ". . . the facts exhibited by the reports of the officers inspecting the South Pass show that the views expressed by many engineer officers, the Chief of Engineers among them, that a new bar would form at the sea end of the jetties, and that it would extend into the sea more rapidly than the old bar, are correct even during the changes going on under the scouring power of the jetties. . . ."[1][2][3]

He concluded:

THE FOREGOING HISTORICAL SUMMARY SUFFI-
CIENTLY PROVES THAT THE RESULTS ACTUALLY
ATTAINED AT THE SOUTH PASS DISPROVE THE
VIEWS ADVANCED BY MR. EADS AND CONFIRM
THOSE OF THE ENGINEER DEPARTMENT.[1][2][4]

Eads made a detailed reply to this absurdity, pointing out all the errors of fact which Humphreys advanced. But he didn't need to do so. Results were all that were necessary. Large, deep draft ships were now regularly using the channel.

The commission which Congress had authorized the President to appoint reported on January 22, 1879. The five Army Engineers, including General Barnard, reached these conclusions:

They had no complaints on his progress to date, substantially agreed with his financial estimate to finish the works, but felt that much more maintenance would be needed than Eads foresaw. They were satisfied with the progress to date, the depth now being 23 feet. They doubted that a permanent channel of more than 25 or 26 feet could be obtained, an assumption which the completed work proved mistaken. They certified the reasonable permanency of the works. As for Humphreys' opinions, they had this to say: "The actual results, therefore, so far as we know them, do not justify the predictions of accelerated bar advance. On the contrary, they show a disappearance of bar material from the front of the jetties."[1][2][5]

As to the main result of their deliberations, a recommendation on the modification of Eads' contract, the Board had some interesting viewpoints. In discussing the history of proposals for the jetties, the Board stated: "The trial of the jetty system at the South Pass, or at least a further study of the subject, before undertaking the construction of a ship-canal, was first recommended in the minority report of the Board of Engineers of 1873...."[1][2][6] This "minority report" was by General Barnard, with an otherwise solid vote of the eight man Board against jetties. They later commented:

> No reason is known why Congress ... should not have left the execution of this work to its own agents (the Engineer Corps) except that the present contractor, Mr. James B. Eads, offered to accomplish the results contemplated by the Board (of 1874) without payment unless these results were secured. It would seem, therefore, that this proposition of payments for results only influenced Congress to award the contract to Mr. Eads instead of leaving the work to its own agents.[1][2][7]

In their bewilderment as to how Congress could *possibly* have refused to give this work to the Army Engineers, the Board, composed of Corps of Engineers members, recommended that Eads only be given a $250,000 advance on his next payment.

Predictably, Eads was indignant at this attitude by the Board. In a long review of the report of the Commission of Army Engineers, Eads took particular issue with the Corps' virtual taking credit for his jetty plan. In May of 1873, he pointed out, he had first pushed the plan of jetties for the Mississippi, long before any Corps member had publicly expressed himself in their favor. The Board of 1874, which recommended jetties, was created purely as a result of Eads' proposal. General Barnard's earlier minority report, he pointed out, recommended only that jetties be *considered* and this *after* dredging had been tried.[128]

Corthell recalled about the Commission of 1874 that all of its members were, at their time of appointment, in favor of a Canal.[129] It was Eads' persuasion that helped convert them.

Fortunately, Congress again chose not to listen to its "own agents," and voted on March 3, 1879 to give Eads an immediate appropriation of $750,000 in addition to easing the conditions for later payments. The rest of this story is now history. With this belated approach to decent financial treatment, Eads' work leaped ahead, and was finished within four months.

By July 10th, 1879, as a result of the construction of Eads' jetties, the South Pass channel had a middle depth of thirty feet, which was four or five feet more than the Corps of Engineers Board, reporting less than six months earlier, had considered to be ultimately probable. This was a greater depth than ever had been required for the nation's number one port, New York harbor. "Eads had won another great victory."[130]

After Successful Completion of the Jetties

Responding to this achievement, within five years the Port of New Orleans jumped from eleventh to second place among American ports in the tonnage of freight carried. Only New York's position as the focus of American life enabled it to keep ahead of New Orleans.[131]

What would have happened at the mouth of the Mississippi if it had been the Corps of Engineers and not Eads, who did the work? A comparison of a somewhat similar work done by the Corps at about the same time is suggestive.

At Galveston, in 1874, the Corps ordered Captain Howell, who had been a particularly vicious opponent of Eads at New Orleans, to draw up plans for jetty improvement of Galveston harbor. He did this, being careful to provide for bar advance, sinking banks and the other catastrophes that General Humphreys had warned of in the case of Eads' project. The Corps' plans drawn up for Galveston were intended to be superior to any that Eads might have made and thus show up his incompetence. These plans placed the jetty walls far apart and submerged below water, rather than above like Eads' type of jetties. This violated fundamental principles of Eads' design, which called for confining the water within the channel and narrowing the channel, thus compelling the confined water to do the work of digging. The Corps plans represented a modest effort, built only to attain 18 feet of depth.[132]

The almost absurd history of this work would make a chapter in itself. By the end of 1879, Howell gave up the work in complete failure. One wall had completely disappeared under water. Some years later, a Congressman went out to investigate, and it took him some time, poking around with a ten-foot pole, to find even the remnants of this "lost jetty."[133]

In 1883, the Army Engineer in charge assured the citizens of Galveston that, if they could raise $100,000, with this he could complete the work and attain a depth of 18 feet. By 1884, the Army Engineers had expended $1,500,000 and attained a depth of only 13 feet.[134] In disgust the citizens of Galveston approached James Eads and asked him to try to secure a contract for the work. Eads made an offer, but he was now 64 years old (he died two years later) and did not have the time or energy to fight the influence of the Corps.* The Corps retained the work, to the regret of the city of Galveston.

*His years of exploring the bed of the Mississippi River under a diving bell, sometimes under the pressure of 70 feet of water, resulted in injury to his lungs from which he never fully recovered, and which apparently caused his death.

A graduate of West Point and former officer of the Corps of Engineers constructed a chart from data in the annual report of the Chief of Engineers for 1887 to show the results of the Corps of Engineers on projects similar to Eads'.[135] (See page 170.) The last column in this table indicates the poor showing of the Corps in the field of channel improvement up to that time. This, of course, is not representative of present conditions which is due in large measure to the excellent hydraulic laboratory facilities of the Corps for model testing of proposed waterway improvements.

As Eads had predicted, the success of the South Pass jetties soon created a clamor to deepen the Southwest Pass. In 1893, six years after Eads' death, Corthell, Eads' chief assistant on the South Pass, made a "no cure, no pay" proposal to Congress for a contract to undertake this work. But Corthell, in dealing with Congress, could not equal the effort of the dynamic Eads, and the Corps of Engineers was smarter now in protecting its domain. The work went to the Corps and the Corps proceeded with a plan dubbed "erroneous" in many features by Corthell.[136] By June, 1914, 21 years after the Corps had defeated Corthell and had kept the job for itself, the Army had succeeded in deepening the Southwest Pass only to 27 feet, and deep water ships still were using Eads' smaller South Pass.[137] As the Chief of Engineers understated in 1924, "The plan [for the Southwest Pass] did not prove to be successful." He added, hopefully, "The ultimate efficiency of the plan, even as modified, cannot be assured, but it is hoped that the studies that are being devoted to the problem will soon bring it to a successful conclusion."[138]

When the brilliant success of Eads' work at South Pass is compared with the work of the Corps at Southwest Pass up to 1914 and elsewhere, it is evident that good results depend not only on correct engineering theory and its application, but also on many intangible factors of technical engineering and construction.

For years after the success of Eads' work at the South Pass was incontrovertibly apparent, the Corps was versatile in

Chart showing the outcome of the Corps of Engineers jetty projects prior to the establishment of the hydraulic laboratory

[Compiled by a former Corps of Engineers' officer from data in the 1887 report of the Chief of Engineers.]

Location	Total Expenditure	Estimate to Complete	Result
1. Galveston	$1,581,782.84	$6,700,000.00	Practically nothing; not an additional foot on the outer bar
2. Galveston Bay	291,923.18	—	Practically obliterated.
3. Trinity River	34,500.00	25,000.00	No increase in depth.
4. Buffalo Bayou	100,676.03	—	Not capable of permanent improvement
5. Brazos River	140,833.94	364,000.00	Not as yet resulted in any useful effect.
6. Pass Cavallo	290,095.16	1,366,780.00	Not as yet resulted in any useful effect.
7. Arkansas Pass	393,556.95	1,571,293.72	Checking the southward movement of the pass.
8. Brazos Santiago	185,204.17	—	Not as yet resulted in any useful effect.
9. Fort Brown	17,000.00	Abandoned	Without result.
Total	$3,035,572.27	$10,027,073.72	

excuses. Eads' positive results at South Pass, coupled with the negative results of similar efforts for more than forty years of the Corps at the Southwest Pass, prompted some Corps officers to make excuses for the Corps. In 1886, an Engineer Corps officer expressed his lingering hope that Eads' jetties might yet fail and the Corps be vindicated. He commented:

As a matter of opinion, I think that there are quite a number of Members of this Society [ASCE] who, while patiently awaiting the development of the next ten years, are not yet prepared to deny that the jetties may still be undermined; that their foundations may still prove unstable; that the bar may still advance more rapidly toward the gulf, that the present channel may fill up rapidly as soon as the present dredging stops; and that the ship canal may finally have to be resorted to as the only permanent method.[139]

At the same time, another Corps officer deplored the method used by Eads in getting his excellent results. While in that case the by-passing of the Corps had been successful, he held that, in other future calls, it might be dangerous. This officer commented:

But suppose the precedent followed, to be applied not to one, but to a dozen harbors. The men most plausible, most reckless in the use of statements, promises and favors, and able to secure the most powerful lobby, would be the ones who would obtain the legislation and secure the contracts. While human nature is what it is, corruption in such a scramble would be inevitable, and all who desire that public moneys shall be honestly used must dread the certain result.[140]

By 1899, an Engineering officer assigned to survey the mouth of the Mississippi was still holding fast against the possibility of the Corps' having been wrong. "Under the very best conditions," he predicted, "the life of the 30-foot channel created and maintained by jetties and dredging will not last at South Pass beyond 1913. . . ."[141] (It still lasts today—1970.)

At long last, by 1932, the Corps acknowledged the success
of Eads' venture. Further denial, after more than half a
century of full, unqualified use, would be nonsensical. The
Corps commented:

> The success of Mr. Eads' project is too well known to
> necessitate description here. Suffice it to say that the
> Eads jetties have, with certain modifications dictated by
> experience, effectually solved the problem of channel
> maintenance at the river mouth.[142]

The Rewriting of History

As the Eads' jetties were everywhere recognized to be fully
effective and long lasting, Corps members, as usual, tried to
rewrite history and recoup lost prestige, by maintaining that
the idea and plan were really theirs in the first place. As early
as 1886, one officer wrote:

> The present method of improvement by "parallel jetties"
> at the mouth of the passes . . . was recommended to
> Congress by the United States Corps of Engineers in
> 1852, before Mr. Eads, as an engineer, had hardly had
> time to find out that the Mississippi River had a bar at its
> mouth. And the present successful results might have
> been obtained years before Mr. Eads took hold of the
> work if Congress had not handicapped the Corps of
> Engineers by specifying that the work must be done "by
> contract." . . . It is certainly unjust to blame the Engineer
> Corps because its recommendations were not fol-
> lowed.[143]

He neglected to mention the long bitter fight of the Corps
against the jetties and in favor of the Fort St. Phillip Canal.

The quoted statement assumes that, if the Corps of
Engineers *had* directed the construction of the jetties at the
time James Eads did, the results would have been equally
favorable. Such is not necessarily the case. If the Corps had
undertaken the job Eads undertook, the results probably
would have been very different. The Corps prevented Eads
from improving the Southwest Pass, where he believed his

work would be most successful. Later, the Corps decided to imitate Eads and to improve the Southwest Pass, the one Eads wanted to work with. What happened?

On May 24, 1928, John R. Freeman, America's foremost hydraulic engineer at the time, outlining the history of the Corps on the Mississippi to the House Committee on Rivers and Harbors, summed up the Corps of Engineers results nearly half a century after Eads began his work. Freeman wrote the House Committee in pleading for the merits of a hydraulic laboratory, which was opposed by the Corps:

> Proceeding down the river to the head of the Passes, abundant work for a laboratory, promising big dividends, can be found in the opening and maintenance of the Southwest Pass. It will be remembered that Captain Eads was earnestly desirous of using this pass, because it presented a cheaper and simpler problem, but was denied this by the Army Engineers. The Army Engineers have now been at work for about twenty years on trying to open this Southwest Pass to big ships, and have expended on this particular job about $20,000,000 [more than twice as much as Eads was paid for correcting the South Pass]. The last time I was in New Orleans I inquired of its success, and was told that the channel bars were continually shifting, and that few if any would venture to take a big ship through it, the course through the Eads jetties continuing to be practically the sole or main passageway for big boats.[144]

With such a record, how could the Corps of Engineers maintain a reputation for excellence and alertness in engineering? By skillfully rewriting its own history. Members of Congress cannot take time to look up the records, nor can the public do so, nor can West Point cadets. What the Corps says of its record tends to be taken at face value.

In 1886, the status of the late General Barnard within the Corps received a bit of rehabilitation, a fellow officer contending, "In fact, Gen. Barnard is really the father of the South Pass jetties, having selected the Pass and the methods of improvement, whereas Mr. Eads wished to make the Southwest Pass."[145]

A statement by a Corps officer in 1908 seemed to reflect a general Corps of Engineers "line" which had emerged on the jetties controversy. This officer stated:

> The plans for the improvement of the South Pass, eventually followed by Captain Eads, were proposed before the Civil War (1852) by a board of engineers from the U.S. Corps of Engineers, and Congress was importuned time and again to give the necessary authority to carry on the work. What would now seem to be an insignificant sum for such a great improvement was at that time too great to obtain from Congress, and not until private enterprise agreed to furnish the money with a guaranteed depth of channel (which incidentally was never obtained) did Congress authorize this important work.[146]

By 1914, a Corps officer held, "The plan for jetties which has been generally credited to Mr. Eads was recommended repeatedly, but Congress would not appropriate the necessary funds. Mr. Eads was a successful promoter and secured funds where others had failed."[147] Again, no mention of the long and bitter fight against the jetties and for the now forgotten Fort. St. Phillip Canal. Apparently, although the Hall of Fame* has deemed Mr. Eads one of America's outstanding engineers, the Corps preferred to remember him as just a "promoter."

In 1921, a Corps officer, testifying that the Corps "has maintained its control of river and harbor works for over a century against all adverse attacks very largely as a result of the high skill and engineering ability of the officers who have had these works. . . ." credited the Corps of Engineers with "conceiving and executing the jetty systems at the mouth of Columbia and at Galveston Harbor . . . to say nothing of the other varied tasks carried out in earlier years, such as . . . the plans for deepening the mouth of the Mississippi."[148]

---

*The Hall of Fame, established in 1900, is a colonnade erected at New York University to contain memorials to great Americans. In 1920, James B. Eads was elected to the Hall.

By this testimony, the officer demonstrated his indoctrination in the highly developed technique of the U.S. Corps of Engineers to rewrite its history, a skill that has been practiced and perfected by a century and a half of active experience. With the passing of time, people's memories dimmed and the Corps' rewriting of history became even more fantastic. Without fear of contradiction by the public and by members of Congress, who seldom took time to check such pronouncements, the Corps could now safely make such statements as that of the Chief of Engineers in 1924 who affirmed:

> *The Army Engineers did not oppose the building of the jetties.* As a matter of fact, the plan for the construction of the jetties was originated by the Corps of Engineers, and Captain Eads merely carried out plans which had been previously discussed. (Emphasis added.)[149]

With such an explicitly false statement, the rewriting of Corps of Engineers history on the subject of the jetties by the authoritative Chief of Engineers would seem to be complete.

What is the conclusion on the South Pass jetties? As a reviewer of the history of the jetties remarked in 1880, "Future readers of the history of the enterprise will wonder at the prominent part occupied by these obstacles, and will see only in the enduring success of the jetties themselves the monument they will long exhibit of the energy and skill of their projector, James B. Eads."[150]

This has proven to be a sound forecast. The jetties built by Eads, then the most significant hydraulic engineering work of their day, still, more than three quarters of a century later, serve the commerce of New Orleans. They have helped it to maintain the position it achieved, following the construction of the jetties, as second port in the nation. They have helped Baton Rouge become an important inland port. They have set the model for many future jetty works in the country. And they indelibly engraved the name of their builder in the annals of great, pioneering engineering. As was said in 1924 in tribute paid him as one of the few engineers in America's Hall of Fame:

James Buchanan Eads was one of the greatest of American engineers, and one of the greatest of all time. A native of the Mississippi valley, he probably did more than any other man of his generation to increase the prosperity, happiness, and wealth of that great basin.[151]

****

For approximately half a century after the completion of the Eads jetties the channel it produced was the main inlet and outlet to the harbor of New Orleans. Then the Corps of Engineers began to make substantial headway in the accommodation of the increasing traffic, first by enlarging the Southwest Pass, and then, in 1965 by completing an additional outlet. With the completion of this last, the harbor of New Orleans has three outlets to the sea: the South Pass, given thirty feet of depth and a width of 450 feet by the Eads jetties; the Southwest Pass, brought to a depth of 40 feet and a width of 800 feet by later widening; and the new shorter and straighter channel with a depth of 36 feet.

notes

1. E. L. Corthell, *History of the Jetties*, John Wiley and Sons, New York, 1881, p. 17.
2. *Ibid.*
3. Florence Dorsey, *Road to the Sea*, Rinehart, 1947, p. 10.
4. Corthell, *op. cit.*, p. 20.
5. Mississippi River Commission, Mississippi River Navigation, November 1965, p. 10.
6. Corthell, *op. cit.*, p. 7.
7. *Ibid.*, p. 19.
8. House of Representatives, Forty-Third Congress, First Session, William W. Belknap, Secretary of War, letter

transmitted by Chief of Engineers A. A. Humphreys, re canal connection the Mississippi River with the Gulf of Mexico, April 15, 1874, *House Document 220*, p. 95.

9. *Ibid.*

10. Corthell, *op. cit.*, p. 24.

11. Dorsey, *op. cit.*, p. 171.

12. Belknap, Humphreys, *House Document 220*, *op. cit.*, p. 15.

13. General J. G. Barnard, letter to Chief of Engineers A. A. Humphreys, re jetties or canal at mouth of the Mississippi, April 29, 1874. National Archives, p. 2.

14. Belknap, Humphreys, *House Document 220*, *op. cit.*, p. 111.

15. Barnard, *op. cit.*, p. 1.

16. Belknap, Humphreys, *House Document 220*, *op. cit.*, p. 96.

17. *Ibid.*, p. 108.

18. Major John G. Parke, letter to R. S. Elliott, Industrial Agent, commending Humphreys and Abbot Report on the Physics and Hydraulics of the Mississippi River, October 11, 1873, National Archives.

19. A. A. Humphreys and H. L. Abbot, *Report on the Physics and Hydraulics of the Mississippi River*, 1861, p. 455.

20. *Ibid.*

21. *Ibid.*, p. 456.

22. Belknap, Humphreys, *House Document 220*, *op. cit.*, p. 109.

23. *Ibid.*, p. 99.

24. *Ibid.*, p. 104.

25. *Ibid.*, p. 99.

26. *Ibid.*, p. 123.

27. *Ibid.*, p. 125.

28. *Ibid.*, p. 124.
29. G. K. Warren, letter to General A. A. Humphreys, January 22, 1874, National Archives.
30. William P. Craighill, letter to Major C. W. Howell, March 23, 1874, National Archives.
31. Brigadier General and Chief of Engineers A. A. Humphreys, letter to the Honorable William W. Belknap, Secretary of War, May 22, 1874, National Archives.
32. C. G. Forshey, letter to Major C. W. Howell, March 23, 1874, National Archives.
33. James B. Eads, Addresses and Papers, Canal and Jetties Compared, April, 1874, p. 145.
34. Gen. J. G. Barnard, letter to the Editors of the *National Intelligencer* (pamphlet), 1862, pp. 5, 10.
35. General J. G. Barnard, letter to General C. B. Comstock, April 18, 1874, National Archives.
36. General J. G. Barnard, letter to General C. B. Comstock, July 5, 1874, Library of Congress manuscript.
37. General J. G. Barnard, letter to General C. B. Comstock, April 22, 1874, Library of Congress manuscript.
38. Barnard to Comstock, April 18, 1874, *op. cit.*
39. *Ibid.*
40. General J. G. Barnard, letter to General C. B. Comstock, April 14, 1874, Library of Congress manuscript.
41. *Ibid.*
42. Barnard to Comstock, July 5, 1874, *op. cit.*
43. Barnard to Comstock, April 14, 1874, *op. cit.*
44. Barnard to Comstock, April 18, 1874, *op. cit.*
45. *Ibid.*
46. *Ibid.*
47. Barnard to Comstock, July 5, 1874, *op. cit.*
48. *Ibid.*

49. Barnard to Comstock, April 22, 1874, *op. cit.*
50. Ulysses S. Grant, *Memoirs*, Vol. II, Webster, New York, 1886, pp. 150-151.
51. Craighill to Howell, *op. cit.*
52. Belknap, Humphreys, *House Document 220*, *op. cit.*, p. 9.
53. *Ibid.*, p. 8.
54. James B. Eads, *Addresses and Papers*, correspondence with businessmen of New Orleans, within review of report of General Humphreys, May 29, 1874, p. 148, National Archives.
55. Corthell, *op. cit.*, p. 37.
56. Eads, *Addresses and Papers*, *op. cit.*
57. Corthell, *op. cit.*, p. 38.
58. *Ibid.*
59. *Ibid.*, p. 40.
60. Corthell, *op. cit.*, p. 43.
61. Robert E. McMath, Letter to Brigadier General A. A. Humphreys, with discussion of Mr. James B. Eads' project for construction of jetties at the mouth of the Mississippi, May 7, 1874, National Archives, p. 1.
62. *Ibid.*, p. 6.
63. Brigadier General and Chief of Engineers A. A. Humphreys, letter to the Honorable William Windom, Chairman, Senate Committee on Transportation, May 27, 1874, National Archives.
64. Corthell, *op. cit.*, p. 48.
65. *Ibid.*
66. James B. Eads, letter to the Honorable Carl J. Schurz, United States Senator from Missouri, June 26, 1879, marked *Personal*, National Archives.
67. Corthell, *op. cit.*, pp. 26-27.
68. Eads to Schurz, *op. cit.*

69. Corthell, *op. cit.* p. 60.
70. Brigadier General and Chief of Engineers, A. A. Humphreys, Report of the Chief of Engineers, House of Representatives, Forty-fourth Congress, First Session, Appendix, January 13, 1875, p. 949.
71. Corthell, *op. cit.*, pp. 63-64.
72. *Ibid.*, p. 62.
73. Humphreys, Report, January 13, 1875, *op. cit.*, pp. 959-975.
74. *Ibid.*, p. 963.
75. *Ibid.*, p. 970.
76. Corthell, *op. cit.*, pp. 64-65.
77. Colonel William E. Merrill, Discussion on "The South Pass Jetties—Ten Years Practical Teachings in River and Harbor Hydraulics," by E. L. Corthell, American Society of Civil Engineers, *Transactions*, Volume XV, April 1886, p. 4.
78. Correspondence between Captain J. B. Eads, Mr. G. W. R. Bayley, New Orleans, and Sir C. A. Hartley, London, on the Mississippi mouths; also speeches on the subject by General W. T. Sherman, U.S. Army, and Captain Eads, 1874-1875.
79. Corthell, *op. cit.*, pp. 65-66.
80. James B. Eads, letter to the Honorable W. S. Holman, Chairman, Committee on Appropriations, House of Representatives, January 29, 1877, New York Engineering Society Library.
81. E. L. Corthell, *The Mississippi Jetties*, Appendix III, Grant from the United States authorizing the construction of the Jetties, March 3, 1875.
82. J. G. Barnard, The Delta of the Mississippi, paper presented March 15, 1875, in the American Society of Civil Engineers publication, *Transactions*, Volume IV, March-December 1875, p. 2191.

83. General C. B. Comstock, letter to General A. A. Humphreys, Chief of Engineers, February 17, 1875, National Archives.

84. Professor C. G. Forshey, Remarks before the Senate Committee on Transportation and the House Committee on Railroads and Canals, "Improvements at Mouths of the Mississippi River," undated, p. 14.

85. E. L. Corthell, *The Mississippi Jetties*, Appendix VIII, letter from James B. Eads to the Secretary of War, 1876, p. 289.

86. General A. A. Humphreys, memo to General Wright, August 27, 1875, Library of Congress manuscript.

87. General A. A. Humphreys, letter to General C. B. Comstock, August 27, 1875, Library of Congress manuscript.

88. Letter of General Humphreys to Senator O. S. Babcock, Pennsylvania Historical Society, August 18, 1875.

89. J. G. Barnard, letter to F. V. Greene, June 8, 1877, National Archives, Record Group 77.

90. Corthell, *History of the Jetties, op. cit.*, p. 96.

91. Humphreys, Report, January 13, 1875, *op. cit.*, p. 948.

92. Corthell, *History of the Jetties, op. cit.*, p. 96.

93. *Ibid.*

94. *Ibid.*, p. 97.

95. *Ibid.*

96. Corthell, *The Mississippi Jetties, op. cit.*, p. 287.

97. Board of Army Engineers, 1852 Hearings, National Archives, Record Group 77, p. 288.

98. Corthell, *History of the Jetties, op. cit.*, p. 98.

99. Corthell, *The Mississippi Jetties, op. cit.*, p. 281.

100. *Ibid.*, pp. 287-288.

101. Brigadier General and Chief of Engineers A. A. Humphreys, letters to Major C. W. Howell and General C. B.

Comstock, June 8, 1876, National Archives.

102. General U. S. Grant, letter to General W. T. Sherman, May 17, 1877, National Archives.

103. Corthell, *The Mississippi Jetties, op. cit.*

104. James B. Eads, Jetties, R. & H, Letters Received, War Department, Correspondence, National Archives, Record Group 77.

105. Corthell, *History of the Jetties, op. cit.*, pp. 101, 102.

106. *Ibid.*, p. 102.

107. *Ibid.*, p. 108.

108. *Ibid.*, p. 116.

109. *Ibid.*, p.118.

110. Brigadier General and Chief of Engineers, A. A. Humphreys, letter to General C. W. Comstock, April 25, 1876, National Archives.

111. Eads, Jetties, R & H, Letters Received, *op. cit.*

112. Corthell, *History of the Jetties, op. cit.*, p. 144.

113. Dwight Goddard, *Eminent Engineers*, Derry-Collard Company, New York, 1906.

114. Corthell, *History of the Jetties, op. cit.*, p. 146.

115. *Ibid.*

116. *Ibid.*, p. 156.

117. Inspecting Officer W. H. Heuer, *Inspection of the Improvement of South Pass, Mississippi River*, (Appendix L of the Annual Report of the Chief of Engineers for 1881), Government Printing Office, Washington, 1881.

118. Eads, Jetties, R & H, Letters Received, *op. cit.*

119. Corthell, *History of the Jetties, op. cit.*, p. 168.

120. *Ibid.*, p. 170.

121. *Ibid.*, pp. 170-171.

122. *Ibid.*, p. 171.

123. E. L. Corthell, *The Mississippi Jetties*, Appendix XIII,

Letter of General Humphreys, Chief of Engineers, United States Army, 1878, p. 324.

124. *Ibid.*

125. Heuer, *op. cit.*, p. 15.

126. *Ibid.*, p. 13.

127. *Ibid.*, p. 17.

128. *Ibid.*, p. 366.

129. Corthell, *History of the Jetties*, *op. cit.*, pp. 194-195.

130. Dorsey, *op. cit.*, p. 11.

131. Goddard, *op. cit.*, p. 147.

132. E. L. Corthell, "On South Pass Jetties," Transactions of the American Society of Civil Engineers, Volume XIII, October, 1884, p. 326.

133. The Honorable Clifton R. Breckenridge, speech in the House of Representatives, February 3, 1885, pamphlet, Washington, 1885.

134. Corthell, "On South Pass Jetties," *op. cit.*, p. 326.

135. Table included in text.

136. E. L. Corthell, "Methods of Creating and Maintaining Channels at Mouths of Fluvial and Tidal Rivers," *Engineering Record*, Vol. 71, No. 2, January 9, 1915, p. 42.

137. *Ibid.*

138. Major General Lansing H. Beach, Chief of the Corps of Engineers, "The Work of the Corps of Engineers on the Lower Mississippi," American Society of Civil Engineers, *Transactions*, 1924, p. 978.

139. Merrill, *op. cit.*, p. 258.

140. *Ibid.*, p. 232.

141. Major Quinn, Report of the Chief of Engineers, United States Army, Appendix V, 1899, p. 1923.

142. Major D. O. Elliott, Corps of Engineers, U.S. Waterways Experiment Station, Vicksburg, Mississippi, "The Im-

provement of the Lower Mississippi River for Flood Control and Navigation," prepared under the direction of Brigadier General T. H. Jackson, President, Mississippi River Commission, May 1, 1932, p. 12.

143. Merrill, *op. cit.*, pp. 255, 259.

144. John R. Freeman, Letter to House Committee on Rivers and Harbors, May 24, 1928, p. 15.

145. Merrill, *op. cit.*, p. 326.

146. *Engineering News*, June 1, 1908, p. 622.

147. Captain C. O. Sherrill, *Professional Memoirs of the Corps of Engineers*, Vol. 6, 1914, p. 6.

148. Colonel William M. Harts, letter, June 22, 1921. (See Department of Public Works.)

149. Office of the Chief of Engineers, War Department, memorandum for the Secretary of War, December 24, 1924, National Archives, Record Group 77, p. 4.

150. E. L. Corthell, "History of the Jetties," review in the *American Architect and Building News*, Vol. 8, No. 261, December 25, 1880, p. 305.

151. George F. Swain, Professor of Civil Engineering at Harvard, Remarks at the unveiling of the bust of James Buchanan Eads at the Hall of Fame, May 13, 1924, p. 1.

chapter 7

opposition of the corps of engineers to the hydraulic laboratory

A hydraulic laboratory is an installation where scale models of hydraulic works are tested, usually under many conditions of flow. Where there is a water condition that needs correction, as in a river channel or harbor, the movement of the water and the shape and conditions of the bed, banks, and obstructions may be reproduced on a small scale model that can be tested in a hydraulic laboratory and the best means of correction determined thereby. Regulation works such as levees, cutoffs, or bank revetments (bank protection) on the small scale model will have substantially the same effects on the movement of water on the bed and banks as occurs under natural conditions.

There are a number of reasons why hydraulic laboratory tests are made. One is because actual flow conditions in nature are far too complex to be calculated theoretically and many of these conditions are so little understood that there are no formulas for their solutions. Also, the element of time works against making observations on natural waterways where it might require many years of waiting for high water to occur of the magnitude used in the design of waterway improvements. But in the laboratory, all desired conditions of flow can be set up at will and tests made.

Also, on a natural waterway such as a large river, the flow characteristics are due to a combination of several factors.

The Nickajack spillway and lock model are part of the Tennessee Valley Authority engineering laboratory complex. This particular test is to determine if the boats can approach the lock satisfactorily during spillway discharge operations. A radio controlled tow is being used in this demonstration. (Photo

Observations of full scale waterways cannot isolate such factors, but the hydraulic laboratory can. By so doing the importance of each factor can be evaluated and, where corrective measures are indicated, the design can be made accordingly.

Another and a most compelling reason for hydraulic laboratory tests is that for great rivers, such as the Mississippi, and for smaller streams as well as for harbors, the "cut and try"* method for the design of works to be built in the waterways is impossible on the natural stream or waterway. This is especially true in complex situations where there is need to try many possible variations in order to arrive at the best solution. Usually it is essential to know how a proposed plan of control or operation will work during several flow situations such as large floods when the safety of the entire system might be at stake, ordinary high water, and low water when navigation conditions are critical. Obviously, on the Mississippi River, which at high water is a mile or more wide and a hundred or more feet deep, observations of such flow conditions or the trying out of a variety of methods to solve complex and crucial problems are impossible. These can be done only on a scale model.

The design of corrective or other works in the hydraulic laboratory is arrived at by the process of intelligent "cut and try,"* starting with a design that judgment indicates might be satisfactory. Using scale models, sometimes *less than one one-hundredth of the natural or prototype scale*, a wide variety of details can readily be worked out and compared. As the best general features are worked out on the model, after trying and comparing many alternative solutions, refinements in detail can be made in the model until it represents rather closely the best possible design for the proposed improvement. Then full scale prototype construction can proceed confidently in accord with the proven design. Long years of experience have shown that the conclusions arrived at by scale model hydraulic laboratory

*The trying of various possibilities.

tests closely parallel performance of the prototype structures.

In essence, the hydraulic laboratory is a place where scale models may be tested to enable the hydraulic engineer to try out and perfect his designs of the water flow features of waterways, dams, locks, harbor facilities, and other structures until the most efficient and most economical design for the intended purpose is determined. Such testing saves large amounts of money in avoiding needless construction works and in preventing structural damage such as that caused by large floods, the repair of which can be very costly. No hydraulic engineer today in charge of important water project design and construction would consider doing the job without the benefit of model tests in a hydraulic laboratory.

But it was not always so, for the Corps of Engineers, U.S. Army, charged with the awesome responsibility for the control of the Mississippi River, for many years stubbornly and unreasonably resisted the idea of a hydraulic laboratory as an essential part of designing proper works for the gigantic task of controlling the great river. This chapter is concerned with the story of this opposition and how it was finally overcome.

Corps Opposes Model Tests

During the last third of the nineteenth century and until 1922, the Corps of Engineers, U.S. Army, notwithstanding repeated criticisms from American civilian engineers, maintained a solid front in holding that it was master of the true and fundamental principles of Mississippi River control. From 1922 to 1928 this assumption, including the Corps' repudiation of the theory and practice of the use of the hydraulic laboratory in working out control measures for the Mississippi River, was challenged by a great hydraulic engineer, John R. Freeman, with the support of the civilian hydraulic engineers of America.

In the early 1920's, the United States was lagging in hydraulic laboratory facilities essential to advancing technical knowledge and as an adjunct to sound hydraulic design.

The Corps of Engineers should have been in a position of leadership in hydraulic theory and practice in this country and in the forefront of the search for more hydraulic knowledge. But this was not the case. Ingrained in the Corps were old theories that had become more and more fixed as time went on. This made change to new and modern ideas, necessitating a reversal of long held ideas and policies, almost beyond the realm of possibility.

Up to that time Colonel Curtis Townsend, Retired, had the distinction of being the one member of the Corps of Engineers to write a book on hydraulics. In the course of that work he expressed a conclusion that he conveyed by letter to the Chief of Engineers:

> There exists in the United States, even among hydraulic engineers, a deplorable ignorance of the fundamental principles governing the flow of water in streams. . . . Some means must be devised to eradicate the alarming ignorance on this subject.[1]

His words fell on deaf ears.

One doctrine that had been long held and vigorously defended by the Corps was that it would be misleading and even dangerous to design works for the Mississippi and other large rivers by means of small scale models tested in a hydraulic laboratory. Such design, the Corps maintained, could only be worked out properly on the river itself. A typical expression of Corps opinion in 1922, which also follows the erroneous theories passed on over a long span of years, is given in a letter to the Chief of Engineers from Colonel G. M. Hoffman of the Corps, dated September 12, 1922:

> The application of model experiments, as proposed by Mr. Freeman, to the solution of flood and channel improvement problems on the Mississippi, Missouri or other large sediment bearing streams would, it is believed, be futile, and it is further believed that this can be demonstrated. Also the establishment of such a laboratory would not only be enormously expensive but might be dangerous in encouraging the substituting of unreliable

determinations from small scale models from those far more accurate deductions that heretofore have been based on the action of the river itself. . . .

When it comes to such a river as the Missouri or Mississippi it can positively be stated that the variable elements affecting the flow will vitiate deductions from model results as to render them valueless. . . . Practically, then, the expenditure of $200,000 to $1,000,000 for an experimental laboratory would be money wasted so far as the solution of our river-control and improvement problems in the Mississippi is concerned. No engineer or scientist experienced in the making or utilization of hydraulic small-scale tests would think of attempting to reach practical conclusions from model tests of such a river as the Mississippi River.[2]

This expression, in its essence, is identical with those of Chiefs of Engineers and other representative members of the Corps, though usually any single expression covered only a part of the ground.

Until the attitude of the U.S. Corps of Engineers on the hydraulic laboratory was attacked from without there is very little reference to it in Corps of Engineers literature. When criticism of the Corps took specific form in 1922, it became clear that the *opposition* on the part of the Corps was unqualified, extreme and unanimous, whereas among United States civilian hydraulic engineers the judgment *in favor of* the hydraulic laboratory was no less unanimous. There were, at that time, about fifty such laboratories in this country with a considerable number of others built for temporary use. There were more than twenty hydraulic laboratories operating in Europe, several of them of large size conducting important operations, working with a wide variety of hydraulic problems from all around the world.

Even so, it required a history-making revolution in the thinking of the Corps of Engineers, brought about from without, with regard to the control of the Mississippi River and other streams to gain acceptance of a hydraulic laboratory. How was this brought about? How was the century-long scientific somnolescence of the Corps disturbed?

Freeman Challenges Corps Policy

Insofar as the change resulted from the acceptance of the hydraulic laboratory and by the marked change in the attitude of the personnel of the Corps which furthered that acceptance, the key figure in the drama was John R. Freeman, one of the great figures in the history of American hydraulic engineering.

Freeman began his training under James B. Francis, the pioneer in American hydraulic research, at the hydraulic laboratory of the Lowell Hydraulic Experiments. Freeman acted as chief consultant in his field for a wide range of cities, states and countries. Not only did he have a very large hydraulic engineering practice, but he did a large amount of careful, disciplined scientific research in hydraulics. For this research, the two leading engineering societies awarded him gold medals, their highest recognition of scientific achievement.*

In 1922, when he was sixty-seven years old, John R. Freeman was elected President of the American Society of Civil Engineers, one of the largest societies in America. In 1905 he had been President of the American Society of Mechanical Engineers, another large American engineering society.

In his inaugural address as President of the American Society of Civil Engineers in 1922, Freeman stated the case for the hydraulic laboratory. No man in America was better equipped than he to judge what was practicable in the field of hydraulics and of river control. No one in America stood higher in the opinion of hydraulic engineers. He was free and competent and was not afraid to "stand up and speak out." As he put it:

> Having all along profited so much from engineering researches from the men who had gone before, and who had broadly published the results of their experience for

---

*In 1923 I visited Freeman at his home in Providence, Rhode Island. I found him living very simply indeed, in such a house as might have been expected for a modestly successful farmer or for a middle-class citizen. This was the only occasion when I talked with him.

the benefit of the whole profession, it was highly proper that I should try to put something back for the benefit of the coming generation.[3]

Freeman thought the greatest engineering job in the United States, the work on the Mississippi, had fallen into the hands of an organization which was overly influenced by tradition and lacking in critical imagination and the motivation to do competent research.

Members of the American Engineering Council, a federation of a large number of the engineering societies of the country, including the large national societies, told Senator Joseph Ransdell of Louisiana of Freeman's concern regarding the subject of the hydraulic laboratory in relation to control of the Mississippi River, and arranged for the two to meet. Senator Ransdell was exceptionally intelligent and well informed. As a result of his meeting with Freeman, he introduced Senate Joint Resolution 209 on June 13, 1922 (Legislative day April 20) in the 67th Congress, Second Session, "To establish a national hydraulic laboratory."*

*S.J. Res. 209
In the Senate of the United States.
April, 20 (calendar day, June 13), 1922.
Mr. Ransdell introduced the following joint resolution; which was read twice and referred to the Committee on Commerce.
JOINT RESOLUTION
To establish a national hydraulic laboratory.
Whereas floods are causing increasing losses along many of the streams of the United States; and
Whereas there is great lack of information on this matter which is of vital concern to the people in various sections of the United States; and
Whereas there is disagreement among the best authorities on fundamental practices involved; and
Whereas systematic research and comprehensive study of flood-control experience and practice in all ages and in all countries promises to be helpful in meeting problems on streams in the United States: Therefore be it
Resolved by the Senate and House of Representatives of the United States of America in Congress assembled, That a national hydraulic laboratory be established in the District of Columbia, in connection

Shortly after introducing his bill, Senator Ransdell wrote John W. Weeks, Secretary of War, asking for arguments in favor of such a hydraulic laboratory, and asking also what agency of the Government the Secretary felt should be entrusted with its administration. This communication was referred by the Secretary of War to Lansing H. Beach, then head of the Corps of Engineers as Chief of Engineers, who drafted the reply for the Secretary of War.

Corps Resists Hydraulic Laboratory Bill

In a confidential memo enclosed with the draft of the letter, the Chief of Engineers informed the Secretary of War that Senator Ransdell's resolution was introduced ". . . at the personal solicitation of John R. Freeman."[4] Without referring to Freeman's vast experience as America's foremost hydraulic engineer, the Chief of Engineers commented that some of Freeman's decisions in work he did on the Yellow River in China ". . . exposed him to criticism from certain quarters."[5] * The Chief of Engineers did not say that the criticism referred to was not from the civilian engineering profession, but was a personal criticism of Freeman's engineering theories in a letter to the Chief of Engineers by a member of the Corps of Engineers who was cooperating with the Chief of Engineers in an effort to discredit Freeman's proposals.

The letter drafted by Chief of Engineers Beach for submission by the Secretary of War to Senator Ransdell covered two and a half pages, single spaced. Rather than giving arguments in support of a hydraulic laboratory, it

---

with such bureau as the President may designate, for the conduct of research, experiments, and scientific studies in connection with the problems of river hydraulics, and an appropriation of $200,000 is hereby authorized for that purpose.[3] A

*Since the correspondence of the Chief of Engineers' office of more than thirty years ago has been transferred to the National Archives, it can now be examined. Practically all the quotations from the files of the Secretary of War and of the Chief of Engineers quoted in this account are from the National Archives.

constituted an elaborate rebuttal, contending that ". . . the art of dam construction is so far advanced in this country that a national hydraulic laboratory is not necessary to advance that science."[6] The main argument was that "the hydraulic laboratory is certainly unnecessary to determine the proper design of levees."[7] Since the doctrine of "levees only" had for many years dominated the policy of the Corps of Engineers, it was obvious to the Chief of Engineers that, having disposed of the hydraulic laboratory so far as levee building was concerned, there was nothing else of importance left to consider.

To make this plain, the Chief of Engineers maintained that " . . . it should be clear that the forces of nature let loose in a flood in one of our great rivers cannot be reproduced in a laboratory. I may go so far as to say I would regret it as a misapplication of government funds to establish such a laboratory for the study of flood problems."[8]

As to what agency should administer a hydraulic laboratory *if one should be established*, the Chief of Engineers, General Beach, was certain that it should be the Corps of Engineers. But he ended his draft letter for the Secretary by reiterating: "I particularly desire to emphasize my opinion that the hydraulic laboratory proposed *would have no value whatever* in solving flood control, and that the government would not be justified in incurring the expense of a laboratory for the investigation of flood problems."[9] [Emphasis added.]

The policy of "levees only" on which General Beach largely based his opposition to the hydraulic laboratory as a means of studying flood problems had been handed down virtually from the time of the building of the first levee on the Mississippi River at New Orleans in 1717. Since then "levees only" had been the one accepted means of protecting against floods. As the levees were built higher and higher, flood waters also came higher and higher and continued to break the levees. The Corps solution, after a major flood had again broken the levees, was to build the levees "another three feet higher." Successive Chiefs of Engineers assured the people that the levees at successive times were adequate for any flood that might come. In 1924, 1925 and again in 1926, the Corps told the Congress that the levee enlargement was nearly completed and *the river was safe from any flood.* Then came the great flood of 1927, the most disastrous in history. The levees failed at many points. Many millions of acres were overflowed, with great loss of property and much loss of life. The assurances of the Corps of Engineers were discredited. The inadequacy of the plan as a whole was disclosed.

Yet the "levees only" policy could not be easily changed. If changes were suggested, some Congressman could bring out the old reports of the Chiefs of Engineers opposing cutoffs, reservoirs and diversions and the suggestion would be cast aside. The entire literature concerning the Mississippi River made it unwise for anyone to question the adopted policy.

The Corps' reflex opposition as evidenced by General Beach's draft letter was two-fold. The first reaction was to deny the need for such research as would be done in the laboratory. Secondly, the Corps showed concern that a hydraulic laboratory not under its control might be used to do independent study of its engineering methods. Particularly, but not solely, on the Mississippi River, the Corps had long maintained and vigorously defended its "levees only" approach to flood control against any other methods proposed by civilian engineers. General Beach, in voicing his opposition to the theory and practice of the hydraulic laboratory was strongly supported by other members of the Corps.

With such determined opposition in the Corps, the task Freeman was tackling for the creation of a national hydraulic laboratory seemed remote of accomplishment. In many situations over the course of time, the political power of the Corps has been practically irresistible. With this great influence in Congress, and with its century-long record of internal solidarity, the Corps had near-control of appropriations dealing with the control of the Mississippi River and its vast number of navigable tributaries, and had defeated the efforts of Presidents and of Congress to curb its power.

In resisting efforts to change its sacred engineering doctrines and its long established habits, the Corps commonly had found it to be little more than a routine process to summarily brush aside opposition. It had been considered necessary only to reaffirm the claim of Corps of Engineers omniscience, as General Jadwin, Chief of Engineers in 1928, did in testifying before the House of Representatives Committee on Rivers and Harbors:

> The Science of River hydraulics in America, both theoretical and practical, as a whole is more advanced than that of any other nation in the world, and this advance is due almost exclusively to the activities of the Army Engineers.[10]

John R. Freeman knew that in every respect the exact opposite of this statement was true. But it was the Corps of Engineers and not he who had the ear of Congress.

Although the official position of the Corps was strongly to oppose the hydraulic laboratory, there were, even in 1922, a few isolated proponents of laboratory research in the Corps of Engineers. But these brave souls publicly expressed their opinions only within the family. Brigadier-General, Retired, Henry Jervey wrote Chief of Engineers Beach his feeling that the proposed hydraulic laboratory would be of "vast benefit" in many fields and that it should be under the Bureau of Standards.[11] The Chief of Engineers took strong issue with this lack of "loyalty" to the Corps.[12] For a *retired* officer, the charge of disloyalty was not so ominous.

Major L. E. Lyon, District Engineer in Philadelphia, wrote General Beach in 1922 that ". . . it is considered desirable to place the Corps of Engineers on record as among the pioneers in applying experimental methods on river models to the improvement of rivers."[13]

Major Lyon's work provided the only example of the Corps' use of a hydraulic laboratory. The Delaware River, of enormous importance to New York City for water supply, and to New Jersey and Pennsylvania for uses which conflicted with those of New York, had been under an intensity of study by the three state governments involved which

,eldom had been given to any other American river. The ;tates of New York, New Jersey and Pennsylvania employed altogether more than twenty of the ranking hydraulic engineers of the country to deal with this thorny problem. Most or all of these engineers were convinced of the value of the hydraulic laboratory.*

Not only did the Corps of Engineers not have the field to themselves on the Delaware as they did on the Mississippi, but also a member of the Corps was being exposed to a group of hydraulic engineers who might lead him to question one of the traditional doctrines of the Corps, and to be interested in the hydraulic laboratory.

On August 2, 1922, Major Lyon wrote a letter to the Chief of Engineers, from which the following is quoted:

> The Engineering Foundation . . . has compiled and issued as of June, 1922, a directory of hydraulic laboratories in the United States.
>
> The directory contains descriptions of 49 laboratories. Of these 39 are maintained by schools and colleges, 7 by manufacturing or commercial concerns, and three by states and by the United States. . . . Only in the following three instances is work pertaining to waterways mentioned . . . Cornell University . . . the University of Iowa . . . and Rose Polytechnic Institute. . . .
>
> While this office does not possess a hydraulic laboratory in the usual acceptance of the term, it is believed that the experiments now under way with a working model of the Delaware River (E.D. 112690/257), entitle its work and equipment to be listed in future editions of this directory, and it is recommended that the Chief of Engineers ask the Engineering Foundation to include the experimental work in progress in this district in future editions of their directory.
>
> It is believed that the model of the Delaware River referred to is the first of its kind to be constructed in this country, and it is desirable to place the Corps of

---

*I represented the State of Pennsylvania on this issue at the hearing of the United States Supreme Court through a Master Commissioner.

Engineers on record as among the pioneers in applying experimental records on river models to the improvement of rivers. . . ."[14]

In the sheet of details enclosed, there is the notation, "Number of persons on regular staff: one."[15] The water supply of the laboratory was 6/1000 of a cubic foot per second, and the scale of the small scale model was one to twenty thousand. Here was a flume fifteen inches wide to represent the lower Delaware River where it was five miles wide—three inches width of flume to represent each mile in width of river. This scale would seem to be inadequate for that purpose. The purpose of the structure was to study tidal action at the mouth of the river.

On receipt of this letter the Chief of Engineers asked that photographs be made and that publicity be given to the engineering press, showing the Corps of Engineers to be at the front of engineering progress.[16]

While this one-man project was probably the first case of the use of the hydraulic laboratory principles in the Corps of Engineers, Major Lyon was mistaken in thinking it was the first for river work in America. Half a dozen or more American engineers had used it on as many projects.[17] *

Among the letters received from members of the Corps of Engineers by the Chief of Engineers in reply to his requests for their opinion there was another which was not adverse to the idea of the hydraulic laboratory. While strongly opposing the use of the hydraulic laboratory in working out specific problems, nevertheless Colonel Curtis Townsend supported its use, but only in engineering schools, for the study of general principles. He wrote:

---

*The hydraulic laboratory of the Miami Conservancy District, of which I was Chief Engineer, was built in 1915. The technical reports on the Miami Conservancy District hydraulics laboratory are included in Part III of those reports, published in 1917. The work of Dr. Gilbert at the University of California preceded by several years that of Major Lyon. Thaddeus Merriman testified to using the hydraulic laboratory on various river projects for over twenty years.

I have suggested to Mr. Freeman that the engineering colleges establish hydraulic laboratories for that purpose. . . .

When an engineer has learned these fundamental principles, the river itself affords a much better means for testing them than any laboratory can create. In fact, erroneous conclusions are liable to be drawn from laboratory experiment, since the volume of the discharge and the character of the river bed are controlling influences which cannot be reproduced in a laboratory.[18]

Even in this unexpected expression of interest in the hydraulic laboratory, Colonel Townsend completely misconceived its function. As leading hydraulic engineers have repeatedly emphasized, the movement of water in rivers is far too complex for theoretical analysis. The findings of the hydraulic laboratory usually are experimental, not theoretical. The century-old theoretical commitment of West Point to theoretical dogmas, with relative disregard for practical experience and research, has long been a paralyzing influence on Corps program and policy.

In 1922 and 1923, although there were some in the Corps who wavered in their opposition to the hydraulic laboratory and dared to express themselves, these were indeed lonely voices crying in the wilderness. Overall, the alignment with regard to the laboratory was in effect: (1) the almost unanimous approval of the method and the use of the laboratory by the representative *civilian* hydraulic engineers of America and of Europe and, (2) the clear-cut opposition to its use by nearly all the Corps of Engineers which had control of the vast Mississippi River system, other rivers, and the national harbors; with, at that time, nearly a monopoly of opportunity for the use of the hydraulic laboratory for stream control. With the introduction of Senate Joint Resolution 209 in 1922 by Senator Ransdell, the Corps clearly and solidly took its position in opposition both to the principles of the hydraulic laboratory and to Senate Joint Resolution 209.

When the Senate Committee hearings on S. 209 were held,

the Corps showed little concern as to the outcome. Why should the Corps be disturbed? It knew that it had sufficient power to prevent the laboratory being approved. For more than a half century, the Corps had defied and defeated the efforts of Presidents and of the Congress to curb its power. A great source of this power lay in the National Rivers and Harbors Congress, an ardent ally of the Corps. This Congress was made up of influential laymen and powerful Congressmen desirous of public works in their home districts. It also included large contractors who worked under the Corps' direction, and depended on Corps approval. In this National Rivers and Harbors Congress, the Corps had a civilian organization which was a fully docile instrument of great political power. The subservient support of this organization could be counted upon to back the Corps' position heavily, whatever this might be.

In considering what strategy to employ in combating the solid support of the nation's leading hydraulic engineers, perhaps the Chief of Engineers thought that the less said by the Corps the better. Yet would the Corps be wise to let the record stand with no expression of its position? Back in 1922 the Corps did not publicize its mental processes. Forty years later the intercommunications within the Corps are on file in the National Archives, where everyone may read them. From that source we can see how the matter was handled.

From time to time in its history, it probably had been considered desirable for the Corps to have among its resources a man of some distinction who could be called upon for special services. The Corps had not left such a need to chance, but had prepared itself for such occasions.

J.A. Ockerson had been an employee of the Corps-dominated Mississippi River Commission for 43 years, since its organization in 1879. Along the way—and certainly with the approval and backing of the Corps of Engineers—he had served a term as President of the American Society of Civil Engineers. He was a large man, of very dignified, imposing bearing. Here was just the representative needed in this case to speak out in opposition to the hydraulic laboratory. He was completely a Corps man. Yet to the general public he was a distinguished civilian engineer.

From correspondence in the National Archives, the story of the introduction of Ockerson into the Senate hearings can be reconstructed. On Tuesday, September 5, 1922, General Potter, President of the Mississippi River Commission, which in substance was an agency of the Corps of Engineers, sent the following message to Chief of Engineers, General Beach:

> Chief of Engineers
> Washington, D.C.
> ReTEL TODAY TELEGRAM FROM SENATOR RANS-DELL RECEIVED PRIOR TO YOURS. SAID HE WANTED ME THERE AND SATURDAY MORNING WOULD DO. WIRED HIM I WOULD BE THERE SATURDAY MORNING. [September 9]
>
> Ockerson[19]

Still another precaution was needed. Time for consultation between Ockerson and the Chief of Engineers was provided.

> Office of Chief of Engineers   FAST MESSAGE
> Lansing H. Beach
> Chief of Engineers
>
> J. A. Ockerson
> Mississippi River Commission
> St. Louis, Mo.
>
> Very important that you should be here before Saturday morning if it is possible to do so. Arrive Washington first train possible to be here.
>
> Beach
Chief of Engineers[20]

> St. Louis, Mo. [Thursday] Sept. 7, 1922
> Chief of Engineers, Washn., D.C.
>
> Ockerson left at noon due in Washington one fifteen Friday [September 8] stop. . . .
>
> Potter[21]

The fact that Mr. Ockerson could get to Washington in time

to be briefed by the Chief of Engineers is important. While to the general public he may have seemed just a distinguished civilian engineer, giving his personal professional opinion, he was, in fact, the one and only representative of the Corps to appear before the Committee. He was there explicitly to put onto the record just what the U.S. Corps of Engineers, and especially what the President of the Mississippi River Commission and the Chief of Engineers, wanted on record. The essence of Mr. Ockerson's testimony is as follows:

> Mr. Ockerson. My name is J. A. Ockerson; address, St. Louis, Mo. I am a member of the Mississippi River Commission and past president of the American Society of Civil Engineers.
>
> Senator Ransdell. How long have you been a member of the commission connected with the work on the Mississippi River, Mr. Ockerson?
>
> Mr. Ockerson. I have been with the commission for 43 years.
>
> Senator Ransdell. That is, you mean since it was created in 1879?
>
> Mr. Ockerson. Yes, sir.
>
> Senator Ransdell. Are you familiar with the resolution we have under consideration to create a national hydraulic laboratory? And if you have any ideas in connection with it, we would be pleased to hear you state them.
>
> Mr. Ockerson. I have read the resolution carefully on the trip from St. Louis, and the idea I get of it is that it is to provide a hydraulic laboratory to consider matters relating to rivers; that is the purpose of the bill. I am here *at the instance of the Chief of Engineers, United States Army, and of the Mississippi River Commission*, representing a majority of the commission that met in New Orleans last week.
>
> Senator Ransdell. We will be glad to hear you make a statement on the subject that you desire.
>
> Mr. Ockerson. I have stated that we met in New Orleans last week.

The impression seemed to prevail there that an extended series of laboratory experiments is needed in order to secure data necessary to arrive at a solution of the problems relative to the regulation and control of the Mississippi River.

After 43 years of active work by a corps of scientific men in nature's own laboratory, the river itself, *it is believed that the commission has accumulated a volume of data covering practically all of the varying phases of the physics of the Mississippi River which are necessary to a full understanding of the regulation and control of the river. There is no "woeful lack" of data, as has been charged.*

It is believed to be wholly impracticable to obtain any further useful data regarding the Mississippi River problems by the use of laboratory models, and the reason for this belief is to be found in the following briefs of conditions to be met with.

When I speak of "models" I speak of the whole scheme of hydraulic laboratory work.

1. The river is so gigantic in all its elements that a practicable model would be too small to duplicate the many elements of the regimen of the river. Then, too, the regimen must be thoroughly understood before it can be incorporated into a model, and this means an exhaustive study of the river itself.

2. The horizontal and vertical scales should be the same, as variations in the proportions give different results. This would give depth and slopes too small to be satisfactorily measured.

The importance of having the proportions of the scale correct is indicated by recent experiments in regard to the Gilboa Dam, where variations in the relative proportions gave quite different results.

Senator Ransdell. Where is that dam, please?

Mr. Ockerson. That is in New York State, connected with the water supply of New York City. It is described in a late paper of the American Society of Civil Engineers, September number of Proceedings, 1922.

3. The present condition of the bed of the river is the resultant of a long period of changes in stage and volume,

passing through many succeeding cycles of high and low water, and a knowledge of all these must be had before intelligent conclusions could be drawn as to the lessons shown by its present condition.

4. In order to reach a fair understanding of the physics of the river it is important that studies should cover a number of cycles of extreme high and low water, and the period of such studies can not be materially curtailed without vitiating the results and involving the conclusions in doubt. This would make the study through models impracticable.

As far as the hydraulic laboratory experiments are concerned, I cannot conceive of anything that it would do that would materially modify the plans that are now under way. [Emphasis added.][22]

Ockerson, representing the Corps, was unqualifiedly opposed to the hydraulic laboratory. The only actual instance referred to by Ockerson in his testimony was that of the Gilboa Dam of the New York Water Supply Commission. The only possible inference of this reference was that small scale models are not to be depended upon. The engineering discussion referred to by Ockerson, and its continuation in the 1923 discussions of the Transactions of the American Society of Civil Engineers (p. 280 et seq.) shows his inference to be distinctly misleading. In effect, the writer of the article referred to by Ockerson stated that the conditions met with at the Gilboa Dam were entirely too complex to be worked out theoretically, and that the small scale model was the only practicable course.

The author of the article referred to by Ockerson had stated:

In making these modifications of the plans for the dam it was found that reasoning was comparatively useless, as the problem was too complicated. . . . It became largely a matter of trying (in the small scale model) anything that did not seem to be too absurd. . . . One hundred and eighty different experiments were recorded. . . . With a full recognition of the fact that there is dissimilarity, the model, if built on a large scale, still remains the most efficient method for determining the most satisfactory section for an overflow dam.[23]

In the discussions of this article in the Transaction of the American Society of Civil Engineers, George G. Honnes, engineer of the New York Board of Water Supply, wrote:

> The writer concurs in the author's conclusion that notwithstanding the fact that the behavior of models will not be exactly similar to the prototypes, the model remains the best means of determining the design of many hydraulic structures. This conclusion is based on experiences with models used to determine the probable behavior of full scale structure in the following instances: Boonton Dam, Boonton, New Jersey . . . Cross River Dam, Katonah, New York. . . . Ashokan Reservoir, Waste Weir, Ashokan, New York.[24]

Robert Fletcher, Director Emeritus of the Thayer School of Engineering, wrote concerning the paper commented on by Ockerson:

> All readers familiar with the principles involved must be impressed by the great value of these remarkable demonstrations of what may be learned by the intelligent use of models.[25]

Engineers Gausmann and C. M. Madden, discussing the same paper commented on by Ockerson, wrote:

> It seems that all discussors agree that models, in whatever sense the word is interpreted, if properly used, may give valuable information for the preparation of designs of engineering work and, more particularly, for hydraulic structures.[26]

Finally, Thaddeus Merriman, one of America's leading hydraulic engineers and author of a foremost hydraulics textbook, and in charge of construction of the Gilboa Dam for the New York Water Supply Commission—the dam mentioned by Colonel Ockerson—wrote:

> On page 477 of the printed proceedings of the hearing,

Mr. Ockerson, in referring to certain experiments on models of the Gilboa Dam, which dam we now have under construction, stated that ... "variations in the relative proportions gave quite different results." In order that erroneous conclusions may not be drawn from this statement, I would like to say that the results of the experiments in question were most satisfactory and that without them we could not possibly have carried the design to a satisfactory conclusion.

I may say further that in order to perfect the design of the spillway of the Ashokan Reservoir we found it necessary to experiment with scale models and that these models were more helpful than all the theoretical considerations we could bring to bear.

Twenty years ago I was connected with the construction of the Boonton Dam for the water supply of Jersey City and the design for the spillway of that structure was also based on experiments with models. Without these experiments the design could not have been brought to the state of perfection which was actually attained.[27]

Thus in the only actual case mentioned by the only witness so carefully selected by the Chief of Engineers to appear before the Senate Committee, the Committee was misled by his testimony.

Ockerson's testimony was substantially in accord with the position taken by the Chief of Engineers in his draft letter to the Secretary of War, though it was given under somewhat more formal conditions and after deliberate consideration. The Chief of Engineers was present at the hearing before this Committee. At a few points in the hearing he made comments, but made no comments on Ockerson's testimony. In this testimony is contained the position of the Corps of Engineers as of the year 1922 on the theory and practice of the hydraulic laboratory: official, concise, unqualified, conclusive, and solidly opposed.

Here was the Corps of Engineers, having charge of the greatest hydraulic engineering problem in the United States and with an amplitude of economic resources to work with beyond those of any other country, speaking out against a hydraulic laboratory. Under these circumstances, the Corps should have been at the forefront of research in that major field of its concern, fully aware of what the rest of the world was doing in hydraulic engineering, and providing active scientific and engineering leadership. That it was not is a black blot on the escutcheon of the Corps.

At the Senate Committee hearings on S. 209, not a single witness appeared in opposition to the proposal for a hydraulic laboratory except Ockerson. As would be expected, John R. Freeman made a clear and effective presentation of the case for the hydraulic laboratory. He was joined by a long succession of witnesses who testified in favor of the laboratory. These included most of the leading hydraulic engineers of this country, who testified that the opinion of American hydraulic engineers was substantially unanimous in favor of the use of a hydraulic laboratory. About forty American engineering societies and associations and the American Engineering Council for these societies formally approved the hydraulic laboratory proposal. As H. N. Eaton wrote later in an historical account, "Rarely had there been such wide-spread interest in any piece of legislation of this nature."[28]

Among the Senate Committee witnesses was Gardner S. Williams, highly respected former professor of experimental hydraulics and head of the Cornell University hydraulic laboratory. He spoke in favor of the laboratory, noting that "The only opposition has been that which appears to have arisen from the Corps of Engineers."[29] Blake R. Van Leer, prominent in river hydraulics, observed later that " . . .no hydraulic engineer of any reputation has expressed public objection to the proposal."[30] Several engineers told the Committee that European river control engineers accepted the hydraulic laboratory as reliable and that its principles and practices had become an essential part of hydraulic engineering in Europe.

Notwithstanding the weight and logic of the nation's top hydraulic engineers in favor of the laboratory, the Corps chose to ignore the united voice of the American hydraulic engineering profession.

In 1922 John R. Freeman was President of the American
Society of Civil Engineers and in his inaugural address firmly
stated the case for the hydraulic laboratory. A year later, at
the Society's Annual Meeting in 1923, perhaps sited in New
Orleans at Freeman's request, he summarized a 60-page paper
entitled, "The Need for a National Hydraulic Laboratory for
the Solution of River Problems." In introducing his talk, he
said:

> One who has seen this mighty river tearing along, in flood
> a mile wide and a hundred feet deep, within a few inches
> of the top of the levee, may well wonder how the
> problem of resisting its angry force can be taken into a
> laboratory, or what can be done in a laboratory about
> disposing of the billion cubic yards of earth per year now
> tumbled into its swirling waters, shifting its strangely
> crooked course and obstructing the navigation channels
> with shoals and snags from fallen trees.
>
> We think of a laboratory as a place of microscopes, of
> delicate balances and little glass test tubes, and far
> removed from giant drag lines and dredges.
>
> What hope is there for an appropriation of only $200,000
> suggested in the pending bill for a laboratory, when for
> more than a century appropriations in terms of millions
> and tens of millions have failed to bring relief?[31]

Between the 1922 and 1923 Annual Meetings of the
American Society of Civil Engineers, Freeman along with his
friends had been active with members of the Congress,
seeking support for S. J. Resolution 209 authorizing the
establishment of a National Hydraulic Laboratory.

But Freeman's efforts were all to no avail. If weak in
engineering, the Corps of Engineers was strong in getting
what it wanted from the Congress. And the Corps wanted S.
209 defeated. The testimony before the Senate Committee
had been overwhelming in support of the hydraulic laboratory. But despite the impressive array of evidence by the
leading hydraulic engineers of this country, despite the
positive statements of several other government departments
and agencies that they had definite need for the laboratory,

and notwithstanding the fact that the use of the hydraulic laboratory had proved itself in Europe and was an essential part of hydraulic engineering practice there, the strategy of the Corps of Engineers proved effective. S. J. R. 209 did win approval of the Senate Committee but was easily defeated in the Congress.

During the five years following the defeat of S. J. R. 209 in 1923, legislation for a hydraulic laboratory was twice introduced into the Congress but met with defeat on both occasions. Such a decisive defeat should permanently have buried the issue of the hydraulic laboratory. It might have done so, but for a single circumstance. That circumstance was John R. Freeman. After being so summarily and conclusively defeated by the Corps of Engineers, what more could John R. Freeman do? Though the highest ranking man in his field in America, still he was only a private citizen.

But for him, this was no ordinary contest. At stake were the saving of hundreds of millions of public funds and the security and well-being of the great Lower Mississippi Delta.

Freeman took account of his position, measured his resources, and for four years prepared for further action. His moves were thoughtful and deliberate. First he went to Europe, where the hydraulic laboratory was fully accepted and relied upon for almost every major problem in river control. He knew there were more than twenty hydraulic laboratories there in operation, a few of them very large and dealing with river control problems of four continents. He made the personal acquaintance of the heads of many of these laboratories, and persuaded several of the foremost authorities in the field to write thorough, scholarly accounts of the theory and practice of their installations. He arranged for these to be published, in 1926, at first mostly in German. To gain the acquaintance and the personal respect and trust of these German leaders so soon after the first world war was itself a masterpiece of personal relations.

Then Freeman extended his studies and acquaintances, until he had masterful statements from the directors of hydraulic laboratories in Austria, Russia, Sweden, Switzer-

land, Italy, Holland, Hungary, and Czechoslovakia. When he
had exhausted the list of those who found time to write of
their own projects, Freeman did not stop. He himself visited
or studied and wrote accounts of still other hydraulic
laboratories in France, Norway, Sweden, and Italy. Parts of
these statements had been published separately, in English.
Finally the whole was translated into English. Returning to
America, he had other papers on the hydraulic laboratory
prepared by half a dozen qualified American hydraulic
engineers. In 1929 all this material was published by the
American Society of Mechanical Engineers with the title,
Hydraulic Laboratory Practice. It included a translation of
the 1926 report of the Verein Deutscher Ingenieur. This
work, with its introduction, constituted a volume of 890
large pages, by far the most complete and authoritative
treatise on the subject ever prepared in any language. This
imposing volume Freeman distributed at his own expense
among the key engineers of the country, including a number
of members of the Corps of Engineers.

But Freeman did not stop. He financed scholarships to an
extent of about $100,000, by means of which ten young
hydraulic engineers made extended trips to Europe to visit
important hydraulic laboratories and to study them at first
hand.

The Corps of Engineers could not be quite so adamant in
its opposition to a hydraulic laboratory as to refrain from
allowing two of its members to accept Freeman scholarships.
Both returned convinced of the value of the hydraulic
laboratory, with the result that the Corps was somewhat
"corrupted" on the subject.

Freeman had one other shaft for his bow. He arranged for
the heads of some of the foremost European hydraulic
laboratories to come to America, where they toured the
country speaking to groups of engineers, in some cases with
members of the Corps of Engineers and members of
Congress. This kind of attack was new to the Corps of
Engineers.

Corps' Position Weakened, Recommends Own Laboratory

As a result of this educational effort by Freeman, the monolithic opposition of the Corps to a hydraulic laboratory was weakened. Within the Corps of Engineers the change came in several ways. Some members of the Corps, while still holding that the hydraulic laboratory was useless for planning control of the Mississippi, began to consider it useful on smaller problems. The Corps, apparently determined to protect itself by having a hydraulic laboratory, if only to keep it out of the hands of other agencies.

In a report issued December 1, 1927, Chief of Engineers General Jadwin did, in fact, recommend such a laboratory. The sections of his report dealing with this are as follows:

143. The establishment of a hydraulic laboratory similar in some respects to such research organizations carried on by certain European governments has been considered. *Measurements and observations on our large rivers supply the best hydraulic data on the flow of such streams since actual experience with full-size structures is preferable to experiment with small-scale models.* However, on occasion questions relative to the flow of water can be worked out by small-scale experiments. Such experiments may be useful in some of our lock and dam designs. [Emphasis added.]

144. In addition, the organization in charge of a hydraulic laboratory may well be charged with the coordination of field data relative to the flow of the Mississippi and other rivers. For instance, we could advantageously take charge of discharge measurements, silt measurements, slope and velocity measurements, etc.,* and make studies and draw conclusions therefrom. It could be a clearing-house for such engineering data and publish the same.

145. It is therefore recommended that the Chief of Engineers under the supervision of the Secretary of War, be authorized to establish a hydraulic laboratory, and that the Secretary of War be authorized to allot the

*These are routine duties, not requiring disciplined capacity for engineering analysis.

necessary funds from annual river and harbor and flood control appropriations to pay the expenses of such a laboratory and for the necessary printing to publish the scientific data collected.[32]

Regardless of General Jadwin's report and recommendations for a hydraulic laboratory to be established in the Corps, there was uncertainty, even within the Corps of Engineers, as to whether the request for the right of the Corps to build a hydraulics laboratory along the Mississippi represented a real interest in a laboratory or whether it was an indirect way to kill the idea. Perhaps some hoped it could be used to dispose of the cutoffs idea. Six months following the report on June 23, 1928, Blake R. Van Leer, a member of the Corps, wrote to General Jadwin:

> . . . You are the first Chief of Engineers of the USA to support (the proposal for a hydraulics laboratory) with any concrete action. . . .
> There is grave danger that the Corps of Engineers will act concerning this proposed laboratory, as some critics say it will, namely secure the appropriation for a laboratory which will for the time satisfy the public demand for such an agency and then so man and equip the laboratory that nothing good or productive will come out of it.[33]

General Jadwin's recommendation for a hydraulic laboratory in the Corps did not mean that the Corps had dropped its opposition to the still pending National Hydraulic Laboratory. On February 11, 1928, the Acting Director of the Bureau of the Budget wrote asking the opinion of the Secretary of War on S. 1710, soon to be submitted by Senator Ransdell. This bill was to provide for the establishment of a national hydraulic laboratory in the Bureau of Standards. The Chief of Engineers, General Jadwin, drafted a reply stating the Corps' usual contention that full-size experimentation was preferable, and that any work done outside of the War Department might lead to "erroneous conclusions" due to a lack of familiarity with "field conditions." "I therefore am of the opinion," concluded

Jadwin for the Secretary of War, "that so far as River and
Harbor works committed to the War Department are concerned, the establishment of a national hydraulic laboratory
under the Bureau of Standards does not appear necessary or
advisable."[3] [4]

Again the Corps had its way in Congress and S. 1710 was
defeated. For the fourth time, Senator Ransdell's bill had
failed to pass.

For the time being, the National Hydraulic Laboratory was
dead. But a very important gain had been made by the
backers of a hydraulic laboratory where problems of Mississippi River flood control could be studied and tested. The
same Congress that had refused the National Laboratory did
authorize, early in 1928, the Chief of Engineers to establish
such a laboratory as recommended by General Jadwin. Thus
in 1929, the Corps was empowered to build its own
laboratory only two or three months after Chief of Engineers
Jadwin in his report had again expressed his firm conviction
that it would not be of value in planning control of large
rivers but could only be assigned conventional routine tasks.
It was evident that General Jadwin had no vision of the vital
part that the Corps laboratory was to play in planning
control of the Mississippi River and many other U. S. water
projects.

Defeated four successive times, a less dedicated and
stouthearted man than John R. Freeman would have been
expected to give up the battle. But not John R. Freeman. So
the struggle continued.

Freeman's Relations With Corps

Reference has been made previously to Freeman's reasons
for disapproval of the Corps of Engineers and its practices.
Since it was Freeman who initiated and sustained the fight to
overcome the opposition of the Corps to a hydraulic
laboratory, it is pertinent to examine in some detail his
relations with and appraisal of the Corps.

At the beginning of his campaign for the hydraulic
laboratory, Freeman dealt rather gently with the Corps. His

aim was to be pro-laboratory, not anti-Corps. In his initial appearance before the Senate Committee on September 8, 1922, his most caustic comment was:

> The steamboat pilot on the river and the scientist in the laboratory each has certain advantages in his point of view. Much of our river training work in America [most of it under the Corps] has been of that scientific quality that might be expected to be produced by a committee of steamboat pilots without training in exact science, and it is now time for more of science.[35]

He repeatedly made it clear that his criticisms were not against individuals, but against the deeply embedded policies of West Point, and of its ranking product, the Corps of Engineers. He wrote, "Personally and apart from the traditions of their Corps, nearly all that I have known are delightful, companionable men. I have had many friends among them."[36]

Toward the end of 1927, when General Jadwin, Chief of Engineers, was asking for permission to establish a hydraulic laboratory along the Mississippi, Freeman wrote him stating that in a vast country like America there would be need for more than one government hydraulic laboratory for river control work, and that there should be no reason why the Corps of Engineers might not well have its own laboratory along the Mississippi. He wrote to the General:

> My own belief is that the Federal Government could with great profit establish at least two of these laboratories, one at the Bureau of Standards, the other at St. Louis or New Orleans, under the U.S. Army Engineers, adjacent to the Engineering School. I believe that both would soon be occupied with problems and would produce results of great practical value.[37]

Within two or three months following this letter, Jadwin had received authority to build a hydraulic laboratory on the Mississippi, though up to the time of receiving that authority early in 1928 he had expressed his long-held disbelief in its value for large scale river planning. He continued to oppose a

National Hydraulic Laboratory, which Freeman sought. When Freeman found his approaches met with rebuff and contempt, he saw that it would be necessary to speak more plainly to the members of Congress. After six years of effort in the interest of the hydraulic laboratory, on May 24, 1928, he wrote a letter to the Chairman and members of the House Committee on Rivers and Harbors. It is significant that this letter expresses the opinion of one of the nation's foremost hydraulic engineers concerning the river control work of the Corps of Engineers and the general competence of the work of the Corps prior to the date of the letter.

The following, quoted from the May 24th letter, indicates some of the basis for Freeman's unfavorable opinion of the Corps. The first quote refers to statements of General Jadwin concerning Freeman's proposals.

I am amazed at the General's statements, at his use of ridicule instead of reason in suggesting that the proposed laboratory would work with water brought in jugs from the Mississippi and "a few barrels of sand" from its bed, and that altho worse than useless for solving river problems, this laboratory might be helpful for things like plumbing fixtures. . . .

I am amazed at [the] apparent conception [of the Chief of Engineers] of what such a laboratory would be like and how it would function. . . . He tells us of what he thinks they lack—initiative in France . . . all with not a word about the marvelous work that has been done during the past twenty years on river, harbor and other hydraulic problems in hydraulic laboratories of Germany, Sweden, Austria and Czechoslovakia. . . . I saw in France four years ago a small but very creditable new hydraulic laboratory recently completed at Grenoble in connection with the hydro-electric engineering college.

Germany today is the most active center for this kind of research, and Sweden, Austria, Czechoslovakia and Switzerland are not far behind. Throughout Central Europe no great engineering problem that has to do with hydraulics now reaches the construction stage without its engineers having submitted many of its elements to the government hydraulics laboratories of those countries for solution and for advancing the state of the art. . . .

I respectfully submit these facts to the intelligence of this committee that a National Hydraulic Laboratory built in a center of research, operated in an atmosphere of scientific surroundings, while maintaining close contact with the problems in the field, cannot be so dangerous to public safety as General Jadwin will have you believe when he says:

The proposed bill (for a National Hydraulic Laboratory) would set up an arrangement that would be fraught with the greatest peril to the best interests of the citizens of the Mississippi Valley, and the progress of river navigation and flood control works thruout the country. . . .

Out of an active engineering experience covering more than fifty years, I assert my strong belief that *in competent and proper hands* a hydraulic laboratory could save tens or hundreds of millions of dollars to the United States and to the residents of this wonderfully fertile Mississippi region in the program now being undertaken. . . . I emphasize the words, "in proper hands."

I understand they have no special facilities for teaching hydraulics at West Point, and that their course in hydraulics is extremely elementary in comparison with those at Cornell, Massachusetts Institute of Technology, Worcester Polytechnic, or the University of Iowa. . . .

The U.S. Army Engineers by education first of all are to be military engineers, by training, office, tradition, and routine of frequent transfer they are not specially qualified for such scientific research. They are in effect chiefly disbursing officers who hire civilian engineers to do most of their designing. They direct supervisions under conditions not adapted to the greatest efficiency. The military method is vastly different from that by which progress is obtained in science.

It is the system which fails to train for research. The personality of the U.S. Army Engineers averages exceptionally high.

Until their sudden awakening by last year's flood

[1927] they were inactive in scientific hydraulic studies, full of strong faith in "levees only" and with a wonderful record for underestimating the cost of finishing their job. . . .

From my knowledge of the river from studies during many years past of pretty much everything I could find in print regarding it, I believe that the science of hydraulics has slumbered all along the great river and its tributaries for more than 40 years, with the one exception of its tributary, the Miami River, where under engineer Arthur E. Morgan and the Miami Conservancy Board, a series of the most outstanding and profitable studies of this kind ever made anywhere in the world was carried out followwing the disastrous flood which wrecked Dayton and other cities in 1913.[3] [8]

Freeman carried his discussion along the Mississippi River, point by point, indicating how and where, in his opinion, the hydraulic laboratory would be effective. We shall illustrate by quoting him concerning two elements of river control. These were the Southwest Pass at the mouth of the Mississippi, and the Greenville bends in the river.

Proceeding down the river to the head of the Passes, abundant work for a laboratory, promising big dividends, can be found in the opening and maintenance of the Southwest Pass. It will be remembered that Captain Eads was earnestly desirous of using this pass, instead of the South Pass, because it presented a cheaper and simpler problem, but was denied this by the Army Engineers. The Army Engineers now have been at work about 20 years [without the use of a laboratory] on trying to open this Southwest Pass to big ships, and have expended on this particular job about $20,000,000. The last time I was in New Orleans I inquired of its success, and was told that the channel bars were continually shifting, and that few if any would yet venture to take a big ship up through it, the course through the Eads jetties continuing to be practically the sole or main passageway for big boats.

I believe that a laboratory, *preferably near at hand*, and similar to that maintained by the German government

beside the former North Sea Naval Base at Wilhelms-
haven, or perhaps a laboratory of the out-of-door type
being developed by Dr. Krey near Potsdam, would solve
the problem of maintaining a permanent passageway for
the larger ships through the Southwest Pass and save
literally millions of dollars; providing the laboratory and
the field work could be put into hands equally competent
with those in charge of maintaining the entrance to
Bremerhaven, where conditions of drifting sand driven
along the sea coast by the wind are almost indescribably
bad. (Emphasis added.)

Another great problem in which a laboratory *under
competent management* could possibly be extremely
profitable, in connection with experiments along the river
is in regard to cutting out some of the great bends, like
those near Greenville for example; or some of the many
others by which the length of the river is increased nearly
50%, and the rapidity of getting the flood water into the
Gulf correspondingly impeded.

I am well aware of the history of trouble that has
followed natural "cut-offs" and the Army Engineers
believe that in preserving the present crookedness at all
hazards, but I do not believe that this problem has ever
been studied in a thorough and scientific way for either
the Mississippi or the Missouri. I am by no means certain
from any *a priori* reasoning as to whether a partial
straightening, from great bends to gentle curves at many
places along the river, could be made feasible. My hopes
that it would be practicable are based on what I have
observed along the River Rhine, where great bends have
been actually cut out at several places in the portion
between Basel and Mannheim, with the result of shortening the river 23% within this distance, and greatly
improving the condition. In about 220 miles the length of
the River Rhine was shortened by about 50 miles.[39]

After covering a number of similar specific cases, Freeman
turned to an examination of the claims of the Corps to
exclusive preeminence in river hydraulics. First quoting the
incumbent Chief of Engineers, he then reported on his own
and others' experience with the Corps.

General Jadwin says:

"The science of river hydraulics in America, both theoretical and practical, as a whole is more advanced than that of any other nation in the world, and this advance is due almost exclusively to the activities of the Army Engineers.

"They have expended over a billion dollars on works of the most varied character. It should be self evident that this could not be carried out without the most extensive theoretical studies.

"The amount of such studies by the Army Engineers has been enormous. It represents a special and highly technical literature, in books, in government publications."

With regard to these and other self-laudatory statements on behalf of the Army Engineers about the very complete data they have collected, I have personally inquired for it at the St. Louis office of the Mississippi River Commission and elsewhere without finding it. I have searched through files of the Annual Reports of the U.S. Army Engineers and have had the explanation given me by a former Chief of Engineers that they were prevented by law from publishing any technical discussions in these reports.

As illustrating the thoroughness with which I searched for these data, some years ago I had a very competent engineer, a professor in one of our engineering schools, spend a large part of his time for eight months in searching through all available engineering libraries of Boston and New York, the Engineering Library in New York and the Library of Congress, the Corthell Library and many others, to compile into convenient form for reference, all facts and opinions given on good authority relative to river hydraulics and the training of rivers. His abstracts comprise more than a thousand pages closely typewritten, but nowhere did he discover the valuable mine of knowledge and wisdom described by General Jadwin.

The general opinion given me by personal contact and

by statements of others, is that the Army Engineers, if they have such knowledge, hoard it as a trade secret for the benefit and preservation of their close corporation, and in their effort to back up their claim that they being the only people who possess this wisdom and experience, should be continued in charge to the exclusion of civil engineers. . . .

Arthur E. Morgan, with exceptional need and exceptional facilities for finding this theoretical and practical data assembled by the Corps has had similar difficulty in finding this.[40]

Freeman quotes General Jadwin, Chief of Engineers, as stating to Congress that the Army Engineers:

Having been the leading hydraulic scientists in this country for over a century, and in many fields they represent practically the only body of organized hydraulic science which now exists in this country.[41]

In his comments Freeman took issue with the prevailing claim of the Corps of Engineers that it provided the intelligence which brought to fruition the Panama Canal. Freeman, in the letter quoted, described in detail how the plans for the Panama Canal were prepared by civilian engineers before the Corps of Engineers was put in charge.

It is my firm belief, based on many years of observation, reading and conferences with many eminent engineers that the activities of the U.S. Army Engineers and their dominating position has a smothering or killing influence on the progress of river and harbor engineering in America.[42]

Hoover Becomes President, Appoints Major General Brown Chief of Engineers

When Herbert Hoover took office as President of the United States at the beginning of 1929, the situation with regard to a national hydraulic laboratory changed radically. President Hoover, himself a great engineer, had become aware of the need for the laboratory while serving as Secretary of

Commerce from 1921 to 1928. He was also familiar with the lower Mississippi River from personal experiences on the river during and after the great flood of 1927 and directing relief in the flooded regions bordering the river. Convinced of the soundness of Freeman's position in advocating a national hydraulic laboratory, he strongly favored the establishment of the laboratory. But as Secretary of Commerce, his opinion was easily brushed aside by the strongly entrenched and politically powerful Corps of Engineers. On becoming President he was in a different position, where he had the power to accomplish his wishes.

He had properly appraised the situation when he wrote to General Jadwin, Chief of Engineers, on June 17, 1927, while he was still Secretary of Commerce, on the subject of the laboratory: "It would no doubt be necessary to have the support of the Engineer Corps to have such a bill passed."[4][3] Since the Chief of Engineers was practically dictator of the Corps, the way to secure such support under new and creative leadership, seemed not impossible to President Hoover.

It was customary, when a new Chief of Engineers was to be appointed, for a recommendation to come from the Corps of Engineers to the Secretary of War, and to be transmitted by him to the President, with recommendation for appointment.

Except for the informal control by "the establishment" within the Corps of Engineers, the Chief of Engineers was largely a one-man dictator. President Hoover informed himself of the personalities and attitudes of those who might be presented to him for appointment. When a name was sent to him he declined to make the requested appointment, and asked for another nomination. When the second request was made, he again refused to make the appointment requested. The same treatment was accorded to the third and fourth, and on and on until he had declined appointment to ten members of the Corps. Finally he found a way to secure the nomination for which he had been waiting. He appointed Major-General Lytle Brown, a man of strong personality who had frequent differences with his superiors, though not to the

extent of General Billy Mitchell, the unfortunate West
Pointer court-martialed for advocating airpower.

Major General Brown, in becoming Chief of Engineers,
brought about a sudden revolution in the Corps of Engineers
attitude toward the hydraulic laboratory. On January 9,
1930, President Hoover wrote three letters to the Secretary
of War, asking that the opposition of the Corps of Engineers
to a National Hydraulic Laboratory cease. To this General
Brown replied on January 21 through the Secretary of War.

> For your own information and for that of the President
> in case you may see the appropriateness of bringing this
> to his information, I wish to state:
>
> I am entirely responsible for all that is done by the
> Corps of Engineers and expect to be held definitely to
> that responsibility.
>
> Nothing that may be done by anyone in the said Corps
> is binding on the Department in any sense unless it has
> the stamp of my approval or is in accord with my
> instructions.
>
> The matter of opposing the proposed hydraulic labora-
> tory at the Bureau of Standards rests entirely with the
> former Chief of Engineers, and not with the Corps of
> Engineers. I favor such a laboratory and have some time
> since informed those who have approached me on the
> subject that I saw no objection to it whatsoever.
>
> I fully understand the President's views, and that will
> insure absolutely that no opposition, direct or indirect,
> private or official, will be found coming from here.[44]

As the newly-appointed Chief of Engineers, Major General
Lytle Brown appeared personally before the House Committee on Rivers and Harbors on February 4, 1930, to present a
point of view diametrically opposite to that long held by his
predecessors. This new attitude astounded the Committee as
it completely reversed the testimony that the Corps had given
in all prior hearings. General Brown's opening statement
read:

> Mr. Chairman and members of the committee, I am of

the opinion that there is a need for a national hydraulic laboratory, as indicated in the bills introduced, I believe, by Senator Ransdell and Representative O'Connor.[4][5]

As the hearings on February 4 proceeded, the responses made by General Brown are most illuminating.

When asked whether he felt that the proposed laboratory should be located at the Bureau of Standards, Brown replied in the affirmative, adding, "The government carries on a lot of work that involves hydraulics, and if you do not have a central place to do it, everybody that is charged with it will do more or less of it himself."[4][6] This unexpected attitude by the Chief of Engineers was quite disconcerting to a committee conditioned to vociferous opposition from the Corps of Engineers.

With one of the Representatives, General Brown had this exchange:

MR. MICHAELSON. May I ask the general if he is familiar with the record made before committee on this question?

GENERAL BROWN. No, sir; I have not read it.

MR. MICHAELSON. Well, I thought so from the fact that you take the position you do. As one of the members of the committee I would suggest that the General familiarize himself with the record as made before this committee, because we have been through this quite extensively, and we have a very extensive record, and the position of the engineers preceding the present Chief of Engineers was totally opposite to the position that General Brown takes now. It makes it difficult for me as one member of the committee, to reconcile the record with what is being stated now.

Later, the following exchange occurred.

THE CHAIRMAN. (Wallace Dempsey) Of course, we asked the General to come. It was probably my fault in asking him to come so promptly. We want to deal with this proposition of the hydraulic laboratory at an early date. I do not think I gave the General an opportunity to glance over this testimony if he wanted to do that.

GENERAL BROWN. I do not want to read any previous testimony. I would not have read it over if I had had the opportunity.

MR. MICHAELSON. Well, the engineers are sort of playing football with the committee, it appears to me. We sat here and had extensive hearings on this question and then the Chief of Engineers comes in and sweeps that all away and puts the committee in a rather doubtful frame of mind as to really what is wanted here.

THE CHAIRMAN. I suppose what the Congressman means, General, is this: We did, at the request of the Engineers' office, and at their request—it was not on our initiative—give very extensive hearings. . . . We had no object in the hearings, except to get the data and information upon which to act intelligently, and it was most elaborate on both sides, and covered a great deal of ground. Naturally in these hearings we are guided by the testimony, and we are obliged to assume that your Corps, when they testify upon any question, are experts, particularly where these men made a study and had gone abroad for the purpose of studying, and then visiting the laboratories here. I suppose that is what Congressman Michaelson has in mind in making the suggestion.

THE CHAIRMAN. It is with all deference, General, and in all kindliness, a little hard for the committee to readjust itself in a moment, in a spirit of discarding all of the testimony which has been given by the Engineer Corps.[47]

Chairman Dempsey, in a ticklish position handling such an abrupt reversal by the Corps, was left no room for doubt after receiving a follow-up letter from General Brown on February 8:

In reference to your advice to me at the recent hearings on the National Hydraulic Laboratory, I wish to inform you that I have gone over a good portion of the previous hearings on the subject, and I am prepared to inform you as to any new impressions that I have. In further explanation of my views before the Committee, I wish to say that I appeared before the Committee as free from the ideas of anyone else as it was possible to do, not wishing to be influenced in any way thereby.

My conviction that a laboratory in the Bureau of Standards for general service is desirable is strengthened. . . .

I am informed by a creditable witness that opposition to the laboratory formerly on the part of some engineer officers was through an impression that the laboratory might be used by irresponsible parties to dictate to the Corps of Engineers as to how work entrusted to its care should be executed, and so be constituted as an origin of controversy, delay and confusion. I see no foundation for that view and have not the least fear of any such evil.[48]

With General Brown's support, there was no further cause for delaying the bill. Senate 3043 and House of Representatives 8299, "An Act authorizing the Establishment of a National Hydraulic Laboratory in the Bureau of Standards of the Department of Commerce and the Construction of a Building Therefor," was passed and signed into law by President Hoover on May 14, 1930.[49]

It was one month short of eight years from the time Senator Ransdell introduced his first bill for creation of a National Hydraulic Laboratory until the law was finally enacted. It had been introduced five times and defeated four times despite the overwhelming—almost unanimous—approval of American hydraulic engineers, but with the powerful opposition of the Corps of Engineers. The bill would doubtless have been defeated the fifth time but for the marked change in the personnel of the Corps of Engineers brought about by President Hoover.

Before continuing our story it may be appropriate to hesitate briefly to shed a tear at the grave of John R. Freeman's hopes for the National Hydraulic Laboratory.

The National Hydraulic Laboratory was not a success. What the present situation is may be seen from a letter I received from Albert Fry, long-time supervisor of the very excellent hydraulic laboratory of the Tennessee Valley Authority, which was initiated under my direction when I was Chairman and Chief Engineer of the TVA. Fry wrote in July, 1967:

> . . . That the National Laboratory did not fulfill the visions of its proponents is due not to any subversion on the part of the Corps but rather to the lack of an effective, vigorous organization and competent staff. There are many unsolved hydraulic problems that the National Laboratory could have tackled had its leadership been aggressive and done so. And these would not have encroached on the work of the Corps at all. As it has been, the National Laboratory has afforded a place to rate current meters and has compiled an annual bulletin of hydraulic research going on in the U.S. This plus a few other studies has been the program of the National Laboratory while other laboratories—the Corps laboratories at Vicksburg and several other locations—the Bureau of Reclamation lab at Denver, the Navy's David Taylor Model Basin in Washington, D.C., the TVA laboratory, plus those at Iowa's Institute of Hydraulic Research, Minnesota's St. Anthony Falls Laboratory, Massachusetts Institute of Technology Hydrodynamics' Laboratory and some others—have all moved steadily forward and expanded to give the United States an outstanding group of hydraulic laboratories. John R. Freeman would be proud of what these laboratories have done and are doing but he would take no pride in what the National Hydraulic Laboratory has failed to do.[50]

Why should this withering of Freeman's hopes have occurred?

As plans developed for the National Hydraulic Laboratory, Freeman considered them to be totally inadequate. He strongly desired that the available funds be used for laying the grounds for a really adequate installation. As those in charge persisted with what Freeman considered completely inadequate provisions, he decided that he could not be a party to the undertaking. His position is clearly reflected in a letter to him from George K. Burgess, Director of the Bureau of Standards, of January 27, 1931, from which the following is quoted:

. . . I am indeed sorry to learn from your letter that we are now "at the parting of the ways" as regards the hydraulic laboratory. My feeling in the matter is that we were never closer together.

I, of course, cannot agree with you when you state we "will produce a mediocre laboratory which can doubtless do routine work admirably for the various departments of the government but will fail almost completely in producing fundamental research and developing formulas and coefficients up to the large depths and quantities required for the reliable guidance of engineers engaged in large projects," nor with your statement that the "laboratory will never become a court of last resort for settling many of the important questions which the new laboratory at Obernach is designed to do, etc."[5][1]

As plans for the National Hydraulic Laboratory got under way, Freeman insisted on using the limited appropriations to lay the basis for an adequate installation and then go back to Congress for enough money to complete a plant which would be an adequate instrument for his large purposes.

But those in charge of the National Hydraulics Laboratory program insisted that the initial appropriation must pay the entire cost of land, building and equipment. Freeman clearly sensed what the outcome of that course would be. He was now an old man. When he saw that his appraisal of the situation was not being given consideration, he withdrew his efforts with what must have been a feeling of frustration and disappointment. However, while his dreams for the National Hydraulics Laboratory were destined not to come true, great credit must be given to him for his long hard-fought battle for the laboratory. This gave a tremendous impetus to the establishment of the considerable number of excellent hydraulics laboratories in the United States which have had such an important part in the planning of America's water development projects in the last three decades.

Hydraulic Laboratory Recasts Plans for Mississippi River

Perhaps the major element of the revolution in the attitude

of the Corps of Engineers towards a hydraulics laboratory was with reference to the plans for the control of the Mississippi River and to the program to be carried out at the Waterways Experiment Station, which, after consideration of possible sites, was located at Vicksburg. With respect to the laboratory, General Brown made radical changes in the position of the Corps and assigned the laboratory a much broader scope of work than had been envisioned by his predecessor. He was aided in this by President Hoover who overhauled the personnel of the Mississippi River Commission* appointing, doubtless at General Brown's suggestion, as President of MRC a modern-minded engineer, General Harley B. Ferguson, who favored a hydraulic laboratory as an important tool to be used in planning control of the Mississippi River.

General Ferguson, an exceptionally vigorous, able and research-minded member of the Corps of Engineers, was an excellent choice to build the hydraulics laboratory at Vicksburg. General Ferguson in turn put in charge of building the laboratory Gerard Matthes who had been a member of the author's staff when the hydraulics laboratory of the Miami Conservancy District was built and operated in Dayton, Ohio, in 1915-1917. Lieutenant Herbert D. Vogel (now Brigadier General, Retired) a Corps engineer who had been the first Freeman Fellow, was made the first Director of the Waterways Experiment Station. Vogel, during his studies in Europe, saw the excellent work being done in the laboratories there and became convinced of the need for such a laboratory in the United States. He was influential in recommending that the Corps should build and operate a hydraulics laboratory. He had an alert, active and investigative mind particularly suited to searching out significant problems and dealing with them creatively, and made an

---

*The Mississippi River Commission consists of seven commissioners appointed by the President of the United States, three from the Corps of Engineers, one from the Coast and Geodetic Survey, and three from civil life, two of whom must be civil engineers. One of the Corps appointees is designated by the President as president of the Commission.

excellent Director of the laboratory. General Ferguson added capable civilian engineers to his staff and this staff has had an important influence extending down through all the years since the laboratory was established.

Since the Corps built the Waterways Experiment Station at Vicksburg and to a large extent as a result of its use in connection with a wide variety of hydraulic problems, several of the basic doctrines of the Corps with respect to the control of the Mississippi River that had been dogmatically held and strongly defended by the Corps for more than half a century have been entirely abandoned or radically revised. Large amounts of money were saved as a result of these changes in attitudes and policies.

One basic Corps doctrine was that of "levees only." As previously set forth, this policy had been the ruling one almost from the beginning of levee building on the Mississippi although such a policy could never by itself accomplish flood control on the River. The hydraulic laboratory in no sense minimized the importance of properly planned and built levees, but did establish that although levees alone could not do the job, levees would continue to be an important feature in the overall flood control plans.

Another reversal in Corps policy took place with regard to reservoirs. A large number of these have been built on the streams tributary to the Mississippi and many more are planned as features in the overall plan for the Mississippi and for many streams within the watershed. Part of the cost of more than a hundred of these reservoirs is allocated to lower Mississippi River flood control. (See reference in Hoover Commission Report, 52.)

The hydraulic laboratory also proved indispensable in testing the diversion floodways provided for in the 1928 Flood Control Act such as the Birds Point—New Madrid Floodway on the west bank just below Cairo, Illinois, and the Bonnet Carre Floodway on the east side above New Orleans. The Corps classic report by Humphreys and Abbot in 1861 rejected such outlets along with cutoffs and reservoirs as unsound.

A third dogma that was upset by the hydraulic laboratory was that of no man-made cutoffs across bends in the Mississippi River. Laboratory tests dispelled the false theories regarding such cutoffs and opened the way for the construction of such cutoffs with large benefits in reduction in river length by more than 170 miles, with consequent reduction in time for passage of river craft and with material savings in miles of levees and protection works. The story of the Corps opposition to cutoffs and how this was overcome is told in the next chapter.

In retrospect, it seems almost incredible that such a vital, progressive policy as that of establishing a hydraulic laboratory could be nullified so long by such a small segment of America's engineering profession. In this instance, America was treated to the spectacle of legislation favored almost unanimously by our civilian hydraulic engineers being stalled for years due to the lack of foresight and to the "establishment" jealousy of the Corps of Engineers. Even after this minority had subdued the vast majority for eight years, it required a change of command and pressure from the President of the United States for the Corps to join the mainstream of thought on the issue. An ironic and fitting postscript to the battle for the hydraulic laboratory was added by Lieutenant Vogel. He wrote with regard to experiments in the laboratory with small scale models ". . . the accuracy of results exceeded all expectation."[53]

Today the Corps of Engineers operates the world's largest and most fully equipped hydraulic laboratory where studies for large scale hydraulic works are carried out by means of small scale models. The Corps' hydraulic laboratories have spread far beyond Vicksburg to Bonneville; Los Angeles; Clinton, Mississippi; Washington, D.C.; and Honolulu. A constantly wider range of hydraulic problems is dealt with. These problems come from every state in the nation. In current publicity officially issued by the Corps of Engineers at its multi-million dollar Waterways Experiment Station at Vicksburg, Mississippi, the Corps states:

An indispensable aid to the hydraulic specialist is the small scale model. . . . Hundreds of investigations have been conducted by the station, and in practically every case the benefits—improved design or better construction at the saving of large sums of money—have far outweighed the costs involved.[54]

With the creation of the Tennessee Valley Authority in 1933, with the author as Chairman and Chief Engineer, a hydraulics laboratory was developed there under the direction of the late Sherman M. Woodward. In 1915, under the author as Chief Engineer of the Miami Conservancy District, Woodward had developed one of the early hydraulic laboratories in America. Later he initiated the excellent laboratory at the State University of Iowa. The TVA Hydraulic Laboratory, for 28 years under Albert Fry, has had a very successful experience through more than thirty years, and has handled many difficult problems.

Another excellent hydraulic laboratory is that of the Bureau of Reclamation at Denver. Established many years ago, it is now one of the world's largest. It was begun with the help of engineers who had been on the author's staff of the Miami Conservancy District.

Good liaison is maintained between the laboratories of the Corps, the TVA and the Bureau of Reclamation and there is also free exchange of technical information and reports between the three organizations.*

*It may be worthy of mention, with regard to modern hydraulic laboratory practice, that the emergence and development of computers offers opportunities for the solution of certain problems that formerly would have been solved by hydraulic models. But the large majority of problems do not lend themselves to computer application, and remain to be solved by traditional hydraulic model techniques. Modern hydraulic laboratories are aware of the value and capabilities of computers and are making use of these wherever feasible. (Albert Fry to Arthur Morgan, March 4, 1968.)

Creative Memory Overlooks Facts

Creative memory is characteristic of the Corps. A Corps of Engineers member illustrates this in the book by Captain Burr W. Loyson, "The Army Engineers in Review." He wrote:

Spurred into action by the disaster [the 1927 flood on the Mississippi], Congress decided that the mighty Mississippi must and would be controlled. To control such a vast waterway, harness and tame its immense power, was one of the greatest engineering projects of all times. Congress called upon the Corps of Engineers to do the job. That was in 1929, two years after the great flood. The rest is typical of the engineers.

At Vicksburg, Mississippi, the Engineers established the Waterways Experiment Station, one of the first of its kind in the world.

What was apparent to the Engineers from the beginning was now made visible. The lower reaches of the river backed up the flood waters by making them flow through a tortuous course whose channel was at times inadequate to take care of the volume of water.

But of greater importance was the fact that the tortuous course could be straightened out on the model, and the effect of this changing of the course of the river determined accurately in advance. [Emphasis added.] [55]

How does this account jibe with the facts of the situation in the 1920's?

First, Captain Loyson writes, "Congress decided that the mighty Mississippi must and would be controlled," as though this was a new Congressional resolve after the great flood of 1927. The fact is that Congress long before gave this assignment to the Corps of Engineers, and the Corps of Engineers repeatedly informed Congress that the job was substantially nearing completion. For a few years before and after 1920 the Corps of Engineers reported to the Congress, through its Annual Report, that the Mississippi Valley had been made safe for all but very great floods. Then, beginning with the Annual Report for 1924, and continuing through the Annual Report of 1925 and 1926, *the Corps removed all qualifications and informed Congress and the nation that the Mississippi Valley was now made safe from serious flood damage.*

The 1927 flood was notice to the country of how greatly the Corps of Engineers misjudged the problem. The 1927 flood, by disrupting the levees all along the river, with much loss of life and vast destruction of property, and with the flooding of millions of acres of land, disclosed how totally inadequate was the protection provided.

Captain Loyson's account continues, "The rest is typical of the Engineers. At Vicksburg, Mississippi, the Engineers established the Waterways Experiment Station, one of the first of the kind in the world." Perhaps Captain Loyson had not heard of the 680-page quarto book by Mr. Freeman describing the more than twenty hydraulic laboratories in Europe or of the nearly fifty in America.[5 6]

Captain Loyson also claimed for the Corps a foreknowledge of the solutions later found with the help of the laboratory model. *"What was apparent to the Engineers from the beginning—"*[5 7] (Emphasis added.) He seems unaware of the long-sustained dogma of the Corps against cutoffs in the river channel, and of their expenditure of millions of dollars to prevent cutoffs. The last brief paragraph, quoted by Loyson, tells how "the tortuous course could be straightened out on the model and the effect of this changing of the course of the river determined accurately in advance."[5 8] As we have seen from quotations of succeeding Chiefs of Engineers, there was almost no point on which the Corps was more obdurate than in their repudiation of the idea of planning cutoffs by means of the hydraulic laboratory.

Perhaps the most remarkable bit of rewriting history is a statement made by General Jadwin, when he had so far changed his position as to call for a hydraulic laboratory under the Corps of Engineers. In the hearing before the House Committee on Rivers and Harbors of 1928 and 1929 General Jadwin stated:

This proposal for a hydraulic laboratory, made by the Chief of Engineers. . . . is nothing in a way of revolution. It is simply a further step in systematizing one particular branch of the theoretical research which the Corps of Engineers has been carrying on for many years. When necessity arises we have been carrying on precisely this type of work.[59]

Perhaps General Emerson C. Itschner, Chief of Engineers, had read this comment by an earlier Chief of Engineers, when, on October 28, 1959, in informing a meeting of the Franklin Institute of Philadelphia of the achievements of the U.S. Corps of Engineers, he said:

The development of hydraulic models for technical studies reflects a major Corps of Engineers contribution to engineering progress over the past thirty years.

Regardless of the confirmed habit of rewriting of Corps of Engineers history by Captain Loyson and numerous others of the Corps of Engineers and of General Jadwin's tongue-in-cheek testimony, the record piled up through the years is clear. The Corps of Engineers early took a position opposing a hydraulic laboratory regardless of the compelling facts that pointed positively to the need for such a laboratory. It doggedly stuck to that position for more than half a century until finally the persistent crusading efforts of a great hydraulic engineer, John R. Freeman, the strong convictions of a great President, Herbert Hoover, and the independent thinking of a brilliant Chief of Engineers willing to break loose from the shackles of tradition, Major General Lytle Brown, combined to bring about a reversal in the Corps' attitude toward the laboratory and toward effective methods for control of the Lower Mississippi River. This is the real story of the Corps of Engineers and the hydraulic laboratory.

notes

1. Townsend, Colonel Curtis (retired), letter to Chief of Engineers Beach, September 29, 1922, National Archives.

2. Hoffman, G. M., Colonel, Memoranda for Chief of Engineers, September 12, 1922, National Archives.

3. Freeman, John R., letter to the House Committee on Rivers and Harbors, May 24, 1928, p. 3.

3A. Joint Resolution to Establish a National Hydraulic Laboratory, S. J. Res. 209, 67th Congress, 2nd Session, by Mr. Ransdell, April 20 (calendar day, June 13), 1922.

4. Beach, Lansing H., Chief of Engineers, memoranda for the Secretary of War, August 9, 1922, National Archives.

5. *Ibid.*

6. Beach, Lansing H., Chief of Engineers, letter submitted by the Secretary of War to Senator Ransdell, August 9, 1922, Corps of Engineers, National Archives.

7. *Ibid.*

8. *Ibid.*

9. *Ibid.*

10. Jadwin, General, Chief of Engineers, statement before the House Committee on Rivers and Harbors, May 15, 1928, National Archives.

11. Jervey, Henry, Brigadier General (retired), letter to Chief of Engineers Beach, October 23, 1922, National Archives.

12. Beach, Lansing H., Chief of Engineers, letter to Brigadier General Jervey, November 13, 1922, National Archives.

13. Lyon, L. E., Major, letter to Chief of Engineers Beach, August 2, 1922. National Archives.

14. *Ibid.*
15. U.S. Engineer Department, Hydraulic Laboratory Data, August 8, 1922, National Archives.
16. Beach, Lansing H., Chief of Engineers, letter to Alfred D. Flinn, Secretary, the Engineering Foundation, August 8, 1922, National Archives.
17. American Society of Civil Engineers, *Transactions*, July, 1923.
18. Townsend, Curtis, Colonel, to Chief of Engineers Beach, September 29, 1922, National Archives.
19. Ockerson, J. A., telegram to Chief of Engineers Beach, September 6, 1922, National Archives.
20. Beach, Lansing H., Chief of Engineers, telegram to J. A. Ockerson, September 7, 1922, National Archives.
21. Potter, General, telegram to Chief of Engineers Beach, September 7, 1922, National Archives.
22. Senate Committee on Commerce, Report 137, pp. 72-73, p. 79, January 6-27, 1930.
23. Gaussmann, R. W., and C. M. Madden, "Experiments with Models of the Gilboa Dam and Spillway," in the American Society of Civil Engineers September proceedings, pp. 1503-1528, September, 1922.
24. Honnes, George G., discussion of Transactions of the American Society of Civil Engineers December 1922, p. 1886.
25. Fletcher, Robert, discussion of "Experiments with Models of the Gilboa Dam and Spillway," Transactions of the American Society of Civil Engineers, February, 1923, p. 241.
26. Gausmann, R. W., and C. M. Madden, discussion of Transactions of the American Society of Civil Engineers, March, 1923, p. 566.

27. Merriman, Thaddeus, statement in "The Need for a National Hydraulic Laboratory," September 6, 1927.

28. Eaton, H. N., "The National Hydraulic Laboratory," in *Commercial Standards Monthly*, June, 1930, Vol. 6, No. 12, p. 1.

29. Williams, Gardner S., statement before the Senate Subcommittee of the Committee on Commerce, Senate Calendar Number 132, p. 100, Report 137, January 10, 1923.

30. Van Leer, Blake, "Need for a National Hydraulic Laboratory," *Engineering News-Record*, January 10, 1929, p. 68.

31. Freeman, John R., "The Need for a National Hydraulic Laboratory for the Solution of River Problems," p. 27.

32. Jadwin, General, testimony before the House Committee on Rivers and Harbors, May 15, 1928, hearing on S. 1710, National Hydraulic Laboratory, p. 63, National Archives.

33. Van Leer, Blake R., to General Jadwin, June 23, 1928, National Archives.

34. Jadwin, General, for the Secretary of War, to the Acting Director of the Bureau of the Budget, March 2, 1928, Corps of Engineers, National Archives.

35. Freeman, John R., testimony before the Subcommittee of the Committee on Commerce, U.S. Senate, on S.J.R. 209, To Establish a National Hydraulic Laboratory, September 8, 1922, National Archives.

36. Freeman, John R., Letter to the Chairman and Members of the House Committee on Rivers and Harbors, May 24, 1928, p. 6, National Archives.

37. Freeman, John R., to General Jadwin, December 2, 1927, National Archives.

38. Freeman, John R., to the Chairman and Members of the

House Committee on Rivers and Harbors, May 24, 1928, National Archives.

39. *Ibid.*

40. *Ibid.*

41. *Ibid.*

42. *Ibid.*

43. Hoover, Herbert C., to General Jadwin, June 17, 1927, National Archives.

44. Brown, General Lytle, to President Herbert Hoover, January 9, 1930, National Archives.

45. Hearings before the Committee on Rivers and Harbors, House of Representatives, on H.R. 8299—National Hydraulic Laboratory, February 4, 1930.

46. *Ibid.*

47. *Ibid.*

48. Brown, General Lytle, to Chairman Wallace Dempsey, File 1870, February 8, 1930, Corps of Engineers, National Archives.

49. S. 3043 and H.R. 8299, An Act Authorizing the Establishment of a National Hydraulic Laboratory in the Bureau of Standards of the Department of Commerce and the Construction of a Building Therefor, National Archives.

50. Fry, Albert, letter to Arthur E. Morgan, July 15, 1967.

51. Burgess, George K., letter to John R. Freeman, January 27, 1931.

52. Hoover Commission Report.

53. Corps of Engineers pamphlet, U.S. Army Engineer Waterways Experiment Station, section on Sources—Hydraulic Laboratory, no. 1, par. 4.

54. Vogel, Lieutenant Herbert D., Hydraulic Laboratory Planned for Mississippi River Studies, in Engineering and Contracting, December, 1929, p. 510.

55. Loyson, Captain Burr W., *The Army Engineers in Review*, E. P. Dutton & Co., 1943.

56. *Ibid.*

57. *Ibid.*

58. *Ibid.*

59. Jadwin, General, before the House Committee on Rivers and Harbors of 1928 and 1929, page 221, National Archives.

chapter 8

shortening the mississippi

View From the Banks of the Mississippi

In the previous chapter, the emergence of the hydraulic laboratory has been followed from the viewpoint of Washington, D.C. The understanding of that occurrence may be increased by noting how it appeared when viewed from the great river and through the eyes of an active minded civilian engineer long resident of the Yazoo District on the river. William E. Elam for forty years was an engineer with the Mississippi Levee Board, Greenville, Mississippi, with the most important of all the levees along the river. He was a member of the American Society of Civil Engineers and in 1938 was President of the Mid-South Section of the Society.

He lived through many high waters on the Mississippi River and observed the behavior of the River at all stages. He was a pioneer student and ardent advocate of artificial cutoffs across bends in the river, a major feature of the plans for flood control on the Mississippi that evolved with use of model tests at the new Waterways Experiment Station hydraulic laboratory, established by Lytle Brown, Mr. Hoover's rebel appointment as Chief of the Corps of Engineers.

Mr. Elam recorded his experiences and ideas in a book, "Speeding Floods to the Sea."[1] Elam observed the extremely obvious fact, ignored by the Corps of Engineers, that the faster water flows in a river, the smaller the channel necessary to carry it, and the lower will be the flood stages. The extreme crookedness of the lower Mississippi River, which doubled its length, resulted in lower velocity and higher flood levels.

Elam's book narrates events in the struggle to overcome the Corps of Engineers' inflexible adherence to erroneous ideas of river hydraulics, and its resistance to cutting off bends in the river. The matter of artificial cutoffs on the Mississippi had been simmering for many years and finally came to a head following the disastrous flood of 1927, just as did the last stages of the conflict for the hydraulic laboratory. It was only after a new and rebellious administration of the Corps of Engineers had conducted conclusive tests in the new and hitherto prohibited hydraulic laboratory that the Corps finally did abandon its long-held sacred policies of "levees only" and "no cutoffs."

Mr. Elam comments on the fact that "Two early reports on the Mississippi River largely influenced the newly organized Mississippi River Commission (MRC) to adopt the 'levees only' policy (in 1879). The first was by a civilian engineer, Mr. Charles Ellet, Jr., who made studies of the Ohio and Mississippi Rivers for the U. S. Government. Ellet's report, made in 1851, recommended among other things the 'prevention of cutoffs'."[2]

The second influence was the massive "Report upon the Physics and Hydraulics of the Mississippi River upon the protection of the Alluvial Region against Overflow and Upon the Deepening of the Mouths," prepared by Captain A. A. Humphreys and Lieutenant H. L. Abbot, Corps of Topographical Engineers,* United States Army (J. B. Lippincott & Co., Philadelphia, 1861; 600+ pages). By 1879, when the Mississippi River Commission was created by Congress, Captain Humphreys had become a General and was Chief of

---

*The Corps of Topographical Engineers had equal status with the Corps of Engineers from 1838 until the Civil War at which time the Corps of Topographical Engineers was abolished by Congress and its personnel transferred to the Corps of Engineers.

Engineers. Naturally his report was accepted by the MRC and became Corps policy. This book, for many years the bible of the Corps of Engineers for the Mississippi River, strongly opposed cutoffs. Captain Humphreys, in transmitting this report, stated, "The effects of cutoffs were likewise the subjects of controversy among engineers, a controversy which the measurements of the Delta Survey must set at rest, since they demonstrate that cutoffs raise the floods below them."[3]

"Protection Against Floods of the Mississippi," Chapter VI of Humphreys and Abbot's treatise, analyzes various flood control plans, including cutoffs, diversion of tributaries, artificial reservoirs, artificial outlets, and levees. A cutoffs plan, it said, ". . .is not applicable, as proposed by hydraulic writers, to large rivers like the Mississippi. . . . where the water often remains for weeks at flood height." The conclusion arrived at is "that a cutoff raises the surface of the river at the foot of the cut nearly as much as it depresses it at the head." Thus, the report finds "The system as a measure of protection for the Mississippi valley is then pernicious."[4]

The conclusions and recommendations of Humphreys and Abbot are based largely on this theory that the water would be raised as much below the cutoff as it was lowered above the cutoff. Fallacious as this theory is easily proven to be by the most elementary hydraulics, it persisted for more than 75 years and never was seriously disputed by the Corps until 1930, when model tests at the newly established hydraulic laboratory demonstrated the truth.

Under "Recommendations" Humphreys and Abbot stated that, "An organized levee system must be depended upon for protection against floods in the Mississippi valley." Quoting from these recommendations:

> The preceding discussion of the different plans of protection has been so elaborate and the conclusions adopted have been so well established that little remains to be said under the head of recommendations. It has been *demonstrated* that no advantage can be derived either from diverting tributaries or constructing reservoirs, and that the plans of cutoffs, and of new or

enlarged outlets to the gulf, are too costly and too dangerous to be attempted. The plan of levees, on the contrary, which has always recommended itself by its simplicity and its direct repayment of investments, may be relied upon for protecting all alluvial bottom lands liable to inundation below Cape Girardeau [Missouri].[5]

It is interesting to note that on the title page of Humphreys and Abbot in very fine print is the following quotation from Benjamin Franklin:

I approve much more your method of philosophising, which proceeds upon actual observation, makes a collection of facts, and concludes no further than those facts warrant.[6]

Perhaps the fineness of the print prevented successive generations of Corps engineers from reading and heeding Dr. Franklin's advice.

"The Jadwin Plan" for the control of the Mississippi River was prepared after the great flood of the spring of 1927, and was enacted into law in 1928. It was hastily prepared, almost entirely following Corps of Engineers tradition and the "findings" of the Humphreys and Abbot monograph on "The Physics and Hydraulics of the Mississippi River," published in 1861. It was presented as covering all phases of Mississippi River control. Mississippi River cutoffs were entirely excluded from that plan.

Following the calamitous flood of 1927, Mr. Elam and others proposed the "cutoff plan" as a valuable feature along with other elements for alleviating great floods on the Lower Mississippi River. But the idea met with strong rebuff from the Corps of Engineers and the Mississippi River Commission (MRC)—which consisted chiefly of Corps membership and was largely dominated by the Corps, and was charged by an act of Congress in 1879 "to make plans and estimates to correct, permanently locate, and deepen the channel and protect the banks of the Mississippi River to improve navigation; prevent destructive floods;" and carry out other duties. Navigation interests, which had sponsored the creation of MRC, were, according to Elam, "afraid to do anything that might speed up the river and make navigation more difficult." The MRC was careful not to oppose these powerful interests.

Even as late as 1927 and 1928, both the MRC and the Chief of Engineers issued reports vehemently condemning cutoffs as part of any plan for Mississippi River flood control. It was anticipated that these two reports would eliminate cutoffs from further consideration. As further support for this position, Chief of Engineers General Edgar Jadwin appointed a Mississippi River Flood Control Board to review his Plan. The General guarded against any adverse opinions by appointing the entire Board, to consist of himself and one other Corps officer and a civilian engineer known to be favorable to the Plan. As expected, this Board approved the Jadwin Plan in every particular.

When the Jadwin Plan came before Congress in 1928, it struck a snag in one essential feature. In the Boeuf Floodway and later in the Tensas Floodway, the westside relief channel, the landowners demanded compensation for rights-of-way for lands that might be flooded. The refusal of Congress to provide such compensation blocked an important part of the Plan and left unsolved the problem of the middle lower Mississippi. The need for an alternate plan might have presented an opportunity for trying cutoffs.

Elam reports that "the 1927 flood disaster helped a great deal in getting thought diverted to some other means of preventing disasters than the levees."[7] Summing up the situation in 1928, he wrote:

> The 1927 flood was the greatest disaster ever to befall the Mississippi Valley. Even after that—which indicated that adopted plans were inadequate—no official with authority recognized the possibility of lowering flood heights by cutoffs and other means. No such program had ever been instituted, and no proof could be given that it would work out as desired. Everyone realized that replanning was necessary, but no one was in a frame of mind to adopt an untried method; nor could the River

Commission make any real laboratory study before time to make their report to the Chief of Engineers and Congress. Immediate planning was essential, and only the early conventional methods of flood control could be used. ALL of these reports violently condemned cutoffs.

Of the general situation, but especially concerning the possibility of cutoffs, Elam wrote:

It takes a great deal of time and careful planning to get a new idea adopted, especially where so many factors are involved—many lives and much property at stake. Little hope was entertained that any help would come from the valley, either engineers or laymen, unless the Army Engineers would adopt the idea [of cutoffs]. This did not appear probable in view of all their reports to Congress, and the certainty that opposition would immediately arise if a complete reversal of ideas should be proposed.[8]

The report of the Chief of Engineers in 1928 on the same subject of cutoffs, which was submitted to the Flood Control Committee of the same Congress, concluded:

The method is too uncertain and threatening to warrant adoption. . . . It is advisable to adhere to the present policy of preserving the river presently in its present form and not to undertake a plan of flood control or improvement for navigation that involves the formation of cutoffs.[9]

General Brown Reverses Old Cutoff Ideas

Early in 1930, the picture changed when General Jadwin was succeeded as Chief of Engineers by Major-General Lytle Brown. The circumstances that brought about this change have been narrated in the previous chapter. General Brown's outlook was vastly different from that of his predecessor in office. He reopened the whole matter of flood control plans for the Mississippi River. Desiring to give consideration to anyone's ideas, General Brown took the course, unprecedented for the Corps of Engineers, of publishing an invitation in the *Engineering News-Record* on February 6, 1930, inviting suggestions on Mississippi River flood control to be sent directly to him.

One of those who responded was Mr. W. E. Elam who, on March 23, 1930, wrote General Brown at some length regarding his ideas for cutoffs and outlets to speed the flood waters to the sea. This proposal met with a favorable response from General Brown, and the two thereafter maintained contact.

Elam, commenting on a conference he had with the Chief of Engineers, General Brown, on a boat trip on the Mississippi, which resulted from this contact, wrote:

> No student of Mississippi flood control could find a single authoritative report that advocated getting the water to the gulf as quickly as possible. If General Brown could overcome this obstacle he had to be good and would need a lot of high powered help to do it.[10]

In December, 1930, General Brown issued an order to the new Waterways Experiment Station to "determine the effects of ten dredged cutoffs in the Mississippi River between the mouths of the Arkansas and Old River." General Brown wrote Mr. Elam to "take any ideas to the research center . . . at Vicksburg and ask that they be tried out by actual experiment."[11]

However, as General Brown sought to restudy and revise the Jadwin Plan, the Mississippi River Commission, as then constituted, recommended "no change at all in the adopted plan." General Brown was legally powerless to order the MRC to carry out any change of the Jadwin Plan, which had been adopted by Congress. But he found a way out.

The Board of Rivers and Harbors was superior in rank to the Mississippi River Commission. General Brown, as Chief of Engineers, probably with the support of President Hoover, directed the Board of Rivers and Harbors to make a trip on the Mississippi River, and to consider the plans for flood control. In that way he avoided the confirmed opposition of the Corps. Never before had the Board of Rivers and Harbors been asked to report on the Mississippi River. When that

Board reported favorably on cutoffs and other changes in the Jadwin Plan desired by General Brown, he used that report in Congress, rather than the adverse decision of the MRC and the Engineer Corps, to gain his objectives. Influenced by this report of the Board of Rivers and Harbors, Congress approved the desired modifications in the Plan, which included cutoffs disguised as "channel rectification and straightening, it having been deemed inadvisable to ask Congress to authorize cutoffs by that name."

Model Tests Confirm Cutoffs Theory

One member of the Board of Rivers and Harbors who reported on the Mississippi-flood-control plans, General Harley B. Ferguson, soon thereafter was appointed President of the Mississippi River Commission by President Hoover. He replaced General Jackson, a vigorous opponent of cutoffs and other changes in the half-century-old Corps of Engineers doctrines. Immediately after General Ferguson's appointment, the cutoffs program emerged from the shadows of oblivion and became a reality. Carrying out General Brown's orders, the Waterways Experiment Station began hydraulic model testing for cutoffs in June, 1931.

Lieutenant H. D. Vogel (now Brigadier General, Retired) was director of the Station and carried out a thorough program of testing aimed at determining the true facts regarding cutoffs. Nearly a year was spent in making the experiments. The tests showed conclusively that the new policy of cutoffs was correct, and disposed of the idea which had been clung to so tenaciously, that the water level would be raised below a cutoff. The action of the river gave conclusive proof that the theories presented against cutoffs for half a century were completely erroneous.

The construction program for making the cutoffs across bends in the Mississippi River, where the laboratory tests showed these to be desirable, followed closely after the hydraulic laboratory tests were made. The performance of the cutoffs on the river confirmed the findings of the model tests. In fact, the flood plane was lowered even more than was predicted by the model tests. The cutoffs reduced the length of the river by more than 170 miles, and lowered the flood plane for long stretches by much more than 15 feet.

Again, quoting Elam:

> The idea of lowering flood heights by opening up the Atchafalaya and passing this lowering upstream by a judicious use of cutoffs was exactly the reverse of the old, accepted theories of flood control of the Mississippi, which were backed up by all the official reports for fifty years.[1][2]

Opposition Still Continued

While President Hoover had been able to introduce a strikingly new leadership in the appointments of Major-General Lytle Brown as Chief of Engineers, General Harley B. Ferguson as President of the Mississippi River Commission and Lieutenant Herbert D. Vogel as Director at the Waterways Experiment Station, there yet remained along the river in various positions a considerable number of old-school U. S. Army Engineers who held firmly to their more than seventy-five year old dogmas concerning the control of the river. The more conservative members of the Corps generally followed the old tradition. These men gave a hard time to the officials appointed by President Hoover.

Elam reported:

> The opponents of cutoffs continued their opposition, perhaps supported to some extent by the navigation interests who had always feared that the increased currents which might result would hinder navigation. It is true that the increased currents in the river, following the beginning of the cutoff period, did give navigation some real trouble, especially when the river was rising rapidly. Then, navigation became at times almost impossible, and there were several periods when navigation was stopped entirely. Even Government boats could not travel upstream against the strong currents. However, this was offset somewhat by making downstream navigation

quicker. The shortened river had its advantages, as all river boats are slow moving, and the many miles saved meant shorter distances to travel, thus, much time was saved.[13]

The unfortunate part of all this opposition was that the men voicing such violent objections were men who had long served on the river, and who occupied positions of high authority. Consequently their opinions were respected. This created a ground swell of uneasiness that undoubtedly made General Ferguson's task extremely difficult and caused opposition both in the Valley and in Congress.[14]

After a few years, when the river had time to scour out an enlarged channel and resume its normal velocity, the navigation interests saw that they had not been hurt, but had actually been helped by the shortened river.[15]

Epitome of Cutoff Battle

In a summarizing chapter, Mr. Elam commented:

The almost miraculous change that has come over the Mississippi River in the last few years has astounded all who have lived under its shadow of ever-present danger.
To those who studied this great flood control problem it had seemed to become more and more hopeless as the years passed and the flood disasters became more destructive. The best brains in the country had worked out a plan of control and the people were told that time and money was all that was needed to complete the job. This situation had arisen before and the same solution was presented, which was a higher levee, plus means for the water to escape from the river when the levees could no longer hold the flood.[16]

And Mr. Elam concluded his book with a eulogy of the Corps. Evidently Elam was not familiar with the battle in Washington which preceded the establishment of the hydraulic laboratory. The work on the river in which he was long engaged was largely under the control of the Corps of Engineers, and he must have known that the Corps had not had an unbroken record of being tolerant with those who oppose them. Perhaps his eulogy of the Corps would mitigate the treatment he otherwise might receive from those who had near life and death power over his professional life. From that point of view his eulogy is eloquent.

This, in brief, is the story of the struggle to gain acceptance for man-made cutoffs in the lower Mississippi River and the overcoming of the stone-wall resistance encountered from the Corps of Engineers over three-quarters of a century. The failure to get Congressional approval of the Boeuf Floodway, an essential part of the Jadwin Plan, helped open the way for consideration of cutoffs. But the circumstance that finally turned the tide in favor of cutoffs was the action of President Hoover in bringing into power General Lytle Brown as Chief of Engineers and General Harley B. Ferguson as President of the Mississippi River Commission, two men who had the courage to act independently of tradition. If this change had not been made, what Elam expresses might have happened: "The Flood Control Act of 1928 would have been carried out as written," and the Lower Mississippi Valley "would have been condemned to another great disaster before any other method would have been tried."

And in the meantime, the Chiefs of Engineers and their staff members would have continued, as for a century preceding, to impress upon the Congress the supreme excellence of the Corps. Thus did Chief of Engineers Jadwin when, in opposing reservoirs, cutoffs and the hydraulic laboratory, he said to the Congressional Committees:

> The science of river hydraulics in America, both theoretical and practical, as a whole is more advanced than that of any other nation in the world, and this advance is due almost exclusively to the activities of the Engineer Corps.[1][7]

This is representative of the confirmed habit of the Corps of Engineers through the years, of fabricating history convenient to its purpose. Congress and the public and especially writers, who of necessity got much of their information from the Corps, were not in position to be aware of this habitual deceit, on which the favorable reputation of the Corps is largely built.

notes

1. William E. Elam, *Speeding Floods to the Sea,* The Hobson Book Press, New York, 1946.
2. *Ibid.,* p. 20.
3. Captain A. A. Humphreys and Lieutenant H. L. Abbot, *Report upon the Physics and Hydraulics of the Mississippi River upon the Protection of the Alluvial Region Against Overflow and upon the Deepening of the Mouths,* J. B. Lippincott & Co., Philadelphia, 1861.
4. *Ibid.*
5. *Ibid.*
6. *Ibid.*
7. Elam, *op. cit.,* p. 38.
8. *Ibid.,* pp. 40-41.
9. *Ibid.,* pp. 57-58.
10. *Ibid.,* p. 68.
11. *Ibid.*
12. *Ibid.,* p. 68.
13. *Ibid.,* pp. 91-92.
14. *Ibid.,* p. 93.
15. *Ibid.,* p. 92.
16. *Ibid.,* p. 8.
17. John R. Freeman, Letter to the Chairman and Members of the House Committee on Rivers and Harbors, May 24, 1928, p. 10.

the army engineers' resistance to reservoirs

At the present time, the Corps of Engineers has constructed and operates several hundred—mostly multi-purpose—reservoirs throughout the country with benefits to flood control, navigation, hydroelectric power generation, recreation, wild life conservation, and other purposes. Such projects constitute a large share of the Corps' civilian activities. But all of this has come about since the early thirties when the era of dam and reservoir building began. Prior to that time, the Corps traditionally and vigorously rejected the concept of the use of such reservoirs, particularly when proposed for control of floods on the Lower Mississippi River. This chapter examines the basis for this opposition, its persistence through the years and the dramatic events leading to the reversal of the Corps' position with respect to flood control reservoirs.

My Search for Basis of Corps' Attitude

In October 1927, after the great Mississippi River flood of the preceding spring, the American Society of Civil Engineers conducted a National Symposium on flood control for the Mississippi. As chief engineer of the only large flood control project in America by means of reservoirs, I was asked to present a paper on reservoirs for flood control on the Mississippi. This paper began:

There has been a fifty-year controversy between the proponents of reservoir control and of levee control for Mississippi River floods. The speaker is not attempting to settle that issue. He does not know the aggregate possibilities for reservoir control, and any estimate made without very extensive and thorough-going investigation can be but a guess.

It is a fundamental principle of sound engineering that, when great issues are at stake, no conclusion of large importance should be left to chance. Actual and definite studies of actual cases are necessary. Until they have been carried to a point where, as nearly as is reasonably possible, all major possiblities have been conclusively determined, there is no adequate basis for far-reaching engineering decision.

If, as is contended by the members of the Mississippi River Commission, the case against reservoir control for the Mississippi has been properly established, it is because a conclusion has been reached in accordance with the evidence. The transmission of an authoritative dogma from one generation to another will not suffice. Somewhere along the way that authoritative doctrine must have been established by scientific methods, and those methods and results must be subject to re-examination.

The writer decided that the best contribution he could make to this discussion was to try to discover the exact nature of the evidence which has led the Mississippi River Commission to reject reservoirs. He has read a vast amount of literature on the subject, especially the writings of the Commission and the Army Engineers, and he has constantly watched for references to other and authoritative opinions and reports.[1]

I then presented my findings based on this research. Covering the Symposium, the Engineering *News-Record* reported:

The surprise of the day came in a paper by Arthur E. Morgan . . . in which he severely criticized the Mississippi River Commission for its attitude toward the whole problem, especially for (1) defective estimates of cost, (2)

errors in estimating the amount of work still to be done
in completing the levee system, and (3) complete failure
to obtain data on reservoir possibilities or flood contingencies. Though couched in polite language, the charges
were so specific and so serious that they caused no little
sensation, particularly as the Secretary of War was sitting
in at the meeting when they were made.[2]

Incidentally the topic for my speech had not been of my
own choosing. It was suggested to me by the Secretary of the
American Society of Civil Engineers, probably because of my
association as Chief Engineer for flood control work of the
Miami Conservancy District in Ohio.

In 1913, when I began the studies for the Miami Conservancy District, I had a conviction that I had acquired from
the authoritative sounding statements of the Mississippi River
Commission and the U.S. Corps of Engineers, that reservoirs
were not feasible for flood control. At that time, only two
flood-control dams could be found in the United States, and
these were small and relatively unimportant. The anti-reservoir thesis held strongly by the Army Engineers had been
very generally accepted by most of America's civil engineers,
myself among them.

Though with little expectation that reservoirs could have
any utility, my associates and I on the Miami project
carefully examined the possibility of reservoirs. We made this
study in the process of carrying out a general engineering
policy of *conclusive engineering analysis*, to which I had long
before committed myself. As detailed in an earlier chapter,
the policy was such that, wherever the importance of the
issue justified, I would not reach an engineering conclusion
until I had examined and compared every possible solution of
the problem, no matter how remote the possibility of its
being the best available. Repeatedly I had found that major
shortcomings of large engineering design had resulted not
from errors of technology, but from failure to persist in
searching for possible alternative methods, and comparison of
possible solutions until every possibility had been adequately
appraised. When the evidence from that process forced me to

change my views, to accept reservoirs as a major element in the Miami Valley plan, and to create five of them, no one was more surprised than I.

Even then, my belief that flood-control reservoirs could never be a helpful part of flood control plans for the Mississippi was only slightly shaken. Assuming the accuracy of the authoritative pronouncements of the U.S. Corps of Engineers, I still supposed that reservoir control could be justified only on small streams. In 1927, but before the above-mentioned Symposium, I wrote an article criticizing the Mississippi River Commission but assuming the Commission to be substantially right in opposing reservoirs. I did say:

> Yet it is not safe to dogmatize. . . . A careful study, such as never has been made, might possibly lead to the development of a few large reservoir projects on the larger tributaries of the Mississippi that would play a minor but valuable and economical part in a flood control program.[3]

The period of history to which I have referred essentially began in 1850. At that time, in conformance with an Act of Congress, the Secretary of War directed a distinguished civilian engineer, Charles Ellet, Jr., a man of broad, informed judgment and creative outlook, who had designed some of the important and pioneering engineering works of his day, including some of the most important suspension bridges, to make surveys and reports on the Mississippi and Ohio Rivers for flood prevention and navigation improvement. In his report in 1852, Ellet proposed, among other measures, a series of reservoirs on the tributary headwaters for flood control for the Mississippi valley. This was the first major proposal made in America to control floods by means of reservoirs.

Though many of the benefits Ellet attributed to this plan were dubious or exaggerated, he did realize that "to bring the proof in detail, will require surveys. . . . Until these surveys are ordered, the further discussion of this subject will be premature."[4] Ellet's proposal aroused considerable discussion. Congress was sympathetic to his plans and was ready to appropriate funds for suitable surveys in the Ohio watershed.[5]

The Corps of Engineers, however, did not accept Ellet's proposal for reservoirs and in 1857, W. Milnor Roberts, a highly respected civilian employee of the Corps, made an extensive report rejecting the feasibility of reservoirs for flood control. He appeared before Congress as representing the Corps, and persuaded its members not to vote money for the necessary surveys. As a result, it was decades before suitable surveys were made.[6] His written report was so persuasive that even by the early part of the next century critics of reservoir schemes often referred to Roberts' report.[7]

Humphreys and Abbot Report Strongly Opposes Reservoirs

In the same year that Congress authorized the Ellet report, it also appropriated funds for a topographic and hydrographic survey of the Mississippi Delta to determine plans for flood control and navigation improvements at the mouth of the river. This authorization, although not so intended by Congress, proved to be one of such ominous import that it resulted in holding back effective flood control for the Lower Mississippi Valley for the succeeding three-quarters of a century. This was because the authorization provided for the decade-long studies of Captain A. A. Humphreys and Lieutenant Henry L. Abbot, that culminated in 1861 in publication of the classic "Report Upon the Physics and Hydraulics of the Mississippi River" which set the pattern for flood control for the Corps of Engineers for the next three-quarters of a century. Subsequent events have proven positively that this pattern was grossly in error; but, nevertheless, the Corps followed it blindly for that long period.

In his *Letter of Transmittal* of the report, one of Humphreys' conclusions was the statement: "Thus every important fact connected with the various physical conditions of the river and the laws uniting them being ascertained, the great problem of protection against inundation was solved." Regarding this, Frank E. Smith, for 12 years a member of Congress and member of the Public Works Committee, and a director of the T.V.A. since 1962, comments in his book "The Politics of Conservation":

> Humphreys' conclusion that the problem was solved was dead wrong, as painful and costly experience was to prove in the years ahead. The tragedy of the conclusion was magnified by Humphreys' using his report as an attack on another report submitted ten years earlier by Charles Ellet, Jr. Ellet's period of study had been far shorter and his compilation of data far less impressive, but his conclusion as to the flood problem solution included the building of reservoirs on the tributary headwaters. . . . in addition to levees. This was the eventual solution in contrast to the Humphreys-Abbot idea of levees only, but the Ellet ideas were to be largely ignored by the Corps for more than 75 years.[8]

The treatment of reservoirs for flood control in the Humphreys and Abbot Report is such that no doubt is left that the two authors positively reject the use of such reservoirs. The recommendations in the chapter "Protection Against Floods" include the statement that "It has been demonstrated that no advantage can be derived . . . from . . . constructing reservoirs." However, in the several pages in the Chapter devoted to *"Reservoirs,"* Humphreys and Abbot stated, "The Plan, in theory, is admirable, and has long been a subject of discussion among European engineers." There follows a discussion of proposals by two American engineers, one of whom is Charles Ellet, Jr. for "the application of a system of artificial lakes to our western rivers." These engineers both advocated the use of reservoirs to improve low water flows for navigation, and Ellet "repeatedly recommended the system for restraining the floods of the Mississippi, even in the delta."

With regard to advantages of reservoirs for navigation, Humphreys and Abbot stated, "It seems possible . . . to effect a marked improvement in the low-water navigation even of the Mississippi itself." Then comes a true but curious conclusion in this report which says, "To what extent this system is practicable and what would be its probable cost, can only be decided by careful and extended investigation and survey . . . a subject with which this report has no connection." If such a careful study is needed to find out whether reservoirs are practicable for navigation benefits, does it not follow that the same kind of studies need to be made to determine whether reservoirs are applicable to flood control for the Mississippi River? Did this ever occur to Humphreys and Abbot? Apparently other considerations led them not to apply the same criterion to flood control reservoirs as they did to those for navigation.

Humphreys and Abbot cite from Ellet's 1851 Report that he proposed reservoirs "to protect the whole delta and the borders of every stream in it, primary or tributary, from overflow." They state, "This subject . . . will be carefully examined," and then proceeded to present calculations showing the errors in Ellet's thinking and why his schemes would not work. With regard to this, the authors wrote, "Little consideration is necessary to make it apparent that this system (that is, the one proposed by Ellet) is not applicable to restraining the floods of all rivers." In concluding the *Reservoirs* section of the Report, it stated:

> To guard against misconception . . . the advantages of a reservoir system upon certain western rivers, for certain objects are not questioned. By it, the low-water navigation of important streams flowing into the Ohio--perhaps even of the Mississippi-- may be improved. The data for deciding whether the advantages accruing from such works would be commensurate with the expense of constructing them have not yet been collected. But the idea that the *Mississippi delta may be economically secured against inundation* by such dams has been conclusively proved by the operations of this Survey to be in the highest degree chimerical.[9] [Emphasis added.]

One gets the impression from reading the Humphreys and Abbot discussion of reservoirs for flood control purposes, that this and the absolute rejection of such reservoirs is based largely on what must have been a rather intense professional jealousy on the part of Humphreys and Abbot, for Ellet and anything he might propose. Had it been otherwise, the two Corps officers might have applied the same rule to flood control reservoirs that they said should be applied to those for navigation. Since they did not do so and because their opposition to flood control reservoirs was so strong, Corps members who regarded the Report on the Mississippi as their bible accepted and perpetuated the false doctrine of rejecting reservoirs.

In fairness to Humphreys and Abbot, their conclusions regarding the applicability of flood control reservoirs for the Mississippi did at the time have some basis in fact. High cost was a principal reason for their objections and, obviously, this resulted from the methods of construction in use at that time. The art of large dam construction as we know it today had not been developed. Portland cement had not been invented. Earth moving methods were primitive and slow as compared to modern giant earth movers. The machines necessary for large construction were developed at a later day. All of these developments, subsequent to the time of Humphreys and Abbot, increased the efficiency of construction with consequent lower costs, as viewed in the perspective of cost levels then and now. Under these changed conditions, flood control and other reservoirs have become economically justified. The shame is that Corps officers accepted and applied the findings of Humphreys and Abbot almost blindly for so many long years after their conclusions had been outdated or disproved.

In 1871, another report of the Corps of Engineers on the Ohio River by W. Milnor Roberts repeated the conclusions he had reached in 1857 in opposition to reservoirs.[10] In 1873, his successor, Major William E. Merrill, accepted Roberts' conclusions without further investigation and repeated the findings of his predecessor to prove the impracticability of reservoirs for the Ohio River.[11] In the same year, Merrill and Major G. Weitzel composed a board of the Corps of Engineers which rejected reservoirs for improving the navigability of the Ohio. They based their conclusions on the impossibility of finding suitable sites, the cost, the effect on commercial interests and the danger of accidents. They concluded, "the board are decidedly of the opinion that *the reservoir plan should be unqualifiedly rejected.*"[1][2] [Emphasis added.]

A landmark in the history of consideration of reservoirs for flood control purposes was the report of a special Commission appointed by President Grant in accordance with an Act of Congress in June, 1874 to investigate and report on a plan for reclaiming the alluvial basin of the Mississippi subject to inundation. This commission was composed of three Army officers and two civilian engineers. With its usual skill, the Corps of Engineers made sure that one of the "civilians" was a West Point graduate member of the Corps of Engineers, their very militant defender, P. O. Hebert, former governor of Louisiana. One of the Army officers was H. L. Abbot, co-author of the Humphreys and Abbot report, which made it unlikely that the Commission would differ from the findings of that report. The three others were Major G. K. Warren, Corps of Engineers, Captain W. H. H. Benyaurd, Corps of Engineers, and Jackson E. Sickels, civil engineer.[1][3]

In its report to the Chief of Engineers, General Humphreys, this Commission paid tribute to Humphreys and Abbot's earlier work, saying "The foundation of the report of the Commission rests upon your invaluable surveys and investigations which, begun in 1850 and continued till 1861, are published in the great work, 'The Physics and Hydraulics of the Mississippi River' . . . and upon the further contributions to these subjects contained in your published official reports in 1866 and 1869."[1][4] The Commission added that it had secured some additional data of its own and considered its report "exhaustive."[1][5]

The Commission did report that it "fully recognizes the advantages sometimes to be derived from a judicious use of artificial reservoirs in moderating the destructive floods of rivers. . . ."[1][6]

For the Mississippi, however, they concluded:

In theory this system is attractive; but in practice it promises no relief to the low lands of the Mississippi, simply because there are no available sites for reservoirs sufficiently large to produce the desired effect. . . .[17]

The Commission went further to apply this conclusion to the Red River. In a resolution passed on their eighth day of deliberation, the Commission concluded:

That, in the opinion of this commission, the examination of Red River, made by the secretary (Col. Charles Fauntleroy), has failed to discover any fit location for reservoirs suited to restrain the floods of that river from injuring the alluvial region of Louisiana below its mouth; and, in the opinion of this commission, *no such localities exist.*[18] [Emphasis added.] *

The Commission felt that:

The question of absolute practicability could only be decided by a series of extensive and elaborate surveys, for which neither funds nor time were available, *nor in the opinion of this commission are they needed.* Here, as elsewhere in the valley, this plan, as an efficient means of restraining the floods of the Mississippi, is in every sense of the word, chimerical.[19] [Emphasis added.] **

Members of the Corps of Engineers, taught at West Point not to critically think, but to follow authority, acting as an important commission on the most important mission in its history, followed its training in unquestionably accepting Humphreys' report, which was found during the Hoover revolution to be entirely wrong. These were not just ordinary

---

*In 1959 General E. C. Itschner, Chief of Engineers, in addressing the Red River Valley Association, mentioned thirteen Red River system reservoirs, in operation or in preparation. Concerning these reservoirs, he told members of the Association: "It is most desirable that we continue a high rate of progress, since these dams provide your first and major line of defense against large flood damage."[20]

**This board estimated the total cost of complete protection of the Mississippi River by levees at $46,000,000,[21] possibly 5% of the cost incurred by the Corps to date for that purpose.

Engineer Corps members, but leaders, placed in the most important commission of the Corps. Yet all of their findings were found by the critical studies of the Hoover revolution to be exactly wrong. Those findings, contrary to Corps tradition, proved so strong that the Corps lived by them ever after.

In the more than fifty years of opposition of the U.S. Corps of Engineers to the use of reservoirs for flood control there are repeated references to "adequate studies" and "conclusive research" to support that position. When we search for these conclusive studies, so pontifically referred to by the Corps, we find that they never were made. The two major bulwarks of the Corps of Engineers' position were the voluminous report of Humphreys and Abbot of 1861, in which reservoirs were dismissed with scarcely the semblance of adequate research, and the report of the special U. S. Corps of Engineers board of 1874, which, after a week or two of deliberation for the settlement of the entire Mississippi River problem, dismissed reservoirs with scarcely a hint of competent engineering inquiry. Repeated references to these and similar studies through the years (and we must include the studies by General Chittenden while he was in the Corps of Engineers as wholly inadequate) had created a veil of conclusive authority which it was impious for the civilian engineer to violate with penetrating questions. And yet practically every major review of the situation by *civilian* engineers referred to this critical lack of definitive study and called for adequate investigation.

Throughout all of these reports emanating from the Corps, the lack of real fundamental data was an outstanding aspect of studies for flood control for the Mississippi Valley and for the possible use of reservoirs elsewhere. Only superficial surveys and investigations constituted the basis for the Corps' opposition to a reservoir system for flood control. In conjunction with one outdated study from France, these made up the bulk of the Army Engineers' studies. It is clear that the Humphreys and Abbot report, though partly justified by the conditions existing when it was written, was not based on thorough investigation. It was almost unquestioned among Army Engineers, and largely accepted on their authority by civilian engineers, that reservoirs were an inefficient method for attaining flood control.

Two other major engineering aspects of the controversy greatly clouded the issue. In the first place, the question was often dealt with as an issue of levees versus reservoirs, as though they were mutually exclusive. Almost certainly the soundest plan of flood control would involve multiple methods. However, the advocates of "levees only"—the Corps' inflexible policy—held sway, and reservoirs were not carefully studied.

The second unfortunate factor was that there were no important cases for comparison until the completion of the Miami Conservancy District works about 1920. It often was contended by the Engineer Corps that, while theoretically preferable, reservoirs were much more expensive than levees. But such a hypothesis had little or no basis in fact, for neither the cost for levees nor the cost for reservoirs was ever adequately determined. The estimates of the Mississippi River Commission, dominated by the Corps, usually were woefully inadequate as to costs of levees, magnitude of floods, and degree of protection provided.

The Corps had an eloquent advocate of their anti-reservoir position in Captain (later General and Chief of Engineers) Hiram M. Chittenden. In later years, I came to know General Chittenden intimately. I have known few engineers for whom I have had greater personal regard. Like such engineer officers as Raynolds and Barnard before him, he had a conscientious dedication to the truth and to his profession which came before his loyalty to the Corps of Engineers. Later I shall refer to him more extensively.

In 1898 Captain Chittenden was assigned to examine reservoir sites for irrigation in Wyoming and Colorado. In carrying out his assignment he went beyond the original order and had a civilian assistant compile a monograph on the effects of reservoirs on Mississippi floods. Unfortunately this Corps of Engineers survey, like its predecessors and successors involved chiefly the compilation of existing data on the subject and certainly was not the thorough study that was needed, but never attempted.

Chittenden's engineering writing showed a more courteous, open approach than that of most advocates of both sides of this question. In this 1898 study he referred to proposed European reservoirs which had never been built, due to their cost From these he concluded that "they disclose the true obstacle to the use of reservoirs for the sole purpose of flood prevention. It is the cost, not the physical difficulties, which stands in the way."[2 2] He went on:

Floods are only occasional calamities at worst. Probably on the majority of streams destructive floods do not occur, on the average, oftener than once in five years. Every reservoir built for the purpose of flood protection alone would mean the dedication of so much land to a condition of permanent overflow in order that three or four times as much might be redeemed from occasional overflow. One acre permanently inundated to rescue three or four acres from inundation of a few weeks once in three or four years, and this at a great cost, could not be considered as wise proceeding, no matter how practicable it might be from engineering considerations alone.[2 3]

In fact, as the Miami Conservancy District reservoir system was later to show, he was in error. In more than forty years of operation, not one per cent of the crops in the Miami Conservancy reservoirs has been lost. The thin deposit of top soil and humus during winter and spring floods adds to the soil fertility and increases the yield.

Captain Chittenden was wrong when he concluded that the only practical uses of reservoirs could be in great multi-purpose systems. Again he was wrong when he concluded that, with the exception of the watershed of the Missouri River, "this large control is hardly one of the possibilities of the future "[2 4] Our great multi-purpose systems, such as the TVA, demonstrate the error of this conclusion.

Captain Chittenden's report conceded many of the possibilities of reservoirs not recognized seriously before, and he concentrated on cost as the chief prohibitive factor. His report became a major weapon in the artillery arrayed against reservoir proponents. Unfortunately, it, like its predecessors, was based on the limited data available and on inadequate thinking on principles of reservoir operations, and not on thorough, first-hand research.

The issue of reservoirs was not prominent again until the conservation crusades of Theodore Roosevelt, 1900-1910, brought it to the fore. The conservationists on this issue were represented by M. O. Leighton, Chief Hydrographer of the U.S. Geological Survey. In his research on the question, Leighton was one of the first to recognize the superficial nature of the criticisms of reservoirs.[25]

Indeed, he felt it necessary to go back to the 1857 findings of W. Milnor Roberts to find specific arguments against reservoirs to attack.

Captain William D. Connor of the Corps of Engineers wrote an extensive reply to Leighton. He referred to the usual old studies of the reservoir question (in this case as it applied to navigation improvements) concluding, "This method of improvement of the Ohio River was for good and sufficient reasons decided against in the early '70's. . . ."[26]

The expressions of public opposition to reservoirs by the Corps continued unabated for several years. In 1909, the elderly H. L. Abbot, Humphreys' former associate, wrote with his usual aggressive finality that the holding of flood waters in reservoirs for release later in the interests of navigation was a "plan often proposed by those not conversant with the technical difficulties involved."[27]

He went on to say that reservoirs as flood regulators "may even tend to aggravate natural conditions on the main river, by promoting a coincidence in the contributions of the great tributaries which is the primary cause of destructive floods."[28]

In this he disclosed a lack of elementary understanding of the fundamental principles of reservoir operation.

In 1909 Major W. W. Harts, Corps of Engineers, wrote a critique of reservoirs used for navigation improvement. His article was a mass of standard Corps cliches. The reservoir system was "seductive at first glance" but presented "insurmountable difficulties."[29]

He discounted multi-purpose plans as being "like the 'combination tool,' the joy of the inventor but the despair of the user." He said that the plan had not "received any favorable comment from experienced engineers. . . . The experience of the past has shown that the theory is impracticable and unsuccessful."[30] Harts concluded with a summary of Corps thinking to that time. He said:

> The use of reservoirs as an exclusive means of improving the navigability of rivers is subject to the following criticisms:
> 1. They have been found inefficient and unsuccessful wherever used.
> 2. Unsafe and attended with great risk, owing to the enormous dams required and quantities of water impounded.
> 3. Of doubtful legality, and a probable source of much litigation, owing to infringement of riparian rights.
> 4. Enormously expensive compared with other methods.
> 5. Slow in construction to a useful stage.
> 6. Soon filled with sediment in many localities.
> 7. Not advocated by river engineers.
> 8. In operation, if they should be constructed, they would present a problem too stupendous and complex for successful operation.[31]

One needs only to look at today's extensive and massive reservoir systems to evaluate the significance of most of these contentions. While his use of the word "exclusive" allows him to argue an extreme case, there is not the least suggestion that reservoirs might be used effectively along with other factors of control as was done a few years later in the Miami Conservancy District, where reservoirs, channel improvement and levees combine to produce an almost ideal solution, or of the TVA reservoirs, which serve flood control, power development and navigation.

In a 1908 meeting of the American Society of Civil Engineers, Lieutenant Colonel Chittenden again joined the fray. As the featured speaker of the occasion, in another thorough review of *existing data* on reservoirs, Colonel Chittenden had found little to add to his paper of ten years before, and quoted from it liberally. He referred to an obsolete French study which he had used in that earlier study as substantiating his case against reservoirs. He again emphasized his conviction that the proposal was too costly for flood control alone and said he doubted the safety of multiple-purpose schemes. He gave an elaborate but not penetrating analysis of Leighton's data.

Chittenden had fallen prey to the usual Corps fallacies once more. His work still was not based on thorough first-hand investigation by anyone. Yet, he stated that the possibility of reservoir flood control for the Ohio River had "often been investigated."[3 2] He concluded that, "The more closely this reservoir proposition is scrutinized, as a scheme for flood prevention, the more impracticable it appears."

What was his alternative? "Take $40,000,000 and reinforce the entire levee system of the Mississippi. That will make it impregnable—as safe as any of the proposed reservoir schemes."[3 3] The flood of nineteen years later (1927) completely discredited this unqualified assertion.

In the discussion that followed Colonel Chittenden's presentation, his courteous, questioning attitude was immediately offset by the comments of the previously mentioned Major Harts. Below are listed some of Harts' comments on reservoirs:

> Its weak points are easily exposed, and its fallacies may be made plain with a little study.[3 4]

> All reservoirs must necessarily be located near the headwaters of the stream.[3 5]

> The effort to combine in one plan the improvement of depths in navigable rivers, the diminution of flood waves to a safe point and the utilization of the stored water for electrical power can never be satisfactory to any single

interest.[36] (This combination has now been proven satisfactory in the TVA and on the Missouri and Columbia Rivers.)

Interestingly enough, R. E. McMath who, in 1874, as a civilian employee of the Corps, had written an attack on Eads jetties for the Chief of Engineers, now stated in this discussion that, while he was employed by the Mississippi River Commission to study reservoirs in 1880-83, he had become convinced of their utility. He resigned from this study at the time, he said, because the "levees only" theory took predominance, and he saw that reservoirs "didn't have a chance with the Corps of Engineers."[37] Chittenden ended the discussion diplomatically, saying that the main purpose of his presentation was to try to blunt visionary proposals and uncertain schemes.[38]

As usual, there was more to this debate than a simple scientific disagreement. Herbert Quick, a participant in that day's conservation crusade, contended that the Corps felt itself in danger of losing its civil works to civilian conservationists. President Theodore Roosevelt envisioned such a unified control of our conservation works, and the Corps had no desire to lose its long-held control of water resources. Hence it offered an almost instinctive opposition to any plan favored by conservationists.[39] Unfortunately, this debate was inextricably tied up with inter-departmental rivalry between the Corps and civilian conservationists, in particular Mr. Leighton of the Geological Survey. Colonel Chittenden, referring to Leighton's reservoir plan, noted that it "is understood to bear the approval of both the Interior and Agricultural Departments."[40] The long time fear of the Corps that these two departments might intrude on their domain is well known.

The Debate Continues

In 1910, an Engineer Officer pointed out that the idea of reservoirs for flood control had been rejected already, in 1866, and painted a picture of the consequences of reservoirs:

At that time the idea was shown to be impracticable, but it has recently been resurrected. . . . In its revised form this project has been made a more attractive pill for the country to swallow. . . . In this scheme large districts are flooded, people are driven from their homes, towns and smiling valleys are ruthlessly turned into reservoir sites; highways and railways are covered with the penned-up waters, farms are turned into forests. . . .[41]

Captain F. W. Alstaetter of the Corps of Engineers viewed the issues as a battle royal. He warned:

If I speak thus strongly against the reservoir project, I do it advisedly, because I understand its friends are girding their loins for a new assault on Congress at the next session; and should they force doubt into the minds of some members of the River and Harbor Committee, we might find the improvement delayed for years while investigations were being made, because Congress is not a body to launch into any large project until they are sure of what they are doing.[42]

The country was to be rescued from "doubt" and "investigations," the very process which might have resulted in thorough, objective study of the reservoir question. As it was the country was saved such inquiry. The Corps went resolutely ahead, without the delay of research. Years later, it reversed itself but only after an enormously disastrous flood, following which President Hoover enforced radical revolution in the operation of the Corps.

In 1912 and 1913 two significant speeches against reservoirs were made by Colonel C. McD. Townsend, Corps of Engineers and President of the Mississippi River Commission. Since public expressions of policy by Corps members must be approved by the Office of the Chief of Engineers, these speeches obviously reflected the Corps' position.

Forty years earlier, in Northern Minnesota, near the source of the Mississippi, the Government, through the Corps of Engineers and at public expense, for the benefit of private timber interests, at two or three locations built rather primitive timber-crib dams such as the lumbermen commonly built for the same purpose.

In disapproving reservoirs for flood control the Corps would refer often to those dams as the largest reservoir system in the world. For half a century almost the only use of the Mississippi River above Minneapolis and St. Paul was for floating logs from the vast northern woods to the sawmills down river at Minneapolis and other down-river locations. Along a hundred miles of the river, and down to within sixty miles of Minneapolis, at low water one could wade across the Mississippi. Vast numbers of logs were stranded on the bottom and margins of the river, requiring extensive construction along the river by timber interests to reduce such loss. An increase of only two feet in the stage of the river might make the difference between poor and fair log-driving conditions.

As a boy I lived at St. Cloud, about a hundred and fifty miles below these timber cribs. Their operations made so little difference in the depth of the river there that the only way a casual observer could easily tell whether the sluices were open was to observe whether the water was deep enough for large logs to float. In my early working years, while cruising timber, I spent more than a month in a camp at the site of the largest of these timber cribs.

Because of the vast area of swamp, flat land and lakes covered, these timber cribs caused a larger reservoir, and stored more water than any other reservoir system in existence, except possibly for similar large primitive log structures and storage areas in similar swamp and flat lands in uninhabited areas of Northern Russia. The only "engineering" skill required in building these timber cribs was in the timber crib building skill of an experienced lumberman. In the widespread lumbering operations of the time, many miles of timber cribs and barriers were built by the employees of lumber companies.

It was this crude, frontier structure, helpful up to seventy-five years ago for floating logs, which for more than half a century went down in Corps of Engineers tradition as the world's largest reservoir system, and enabled the Corps to speak with seeming authority on the technique of designing, building and operating flood control and navigation reservoirs. When in engineering history has such a crude, backwood development been so used to support the professional reputation of a large and powerful organization? This expression by one of the Corps' major members is a typical example of habitual unashamed misrepresentation by major members of the Corps.

The Corps' descriptions of the working of these reservoirs ran far beyond reality. For instance, Colonel Townsend, in some of the speeches referred to, informed his audiences that:

> ... on the Upper Mississippi the Corps of Engineers has constructed the largest system of reservoirs for regulating rivers that has been built in any country.... These reservoirs have been most successful, not only for increasing the low-water discharge above St. Paul, the purpose for which they were constructed, but also for reducing floods in that portion of the river.
>
> There is therefore, nothing novel to the river engineer in the proposition to control rivers by reservoirs. We have not only studied its advantages, but we know its limitations.[43]

In early 1913, Colonel Townsend made another speech in which he showed a fundamental misconception commonly maintained by Corps officers, as to how a reservoir system would operate. Said Townsend: "To control the flow of every stream in the Mississippi Valley by reservoirs is a pretty large job ... but that is what the control of the Mississippi during floods by reservoirs signified."[44] Of course this was a fallacy.

Townsend offered the Corps' usual alternative to new methods, saying, "While the use of forests or reservoirs as a means of flood control is still in an experimental stage all over the world, the employment of levees for this purpose has been tested for centuries."[45]

Thus was the country to rely on "levees only" and be saved from experimentation. Townsend concluded:

While the control of the lower Mississippi by reservoirs is impracticable, there are numerous smaller streams where they can be used with excellent results.

It is questionable, however, whether such reservoirs should be built with the control of our rivers the first object of consideration.[46]

It is interesting that he should make this unexpected remark just about the time of the initiation of Miami River flood control works, after the great flood of 1913. The length to which a leading member of the U.S. Corps of Engineers and president of the Mississippi River Commission would go to impress his audience is illustrated from Townsend's address before the National Drainage Congress, as reported in the *Engineering Record:*

Reservoirs.

To have retained the Mississippi flood of 1912 within its banks would have required a reservoir in the vicinity of Cairo, Ill., having an area of 7000 square miles, slightly less than that of the State of New Jersey, and a depth of about 15 feet assuming that it would be empty when the river attained a bank-full stage. If the site of such a reservoir was a plane surface the quantity of material to be excavated in its construction would be over 100,000,000,000 cu. yds. and its estimated cost from 50 to 100 thousand million dollars.[47]

Miami Valley Decides on Reservoirs

On March 20, 1913, floodwaters of the Miami, Stillwater and Mad Rivers swept through Dayton and the entire Miami Valley, killing more than 300 persons and doing more than $100,000,000 damage. There arose immediately a general cry for Federal help, and President Woodrow Wilson appointed a board of Army Engineers to investigate the problem. This board made a preliminary report seven months later, and wisely reported that any conclusions that it reached would only be tentative due to the lack of data and time for concentrated study.[48]

The Board did discuss briefly the possibility of reservoirs and did not find them promising.

In transmitting this preliminary report to the Secretary of War, the Chief of Engineers commented:

> It is the present opinion of this office that very little expenditure of money on reservoirs in the Ohio Valley will be found to be justified in the interest of flood prevention alone. On the other hand, it is believed that, as recommended by the board, further investigation should be made at least of the more favorable sites if for no other reasons than to make sure that all plans which have been advanced have received thorough consideration.[49]

The citizens of the Miami Valley could ill afford to wait for Federal action. They formed a Flood Prevention Committee, supported by a voluntary fund to start plans for flood control. In early May, 1913, the Morgan Engineering Company* was engaged to prepare such plans. The known disapproval of reservoirs by the Corps of Engineers was a formidable hurdle, but did not prevent thorough examination of all methods of flood relief.

Many detailed studies were made in order to find the one that would do the thorough job demanded by the project. As months passed with the flood control plans still incomplete, citizens in the area grew understandably impatient for action. One "Letter to the Editor" in a local paper read:

> Things are going painfully slow . . . We have no objection to 60 young fellows dressed like cowboys going out every morning with a great parade . . . collecting data. Do some cleaning out, and let boys go on "collecting data" if that is any source of amusement to them.[50]

It was considered essential to withstand such pressure, in favor of a thoroughly examined approach to the plan that would be most satisfactory.

When we undertook the study of the Miami Valley flood situation, we were far from convinced of the feasibility of the use of dams for flood control. We included a careful study of

---

*The author was President of the Morgan Engineering Company when these studies were being made, and later personally Chief Engineer of the Miami Conservancy District.

that possibility because of long time commitment to the principle of conclusive engineering analysis. By that process we arrived at the use of dams as the major feature of the overall plan for the protection of the nine cities in the Miami Valley. Interestingly, of the five reservoir sites proposed and used, not one had been discovered by the Corps of Engineers board which had preceded us at the direction of President Wilson.

Desiring to disclose any weakness in so important and unconventional a program, we assembled two boards of consulting engineers, first one of three hydraulic engineers, and then a second board of nine. So far as we knew, only one of these, Morris Knowles of Pittsburgh, had taken interest in reservoirs as a feasible means for flood control. Four of these consultants, three of them ex-Chiefs of Engineers Bixby, Ernst and Chittenden, and one ex-President of the Mississippi River Commission, Ockerson, had long opposed reservoirs. Some of the others were definitely skeptical. One of the ex-Chiefs of Engineers, General Bixby, while he testified strongly in favor of the plan, was not able to be present to sign the report. Aware of their previous opposition, but confident in the validity of our plans, we wanted to subject the plans to review by these principal opponents of reservoirs since their approval would lend added weight for the acceptance of the plans.

We were particularly pleased to secure Chittenden, ex-Chief of Engineers, as a member of the consulting board. He was considered the foremost opponent of reservoirs for flood control by the Corps of Engineers, and his writings were perhaps the chief authority of the Corps on the subject. Since the Miami River Consulting Board's decision approving flood control reservoirs seemed to negate his chief contribution to engineering literature, Chittenden gave a very thorough personal examination to the plans and spent months as a special consultant in that examination. From six to twelve of the engineering staff of the project commonly were employed in supplying and organizing data, and in making calculations for him. He spent a considerable part of each day in interviews with men in charge of different parts of the planning.[51] Chittenden was a very straight-minded man, yet one wonders whether if he was still a member of the Corps he could have broken loose from Corps discipline, to make such an independent report, at variance with the half century discipline of the Corps. He was, however, a tough-minded man. When President Theodore Roosevelt commanded his top Corps officials to ride on horseback fifty or a hundred miles in a day to prove their fitness, he made the ride, though it crippled him for life. He was that kind of a man.

When he had fully satisfied himself as to the soundness of the plan, he endorsed it fully and gave it his active support. His last professional effort before he died was a contribution to the *Transactions* of the American Society of Civil Engineers, pleading for an open mind on the subject of reservoirs.[52]

The consulting board, after due consideration and review of the plans for the Miami Conservancy District, made a unanimous report giving approval to the plans and stating that "channel enlargement alone is impracticable" and that "detention basins, supplemented by limited channel improvement, do offer a satisfactory solution of the problem."

The *Engineering Record* in an editorial on March 28, 1914, entitled "Reservoirs on the Ascendant," commented on the Miami plans and some similar studies done earlier by the Pittsburgh Flood Commission. Said the *Record*:

> It is a safe statement that until the Pittsburgh and the Dayton conditions were studied, American engineers, with few exceptions, were prejudiced against reservoirs and gave them but scanty consideration. This was due, no doubt to the attitude of the majority of the Army Engineers.[53]

In April of 1914, H.A. Petterson, a civil engineer of San Francisco, had a series of long, thorough articles in the *Engineering Record* studying various methods of flood control. In these, he anticipated by several years my own thinking on the question of reservoirs as a generally applicable method for handling floodwaters. At the time I still shared the Army Engineers' skepticism about any widespread value in the reservoir system as a factor in flood control for larger river systems. Petterson concluded:

A rather thorough study of flood literature has convinced the writer that there has been too much of a partisan spirit and too little of a real scientific spirit displayed by advocates of particular systems of flood control.[54]

He recognized that:

A study of any river system, for the purpose of devising the most feasible means of preventing floods, or inundation therefrom, will be incomplete unless the possibilities of all the systems are taken into consideration. A combination of two or more systems may often prove the most feasible and productive of the greatest benefits.[55]

Concerning the "authoritative" report of the 1874 special Presidential Commission dominated by the Corps of Engineers, Petterson had this to say:

It has often been stated that this commission had thoroughly investigated the feasibility of reservoir construction for reducing flood heights on the lower Mississippi. Its reports bear no evidence of any exhaustive investigation whatever except for a lake near Shreveport. Reservoirs were rejected because this commission believed no adequate sites for reservoirs existed.[56]

He concludes:

The writer does not pretend to state that reservoir control is practicable for the Mississippi. He can state with positive assurance, however, that no one else, not even the members of the Mississippi River Commission, can disprove the practicability of reservoirs, and furnish convincing proof. The data to prove or disprove the case are not available, because the necessary engineering surveys of various kinds have not been made. There never has been a thorough investigation of the subject. All previous decisions of engineering boards have been based on opinions.[57]

Corps Opposition Weakens

On the Miami Conservancy District Consulting Board, the concurrence of the three former Chiefs of Engineers and an ex-President of the Mississippi River Commission with all the other members of the large board, in approving of the plans involving principally flood control reservoirs, was a complete reversal of their former opposition to such reservoirs. This action may have shaken the sure conviction of the Corps on the matter of reservoirs. After the successful realization of the Miami Conservancy District plans, opposition to reservoirs within the Corps of Engineers with regard to reservoirs began to shift.

That tendency of Engineer Corps opinion toward a change of position is reflected in a 1914 paper on flood prevention by Major J. C. Oakes. He commented: "There are without doubt many localities that may be protected by a reservoir or reservoirs."[58] He mentioned Columbus, Ohio; Dayton, Ohio; and Pittsburgh, Pennsylvania as examples. Major Oakes still rejected their possible use on larger rivers, such as the Mississippi and the Ohio, and stated definitely that multipurpose reservoirs are not feasible.[59] He conceded the necessity for more information, stating that, on the basis of a year's experience with a board looking into the subject, "it is remarkable to find how little information there is upon which to base authoritative computations."[60] However, he still favored levees as being tried and true.[61] This position was quite generally that of the Corps at that time.

Another factor that emerged with the success of the Miami Conservancy District probably had an influence in changing the attitude of the Corps toward flood control reservoirs. Up to and including 1916, the duties of the Corps of Engineers were still largely those concerned with rivers and harbors. The Corps must have noted the attention attracted by the Miami Conservancy District, where nine cities were preparing to carry through a unified program of flood control, the first of its kind in America, and to pay for the work themselves. The Corps may have begun to ask questions. What if this attitude of self-help should spread? If an independent Miami Conservancy District should be repeated elsewhere, it might start a trend. In its whole career the Corps of Engineers had almost entirely been a bearer of free gifts. It improved harbors at the cost of the national government. It improved river navigation entirely at the expense of the federal government so that river traffic could compete with the railroads, which had to pay their own costs. The farm lands along the Mississippi were being protected from flood, and the great lumber companies and planters along the river were having vast wealth added to their property at government expense. What if Congress should take notice and require the interests directly benefited to share in the cost? The status of the Corps as the bearer of free gifts, a chief source of its power and of the "pork barrel," would be endangered.

A more favorable attitude toward reservoirs began to emerge, but the West Point mind moves slowly, and a half century of docile, uncritical acceptance of Humphreys and Abbott and of the Commission of 1873, was not quickly overcome. Then there was the Constitution of the United States.

Section 8 of the Constitution provides that:
   The Congress shall have power. . . . To regulate commerce with foreign nations, and among the several states and with the Indian tribes.

Especially before the coming of railroads, some commerce was carried on rivers, and it came to be held that, in the interest of commerce, the national government could properly improve "navigable rivers." For more than a century this function had been strictly defined, though it came to be recognized that in some cases flood control benefits would incidentally follow. In time the "incidental" of flood control came to weigh more than the recognized function of navigation.

After this anomalous course had been followed for many years, on March 1, 1917, Congress passed the first flood control act. This recognized flood control as a proper function of the Federal Government. Since this action never was effectively challenged, action in accord with it constituted an unconventional amendment to the Federal Constitution. The range of activity under that general change has greatly increased through the years.

That act of Congress extended the jurisdiction of the Mississippi River Commission to all the water courses connected with the Mississippi River, to the extent necessary to keep flood waters out of the upper delta basin. In approving flood control surveys for the Sacramento River in California, the Government extended the federal flood control activities out of the Mississippi watershed for the first time. The Rivers and Harbors Act of 1917 authorized the surveys of rivers for flood control purposes and required the Corps to give consideration to all related water uses.[62]

Fiske Envisions Multi-purpose Reservoirs

By 1924, Major Harold C. Fiske was making a fairly extensive study for the Corps of the reservoir possibilities of the Tennessee River system. In reply to a request by Senator Joseph Ransdell for information on the subject of reservoirs, Fiske gave his views. While necessarily, as a member of the Corps of Engineers, adhering to the "levees only" doctrine of the Corps, he did have a more favorable attitude toward the eventual combination of power development and flood control from the same dam, though he added, "Optimistic as I am, however, I cannot conceive that even under the most unexpectedly favorable conditions such a result would in fact be attained during the lifetime of any person now living."[63]

The Engineer Corps, though they did approve his letter for transmission, twitted Colonel Fiske for this heresy. Said General H. Taylor, Assistant Chief of Engineers, "However, there was one very important consideration in the use of reservoirs which is not referred to in your letter, or at least not sufficiently emphasized, and that is the fact that the use of reservoirs for flood control purposes and for power purposes are *diametrically opposed* to each other as you will

readily see if you will give the matter a little consideration."[6][4] (Emphasis added.) He reinforced his viewpoint by
saying:

> If you could be in this office for a short time and see a
> few of the complaints that come in concerning the
> operation of the reservoirs on the Mississippi, or the
> control of Lake Winnebago at the headwaters of the Fox,
> you would realize that flood control, power develop-
> ment, navigation and land reclamation are four entirely
> separate subjects, but with all of which reservoirs are
> intimately connected.[6][5]

In reply, Fiske gave a long, well-reasoned exposition of his
optimism. His vision of a multi-purpose reservoir development in the Tennessee basin in many ways forecast the
eventual developments in T.V.A. He was ahead of the
thinking of the rest of the Engineer Corps.

This exchange illustrates one of the major defects in the
Corps' method of developing flood control plans. The fact
that he had to clear his letter to Senator Ransdell with the
Chief of Engineers' office before mailing it indicated that
policy was being determined by administrative discipline
rather than by scientific analysis. Patronage was determined
by the administrative head of the Corps. How much Fiske
toned down his actual convictions in regard to reservoirs to
suit the convictions of his Department cannot be known. The
late E. W. Lane, Honorary Member of the American Society
of Civil Engineers, all of whose early work was as a member
of my staff, was dismayed at what he observed while working
for five years for the Corps on the Mississippi. He later (in
1929) expressed to me his opinion that, if any Army
Engineer should approve reservoirs as part of a flood-control
project, that person would at once be demoted, and his
career as an Army Engineer would be at an end. The earlier
experiences of Colonel Raynolds and Colonel Barnard,
discussed in "The Mississippi Jetties" chapter of this book, in
trying to introduce engineering progress in other areas
independently of the opinion of the Corps of Engineers,

would tend to substantiate this opinion. General Chittenden was retired at the time that he approved reservoirs for flood control and could then be independent in his engineering conclusions, while acting as a consultant on the Miami Conservancy District.

The viewpoint of the Department was again expressed strongly by Colonel Charles L. Potter, President of the Mississippi River Commission, who, in 1925, in an article giving the definitive defense of the "levees only" theory wrote:

> If the [Mississippi River] commission had unlimited funds and if it were economically justified in destroying large areas of valuable farming lands, the flood problem could be solved by reservoirs, but the solution would be thoroughly unreasonable from either standpoint.[6 6]

He repeated references to an extremely primitive and inapplicable case in writing:

> An illustration of the futility of trying to affect floods by isolated reservoirs may be had from the system of reservoirs which the government has built at the head-waters of the Mississippi.[6 7]

Great 1927 Flood Shatters "Levees Only" Doctrine

But the Corps was not yet ready to accept reservoirs as of more than theoretical, but not practical, interest. Assurances continued to be given that the protection of the Mississippi delta from floods by means of "levees only" was "substantially complete." The Annual Reports of the Chiefs of Engineers were the considered and authoritative pronouncements of the Corps. By the early 1920's these Annual Reports conveyed the welcome information that dependable protection was being approached. They stated that the Mississippi Valley was now *safe from any but the most extreme floods.* (Emphasis added.)

That qualification of *"the most extreme floods"* is important to note. In three successive Annual reports of the Chief of Engineers, beginning in the Annual Report of 1924, even that qualification was removed. The Congress and the people of the United States were authoritatively and unqualifiedly assured that the lower Mississippi Valley was now safe from serious flooding.

Then came the great flood of 1927, which broke through the levees in many places, flooded many millions of acres of fertile land, inundated thousands of homes to the very eaves, took numerous lives, caused widespread destruction, and resulted in many millions of dollars of loss—the greatest flood disaster in the nation's history. The fifty-year-old sacred "levees only" doctrine had been proven false. The Corps of Engineers by the circumstance of this great flood, had to take a new look at the flood problem.*

* The following are excerpts from "The Development of the Federal Program of Flood Control on the Mississippi River," by Arthur DeWitt Frank, Ph.D., Columbia University Press, New York, 1930, pages 192-193, concerning The Mississippi Flood of April, 1927.

". . . more than 700,000 people were driven from their homes and had to be assembled in refugee camps or in places where they could be cared for by the Red Cross and other agencies. How well the work was done is shown by the fact that 330,000 people were actually rescued from levee tops, trees, house tops, and other points of temporary safety and that more than 607,000 were carried to Red Cross refugee camps. The actual loss in life will never be known because of the large area inundated and the transient nature of much of the Negro population of the delta. After the waters receded many human bodies were found in some sections. However, the official reports show a total loss of life of less than 250. . . .

. . . in the words of Secretary Hoover, "This flood has been the greatest disaster of peace times in our history."

The U.S. Weather Bureau estimated the direct property loss at $363,533,154.00. . . . The terrible toll fell on . . .people in all walks of life . . . But of all classes the owners of land suffered most in property damages and the Negro tenant farmers most in loss of lives. The Negroes more frequently than the whites lost all the property they had, but they owned practically nothing in most cases except very meager household furnishings. The fare in the refugee camps and the supplies furnished by the Red Cross as they returned home seemed to satisfy most of them."

Would the shock of a vast, disastrous flood stir the Corps to a really critical and adequate study of the entire problem, or was there something in the West Point training which was fatal to the attitude of critical, adequate inquiry? Would reservoirs now be recognized as a vital element in an overall plan for Mississippi River Flood control? The answer is clear, as in the case of the pretended investigation of reservoirs later in this chapter.

Soon after the 1927 flood the Chief of Engineers, General Edgar Jadwin, did go through the motions of undertaking to determine the feasibility of reservoirs for Mississippi River Flood control but that formality only emphasized the farce of pretended research. He set up a Board of officers of the Corps of Engineers to make such a study, and undertook the appearance of providing them with the essential data. Late in 1927, at the time of the Symposium on Mississippi River Flood Control arranged by the American Society of Civil Engineers the report of this Board was completed but not yet published. The Chairman of the research board reported the finding to the Symposium, and the full report was available in time to be referred to by those who read and later commented on papers at the Symposium. The report was presented as an authoritative finding to be a basis of longtime public policy on the most important subject in the history of the Corps. The finding was definite. The conclusion was that reservoirs were not feasible for Mississippi River flood control. In my paper, published by the ASCE following the Symposium, I criticized that report as inadequate in its thinking and in its data. At that time, I had nothing to go on but the report of the Corps of Engineers Board itself, and the statements of its chairman. But today, more than thirty years later, the Government Archives in Washington, D.C., have on file the correspondence of the office of the Chief of Engineers at that time, and we can get a first hand look at just how the evidence for this Board of inquiry was assembled. Even with my critical opinion of the Corps in 1927 I was not aware of the sheer bungling inadequacy of what was done and was reported as conclusive evidence.

Reservoirs Study Extremely Hasty and Wholly Inadequate

The Archives records show that on May 21, 1927, shortly after the 1927 flood had subsided, the Chief of Engineers sent orders to all District Engineers in the Corps' Central Division (excepting one) to study reservoir possibilities for the purpose of ameliorating or reducing floods in the Mississippi Valley. "Time is an important element," read these orders, "and no field work, topographic or hydrographic, will be undertaken." Only existing data was to be used in these studies. Cost estimates were called for, these to be based on "such information as is readily available."[68]

The response was as might be expected. One District Engineer reported that "Unless some field data can be secured, the results to be submitted will be little better than guesses." He asked for money to conduct more thorough investigation, and requested some maps. Only the request for maps was approved.[69]

Another District Engineer wrote: "An effort will be made to secure whatever data is available from State and private sources but the outlook is not encouraging." Still, this officer wrote that he estimated he could get his report in by August 1st only two months hence.[70] Another engineer wrote that he felt it would take him four months to complete the work. His letter was forwarded by the Division Engineer with the comment that, "This would appear to be too late for carrying out the intentions of the Chief of Engineers, as I understand them."[71]

The above quotations are typical of letters received from engineers responsible for assembling the data. On June 16th, supplemental instructions went out from the Chief of Engineers' office. These read, in part:

> While the Chief of Engineers calls for a study that will include "all possible reservoirs" it is to be understood that if time available does not permit a literal compliance with these instructions, preference should be given to those reservoirs that give the greatest promise from an economic standpoint.[72]

In a later paragraph he added, "What is desired is as complete a study of the subject as may be practicable in the time available."[73] The orders of June 16th called for submission of reports by July 15th. From May 21 to July 15 to assemble the data (and study reservoir possibilities) for this vast project!

When one District Engineer said he could not get his report in until August 15th, he was advised, "Work upon these studies must be expedited and outline maps, costs and graphs of reservoirs and reservoir hydrographs must be submitted so as to reach this office not later than August 5. The personnel of your office should be expanded, if necessary, to meet this requirement "[74]

With all this haste, did the Corps hope to do a thorough study of reservoir possibilities? A letter of Chief of Engineers Jadwin to Colonel Potter, President of the Mississippi River Commission would so indicate even though Jadwin must have known that this was impossible. Jadwin wrote:

> The Department not only must be in a position to submit complete information to Congress in support of the plan it recommends, but at the same time it must be prepared to show that other plans have been considered, and to give the reasons and computations for not recommending them.[75]

The accuracy of these hasty studies can be judged by the letters accompanying reports from the Districts. One District Engineer wrote: "The report submitted by this office on flood control reservoirs for the Tennessee Basin, dated August 20, was prepared in a great hurry and forwarded before the data contained in the appendices had been checked and properly analyzed." He enclosed corrections.[76]

Major R. C. Williams, District Engineer at St. Paul, Minnesota, wrote:

> It is believed that the results of the following studies approximate average conditions, but no great accuracy can be attributed to them. This follows because the short time in which the report was prepared made necessary

the use only of data immediately available and the exclusion of some studies which should accompany this report.[7 7]

Another engineer objected to the method used for estimating the amounts chargeable to water power and proposed an alternative, but added, "with the limited data and limited time available any evaluation of that nature would not be anything more than random guessing, therefore, this office preferred to look on the subject from the one viewpoint of flood control."[7 8]

As late as December, 1927, when the "Jadwin Plan" for the Mississippi was practically complete, when some question was asked by the Chief Engineer's office concerning data submitted by a district office, an engineer of the District office telegraphed: *"Reservoir sites in Oklahoma were accepted as Recommended by state Commission of drainage irrigation and reclamation. . . . I did not personally visit sites nor did I have field reconnaissance made."* Another engineer from that office wired: *"I visited none personally. . . . Cannot answer as to assistants until return to Memphis. Stop. Some were visited by an assistant no longer in service."*[7 9]

The President of the Mississippi River Commission, Colonel Potter given even more superficial data to work with, said he believed that reservoirs "were the most feasible method." Still, he was not ready to recommend such a plan, and was highly critical of the Chief of Engineers for submitting a plan based on insufficient information.[8 0] The traditional unwillingness of the Corps to consider reservoirs was maintained when even the Corps of Engineers' President of the Mississippi River Commission, previously a strong "levees only" man, had finally become convinced of the necessity for thorough study before adoption of a plan.

General Jadwin was not swayed by Colonel Potter's opinion and in his comprehensive report (that came to be known as the "Jadwin Plan") stated categorically that "the surveys and studies already made are in sufficient detail to *determine conclusively* the merit [or the lack of merit] of reservoirs for Mississippi River control. . . ."[8 1] (Emphasis added.) The "Jadwin Plan" was basically "levees only," supplemented by floodways and diversions at appropriate locations. Both reservoirs and cutoffs as elements in the Mississippi River flood control plan were rejected. In his report Jadwin gave what he considered conclusive evidence of the excessive cost and inadequacy of the reservoir system. He specifically rejected reservoirs for either the headwaters, the valley above Cairo, or at the lower reaches of the several tributaries of the Mississippi. (Today, following the temporary revolution brought about by President Hoover, reservoirs on the tributaries are an essential part of the Corps of Engineers program for Mississippi River control.)

Jadwin's general viewpoint as to reservoirs was that expressed regarding headwater reservoirs: "These reservoirs would afford inadequate relief at a cost four times as great as the cost of the plan for complete protection herein. . . ."[8 2]

In commenting on the difference between his views and those of Colonel Potter, Jadwin gave this expression of the engineering philosophy of the Engineer Corps:

> Proposals have been made that the whole question of Mississippi flood control be left in the air, *without final and decisive action by Congress*, until further elaborate studies are made. I have recommended strongly against such delay in coming to the relief of flooded areas. The Mississippi has been under study for more than fifty years. The data collected during the last flood have been studied with the greatest care, by hundreds of competent engineers army and civilian, and an *adequate and comprehensive* project has been worked up on the basis of these studies. It is time that we got to work to solve the problem, while the interest of Congress and of the nation is still focussed on the subject, instead of waiting for an indefinite period for a commission or other agency to collect additional *needless* data.[8 3] [Emphasis added.]

Conflicting Corps and Civilian Policy for Decision-Making

Here was the greatest engineering project in the United States. The Corps of Engineers year after year had repeated to the people of the Mississippi Valley and the United States the most unqualified assurance that the "levees only" protection works, made the lower Mississippi Valley secure from flood damage even in the event of the maximum possible flood. But despite these assurances, when the great flood of 1927 came, the unlimited assurances of the Corps proved to be entirely false. The protecting levees were broken in many places over the length of the delta. Vast areas of land, including many cities and towns were inundated, causing great loss of life in this the most terrible flood disaster in the history of the country. And floods even larger than 1927 are considered possible by competent hydraulic engineers. Clearly a restudy of the problems of Mississippi River flood control was called for. Apparently rising to the challenge, before beginning this entirely inadequate study, the answer must be "final and decisive" and the resulting plan should be "adequate and conclusive." The fact was that the policy adopted should be good for generations to come. The plan would cost many hundreds of millions of dollars and it should insure the safety of life and property in the Lower Mississippi Valley.

What would constitute adequate and suitable study and research for the preparation of a sound plan for flood protection on the Lower Mississippi, and for the momentous decisions involved in the making of that plan? How would the Corps of Engineers answer this vital question? Through the circumstances that the records in the National Archives in Washington, D.C., are available, direct first-hand evidence as to what the Chief of Engineers considered to be adequate study is provided by the orders of the Chief to his staff and from the correspondence between them. As to whether the measures he took were sufficient to enable a sound plan to be made and to give him a suitable basis for long time, far reaching decisions, any competent, experienced engineer can judge for himself. The decision as to feasibility of reservoirs must cover all branches of the Mississippi extending to New York and Pennsylvania on the East, and to Minnesota, Wyoming and Colorado on the West, and involving hundreds of possible reservoir sites.

The conclusion reached was not just the decision of an individual, in the powerful and arbitrary position of Chief of Engineers. It was the expression of a now century-old policy drilled into the cadets of West Point, and by them transmitted to the civilian staffs they controlled.

Need for Conclusive Analysis

At the time that the author gave his paper on reservoirs for Mississippi River flood control at the American Society of Civil Engineers Symposium in October, 1927, referred to earlier in this chapter, the "Jadwin Plan" was nearly completed and ready to submit to Congress. In the preceding months the Chief of Engineers had appointed the special Board of Corps members, to review the plan.

In 1927, my designation in my ASCE paper of that Board's report on reservoir control for the Mississippi as totally inadequate was based solely on the content of the report itself not on knowledge of how it was arrived at. The later complete repudiation of that report by General Lytle Brown as Chief of Engineers is a commentary on the validity of my criticism.

Several extracts from my Symposium paper of October, 1927, will illustrate:

> . . . until recently there has not been even a remote effort on the part of the Commission to discover and to estimate the cost of the most favorable opportunities for reservoir control. Thus, there is the remarkable situation of fifty years of insistence of the superiority of levees over reservoirs, without a thoroughgoing engineering analysis of the cost of either.
>
> Perhaps, however, the members of the Mississippi River Commission are so thoroughly informed concerning the principles and facts of reservoir control that their informal judgment is sufficient. The writer has searched their writings of nearly half a century to find evidence of that clear understanding, but he finds it to be almost completely lacking. They have many times given their reasons for rejecting reservoirs, the more important of which will be mentioned.[8 5]

There follow comments on false statements and inaccurate inferences by members of the U. S. Corps of Engineers and the Mississippi River Commission. (We repeat, the thinking of the Mississippi River Commission was dominated by its Corps of Engineers members.)

Contrary to the frequently repeated statements of the members of the Mississippi River Commission, suitable sites low down on the main tributaries probably do exist.[86]

Since I made these remarks in 1927, a considerable number of large and important reservoirs have been located and built on the lower tributaries. Conspicuous among these are the reservoirs built by the T.V.A. and the adjoining reservoir on the Cumberland, built by the Corps.

The assumption that sites for flood-control dams can be found only on head-waters permeates the thinking and writing of the Army Engineers and members of the Mississippi River Commission and largely destroys any value their studies might otherwise have had.[87]

Another member of the Mississippi River Commission states, 'Nature has greatly simplified the problem of flood control by making the drainage of the flooded lands, in the larger basins, comparatively simple.' Yet it is a fact that there are few more difficult problems of drainage and flood control than are found in these basins. In the Great St. Francis and Yazoo Basins there are four or more streams emerging from the hills, each of which has a maximum flood flow of 100,000 to 150,000 cu. ft. per sec., with an initial channel capacity in the delta of less than 5% of that amount. Control of these streams by reservoirs is feasible and in most cases probably is the only feasible method within reasonable cost. Such reservoirs would help solve the general Mississippi problem, and without them much of the land protected by levees will still be subject to destructive local flooding after the great river is controlled.[88]

This judgment in conflict with that of the Corps, was made in 1927. Since I made the speech from which this is quoted, these flatlands have largely been made safe from floods by reservoirs on the lower tributaries.

... In the writings of the Army Engineers and of the Mississippi River Commission for forty years one finds scarcely a hint of this great problem. It nearly always has been ignored in their general plans.[88]

(From my acquaintance with Engineer Corps methods through the years, I undertook to give a bit of advice to the Corps:)

In the practice of engineering there are two fundamental processes, both of them invaluable, which should supplement, and not compete with, each other. One method is that of perfecting and refining existing methods; of letting future policies grow gradually out of past experience. The other method is that of fundamental scientific analysis and engineering design.[89]

The employees of the Mississippi River Commission, and the Army Engineers working under its direction, sometimes have used excellent scientific methods in their work, but in its larger aspects the whole policy has been that of the practical rule-of-thumb man, and has almost entirely lacked thoroughgoing analysis of the larger engineering problems.[90]

I referred to the Miami Conservancy District which is a subject of thorough, careful planning, for which in fifty years, with repeated reviews by foremost engineers, had never been found lacking in any significant element. That favorable state continues to the present.

On the Miami Conservancy project there were at first the same conflicts of opinion, but the technical studies of the district settled nearly all mooted questions, and the technical design adopted has been generally approved by American engineers. Similar unity concerning the Mississippi problem will follow a proper study of the facts. No other policy than long continued, thorough-going, comprehensive analysis will bring that unity. The country should not be committed to a far-reaching flood-control policy without such study. At some time, the fact of lack of information must be acknowledged and this policy of thorough-going analysis adopted. It will then take years of such study to arrive at a dependable decision.

In conclusion, the writer would emphasize the fact that he is not an advocate of any specific degree of reservoir control as a proven method of flood control for the Mississippi. He does not know to what extent such control is feasible; but he does advocate a deliberate and conclusive study of the subject, which, he believes, never has been made.[91]

At the meeting at which I made this speech, on October 13, 1927, the Chief of Engineers, General Edgar Jadwin, was Chairman. I stood at his side while I read the paper, and he paid close attention. The next day, I now know from referring to the National Archives records, he sent the following letter to the District Engineers at Cincinnati and Louisville:

1. In the paper delivered before the American Society of Civil Engineers at its meeting in Columbus, Ohio, on October 13th, Mr. Arthur E. Morgan stated that the reservoir studies being made by the Department were not complete in that many good sites were not included. He mentions specifically a reservoir in the bed of the Ohio that would be efficient for the control of floods. He suggested a dam at Paducah, Ky. (for Louisville); Maysville, (backing up water up to the vicinity of Portsmouth, for Cincinnati).

2. This reservoir site will be investigated by you. Complete data called for by previous letters of instruction in regard to the study of reservoirs as a means of Mississippi River flood control will be submitted at the earliest date practicable. Report is desired as to when these data will be submitted.[92]

These letters were written three months after the date set for completing field studies, and after the conclusion of Jadwin's Reservoir study board had been reached, rejecting reservoirs. The District Engineer at Louisville wrote back that this would require a great deal of work, and take at least two months. This was about as much time as the original reservoir studies had taken.[9 3]

The next day General Jadwin, this time without mentioning the incentive of my speech, sent out orders for more reservoir studies to four additional District Engineers. Was it possible that an objective, thorough study was finally to be made?

In three of these letters, General Jadwin included the phrases:

> To meet the arguments of the proponents of a reservoir project it is necessary that we be able to state that such sites have been considered and to show that the cost is disproportionate to the benefits, if such be the case.

The same day, Jadwin had sent a telegram to the engineer at Vicksburg, Mississippi, amplifying on a telegram of the previous day, mentioning some of my specific criticisms and stating, "It is urgent that our reservoir studies shall not be open to such criticism. . . ."[9 4] and he ordered additional study.

Later that month, General Jadwin, Colonel Kelly, who was in charge of the Corps' reservoir studies, and Major Lee of Vicksburg all wrote me to try to obtain the data which lay behind my criticisms. The Corps of Engineers had a policy of secrecy with regard to its own internal communications. I questioned whether a one-way flow of information would be constructive. In perplexity, I wrote a letter to John F. Stevens, President of the American Society of Civil Engineers, and the real master mind of the Panama Canal, the credit of which went to the Corps, asking his opinion in the matter. Stevens replied by saying, "My judgment is that I would give them no data whatever. They simply want to be prepared in advance to demolish if they can any arguments which may come up against them."[9 5] At that time I did not know the superficial manner in which the studies were being conducted by the Corps, but judged it must have that character. As it turned out, Stevens' judgment was remarkably accurate.

It was clear that the reservoir studies made by the Corps of Engineers were demonstrably inadequate and lacking in quality. The House Committee on Flood Control agreed with me, reporting in April, 1928 that, "In the limited time since the 1927 flood it has been impossible for Federal engineers to make an adequate survey and study of reservoir sites on which to base a suitable recommendation."[9][6] Still, General Jadwin publicly proclaimed the "conclusiveness" of the Corps' studies and had enough political muscle to push his inadequate plan through Congress.

At the national Symposium on Mississippi Flood Control in October 1927, Colonel Kelly, Chairman of the Corps of Engineers' board study of the possibility for using reservoirs for Mississippi flood control, made his report. I criticized that report as inadequate, and as not providing a sound basis for opinion. Discussion was continued in the "Transactions" of the A.S.C.E. for 1929. Colonel Kelly took me vigorously to task for my criticism. (He did not need to mention my name.) I quote from his expression:

> Considerable criticism has been launched against those studies, on the ground that they are inadequate and based upon incomplete data. They have also been attacked on the ground that the U.S. Corps of Engineers long ago took a stand against reservoirs and could not now be expected to reverse itself . . . the studies . . . were efficiently and honestly made in such a way that the probable errors would favor the reservoirs. Had they shown any reservoirs that offered even a remote chance of economical use as part of a solution of the Mississippi flood problem, accurate and complete surveys thereof would have been recommended. . . .there is no reasonable hope that undiscovered reservoirs might overcome this difference in cost . . . the writer is convinced that thie preliminary surveys made are sufficient to justify the conclusion that the expense and delay necessary for more accurate surveys of reservoir possibilities for Mississippi floods are not warranted.[9][7]

This statement was made just after the A.S.C.E. meeting in

October 1927, and after Colonel Kelly had been made aware of possible limitations, and when he might have exercised caution. His unqualified statements might seem to discredit his critics. He continued to assure his audiences. He proceeds then to laud the Corps for objectivity and candor. As an illustration he cites the unanimity of the conclusions of the Corps against reservoirs as an example of critical writing. The hundreds of reservoirs built by the Corps when the tremendous errors of his writing of the condemnation of reservoirs was discovered by President Hoover's appointment of the rebel, General Lytle Brown, as Chief of Engineers. The hundreds of reservoirs built by the Corps of Engineers since then show how the reputation of the Corps is bolstered and preserved by the "esprit de corps" of the Corps.

In regard to the second criticism, during thirty years of experience in the Corps of Engineers, the writer has never encountered a case where pride of Corps has affected the professional judgment of its members. On the other hand, such pride as the Corps has, is in its success in upholding its professional proficiency and integrity. The officers of the Corps are no different from other engineers. They are trained to seek facts and to form independent judgment therefrom and are never backward about expressing differences of opinion with each other. The fact that heretofore they have independently but uniformly reached a conclusion against reservoirs as a cure for Mississippi floods is a fairly good guaranty that under the conditions that have existed up to the present, reservoirs could not be economically used to relieve the Mississippi Valley.[9][7]

This unqualified praise of the work of the Corps and unqualified condemnation of my criticism was issued shortly after the symposium of the American Society of Civil Engineers on Mississippi flood control in October 1927. It seems probable that Colonel Kelly's superiors and associates felt some misgivings. I received personal letters from Chief of Engineers Jadwin, Colonel Kelly in charge of reservoir studies, and Major Lee of Vicksburg, all of whom wrote me to try to obtain the data which lay behind my criticism. It evidently was considered tactful and desirable to make a few hurried additional reservoir studies, so as to have something to report, beyond the completely negative report of the Chairman of the Reservoir Committee, Colonel Kelly, as it had been approved by the Chief of Engineers, General Jadwin. After my talk the Report was hastily revised, with some small admissions on the value of reservoirs. After his reply to my talks, in which he had refused to admit any possibility of reservoirs, the hurried further study for a revised report on the conference made an admission:

> As a result of this experience the writer, while not accepting reservoirs as cure-alls, believed that they might form a valuable part of a complete Mississippi flood project.⁹ ⁷ᴬ

After this hasty amendment of the Report of the Commission on Reservoirs was made, the few tentative admissions showed a similar lack of conclusive engineering analysis. For instance, they drew attention to the fact that the Miami Conservancy reservoirs would not help the lower Mississippi. They did not mention that at the very mouth of the Miami River, below all the Miami reservoirs, was a site just at the mouth of the river just west of Cincinnati, which should be used for reservoir purposes to hold back Miami River water from the Mississippi during floods, but unless so used promptly would soon be occupied by improvements which would make it no longer available. This possible reservoir would have a dam very near the mouth of the Miami River, with possible dikes along the eastern border to increase capacity. Railroads and highways would be carried across the Miami on the top of the dam. In addition to being available to hold back rare floods, the reservoir area would supply Cincinnati with a rare area of forest and recreation land and with space for truck crops for Cincinnati. In the fifty years of the Miami reservoirs, not more than one or two per cent of the crops have been lost by floods, and the deposit of humus has materially increased productiveness. The same would be true of this reservoir at the mouth of the Miami. This very large possible reservoir at the mouth of the Miami was gradually growing less available, while the Corps was drawing attention to the fact that the Miami River reservoirs would not help the Mississippi. By now this excellent reservoir site, fifty years later, has probably become practically unavailable.

The Yazoo River in Mississippi is represented as not having reservoir sites at its mouth. Most of the drainage area of the Yazoo had reservoirs available in the hills to the west, from which flood water came. I personally planned a reservoir near the headwaters of the Yazoo, which with a steep, rapid discharge into the Mississippi near the line between Mississippi and Tennessee, would have emptied the floodwater very quickly into the Mississippi, taking it entirely out of the Yazoo basin and sending it down the Mississippi well in advance of the great bulk of the flood waters from the north. I consider the omissions of this reservoir by the Corps, and the adoption of much more expensive and unsatisfactory storage to be a sad error. On the whole, the Report published in the 1929 *Transactions* of the American Society of Civil Engineers is a weak semi-apology of the levee board, to make its direct condemnation of my statements seemingly more complex and reasonable.

After thirty years, federal executive "correspondence" is transferred to the Government Archives, and is accessible to the public. There we found it. There was disclosed a fragmentary, careless and greatly inadequate process of inquiry. It is evident that very little confidence could properly be placed in the results. Within three years of the time that Colonel Kelly made his unamended report to the Symposium, a revolution was brought about in the leadership of the Corps by President Hoover. A study concerning reservoirs was made, and after more than fifty years of blind adherence to the "levees only" doctrine the building of flood control reservoirs began, and never has ceased. Within about 20 years of the above criticism the Hoover Commission and Task Force reported that the Corps had built more than 100 reservoirs for flood control, at least part of the cost of each of which was charged to flood control for the Mississippi River.

To illustrate how extremely far astray a leading Corps officer could go in giving assurances of the work of the national Board of the Corps on reservoir possibilities, and in his pontification concerning the merits of the Corps, note how far the Chief of Engineers has come from the half century of rigidly dogmatic holding to the doctrine of "levees only, and no reservoirs." In 1956, the Corps had 222 reservoirs in operation, and more in process. The Chief of Engineers told an Ohio Valley audience:

> *These dams provide your first and major line of defense against large flood damage.*[98] [Emphasis added.]

He also said that *some areas needed "supplementary" protection "such as levees and flood walls."* [Emphasis added.]

New Chief of Engineers Reversed Corps Flood Control Policies

Fortunately, after Jadwin had finished his tenure as Chief of Engineers in August, 1929, only two years later the new Chief of Engineers, General Lytle Brown (who took office in September, 1929), considered it necessary to re-do the reservoir studies. Under General Brown an indirect, though conclusive critique of the 1927 studies was conveyed in a set of "Comments on Plan for Carrying out Reservoir Studies," written by a staff member in the Chief of Engineers' office. This read:

> It appears that the determination of the most effective and satisfactory method of operating reservoirs for Mississippi flood control is by far the most important part of the investigation. It is the part which will be most seriously attacked by outside parties. It is also the part in which it will be easy to get involved in serious errors. The discovery of reservoir sites and the estimating of their cost and capacity is routine engineering work while the use of this data in working out a consistent, satisfactory and workable plan requires the highest degree of skill and

imagination and the results obtained will have to be defended against vigorous attacks.

The method adopted by the Reservoir Board of 1927 was only one method. When the Board was organized it found that some work had already been done along this line and the Board decided to continue the same method. There was not time to start from the bottom and work out several schemes. Mr. Arthur A. (sic) Morgan stated that the plan adopted was the least efficient method which could be devised. This was an *exaggeration*. Other schemes can be tried. (Emphasis added.)[9][9]

Thus, although General Jadwin's Board, in 1927, disapproved of reservoirs, between 1929 and 1935 following the further studies under Chief of Engineers General Brown, the attitude of the Corps of Engineers Board toward reservoirs changed significantly. As indicated in greater detail in the chapter on the hydraulic laboratory, the great change in outlook and policy which took place in the Corps at that time did not represent a normal evolution in the attitude of the Corps. It was in large degree a sudden revolution imposed on the Corps from without, as I mentioned in the chapter on the hydraulics laboratory. When Herbert Hoover became President and was called upon to appoint a successor to General Jadwin as Chief of Engineers, he did not follow the conventional course of accepting the recommendation of the Corps, but passed over ten of the leading Corps officers and appointed the man he wanted, General Lytle Brown, not a Corps of Engineers man, who had repeatedly differed from his military superiors.

Almost immediately on his appointment to be Chief of Engineers, General Brown made striking changes in Corps of Engineers policy and personnel for Mississippi River flood control; in fact greater changes in policy were made under him from 1930 to 1935 than had been made during fifty years preceding. Reservoirs now became an orthodox method of flood control and were included in most Corps flood control plans, particularly those made under the provisions of House Document No. 308, Sixty-ninth Congress, First

Session, approved January 21, 1927, covering the flood control needs of the nation as a whole, and the additional provisions of the Flood Control Act passed May 15, 1928. The latter directed the Corps of Engineers "to prepare and submit to Congress at the earliest practicable date projects for flood control on all tributary streams of the Mississippi River system subject to destructive floods. . . .and the reports thereon. . . . shall include the effect on the subject of further flood control of the lower Mississippi River to be attained through the control of the flood waters in the drainage basins of the tributaries by the establishment of a reservoir system. . . ."

In 1955, a Task Force of the Second Hoover Commission on Organization of the Executive Branch of the Government reported that the Corps of Engineers was using benefits for the Lower Mississippi River to economically justify 112 separate reservoirs.[100] The Task Force commented, "This is equivalent to claiming that the great floods of the past would have been virtually eliminated had the reservoir system been in existence when they occurred."[101] Then the Task Force proceeded to sound a rather sour note by stating, "As a matter of fact, this claim implies that a vast sum has been wasted in constructing levees to a much greater height than necessary. The task group does not accept this implication. In its opinion, the levees are not too high; rather, the effectiveness of reservoirs has been greatly overestimated."[102] The latter statement is moot but the significant fact remains that the Corps, somewhat paradoxically, is now in direct opposition to its long-held position of "levees only," and recognizes the value of reservoirs as essential to adequate flood control for the Lower Mississippi Valley. Ironically, the Corps is now on the other side of the fence and is likely to be attacked for not giving enough emphasis to other methods. On one major issue after another, after the Corps has been defeated from its extreme efforts, new and greatly different methods have been established with such great success that the Corps was compelled to acknowledge them. The Corps meets the issue by claiming credit for these policies forced upon it and by praising itself for its wonderful acumen and achievements. This has been true with reference to the Hydraulic Laboratory which is now the largest in the world, to Cut-offs on the Mississippi and to Reservoirs.

In 1959, a former officer of the Corps of Engineers, in describing the Corps' program for the Mississippi River flood control, gave "reservoirs on the tributary streams both within and outside the alluvial valley, to hold back flood flow so far as practicable. . . ." as number one among the methods used.[103]

Today, reservoirs are one of the Corps' main methods of protecting against floods. In 1965, the Corps had 222 flood control reservoirs in operation and about 200 more authorized or under construction.[104] In the Ohio Valley, which the Corps for so long termed "unsuited" to reservoir control, there were 33 Corps reservoirs operating in 1959.[105] To repeat what we stated on page 298: *"These dams,"* the Chief of Engineers told an audience, *"provide your first and major line of defense against large flood damage."*[106] He said that some areas needed "supplementary" protection, "such as levees and floodwalls."[107] (Emphasis added.) This is a far cry from the earlier half century long anti-reservoir attitude of the Corps of Engineers.

Contrary to earlier Corps pronouncements, reservoirs have played a significant role in navigation improvement, as any shipping firm utilizing the TVA reservoirs would readily testify. In late 1953, a news report read, "The Missouri River would have been 'dangerously low' now except for upstream reservoir controls, Army Engineers would have said today."[108]

Multi-purpose projects are now the order of the day. By 1952, a Corps pamphlet on flood control ran directly against the Corps' earlier assertions. It reads:

> "Storage for flood control may often be combined with storage for other purposes—such as hydroelectric power production, irrigation, water supply, pollution abatement, fish and wildlife conservation, recreation, and similar uses. . . ."[109]

In 1965 the retiring Chief of Engineers commented that, "The single-purpose reservoir has become virtually a thing of the past. The multiple-purpose project now dominates water resources development."[10] The experience of more than thirty years of TVA, of which I was first Chairman and Chief Engineer in charge of unified river control, is conclusive evidence of the soundness of multi-purpose development.

Looking back on the long struggle to bring about the Corps of Engineers change in its traditional opposition to flood control reservoirs, this covered nearly three-quarters of a century from the time of Humphreys and Abbot in the 1850's and 1860's until the advent of Herbert Hoover as President of the United States in 1929, and the appointment of the rebel General Lytle Brown as Chief Engineer of the Corps, against the overwhelming disapproval of the Corps membership. During all of this time, large floods came and went on the Lower Mississippi River, some of these very devastating. The "levees only" policy of the Corps of Engineers as propounded by Humphreys and Abbot became more and more firmly entrenched. Finally, it took a great flood and a great President to break the traditional position of the Corps and force it to accept reservoirs as essential to flood protection for the Lower Mississippi Valley and other areas. The widespread use of reservoirs today by the Corps, and the effectiveness of reservoirs in preventing flood losses, is ample evidence that the persistence of those who, through the years envisioned the benefits of flood control reservoirs, has been well worthwhile. As planner and chief engineer of the construction of the first flood control reservoirs in America, it is natural that I have a certain satisfaction in this development.

notes

1. Arthur E. Morgan, "The Basis of the Case against Reservoirs for Mississippi Flood Control," American Society of Civil Engineers, *Transactions*, Vol. 93, 1929, p. 737.

2. Editorial: "Civil Engineers Consider Mississippi Floods," article in the *Engineering News Record*, Vol. 99, No. 16, October 20, 1927.

3. Arthur E. Morgan, "The Mississippi: Meeting a Mighty Problem," *Atlantic Monthly*, Vol. 141, 1928, p. 668.

4. Charles Ellet, Jr., "Reports on Overflows of the Delta of the Mississippi," Senate Executive Document, No. 20, Jan. 21, 1852, p. 101.

5. H. A. Petterson, "Comparisons of Systems of Flood Control," *Engineering Record*, Vol. 69, May 1914, no. 15, p. 560.

6. *Ibid.*

7. N. O. Leighton, "Relation of Water Conservation to Flood Prevention in the Ohio River," *Engineering News*, Vol. 59, No. 19, May 7, 1908, p. 1.

8. Frank E. Smith, "The Politics of Conservation," Pantheon Books, 1966, p. 17.

9. Captain A. A. Humphreys and Lieutenant H. L. Abbot, "Report on Physics and Hydraulics of the Mississippi River," Washington, 1876, first published, 1871, p. 411.

10. W. Milnor Roberts, "Survey of the Ohio River," *Executive Documents*, 41st Congress, 1870-71, p. 29.

11. Major William E. Merrill, Corps of Engineers, *Report of the Chief of Engineers*, Appendix M, 1873, pp. 498-501.

12. Major William E. Merrill and Major G. Weitzel, *Report of the Chief of Engineers*, N. 2, 1873, pp. 540-541.

13. *Report of the Chief of Engineers*, Part 1, Appendix O, 1875.

14. *Ibid.*, p. 537.

15. *Ibid.*, p. 538.

16. Proceedings of the Commission appointed under the Act of Congress approved in June 1874 "to investigate and report a permanent plan for the reclamation of the alluvial basin of the Mississippi River subject to inundation," p. 137.

17. *Report of the Chief of Engineers, op. cit.*, p. 540.

18. Proceedings of the Commission, *op. cit.*, p. 141.

19. *Report of the Chief of Engineers, op. cit.*, p. 541.

20. Address by Major General E. C. Itschner, Chief of Engineers, before the Red River Valley Association, Shreveport, La., March 30, 1959, p. 7.

21. *Report of the Chief of Engineers, op. cit.*, p. 563.

22. Captain Hiram M. Chittenden, to Lt. Col. Amos Stickney, *Report of the Chief of Engineers*, 1897, p. 2860.

23. *Ibid.*

24. *Ibid.*, p. 2861.

25. Leighton, *op. cit.*, first page.

26. Captain William D. Connor, Corps of Engineers, *Engineering News*, Vol. 59, No. 24, June 11, 1908, first page.

27. H. L. Abbot, Professor of Hydraulic Engineering, late Colonel, Corps of Engineers, "Regulation of Rivers in the Interests of Navigation," lecture before postgraduate engineering students, George Washington University (March 17, 1909), p. 224.

28. *Ibid.*, p. 228.

29. Major W. W. Harts, Corps of Engineers, "Improvement of Inland Rivers," *Professional Memoirs, Corps of Engineers*, April-June 1909, p. 78.

30. *Ibid.,* p. 80.

31. *Ibid.,* p. 84.

32. Lieutenant Colonel H. M. Chittenden, Corps of Engineers, "Forests and Reservoirs in the relation to Stream Flow, with particular Reference to navigable rivers," *Transactions* of the American Society of Civil Engineers, Vol. 62-63, paper no. 1098, 1909, p. 304.

33. *Ibid.*

34. *Ibid.,* p. 348.

35. *Ibid.,* p. 351.

36. *Ibid.,* p. 353.

37. *Ibid.,* p. 432.

38. *Ibid.,* p. 506.

39. Herbert Quick, *American Inland Waterways,* Putnam, 1909, Chapter 7.

40. Chittenden, "Forests and Reservoirs in the relation to Stream Flow," *op. cit.,* p. 296.

41. Captain F. W. Altstaetter, Corps of Engineers, address delivered at Wheeling, W. Va., Nov. 3, 1909, in *Professional Memoirs, Corps of Engineers, U. S. Army and Engineer Department at large,* Vol. 2 (Jan.-Dec., 1910), pp. 38-39.

42. *Ibid.,* p. 39.

43. Col. C. McD. Townsend, "Controlling the Mississippi River," *Engineer News,* Vol. 68, No. 18, Oct. 31, 1912, p. 832.

44. Col. C. McD. Townsend, Corps of Engineers, president of the Mississippi River Commission, address to the National Drainage Congress in St. Louis, Mo., April, 1913, *Engineering Record,* Vol. 67, May, 1913, p. 506.

45. *Ibid.*

46. *Ibid.,* p. 500.

47. *Ibid.*

48. Preliminary Report of the Army Engineers on the Central States Floods, *Engineering News*, Vol. 70, No. 15, October 9, 1913, p. 725.

49. *Ibid.*, p. 726.

50. Arthur E. Morgan, *Miami Conservancy District*, McGraw-Hill, 1951, p. 155.

51. *Ibid.*, p. 292.

52. Hiram M. Chittenden (General, Retired), "Detention Reservoirs with Spillway Outlets as an Agency in Flood Control," Paper No. 1423, *Transactions* of the American Society of Civil Engineers, 1918, Vol. I, No. LXXXII, p. 1473.

53. *Engineering Record*, No. 13, March 28, 1914, p. 350.

54. Petterson, *op. cit.*, p. 391.

55. *Ibid.*

56. *Ibid.*, p. 392.

57. *Ibid.*, p. 502.

58. Major J. C. Oakes, Corps of Engineers, address on "Flood Prevention," *Professional Memoirs of the Corps of Engineers*, Vol. 6, May-June, 1914, p. 427.

59. *Ibid.*, p. 432.

60. *Ibid.*

61. *Ibid.*, p. 433.

62. *Ibid.*

63. Letter from Major Harold C. Fiske, Corps of Engineers, to Senator E. Ransdell, April 28, 1924, p. 5.

64. Letter from General H. Taylor, Assistant Chief of Engineers, to the District Engineer, Chattanooga, Tennessee, May 1, 1924, p. 1.

65. *Ibid.*

66. Charles L. Potter, Colonel, Corps of Engineers, President of the Mississippi River Commission, St. Louis, Mo., "Some Suggested Ways of Controlling the Missis-

sippi Floods," *Engineering News-Record*, Vol. 94, No. 14, April 2, 1925.

67. *Ibid.*

68. Letter from Colonel C. W. Kutz, Division Engineer, Corps of Engineers, to the District Engineers, Central Division (except Florence, Alabama), May 21, 1927, p. 1.

69. Letter from Major C. C. Gee, District Engineer, Corps of Engineers, to the Chief of Engineers, Washington, D.C., May 25, 1927, p. 1.

70. Letter to W. H. McAlpine, Senior Engineer, Corps of Engineers, Louisville, Kentucky, to the Chief of Engineers, Washington, D.C., May 28, 1927, p. 1.

71. Letter from Col. Charles L. Potter, Corps of Engineers, Pittsburgh, Pa., to the Chief of Engineers, May 25, 1927, p. 1.

72. Letter from Col. C. W. Kutz, Division Engineer, Cincinnati, Ohio, to District Engineers, Central Division (except Florence, Alabama), June 20, 1927, p. 1.

73. *Ibid.*

74. Letter from Brig.-Gen. Herbert Deakyne, Acting Chief of Engineers, to District Engineer, Cincinnati, Ohio, July 22, 1927, p. 1.

75. Letter from Maj.-Gen. Edgar Jadwin, Chief of Engineers, to Col. Charles E. Potter, President, Mississippi River Commission and Division Engineer, West Division, St. Louis, Mo., June 15, 1927, p. 1.

76. Letter from Major Lewis H. Watkins, District Engineer, Chattanooga, Tennessee, to the Chief of Engineers, Sept. 1, 1927, p. 1.

77. Major R. C. Williams, District Engineer, St. Paul, Minnesota, "Study of Flood Control Reservoirs," August 30, 1927, Item 43.

78. Letter from Major Donald H. Connolly, District Engineer, to Chief of Engineers, October 1, 1927, p. 2.

79. Telegrams from Corps officers Lee (Vicksburg, Mississippi) and Connolly (Fort Smith, Arkansas), to Chief of Engineers, Washington, D.C., December 16 and 17, 1927.

80. Senate Report no. 448, 70th Congress, First Session, Committee on Commerce, March 2, 1928, pp. 2-3.

81. Letter from Maj.-Gen. Jadwin, Chief of Engineers, to the Hon. Frank Reid, Chairman, Committee on Flood Control, House of Representatives, Feb. 9, 1928, p. 1.

82. Senate Report no. 448, *op. cit.*, pp. 2-3.

83. Letter from Maj.-Gen. Jadwin, Chief of Engineers, to R. F. Danner, A. A. E., Oklahoma City, Okla., March 16, 1928, p. 1.

84. Gilbert A. Youngberg, "The Civil Activities of the Corps of Engineers," *Military Engineer*, Jan.-Feb. 1921.

85. Arthur Morgan, "The Basis of the case against Reservoirs for Mississippi Flood Contorl," *op. cit.*, p. 739.

86. *Ibid.*, p. 740.

87. *Ibid.*, p. 741.

88. *Ibid.*

89. *Ibid.*, p. 750.

90. *Ibid.*

91. *Ibid.*, p. 754.

92. Letter from Major-General Jadwin, Chief of Engineers, to District Engineers in Louisville and Cincinnati, Oct. 14, 1927, p. 1.

93. Letter from Lt. Col. George R. Spalding, District Engineer, Louisville, to Chief of Engineers, Oct. 24, 1927, p. 1.

94. Telegram from Major-General Jadwin to Major Lee, Vicksburg, Miss., Oct. 15, 1927.

95. Letter from John F. Stevens, President of the American Society of Civil Engineers, to Arthur E. Morgan, Nov. 13, 1927, p. 1.

96. House Report No. 1100, 70th Congress, 1st Session, Committee on Flood Control, April 2, 1928, p. 14.

97. Col. Kelly Letter, *Transactions*, American Society of Civil Engineers, 1929, pp. 954-955.

97A. *Ibid.*, p. 724, "Reservoirs for Mississippi River Valley Flood Control Protection."

98. Address by Major Gen. Itschner, before the Red River Valley Association, *op. cit.*, p. 7.

99. Major J. C. Gotwals, District Engineer, St. Louis, Mo., "Comments on Plan for Carrying out Reservoir Studies," Sept. 20, 1929, p. 1 (enclosed with letter from Brig.-Gen. T. H. Jackson, Division Engineer, Western Division, to Chief of Engineers, Washington, D.C.)

100. Report of the Second Hoover Commission, 1955, p. 805.

101. *Ibid.*, p. 806.

102. *Ibid.*

103. Maj.-Gen. Hohn R. Hardin (retired), "Evolution of Mississippi Valley Flood Control Plan, paper no. 2973 in the *Transactions* of the American Society of Civil Engineers, Vol. 124, 1959, p. 217.

104. (1) *Engineering News-Record:* (1929, August 8), p. 235. (2) *Engineering News-Record:* (1929, Sept. 26) pp. 479, 513.

105. Address by Major General E. C. Itschner, Chief of Engineers, before Ohio Valley Improvement Association, Cincinnati, Ohio, Oct. 26, 1959, p. 4.

106. Address by Itschner before the Red River Valley Association, *op. cit.*, p. 7.

107. *Ibid.*

108. U. P. Report from Omaha, Nebraska, Sept. 28, 1953, "Controls help Missouri's Flow," in *New York Times*, Sept. 29, 1953, p. 31.

109. "Floods and Flood Control," Corps of Engineers pamphlet, Omaha, Nebraska District, Jan. 1952, p. 44.

110. Lt. Gen. W. K. Wilson, Jr., Chief of Engineers, before the Sub-Committee on Flood Control and Rivers and Harbors of the Committee on Public Works, U.S. Senate, March 22, 1965, p. 3.

chapter 10

the
upper
allegheny

Pittsburgh early became an industrial city and a gateway to the West by way of coal and steel and railroading. Because of its location Pittsburgh suffered from floods. It was natural that industrialists and engineers should desire to create suitable living and working conditions for the community. The very nature of the physical setting of the city, with the Allegheny and the Monongahela Rivers coming out of the mountains and converging on the city to form the Ohio River, compelled the conclusion that there was no local, simple way to deal with flood waters. They had to be held back *before* they reached the city.

In February 1908 a number of Pittsburgh's foremost citizens, through the medium of the Pittsburgh Chamber of Commerce, organized the Flood Commission of Pittsburgh. Practically every widely experienced engineer in the city (including a number with national reputations) was on the Engineering Committee of the Flood Commission. The actual conduct of the engineering work was in the hands of Kenneth C. Grant. He made an extended trip to Europe, covering nearly every part of the continent in search of any practical or theoretical light on the Pittsburgh problem. He later became an employee of the Miami Conservancy District and turned over his European findings to us. The President of the Commission was the industrialist, H. J. Heinz, whose plant was especially subject to flooding.

Four years later, in April 1912, the Flood Commission of Pittsburgh published a 700-page report of its studies, and a separate large volume of its maps. Reservoirs were the chief method of flood control recommended. This was a year before the great Dayton flood and so the proposal for Pittsburgh was the pioneer American plan recommending reservoirs for flood control.

When the Flood Commission sought the help of the federal government in its problem, it came in conflict with the fifty-year long opposition of the U.S. Corps of Engineers to reservoirs for flood control. The Corps was still wedded to the ideas of Humphreys and Abbot, whose massive "Physics and Hydraulics of the Mississippi River" of 1861 was the scripture of the Corps.

From 1911 until 1924 the Flood Commission of Pittsburgh sought in vain to win the interest of the Corps of Engineers which vigorously defended itself against the heresy of reservoirs. Finally in 1924 Pittsburgh persuaded the State of Pennsylvania, under the liberal and progressive Governor Gifford Pinchot, to appropriate $25,000, and secured a similar appropriation from the Federal government for the Corps of Engineers to make a study of the subject. Thus the Corps was led reluctantly into a study of reservoirs for flood control. A report on that study was made in 1928.

What happened during the period from 1924 to 1928 is not clear. The records of the Flood Commission of Pittsburgh were lost in the flood of 1936, and only its printed reports remain. The Flood Commission and Governor Pinchot may have influenced this study. Also, for a part of that period General Hartley B. Ferguson, a rebel against the Corps of Engineers' traditions, was in charge of the Ohio division of the Corps of Engineers. The plan which first emerged was for a combination of power development and flood control, with $54,000,000 assigned to power development and $14,000,000 to flood control.

At that time divergent influences existed. The private power interests of Pittsburgh were intensely anti-public power. And the effort for flood protection for Pittsburgh proceeded in a tangle of conflicting interests on the subject of public and private water power.

Evidently the Corps did not consider its 1928 Report to be one of its classics. Toward the end of the Report, where one would expect to find the conclusion, a page is cut through the middle, and the rest of the Report is missing. The Flood Commission of Pittsburgh printed a criticism of the Corps, in which it quoted this conclusion of the Corps, so we know what had been cut out:

> A combination project for flood control and power has been studied. The benefits to be derived have been given, together with the gross and net costs for flood control. In order that the greatest flood benefit may be obtained from the most economical investment at the location selected, it is necessary to study a plan which has flood control only as its basis.
>
> *Location.* It is proposed to locate the reservoir on the Allegheny River at the same place selected for power development. Diversion of water to Lake Erie is not intended in this project and as the Conewango Reservoir was needed only for power purposes, that development would be omitted, together with other dependent structures. Flood control on the Conewango basin is not contemplated.
>
> *Flood control only.* Gross cost: interest, taxes, engineering, legal administration, superintendence, added—Total cost for flood control, $18,694,700.[1]

The controlling element of an optimum plan for the protection and increase of low-water flow without any question was the use of the Conewango basin. To entirely leave the Conewango basin out of this study would be a fatal omission. Therefore such a study would be condemned at the start. A careful study of the Conewango possibilities is the very heart of the solution. Even at the time of the work of the Consulting Engineers for the Corps in 1958, though I urgently pointed out to the Corps and their consultants the imperative need for such a study, the Corps and the consultants persisted in omitting large elements of the study, some of which would have become an integral part of any adequate treatment of the problem.

That part of the Corps of Engineers Report of 1928 which deals with the Upper Allegheny River is Appendix 14, Project B. There are two parts to this: a plan including water power and flood protection, and a plan for flood control only. For the Conewango Project the estimated cost for power was $43,000,000, and for flood control was $14,000,000.

The general finding of the Corps of Engineers Report of 1928 can be reconstructed from the following quotation from it and the references to it in the letter of 1930 quoted to the Chief of Engineers.

The following statement is from the Flood Commission's Review:

> Having apparently proved that its proposed system of complete protection by reservoirs is uneconomic, (sic) the Report fails entirely to discuss whether any less degree of protection of reservoirs is economic. It would seem that this omission constituted a failure to adequately comply with the intention and authorization of the work. (X1, p.4)[2]

The Flood Commission of Pittsburgh quoted as follows from that part of the Corps of Engineers Report which was later cut from the Corps of Engineers Report, presumably by the Corps:

> 29. Although it is possible to remove the flood menace from the Allegheny, Mononghahela, and Upper Ohio basins by reservoirs, the excessive cost of such a project renders it uneconomical. On a simple investment basis it would appear more practical to sustain the losses, or were it possible, to invest $26,000,000, the approximate capitalized value of future flood damages, and use the return thereon to pay the damages, rather than to suffer a greater annual loss in carrying charges on an investment of $60,740,000, which is the difference between the cost of the reservoir plan and the value of the increased benefits other than relief from flood damages received. 32. From the viewpoint of economy only, there is strong

argument in favor of the more primitive method of protecting locally the individual property interest of those limited and concentrated areas subject to excessive flood damage where local protection is economically feasible. (XI. p. 9)[3]

Another quotation from the 1928 report of the Corps has the same thrust:

While flood control by any plan of reservoirs is found to be uneconomical, it is nevertheless recommended in all future construction for navigation improvement, water power development, etc., by the Government or private enterprise, their execution with a view to securing the maximum incidental flood protection shall be provided for. . . .(XI, p. 10)[4]

The report of the Corps on the Allegheny was not satisfactory to the Flood Commission of Pittsburgh. At first the Flood Commission saw no further feasible action. In 1930, however, when President Hoover brought about a revolutionary change in the leadership of the U.S. Engineer Corps by appointing General Lytle Brown as Chief of Engineers, striking changes occurred for the time being in the administration of the Corps. A few months after the appointment of General Lytle Brown, the Flood Commission of Pittsburgh, in hopes of a more favorable response, again wrote the Chief of Engineers on April 30, 1930.

Maj. Gen. Lytle Brown, Chief of Engineers
Department of War
Washington, D.C.

Dear Sir:

There is transmitted to you herewith, for the consideration of the Board of Engineers for Rivers and Harbors, a review based upon the survey of the Allegheny and Monongahela Rivers, with a view to the control of their floods . . .A long period of time has been spent in analyzing the Report in close detail and as will be observed, the principal points which we emphasize are (1) that the Report recommends a volume of storage in excess of what we believe to be the requirements, thereby increasing the cost, and (2) that the benefits arising from the construction and operation of the storage reservoirs have not been studied with sufficient comprehensiveness and are generally too low.

This organization has spent twenty active years in promoting the regulation of the Allegheny, Monongahela and Upper Ohio Rivers, which converge at Pittsburgh. It is our suggestion that the contents of the appended review be used as a basis of a more detailed study of this problem looking toward a revision of the Report. . . .

Respectfully submitted,
Flood Commission of Pittsburgh
George S. Davison, President

As evidence of the caliber of the Flood Commission at Pittsburgh, at about this time Davison was President of the American Society of Civil Engineers.

The Corps of Engineers never assembled the data necessary for a conclusive engineering analysis of the problems of Pittsburgh, for the Kinzua Reservoir or other solution. This city's flood control experience belies the claim repeatedly made by the Corps that it has examined all important alternatives, in search of the best. The Corps has been entirely unaware of some of the most important and most promising alternatives. The Corps never made the necessary explorations or assembled the data which would would made it possible for it or anyone else to come to a dependable conclusion as to which of various possibilities was best. It is a very definite conclusion certainly that the Kinzua Reservoir was far from the best solution.

The Upper Allegheny River Control: The Author's Involvement

All previous chapters of this book which describe specific projects or methods have been gleaned from history. These accounts have been reported, largely as recorded by those who took part. These accounts of the Corps of Engineers projects through the course of a century demonstrate a striking uniformity of attitude, spirit and method.

In the case of the control of the Upper Allegheny, I can report an actual first hand account of my personal experience. In this chapter these direct personal experiences with members of the Corps are recorded in intimate detail.

The incompetence of the Corps on the Upper Allegheny was not come upon by a search among many projects for one badly managed. It was simply come upon by chance. If I had not responded to a plea of the Seneca Indians this project would have gone to completion without criticism. The Corps is careful not to have its work examined by independent outsiders. Its principal consulting firm was founded, partly staffed and dominated by men who were previously members of the Corps of Engineers.

Few of the inadequately studied projects of the Corps are publicly recognized as such, because few are independently examined. I will cite but one such project.

In the early days of the Tennessee Valley Authority the State Engineer of New York came to me in distress. He wanted to get a message to President Roosevelt but did not feel free to go to him personally. His message concerned the Passamaquoddy project for tidal power. He said that in his opinion the plans for that project prepared by the Corps of Engineers were totally inadequate, and if followed in building would be a great embarrassment to the President. Would I carry that message to the President? I knew nothing of the merits of the issue, but on seeing the President a few days later I gave this message as I had received it. President Roosevelt did not need this warning, for he had been warned by other sources, and was preparing to cancel the undertaking. But the President gave me his appraisal of the Corps. His closing comment was, "Why do they do that way? (Sic.) Do they do it on purpose, or are they just dumb?"

The result of the failure of the Corps to practice intensive engineering analysis in the Upper Allegheny River project resulted in inadequate flood protection for a region that includes the cities of Warren, Pittsburgh, and other industrial cities, as well as extensive industrial areas. It meant also a great waste of water for low water river regulation. Enmeshed in these results are estimates of financial costs and losses over and above those necessary, as well as human costs—the loss of areas of recreation and the loss of the lands of the Seneca Indians for habitation.

Two methods were proposed for the control of the Upper Allegheny River: the Conewango plan, which was developed by me and my associates, and the Kinzua plan—developed by the U.S. Corps of Engineers.

The capacity of the Kinzua Reservoir site is inflexibly fixed and limited by the fact that there is only one short stretch of the Allegheny where it is feasible to build the dam, while the location of the city of Salamanca upstream in the bottom of the Allegheny River Valley sets a definite limit as to how high water can be stored in the reservoir. No amount of engineering study can change this hard fact.

My first acquaintance with the project in 1956 was the result of a telephone message from Cornelius Seneca, president of the Seneca Nation of Indians in New York State.

Taking into account my engineering experience in flood control, my interest in the improvement of small communities and small cultures, and my connections with the Society of Friends, it was natural for a leading Friend to suggest to Cornelius Seneca that he consult me concerning the impending disruption of the Seneca Reservation by the construction of the Upper Allegheny-Kinzua-Reservoir. I never had worked with the American Indians, had not taken a very active interest in them, and indeed did not know of the existence of the Seneca Nation. Neither was I familiar with the Upper Allegheny River project of the U.S. Corps of Engineers. The experience with the Senecas was somewhat duplicated when I came to examine conditions on the Upper Missouri.

Cornelius Seneca hoped that I might help find that the taking of their reservation as decreed by the Corps was not necessary to the river control program underway.

In 1794 the Senecas had made a treaty with the United States government whereby they surrendered ownership to most of their long-held domain, and in return had received absolute, unqualified promise from the American government, that the small remaining reservation would be theirs, "so long as the sun rises and the river runs." This treaty—known as the Pickering Treaty—was the oldest existing treaty signed by the United States of America. It was signed and ratified during the Presidency of George Washington.

It was under these conditions that Cornelius Seneca came to me, by suggestion made without my knowledge through our common relations with the Quakers, for help in preventing the construction of the Kinzua Dam and Reservoir.

I advised Cornelius Seneca that the Seneca Indians would do well to participate in an open-minded study of the problem, and that if there should be no other reasonable way to protect Pittsburgh and to get the other major benefits of the proposed reservoir, his people should accept the course which would be of the greater public benefit, and then should try to work out with the Corps of Engineers the overall most useful solution.

While most of the alternatives proposed by the Senecas seemed impractical or inadvisable, Cornelius Seneca mentioned one possibility about which I was not informed. It was that the flood waters of the Allegheny, beyond the amount that could be stored, could be diverted to Lake Erie. That solution seemed to have limitations, but I said it was an alternative which I thought deserved study.

When Cornelius Seneca left my office, he was in a quite different state of mind. He said that the Seneca nation would make a public announcement that, unless some suitable alternative should be found, the Senecas would accept the reservoir and try to make a suitable settlement with the Corps of Engineers. Not long after his visit the governing body of the Senecas did announce publicly that, if there were no reasonable alternative, the Seneca nation would withdraw its objection to the construction of the Kinzua reservoir.

I had controverted so nearly all of Cornelius Seneca's ideas and proposals that when he left my office I did not expect to hear from him again. However, he did request me to make a first-hand study of the situation including a study of the prospect of diversion to Lake Erie, and to give the Senecas my opinion.

It was not easy for the Senecas to arrange for an independent study. Legislation had been enacted prohibiting the Senecas from using tribal funds, except on specific governmental approval. This would prevent the Senecas from using their own tribal funds for making an independent inquiry or from trying to protect themselves. How under such circumstances could they have an independent inquiry made? Those who promoted this legislation had not depended on general terms, but had endeavored to list and to prohibit the unapproved use of each specific type of income, such as rental income on tribal land, royalties on sale of gas and oil, and other sources. The Senecas searched for some source of income, the use of which was not prohibited for making an independent examination. Otherwise they would be at the mercy of the Corps of Engineers for statements of fact. It occurred to them that there was no prohibition from using income from the sale of sand and gravel. That source of funds may have been overlooked, or, since there was no large market nearby for sand or gravel, perhaps it did not seem worth mentioning. The Senecas sold some sand and gravel in order to arrange for my employment.

After a year or so of working with the Senecas, as I became acquainted with the conditions and saw the prospect of a waste of more than a hundred million dollars in the plans of the Corps, my center of interest changed. Such a chance to be of service in saving such an amount of money for the public does not occur very often. If I could do that, I would have compensated my country for the privilege of citizenship. I decided to make a major effort. I therefore wrote a letter to the Seneca Nation, resigning my association with them, and thereafter worked without compensation, and at my own expense, with colleagues of my own choosing, who were experts in their fields.

I learned on a study of the situation, that a great saving could be effected by using the vastly larger capacity of Conewango reservoir for storing the Allegheny River's entire year's flow, even during most large floods, and using the entire storage for increasing low water flow. This would entirely remove any flood flow from the Upper Allegheny River.

Exploration of Conewango

In 1924-1927 the Corps of Engineers took a quick glance at the Upper Allegheny, and tentatively planned a power development and flood control project. At that time the Corps was made slightly aware of the existence of the great Conewango basin as a reservoir for power and flood control. This was the first—and very unwilling—departure from the Corps' opposition for more than half a century to flood control reservoirs. In the years since that first look there had been abundant time to make a thorough-going conclusive engineering analysis of this area.

But the curiosity and the tradition of penetrating inquiry were not in the Corps. For more than 30 years the art of plausibility was practiced with all the air of finality by the Corps, with near total disregard for the realities. The Corps repeatedly stated that thorough studies had been made, when none such existed. It seems almost incomprehensible that for more than 30 years this great glacial depression of Conewango was less than ten miles away from the Allegheny River, and that yet the members of the Corps were completely unaware of its major alternative possibilities. But reservoir sites are usually in river valleys. What significance could there be in a depression dug by a glacier? Where is a glacier mentioned in the text books or in West Point classes?

During the early period of my inquiry I had as assistant and associate, Barton M. Jones, who had been chief designing engineer of the TVA during its early years, and for a time was Chief Engineer of the Miami Conservancy District. He died suddenly in 1957 while engaged on Conewango, and I had difficulty in securing his field notes. He had been helpful in the technical design of a plan for the Conewango Reservoir project.

Late in October 1957, shortly after Barton Jones' death, an

agreement was reached between Colonel R. E. Smyser, Division Engineer of the Ohio River Division of the Corps of Engineers in Cincinnati, and the Seneca Nation of Indians, from which the following is quoted:

> The Corps of Engineers will contract with an independent civilian engineering firm, Tippetts-Abbett-McCarthy-Stratton, New York City, to review and re-evaluate the engineering data on a comprehensive basis between the proposed "Kinzua Dam," and the diversion canal and dam in the Conewango Valley as advanced by Dr. Arthur E. Morgan at the Congressional hearings this past June.[6]

When Col. Smyser suggested an examination of my proposal for the Conewango reservoir he said it would be by an *"independent, civilian engineering firm."* He did not tell me that the firm was founded by a man who was a member of the Corps until he resigned or retired to set up this firm, or that of the four partners of the firm, three were ex-Corps members, nor did he tell me that for twenty years or more the Corps had been by far the most important client of the firm. Since the Corps already had strongly condemned my proposal it might be embarrassing for this consulting firm to make a contrary finding.

Just before beginning its work, two representatives of the Corps' consultants, Tippetts, Abbett, McCarthy, Stratton, hereafter referred to as TAMS, visited my office to have my verbal description of my proposed plans. In about a two hour session with TAMS representatives, I outlined the situation in general.

Conewango basin did not supply just a single plan. Its large, rough, forested margin near the drop off into Lake Erie, and the discharge of Conewango Creek into the Allegheny River, gave at least half a dozen alternative solutions to the problem of using the Conewango basin as a reservoir site, each of which possibility called for definitive study before a decision should be made. I explained to the TAMS representatives in some detail the use of one possible outlet to Lake Erie, and proposed three different treatments of the one route; these treatments TAMS designated Plans No. 1, 2 and 3.[7] I had examined this possibility quite thoroughly. I asked also that a determination be made of the maximum usable capacity of the Conewango basin for a reservoir. TAMS made such a determination of the maximum capacity of the Conewango basin and called it "Plan No. 5."[8] I did not specifically request that the three different treatments I suggested be applied to the maximum reservoir capacity.

After these representatives had left my office I felt that I had not sufficiently emphasized the need for a thorough examination of each of the alternatives of the Conewango reservoir. Shortly afterward in November I sought a conference with the TAMS firm but was asked to postpone it from November until sometime in January. At that time they were beginning their field work whereas in January there would be only a few weeks left during which new ideas would be received. I therefore wrote them a letter, dated November 18, 1957, outlining in some detail my suggestions up to that time and emphasized the necessity for examining all possibilities. I wrote:

> The earlier field work and calculations for this study were largely made by my long-time friend and associate, Barton M. Jones. On his sudden death a few weeks ago I located such of his papers as I could and have continued the study. He commented frequently that the project has such a variety of promising alternatives that when the possibilities and economies are fully worked out the plans may have little resemblance to the ones he prepared. There has been expended only about three thousand dollars altogether on our study. It is hoped that as Tippetts-Abbett-McCarthy-Stratton make their study with more adequate resources they will not simply determine the feasibility of the elements we propose, but will be alert to see further possibilities and economies, as well as any weak spots in our proposals.[9]

The Tippetts engineers did not make any general survey of possibilities, but, with the exception of Plan No. 4, only looked into the very first suggestions I made to them. In their

Plan No. 4 TAMS proposed the use of the Conewango basin but suggested that excess flood waters could be carried from the basin back through the diversion channel into the Allegheny River. There was no provision for an outlet channel to Lake Erie in Plan No. 4. When I asked them to look into other possibilities they replied that they could not look further. The TAMS report states:

> . . . the scope of this review has been expanded to cover as much of Dr. Morgan's revised views as available time permitted. (p. 3)[10]

Evidently Col. Smyser assumed that the Conewango prospect was like Kinzua in being simply the building of a dam across a channel, with only one clear answer, and so he gave instructions and limitations to his consultants in accordance with that understanding.

The two situations, however, were greatly different. The Kinzua prospect presented only a narrow river channel to be closed by a dam in a definite place, whereas the Conewango basin was unique. It was a large irregular basin excavated by a great glacier with its long northern margin not far from Lake Erie. Also, it had a ready made channel for an outlet through the deep pre-glacial gorge of Cattaraugus Creek and one of its branches to Lake Erie, which TAMS did not discover. The Conewango basin offered half a dozen alternative solutions, which required definitive study to determine which would be best. In limiting the consultants in time and funds the Corps compelled them to miss entirely two or three of the best solutions, and to be entirely unaware of the existence of the two best.

The consultants saw their assignment to be only to consider benefits "comparable to that of the authorized Allegheny River reservoir project" adopted by the Corps. This was again expressed, "providing substantially the same flood control and low-water benefits as those of the authorized Allegheny River Reservoir project." They did not seek the greatest possible values of the Conewango project. Thus it was not a failure to fulfill their specific assignment to overlook very great values, as it was in failing to provide a relief channel for their Plan No. 5.

This omission of a diversion channel to Lake Erie for use in extreme floods such as might occur at intervals of a century or more, was a very grave limitation of TAMS Plan No. 5. However, my Plan No. 6[11] called for revision in that one respect. By later correcting TAMS' inadequate estimate of the full use of the capacity they had found for Conewango Reservoir, the vastly greater capacity of Conewango is made evident. With their Plan No. 5 left in that condition it would be necessary to leave half the capacity of that reservoir unused for one or two centuries at a time in order to have available capacity for holding the excess of the extremely rare but extremely disastrous floods. By amending TAMS Plan No. 5 and adding an emergency channel to Lake Erie to carry for a few days the excess of the extremely rare great flood, almost the entire maximum capacity of Conewango Reservoir could at all other times be available for storing decade after decade the entire year's flow of the upper Allegheny River and for increasing the low water flow at Pittsburgh and down the Ohio River.

At the rate of $100 per acre foot of storage for increasing low water flow (which was actually incurred in building Kinzua) the great storage capacity of Conewango would be worth an added $150,000,000 more than Kinzua for low water storage.

The need for that greater storage for increasing low water flow down the Ohio River is almost unlimited. In fact the TAMS report stated:

> It is anticipated that the need for a regulated supply of water in the Ohio River Basin for industrial use and other purposes will eventually increase to a point where all available sources will be fully exploited. The benefits resulting from using Conewango Reservoir to develop fully the water resources of the Allegheny River would therefore continue to be increasingly important.[12]

It is almost certain that the land along the Ohio River will be one of the world's greatest centers for chemical industry.

The narrow flat valley along the Ohio River is rapidly being purchased for that use. General Itschner, Chief of Engineers, referred to this area as "The Ruhr of America."[1][3]

Underneath the Ohio River and its valley is one of the world's greatest concentrations of salt deposits—a prime need in chemical industry. By barge transportation through the coal region, coal can be delivered along the river as cheaply as anywhere in the world. Sulfur from the great deposits of Louisiana and the Gulf coast can be delivered by barge on the Mississippi and Ohio very cheaply. Coal and sulfur are imperative elements in chemical industry. South of the Ohio River in the hills of West Virginia and Kentucky is more available labor needing employment than almost anywhere else in America. In few localities are conditions for chemical industry so favorable, and a major factor for chemical industry is abundance of water of good quality. By greatly restricting the flow available for low water periods in the Ohio, the Corps sacrificed the possibilities of industry in addition to reducing the quality of water, and generally losing the value of a much greater low water supply.

I had asked the House Appropriations Subcommittee to provide for an impartial, disinterested comparison of the two alternatives. The Corps opposed such an independent, impartial comparison. And after being ordered by the House Appropriations Committee to make a comparison of the two alternatives, the Chief of Engineers made a report opposing Conewango and favoring Kinzua. [He stated] Concerning the larger capacity of Conewango:

> It is not practicable under present authorities to assess benefits for conjectural, possible future water supply needs as a basis for justifying additional water supply storage. . . .That additional investment [for Conewango] could not be justified on the basis of additional benefits that can now be evaluated.[1][4] *

*In a list of polluted rivers (*Look* Magazine, May 4, 1971, p. 25) the Ohio is referred to as "America's filthiest." But for the gross over-estimate of Conewango Reservoir to cover up the facts of

This is the Chief of Engineers, speaking against Conewango. But note what the same Chief of Engineers a few months from that date said of such storage, when he was addressing the Ohio Valley Improvement Association:

> The cost of acquiring land for reservoirs is rapidly becoming one of the most serious and expensive items of water resource development throughout the country. . . . The states and localities should take proper measures to discourage or prevent further expensive development, *particularly public improvements* such as dual highways, airports, and utility lines within such areas. . . .
>
> A third and highly important matter is that of combining wherever possible, provision for local and area water supply with Corps of Engineers reservoirs *built primarily for river control.* This is a means by which, we can reduce the costs of both flood control and water supply. (Emphasis added.)
>
> It has been estimated that by 1980 the use of water in this valley (less Cumberland and Tennessee) will be about three and a half times the present use. Allowing for the re-use of water, the total demand in 1980 is expected to be some 13 times greater than the present dependable discharge of the lower Ohio River. While accurate conclusions cannot be drawn for specific areas from this prediction it does emphasize the probability that competition for the use of water will become keen in the future. It also makes clear the necessity for providing storage to increase the dependability of existing supplies.

---

atrociously inaccurate work of the Corps, the four hundred per cent greater storage capacity of Conewango for reducing Ohio River pollution would have cost no more than the inferior capacity of Kinzua. The extreme incompetence and inadequacy of the Corps in plans for controlling the Upper Ohio was not found by hunting for an extreme case, but by looking into this particular case at the request of the Seneca Indians, because of the Corps' callous disregard of their treaty with the United States. The extreme incompetence of the Corps in this case almost immedialy adjoining the Corps' major Pittsburgh office is a hint of what might be found in a search of its hundreds of projects over the country.

Studies indicate that the future water demand-supply relationships in the Ohio Basin to be one of the most critical in the most humid east.[1 5]

And, in the *Saturday Evening Post* for June 5, 1959, only a few months from the time he made his adverse report on Conewango to the Appropriations Committee, General Itschner said:

We face a critical problem of reservoir sites. Good locations for major impoundments are already being lost at an alarming rate as improvements of one kind or other industrial plants, housing projects, highways, public utilities and other facilities are built in the very places reservoirs should be located.

Again he wrote:

As the natural occurrence of water in this basin will no doubt remain about the same as it has been in the past, the needs generated by increased activities will obviously call for a considerably higher rate of water resources development than heretofore.[1 6]

Conewango is the only unoccupied reservoir site on the whole Ohio River system where similar preservation of its entire capacity for low water increase is possible.

It was not only in Ohio that Chief of Engineers General Itschner carried his message. Wherever he went, it was the same message. Speaking before the Water Supply Conference, Illinois State Chamber of Commerce, on August 27, 1958, three or four months after he presented his adverse report on Conewango to the Appropriations Committee, the Chief of Engineers said:

We may find at an earlier date than we realize that the availability of water and the provisions made for its utilization will become one of the major limitations on our growth, prosperity and strength. Our efforts and progress must be constantly reviewed and improved in that light and with full consciousness of their importance to national survival.

We have already reached a critical point where our overall water resources efforts must be placed on a more orderly basis. *We must avoid irrevocable actions,* that would establish a ceiling to our growth at a lower point than necessary. (Emphasis added.)[1][7]

And so one might go on and on, quoting from Chief of Engineers General Itschner and his predecessors and successors, on the same subject, and to the same end. How could such expressions so completely contradict their statements to the Appropriations Committee?

Conewango Reservoir is by far the greatest and least expensive unused reservoir site along the Ohio River. I undertook personally an exploration of the entire margin of the Conewango basin; and thus I found an additional and very much superior route for an outlet from Conewango to Lake Erie.

To find it, I travelled around the margin of the Conewango basin. I tramped on foot through the woods and gullies, following up each hint of a prospect, and found one very much superior to any TAMS had explored. Then I located the men who had drilled for water, gas and oil in that area, and went over the ground with them personally, while they, and the few farmers who had wells, told me about the underground structure. Following along a gully, it was possible to locate definitely the border line between the rock of the mountainside and the sand, gravel and clay of the glacial deposit. The elevation of the clay layer could be observed, and largely avoided. By careful observation one could keep just far enough from the mountainside to avoid rock excavation, yet close enough to have rock foundation for outlet works.

The ranking officers of the Corps later were eloquent with regard to the unknown difficulties I would face, and in light of these difficulties, they raised my estimates. The farmers along the route told me there had been no Corps' surveyors or investigators over that route, though on one occasion two Corps men drove by on a nearby highway. The Corps had not made a first hand conclusive study, and in their criticisms and assertions in opposition to my proposals they may have assumed that I was as uninformed as they were.

A habit of conclusive engineering analysis would have led the Corps to look into the proposal to find whether there might be something of value, especially as to outlet from the Conewango basin. But, aside from the survey of the consulting firm, which made no such thorough study, there was not in evidence any spirit of inquiry. The aim seemed wholly not to explore the prospect, but to discredit it. In my opinion, even the partial disclosures of that survey by the TAMS consulting firm, limited though it was by the instructions of the Corps under which it worked, still gave strong evidence of the superiority of Conewango over Kinzua, and were clear enough to have led the Corps at least to a careful exploration.

Frequently, in their concern to find reasons against Conewango, the Corps has stated that it would not be possible to make a diversion into the International waters of Lake Erie because of international relations. Yet, if the entire rainfall of a maximum storm on the Upper Allegheny watershed were put into Lake Erie all in an instant, which of course would be impossible, it would raise the Lake's level less than three inches.

Brigadier General Roy T. Dodge, Division Engineer of the North Central Division of the Corps of Engineers, said to the Great Lakes Commission at Chicago in a speech in reference to international cooperation on January 25, 1965:

> Any action or proposed action along these lines would require full co-ordination with Canada. And I might say here that, based on my association with the International Boards which deal in these matters, I consider work in this area to be a model of international cooperation.[18]

In this case, as elsewhere, the freedom of the Corps in making the statements which explicitly contradict each other cavalierly risks that some members of the public, as members of the public, would not hear their diametrically opposite assertions.

Indeed with Conewango and with a safety valve to Lake

Erie there would have been no need for concern about such complications. Conewango would provide the necessary flood protection without difficulty. Moreover, Canada would be eager for such a connection, since, it would be possible to supply emergency water for sudden needs in Lake Erie, water which, in the absence of Conewango Reservoir, would be solely a flood season threat.

Very great floods are very rare occurrences, possibly not even as often as once in a century. But, as Colonel Smyser, head of the Ohio River Division of the Corps of Engineers, testified concerning the attempt to get all possible capacity for Kinzua, "even if a flood be due but once in 300 years, that once may be tomorrow." A modern foresighted nation should not leave a densely populated area subject to a flood disaster even once in a century, *especially if a completely adequate and safe alternative is fully available,* as was the case with Conewango.

The Letter of Transmittal

When the work of the consulting firm had ended, its report was delivered to the Ohio River Division of the Corps of Engineers at Cincinnati. As made public the Report was introduced by a *Letter of Transmittal.* In my opinion, this Letter of Transmittal was drafted in the office of the Corps of Engineers with the collaboration of the consulting firm and the Corps. The Letter of Transmittal was made public by a news release by Col. Smyser, head of the Ohio River Division of the Corps of Engineers. Without having informed me that the Report was ready, or giving me a chance to comment on it, they approved this Letter of Transmittal:

Tippetts-Abbett-McCarthy-Stratton
Engineers
62 West 47th Street
New York 36, New York
April 1, 1958

Colonel R. E. Smyser, Jr., Division Engineer
U.S. Army Engineer Division, Ohio River
P. O. Box 1159
Cincinnati, Ohio

Dear Colonel Smyser:

In compliance with our contract No. DA-33-017-CIVENG-58-7, dated October 22, 1957, we are pleased to submit our report on the Allegheny Reservoir Project—Authorized Plan and Alternatives.

During the past five months, we have made an engineering study and review of the features and costs of the Authorized Project, and of five alternative plans that cover the principal possibilities for storage in the Conewango Valley and for diversion through the Conewango Valley to Lake Erie. One of these provides for diversion of Allegheny flood waters to Lake Erie substantially as proposed by Dr. A. E. Morgan to the Appropriations Committee of the U. S. Senate on May 22, 1957. Two of the plans would have lesser rates of diversion to Lake Erie, and two would not involve diversion out of the Allegheny Basin.

During the course of our studies, we have reviewed data furnished by you on the Allegheny Reservoir Project and have held several meetings with you and your staff. In a series of field reconnaissances, on one of which we were accompanied by Mr. Cornelius Seneca, President of the Seneca Indian Nation, we examined field conditions in the alternative-project area, with particular reference to the problem of railroad and highway relocations and the cost of land taking. We met several times with Dr. Morgan, consulting engineer to the Seneca Indian Nation, and have reviewed and studied a number of suggestions that he furnished us.

Our occasions of contact were few. We never were informed of the conclusions they had reached. We wrote asking for occasion to meet them in their office, but were told it was not convenient. We were not allowed to see the report which was nearing completion. We met at the office of the consultants only once, when the report was almost complete except as to one particular. In some respects they did not take the trouble to learn the nature of our plans, and totally misrepresented those plans in discussing them. For instance, in describing in their Report our plans for the removal of the Pennsylvania Railroad, they definitely assumed an extremely inefficient method entirely different from what we had planned and vastly more expensive.

We discussed pertinent problems with County and State officials, with representatives of the railroads, and with experienced earth work contractors. We had four borings made, under our supervision, to investigate sub-surface conditions.

TAMS did make four borings at our suggestion but otherwise declined to consider nearly every one of our urgent suggestions and requests, especially all those relating to the examination of further alternatives to which we had urgently drawn their attention. They did not want us to know the nature of their conclusions, or to make any criticisms of their suggestions, which might have corrected their errors.

Our findings are contained in the attached report, together with a description of our studies, and are summarized in the section of the report entitled "Summary of Major Findings." In brief, we find that:

1. The storages allocated in the Authorized Project for winter flood control and summer low-flow augmentation are adequate but not excessive and are economically justified.

2. There is no engineering or construction reason why either the Authorized Project or any of the alternative plans cannot be built, and either the Authorized Project or any of the alternative plans could be operated to meet the requirements established by the Corps of Engineers for flood control and low-flow augmentation in the Allegheny River.

3. The alternative plans would cost from 25% to 38% more than the Authorized Project.

4. The alternative plans would require the dislocation of from 51% to 108% more land than the Authorized Project.

5. The alternative plans would require the dislocation of from 150% to 180% more people than the Authorized Project.

6. Three of the alternative plans studied would divert flood waters to Lake Erie that could be used to generate an additional 115,000,000 kilowatt-hours annually at Niagara Falls, worth about $230,000.

7. Two of the plans studied would provide a conservation pool 500,000 acre-feet larger than that of the Authorized Project. This additional storage would be available for low-flow augmentation purposes, if desired.

This has been an interesting and challenging assignment, and we trust that the findings of our report will be of assistance to you. We wish to thank you for the full cooperation we have enjoyed from you and your staff.

> Very truly yours,
> TIBBETTS-ABBETT-McCARTHY-STRATTON
> Gerald T. McCarthy

This letter of transmittal was the only part of the TAMS report generally made public by the Corps.

While the report was officially an appraisal of my proposal, I was not allowed to see it until it had been presented to the Chief of Engineers with the inference that it was unfavorable to my proposal, and that the plans of the Corps were preferable. From that time on the Congress and the public were informed that the consultant's report was favorable to the Corps' plan and that my report was markedly inferior. Probably 90% of the quotations from the report made by members of the Corps in their statements concerning the report were from the numbered paragraphs of that Letter of Transmittal. *Actually the consultant's report did not express any preference for either the Kinzua or the Conewango plan.*

The only comments made on these points by Col. Smyser in his news release, so far as they related to the Conewango plan, as to the adequacy of the provisions for low water augmentation, were quite in contrast to the repeated appeals of the Chief of Engineers and of his predecessors and successors.

Here is a case where the consulting firm, without making a factual misstatement, could convey a grossly false impression. Naturally the Engineer Corps in planning the Kinzua Reservoir planned only for the actual capacity of that reservoir. There would have been no sense in planning for a capacity which did not exist. In the Letter of Transmission, the consultants did not state that either one of the designs would be adequate. They stated that:

> There is no engineering or construction reason why either the Authorized Project or any of the alternative plans cannot be built, and either the Authorized Project or any of the alternative plans could be operated *to meet the requirements, established by the Corps of Engineers* for flood control and low flow augmentation in the Allegheny River. (Emphasis added.)

There is no statement that the plans are *equally adequate*, but only that either would meet "the requirements established by the Corps."

In the consultants' estimates for Conewango plans Numbers 1, 2 and 3, the plans were completed with emergency diversion channels to Lake Erie. Plan No. 5, however, was left incomplete, without such a diversion channel. If Plan Number 5 were completed in the same way as the others, the results would be that Conewango Reservoir would have flood control capacity much more than twice as great as Kinzua, and would have four times the capacity for storage for low water use as would Kinzua. A plain statement of the reality by the Consultants would have been that Conewango would have more than twice the flood prevention capacity of Kinzua and four times the capacity of storage for low water use.

Kinzua would do less than half what Conewango would do. In fact, in outlining the work of the Consultants, the Corps had asked only whether Conewango would perform equal service. It was not necessary for TAMS to draw attention to the fact that Conewango would have twice the capacity of Kinzua, for flood control, and four times as much for low water storage. If TAMS' report is carefully examined, the information of the superiority of Conewango is there, but inconspicuously stated. The Letter of Transmittal buried that important information in misleading statements, so that Congress and the public would be quite unaware of this important information. In ordinary life such a course might be called misrepresentation, or it might be given even a harsher designation. Let us examine the numbered paragraphs of the Letter of Transmittal.

The first numbered paragraph which relates to Kinzua is a finding of the Corps, not of the consulting firm, which states:

> The storages allocated in the Authorized Project for winter flood control and summer low-flow augmentation are adequate but not excessive and are economically justified.

There is no evidence that the consulting firm made studies which would have justified that conclusion. As to the adequacy of provision for low water augmentation, the repeated appeals of the incumbent Chief of Engineers, and his predecessors and successors, which I have quoted, as well as the statement of TAMS in its report, are striking, direct evidence to the contrary. The Kinzua provision for flood control, according to the Corps of Engineers, sufficient to care for 40 to 60% of the maximum flood, not providing for such exigencies as heavy winter snow in addition to rain, double crested floods and other complications which I mention elsewhere, is a repetition of the finding of the Corps.

Paragraph 2 states that:

> There is no engineering or construction reason why either the Authorized Project or any of the alternative plans cannot be built, and either the Authorized Project or any of the alternative plans could be operated to meet the requirements established by the Corps of Engineers for flood control and low-flow augmentation in the Allegheny River.

This paragraph, a clear recognition of the feasibility of using the Conewango basin, controverts the position of the Corps for 30 years until my proposal was made in 1957. For instance, until 1957 the Corps had taken the absolute position that:

A major reservoir on the Allegheny would be required in connection with any plan of diversion, flood control or power generation.

That assertion is controverted by Paragraph 2 of the Letter of Transmittal.

Paragraph 3 reads:

The alternative plans would cost from 25% to 38% more than the Authorized Project.

I have commented elsewhere on the improper use of unit cost estimates under circumstances very different from those for which they had been originally adopted. A good many millions of dollars are involved in this wholly improper misuse of estimates of unit cost. Their estimate for excavation of the Kinzua Reservoir was largely on steep rocky mountain sides where maximum costs would be expected. The consultants transferred these unit costs to the relatively flat glaciated areas around the Conewango reservoir and high fills across the reservoir for highways, for all of which the cost per yard of excavation would probably be not more than half the cost incurred for Kinzua.

Paragraph 4 discusses the taking of more land for Conewango:

The alternative plans would require the taking of from 51% to 108% more land than the Authorized Project.

A large part of the Conewango basin is flat, wet, hard pan, bottom land, useless for agriculture and covered by brush and small trees which were left when the merchantable timber was cut, or was in use for low grade pasture or meadow. The TAMS report refers to it as:

A predominant type of poorly drained or hard pan soil, the principal use of the land is for pasture and hay.... The economy of the area is generally depressed. Many farms and farm buildings have been abandoned or are in need of rehabilitation.

The Corps in its 1928 report on the use of the Conewango

basin for power development, reported:

> The Conewango reservoir is so situated that a great portion of the valley floor is occupied by swamp land which is of little or no value.

It would be a good fortune to the owners of land in this area to have it purchased as a reservoir. The relative values and the interests of the residents are exactly the opposite of those implied in the Letter of Transmittal. Yet no part of the report was quoted more often by the members of the Corps in their effort to discredit Conewango.

In contrast, the land along the Allegheny River, not included in the Seneca Reservation, was a popular summer vacation area. There were hundreds of summer homes, cabins or cottages along the river. If Conewango had been built, removing flood danger from this stretch of river and insuring a good summer flow, instead of a river that in summer was nearly dry, this would have been one of the choice summer home areas of western Pennsylvania.

notes

1. Pittsburgh Office of the U.S. Corps of Engineers, Report of the 1928 study of the diversion project for power and flood control on the Upper Allegheny, and of a flood control project on the Allegheny, p. 54. (Quoted by the Flood Commission of Pittsburgh.)

2. Flood Commission of Pittsburgh, Pa.: "Review of Report of the U.S. Corps of Engineers on Flood Control Survey, Allegheny and Monongahela Rivers," Pittsburgh, Pa., April 30, 1930, 6: "Possible Combination of Flood Control and Power Development on the Upper Allegheny."

3. *Ibid.*

4. *Ibid.*

5. George S. Davison, Flood Commission of Pittsburgh, in a letter to Major-General Lytle Brown, Chief of Engineers, April 30, 1930.

6. Col. R. E. Smyser, Division Engineer of The Ohio River Division of the Corps of Engineers, quoted by Cornelius Seneca, President of the Seneca Nation of Indians, in a letter to Col. Smyser, Nov. 1, 1957.

7. Report of Tippetts, Abbett, McCarthy, Stratton, Consulting Engineers: "Plans 1, 2, 3: Allegheny River Reservoir: A Review of Authorized Plan and Alternatives, for the U.S. Army Corps of Engineers Division, Ohio River," (April, 1958, New York), pp. 9-15.

8. *Ibid.*, Plan No. 5., p. 16.

9. Letter of Arthur E. Morgan to TAMS Consulting Engineers, Nov. 18, 1957.

10. TAMS, *op. cit.*, p. 3.

11. Arthur E. Morgan: "Memorandum to Gen. E. C. Itschner, Chief of Engineers, U.S. Army, On the Conewango Reservoir Diversion Project for Control of the Upper Allegheny River," Oct. 13, 1958.

12. TAMS, *op. cit.*, p. 32.

13. Gen. E. C. Itschner, Speech to the Oklahoma City Chamber of Commerce, Jan. 23, 1958, p. 5.

14. General E. C. Itschner, Analysis of Allegheny Reservoir and Alternate Proposal of Dr. Arthur E. Morgan, to the Sub-committee on Public Works of the House Appropriations Committee, 1958.

15. General E. C. Itschner, Address to the Ohio Valley Improvement Association, Cincinnati, Ohio, Oct. 26, 1959, pp. 6, 7, 8.

16. General E. C. Itschner, article in the *Saturday Evening Post*, June 5, 1959.

17. General E. C. Itschner, to Illinois State Chamber of Commerce, Aug. 27, 1958: "Water Resources in a Growing America."

18. Brigadier-General Roy T. Dodge, Division Engineer of the North Central Division of the Corps of Engineers, to the Great Lakes Commission at Chicago, on "Great Lakes Water Levels," Jan. 25, 1965.

chapter 11

the kinzua
dam

The larger area of Conewango Reservoir would have provided a lake four times the size of Kinzua, with twice the total storage capacity. The lakeside lots resulting from the newly created shore line would greatly enhance the value of the property thus improved. The actual balance of values would have been just the opposite of those stated in the Letter of Transmittal.

Paragraph 5 expresses the most primitive and tragic decision of the consultants and of the Corps:

The alternative plans would require the dislocation of from 150% to 180% more people than the Authorized Project.

Around the margin of Conewango basin are four villages and a few small hamlets. Each of the villages has populations from 500 to 900, except for Randolph, which has about 1500. If the Conewango Reservoir had been built the homes in these villages which would be flooded could have been moved above water, where they would have been on the shore of a large lake with pleasantly sloping shores. They would become popular recreation centers. The largest town, Randolph, is now in a highly precarious position. The lower part of the town is at the outlet of a mountain stream which comes down with a fall of 100 feet to the mile. As sure as fate, Randolph will some day have its turn with an intense summer rain storm which will rush down the mountain, producing one of those intense local disasters. In removing the low lying buildings which otherwise would be flooded by the reservoir, this certain risk would be removed, and the town made safe. Randolph is the only community along the shore of Conewango basin which has its own industrial life, nearly all located in the area subject to local flood. To brusquely extinguish the homes of these 4,000 people around the margin of Conewango basin as proposed and to leave them to readjust their lives as they could, would be a last desperate measure. Humane engineers practicing conclusive engineering analysis find better methods. It is only by assuming such ruthless practice that there could be any truth to this statement.

With a normal human treatment many more persons would be displaced by Kinzua than by Conewango, and under far more difficult circumstances. Down stream from the Seneca reservation the Kinzua reservoir lies between very steep, rugged mountain sides. The slope of these mountain sides is stated by the Corps to be 1½ to 1. There was no chance for the village of Kinzua and other villages to move up the steep slope to new locations above flood level. They had to be abandoned. If Conewango had been chosen, this destruction would not have been necessary.

To illustrate what might have been done in a situation more difficult than Conewango, let me illustrate the course taken on one of my projects.

In the planning and building of the Huffman Dam and reservoir in the Miami Valley Conservancy District in Ohio there was in the way the village of Osborn, population about 1,000. Also the village of Fairfield would be damaged in very great floods. A mile or two away from each we laid out a new town site in a competent modern way. We retained a hundred foot wide connecting strip of land, so that the legal continuity of the corporations never was interrupted. Then with a large scale moving program we very economically moved all the houses worth moving from the old site to the new. After the new site was established the old site was vacated, with no break in official continuity.

This location was so favorable that we recommended it to the government as the location for a federal research project. The recommendation was adopted, the undertaking was successful, and today the combination of these two villages is a thriving community of 30,000 people called Fairborn—the largest community in the county.

In the case of Conewango the villages would still be largely above water after the construction of the reservoir. It would be necessary only to move the low lying parts of the villages to adjoining higher areas as extensions of the villages, where the topography is very well suited to residence or economic use. In striking contrast, the villages displaced by the Kinzua Reservoir could not be moved and had to be entirely destroyed. As a matter of fact, the damages with reference to moving villages was far more serious for Kinzua than for Conewango, yet the Letter of Transmittal states the exact opposite.

Paragraph 6, relating to power at Niagara Falls, is of no concern here.

Paragraph 7 states:

Two of the plans studied would provide a conservation pool 500,000 acre feet larger than that of the authorized project.

If TAMS Plan No. 5 had been completed it would have shown that the conservation pool of Conewango would be, not 500,000 acre feet larger than Kinzua, but 1,500,000 acre feet larger. At the cost of $100 per acre foot, which was the cost of conservation storage for Kinzua, this one item would be worth $150,000,000 more than indicated by the Letter of Transmittal. The very great increase of storage for low water use, if estimated at the unit cost of low water storage for Kinzua, alone would pay the whole cost of flood control.

It is not only storm rainfall for which Kinzua reservoir would have to serve, but sometimes also the winter snow which may not have melted until the rain came. The Pittsburgh Flood Commission wrote:

It was the warm spring rain on the accumulated snow which caused the most disastrous flood which ever occurred on the Allegheny River, that of March 1907.[1]

The Letter of Transmittal did not draw attention to the fact that whereas Kinzua would care for half the maximum flood, though not in case of heavy rainfall with snow on the ground or with many other possible contingencies, Conewango would care for *all* flood contingencies. Yet probably more than 90% of all Engineer Corps' references to the consultant's report were only to the Letter of Transmittal, which for the most part is a collection of strikingly misleading statements. The art of plausibility is highly developed with the Corps.

The Corps and Flood Control

Handling floods has been a major concern of the U.S. Corps of Engineers. For more than a century the training ground of the Corps has been the U.S. Military Academy at West Point. And even in the 1968-1969 year, the U.S. Military Academy Catalog has no reference to public works. There is no department relating to this field. There is but one relevant course, technical engineering, offered which may prepare a cadet for public works such as flood control. Quite in contrast, West Point is a training place for war, as it was a century ago, and military considerations rule the program.

It cannot be over-emphasized that the process of war is very different from the process of internal improvements. It has not been clearly realized that the conditions of conducting a war, as they have long been presented by traditional West Point military doctrine, are strikingly different from the demands of civilian human relations in planning and construction of public works programs.

Thorough-going conclusive analysis, to the end that all factors and prospects have been deliberately mastered and compared, has been strikingly absent for a century. The case of the Upper Allegheny is evidence that, especially with engineer officers who graduated more than twenty years ago, and who are at the peak of their prestige, the century-old ways still hold. The young men of later classes, while adding to the quality of technology, are not yet in control of policy, and tend to be under servitude and intensive indoctrination to the century-old "establishment."

Our country still is young. Probably since its settlement by Europeans no area subject to flood has as yet undergone the greatest flood which sometime may come to it. Probably on many streams the "greatest flood on record" may occur, only to have that record broken again and again. That does not imply a tendency toward increase of undesirable experience, but simply of increased length of experience.

During a recent period of 42 years, on three occasions our country has experienced the greatest flood disaster in the nation's short history: in 1913—the Miami River Flood, in 1927—the Mississippi River Flood, and in 1955—the New England Flood. Each flood broke the national record up to that time.

The first of those three disasters was known as "The Dayton Flood" which in March 1913 struck ten cities of the Miami Valley. The City of Dayton and other communities of the Valley had been suffering from Miami River floods for a century. When a large flood occurred in 1898 the people of Dayton decided to put an end to flood losses. They employed a well-known hydraulic engineer to prepare plans. His aim was to be adequate, but not excessive. He planned to make Dayton safe against a flood of 90,000 cubic feet per second. The plans were approved, and contractors were installing equipment to do the work when the flood occurred, not of 90,000 cubic feet per second, but of 250,000 cubic feet per second. More than 200 people were drowned and property damage was estimated at $200,000,000. The occurrence was rated as the greatest flood disaster in the history of our country.

Up to that time no thorough and adequate study of rainfall possibilities had been made in our country. I directed the first such studies. As Chief Engineer for the project of protecting Dayton and the whole Miami River Valley (The

Miami Conservancy District) from flood damage, I initiated the most extensive and thorough study of rainfall possibilities in the history of America. Examination was made for the eastern half of our country of the entire records of the U.S. Weather Bureau, its predecessor, the Signal Corps, and such fragments of older records as could be found by a staff of men during the years 1913-1917. One of the ablest theoretical engineers and hydrologists in America, S. M. Woodward, assisted with a parallel theoretical study of rainfall possibilities. The whole was published by the Miami Conservancy District under the title "Storm Rainfall in the Eastern United States." It became at that time the standard authority on the subject.

In 1958 the Chief of Engineers took credit before the House of Representatives Subcommittee on Appropriations for Public Works for the method of making rainfall studies in 1936. The Corps used the U.S. Weather Bureau to make these studies. They neglected to mention the first such studies I had made many years before.

Sometime after the Miami Conservancy District (Dayton Flood Control) work was finished, my engineering firm became Chief Engineer for the Muskingum Conservancy District, a $50,000,000 project to control the Muskingum River in Ohio. In 1933 I resigned from that position to become Chairman and Chief Engineer of the Tennessee Valley Authority (TVA). I was followed on the Muskingum project by the U.S. Corps of Engineers. This became the first actual experience of the Corps of Engineers in administering the construction of flood control reservoirs. For the Muskingum project we had established standards for maximum flood rainfall by which we worked. When the Engineer Corps took over the project they reduced our estimates of flood rainfall protection from 9 inches to 6 inches. During the progress of the work, through the influence of some of my former men who stayed on the job, the Corps decided that they had been mistaken in making that reduction in estimates of rainfall and revised their standards upward, but only to 7 inches. So, inadequate flood control protection is not new to the Corps.

The second breaking of national records by a flood disaster was on the Mississippi. For 75 years the Corps of Engineers had been planning and constructing works for the Mississippi River. I believe that during the 75 years period of the Corps' control of that region no thorough rainfall studies had been made by the Corps.

Gradually the Corps, by a protection system consisting chiefly of levees, reached the conclusion that the Mississippi River was almost safe from serious flood damage. For a few years up to and including 1923 in each of the annual reports of the Corps there was the announcement that the Mississippi was now safe from serious flood damage, "except from the most extreme floods." Then, beginning with the Annual Report for 1924, and continuing in the reports for 1925 and 1926, all qualification was removed. The country was assured that "the Mississippi is safe from serious flood damage."

Then came the great 1927 flood, far greater than any previous flood disaster, and far greater than anything the Corps had anticipated. It tore up the flood protection system of levees for hundreds of miles, drowned many people, and destroyed a vast amount of property. It was the greatest flood disaster of America up to that time (as before stated).

The third case in 42 years of breaking the national record for a flood disaster occurred in New England in 1955. It was a very great flood which in its effects exceeded anything in the 250 years of the settlement of New England, and was the greatest flood disaster in our nation's history. Such a storm would seem quite "improbable."

Should such "improbabilities" be protected against? That should depend somewhat on circumstances. To protect New England completely would cost many hundreds of millions of dollars. On the other hand to give full, unlimited protection under all conditions from Upper Allegheny floods by use of the Conewango basin plan, would have cost little, if any, more than the very incomplete protection provided by the Kinzua plan.

In the case of the very great, though very infrequent flood disasters against which a nation such as the United States should protect itself, the ordinary conditions of rain and flood forecasting may not be adequate. By what might have been the good fortune of the U.S. Corps of Engineers, the use of the Conewango reservoir site could have protected against, not only the 40%-60% of the estimated maximum probable flood flow, which the Corps officially estimated, but against a full 100% of the extreme maximum calculated flow. If even half of the estimated maximum rainfall, occurring in February or March, should fall upon the winter's accumulated snow, adding 50% to the maximum runoff from extreme rainfall, Conewango "Plan No. 5," provided with a diversion channel to Lake Erie, could take care of the extreme flood of once in one or two centuries. In addition, it would have provided 2,000,000 acre feet of storage space available for increasing low water flow. Conewango thus could have made an exceptionally large contribution to the reserves of water supply storage for which the Chiefs of Engineers for a decade have been pleading so urgently.

Difficulties of Estimating and Forecasting Floods

The Pennsylvania Department of Forests and Water, in cooperation with the U.S. Geological Survey, issued a publication entitled, "The Floods of March 1946 in Pennsylvania," from which the following is quoted:

> Just prior to the general storm of March 11 and 12, there was snow on the ground in most of the headwaters of the Susquehanna and Delaware Rivers in New York— and the eastern tributaries of the Allegheny and Monongahela rivers. Preliminary estimates indicate . . . that in certain of the Susquehanna and the eastern tributaries of the Allegheny and Monongahela Rivers the snow cover equalled more than four inches (of water).[2]

Four inches in depth is about four-tenths of a maximum rainstorm in that region of the size of the Upper Allegheny.

At Harrisburg on February 17 there had been 35 inches of snowfall, and on that date there was 12" of snow which had a water content of 3.94". This decreased to

1.5" on March 2. On March 3 it increased to 4.3"—and in the afternoon all snow had disappeared.

The general melting of accumulated snow and its entire disappearance on extensive areas prior to the advent of heavy rains on and subsequent to March 11, greatly alleviated a most threatening condition. (Emphasis added.)[3]

There may be some rare cases in which a heavy snow will not have melted until a great rain may occur and produce a rare and disastrous flood. "Unusual conditions" are unusual. To take another nearby case, the 1928 report of the Corps of Engineers (Appendix 3, paragraphs 1-5), mentions a storm on the Monongahela and Allegheny Rivers on March 1, 1902, in which there was light rain on deep snow. The runoff was 232% of the rainfall. It is only a matter of time until a heavy rain falls on a heavy snow, such as the collection of 100 inches of snow in March, 1910. (Report of Pittsburgh Flood Commission, p. 47.) Fortunately March 1910 had less than 1 inch of rain. Had the usual March rainfall of about 5 inches occurred, the resulting flood might have been the greatest on record. If there should be such a snow cover in case of a storm even half as heavy as the maximum probable rainfall, the resulting flood would approximate the maximum probable, and would overtax the Kinzua reservoir. This, according to the Corps of Engineers' method of calculation, probably would do many millions of dollars of damage at Pittsburgh and below.

Comparison of Kinzua and Conewango flow Considerations

Kinzua provides no margin of safety from a great storm. The runoff from such a storm might be much greater than that estimated by the Corps of Engineers, or by the Tippetts Engineers. They estimate that in case of a storm 44% as large as the maximum probable, two-thirds of the rain will run off. In the case of the Dayton, Ohio, flood, from an area of similar size, on much flatter ground, 91% of the rain ran off. Earlier rains had saturated the ground, but there was no snow cover. If the runoff from the "standard design flood" should be 90% instead of the 66% estimated, the damage at Pittsburgh would be heavy. In the case of using Conewango basin for a reservoir such a large runoff would be completely taken care of, and would cause no flood discharge at Warren or Pittsburgh from the Upper Allegheny. This is a fundamental and very serious limitation to the value of the Kinzua Plan which has not been faced in the discussions of the Corps of Engineers or of the Tippetts engineers. We shall illustrate this limitation, from the published conclusions of the U.S. Weather Bureau, the Corps of Engineers, and the Tippetts engineers, and from actual cases.

The Corps of Engineers has estimated the value to Pittsburgh and vicinity which would result from the Kinzua Dam in case of each of the 27 floods which have occurred from 1860 to the present.[4] So far as explicit data is available, these estimates of benefits assume that the entire flow at Kinzua would be held back in each case, and that the full effect of that diminution would be secured exactly on schedule at Pittsburgh 176 miles and two to four days away. This is not strained or figurative language, but actually represents the assumptions of these estimates of benefits. To obtain such estimates would call for weather forecasting and flood wave estimating of a high order. My own intensive study of rainfall and runoff came to fruition in 1913, when for the Miami Conservancy District I brought about a study of storm rainfall in the eastern U.S. which has been followed as a type treatment of the subject since then, in most engineering projects including the Weather Bureau and the Corps of Engineers.

Let us assume that such a high degree of accuracy is actually achieved. These published estimates of benefits which would be received assume that there never would be a problem of whether to store or not to store water at any time. That is a mistaken assumption, especially in case of very large floods.

The type of rainfall which could produce the maximum probable flood, as developed by the U.S. Weather Bureau and

the Corps of Engineers, and as used by the Tippetts engineers
in deciding what size flood the Conewango should protect
against, is shown by the curve on the plate in the Tippetts
Report. This was prepared by the Corps of Engineers. *It
shows two storm crests, the first and smaller one 60% larger
than the 1936 flood and the second a week later, much
larger. Smaller floods can and sometimes do have this
character of a double flood, the crests following each other
from two or three days to ten days apart.* (Plate 7, TAMS
Report, Apr., 1958)[5] (Emphasis added.)

Such double-crested floods are not very unusual. Some of
the very greatest floods in the country have been of that
nature. The flood records of Pittsburgh include such a case.
Now assume for such a flood, as is assumed by the Corps of
Engineers in the table of benefits referred to above, that the
Kinzua gates should be kept closed during the first flood and
all the water held back. For a few days Pittsburgh would get
the relief assumed in that table of benefits, that is—in
1936—of $30,058,000. But then when the really great flood
did come, that much storage space would have been used up,
and would not be available for storing the larger flood. The
large flood would quickly use up the limited remaining
storage, and then pour down on Pittsburgh with much greater
damage than though the gates had been left open during the
first flood and the city had been allowed to suffer its
$30,000,000 damage. This is by no means a strained or
imaginary case. Such floods actually happen.

In the case of the Kinzua Reservoir, each time a moderately
large flood should occur the engineer must gamble as to
whether the present flow is the whole of the flood and can be
safely withheld, or whether it is the precursor of a much
greater—or even somewhat greater—flood that might be
disastrous to Pittsburgh, if Kinzua holds back the smaller
flood but is unprepared for the greater. No flood forecasting,
and no weather forecasting, can be sure, in a period favorable
to great rainfall, what will occur a week later. Usually the guess
that a very great flood will not occur works out well, because
such floods are very exceptional. But it is chiefly very

exceptional floods which cause great flood disasters.

One of the most serious limitations of the Kinzua Project is that, while under certain favorable conditions it would protect Pittsburgh from Upper Allegheny River floods of moderate size—such as those which have occurred in recent decades, under other conditions it could not be counted on.

The real question is: Should Pittsburgh be content to accept relief from moderate and fairly large floods from the Upper Allegheny, leaving itself wide open to the exceptional conditions which produce great flood disasters, or should it endure without relief much of the damage of moderately heavy floods with damages up to $30,000,000, so as to be prepared in some degree against the kinds of great floods which cause great flood disasters? Should Pittsburgh have insisted on the kind of project, fortunately, then available, in this case, with Conewango, which would fully and completely protect it from both kinds of flood, and from every kind of flood from the Upper Allegheny watershed?

With a practically perfect project available with Conewango, should saving the face of the Corps control the embarrassment of recognizing and correcting a mistake? The Conewango project, by discharging surplus flood water through the commodious preglacial channel of the Allegheny River (Cattaraugus Creek) or through a channel and down Big Indian Creek which enters Cattaraugus Creek nearer its mouth, and then into Lake Erie, could have fully and completely accomplished both purposes.

Now let us consider cases of storms with two crests several days apart, or as they might be called, two storms in rapid succession. This circumstance has been responsible for several disasters.

The storm of March 1936 had two separate crests in eastern Pennsylvania, one on March 11 and the larger on March 20. Pensacola Dam on the Neosho River in Oklahoma is an even more striking case. It was completed in 1941. The largest flood on record up to that time was 215,000 cubic feet per second. A very large flood occurred on May 11, 1943, the greatest on record up to that time, and was stored to protect the land below. Then on May 21, before the reservoir had been emptied, occurred another great flood, by far the greatest on record, which did very great damage below. The great New England storm of 1955 had two crests a short time apart. Except for the bungling of the Army Corps of Engineers, Conewango would have made the Upper Allegheny free from such threats as these.

Another limitation of the Kinzua project is that, since there is inadequate margin of safety in the storage capacity of Kinzua Reservoir, the Corps of Engineers would be compelled to rely on the precision and accuracy of weather forecasting. For the previous discussion we have assumed a high degree of accuracy in weather forecasting. This I consider to be beyond reasonable possibility, especially in case of a very great storm rainfall, for which there was little precedent. If such forecasts were not accurate, then vast damage to Pittsburgh might result. Where there is an abundant margin of safety, as would be the case with Conewango, this elaborate forecasting is of little consequence. Even in the case of a total miscalculation in weather forecasting, the Conewango Reservoir with its emergency outlet into Lake Erie would leave Pittsburgh and Warren fully protected.

Cost of Earth Work and Timber Clearing

The two reservoir sites, while not far apart, are very different in physical character. Kinzua Reservoir site, which is just beyond the limit of glacial action, especially the southern part where nearly all the construction work for Kinzua is located, is typical mountain sides. Rocks protrude through the thin soil. The price set by the Corps of Engineers for moving this material, $1.00 per cubic yard, is reasonable.

In marked contrast, the Conewango basin and its environs is an area which has mostly been worked over by the glacier. The mountains have been ground into sand, clay and gravel, such as are familiar in northern Ohio and the adjacent parts of western New York and Pennsylvania. Probably nine-tenths of all the excavation considered for creating the Conewango

Reservoir is sand, clay and gravel, such as commonly is met with south of the Great Lakes all the way from the Mississippi River to the east end of Lake Erie. This is just such material as modern excavation equipment is fit to handle economically.

In accord with the art of plausibility which the Corps of Engineers has long practiced, what could be fairer than to estimate the two projects with the same unit cost—$1.00 per cubic yard? The consultants and the Corps did not take into account the fact that most of the earth moving for Conewango was with sand, clay and gravel for which normal excavation costs would not be $1.00 per cubic yard. Most of the heavy earth work for the Conewango project could be done with large scale excavation equipment and probably could be contracted at less than 30 cents per cubic yard.

(My estimates of this excavation were made by George J. Schmidt, perhaps the foremost man in America in estimating heavy earth excavation for large contractors. I have his careful detailed estimates giving the capacity and range of each piece of excavating equipment, and even the staffing of each piece of equipment, and the detailed cost of the operation, down to the individual members of the crews. Even the soil conditions were carefully observed and appraised. A measure of his competence is the fact that many of the large contractors of the country make their bids on his judgment.)

Yet, earth moving was not the only element of the Conewango project in which the Corps could practice the art of plausibility.

The excess of estimate for timber clearing of the Conewango site in the consultants' report was more than $2,000,000. The Corps of Engineers' officer who questioned my estimate had been practicing plausibility. He probably never had seen the Conewango basin.

Criticism and the Corps of Engineers

When Colonel R. E. Smyser, head of the Ohio Rivers Division of the U.S. Corps of Engineers, asked for a consultants' examination of my proposal, he seemed to show a spirit of open inquiry which has not been characteristic of the Corps. His act gave promise of value, yet in some respects the manner of its use by the Corps suggested, not a search for possible additional light, but a desire to discredit criticism.

In two or three cases on the Upper Allegheny project, I had relations with members of the Corps in responsible positions, where I felt that I might be dealing with honorable men, acting with honor. Yet when these men came to act in company with the Corps as a whole, I found them taking actions lacking in integrity and general fair dealing. In two cases in particular this occurred. I came to the conclusion that a member of the Engineer Corps, even to the very top, was not a free agent, but that the general lack of honest and honorable dealing put upon even these men a compulsion to act according to the nature of the Corps. I have no doubt that there are members of the Corps here and there who persist in acting independently under all circumstances. But there is a strong group influence to compel them to follow the Corps pattern. The training and compulsion for such action is inherent in West Point, part of whose graduates join the Corps of Engineers. Most of the others go into the Army. A striking case of compulsory unity among graduates of West Point occurred recently in a case where mass murder was committed on women and chidren in Viet Nam. This action was so completely hidden from the public by West Point "discipline" that it was only by accident, after a long period, that the facts emerged. That massacre was covered up by officials from highest to lowest. The fact that this training begins early at West Point was evidenced by the fact that when the disclosures involved the Superintendent of West Point and when public opinion called for his elimination from his position, he received a great ovation from the student body of West Point. The American public is not yet fully aware of the near universality of the prevalence of this trait. There are, I am certain, West Point graduates who have successfully resisted this process of indoctrination. Those who condemn the Corps should always recognize and rejoice in such occasional exceptions. At West Point from its early origin, from Napoleon's generals and admirers who assumed the responsibility of developing military training in America, under a largely secret regime, these characteristics have been present beyond public knowledge.

A striking case of a grossly misleading and thereby deceptive statement was presented by the Chief of Engineers to the Subcommittee on Appropriations for Public Works. To infer great inadequacy in my estimate of the cost of the dam and outlet from Conewango basin to Lake Erie, the Chief of Engineers quoted TAMS estimate for that work, and then quoted my very much lower cost for achieving the same result. There was no reason for including and comparing these two estimates except to imply that my much lower estimate must have been greatly inadequate, and therefore incompetent. The quotation and the comments did not hint that the two estimates referred to locations several miles apart, and under very different physical conditions. This quotation follows:

> TAMS outlet to Lake Erie via Silver Creek $28,678,000 versus Morgan's outlet via Cattaraugus Creek $7,387,000. Morgan's scheme is hydraulically inferior. . . . A detailed survey and hydraulic analysis would be needed to support his scheme before it could be accepted as cheaper than the route studied by TAMS.[6] *

The two suggested locations of a combination gates and outlet channels are miles apart, with extremely different physical conditions. To mention the great difference in total estimates without disclosing the great difference in conditions had the intended result of raising doubts and discredit-

---

*When TAMS discontinued their study of Conewango without making any studies except of my original tentative suggestion, I took up the work again to study other possible outlets to Lake Erie which TAMS had not taken time to examine. The U.S. Corps of Engineers criticized the time required, implying that I was purposely delaying the proceedings. I therefore reported on the cost of Plan No. 6 before I had completed the estimate of carrying the discharge past the two railway bridges, and into Lake Erie.

ing the responsibility of the lower figure. This is especially true where there is a succession of such inferences and innuendoes by the Corps of Engineers, constantly implying inadequacies or incompetence.

In fact, the comparison which the Corps made in its formal report is a striking example of the failure of the Corps to require conclusive engineering analysis. Knowing the century-long failure of the Corps in this respect, I had emphatically warned TAMS to be careful not to omit any of the several alternatives for the solution of this problem of disposing of flood waters from the Conewango Basin to Lake Erie. I was particularly emphatic against oversight in this case where there were more alternatives than are usually met with. In reference to this particular problem I had written TAMS just before they began their survey that:

> . . . My major engineering associate has written "The project has such a variety of promising alternatives that when the possibilities and economies are fully worked out the plans may have little resemblance to the ones we had prepared." It is hoped that as TAMS make their study with more adequate resources they will not simply determine the feasibility of the elements we propose, but will be alert to see further possibilities and economies, as well as any weak spots in our proposals.[7]

Could my warning have been clearer? But the Corps had set limits of time and money to this study which made a conclusive engineering analysis beyond the limits of TAMS. In these circumstances, TAMS replied to me that they did not have time or funds to make any additional studies. That

---

As soon as that element was estimated I sent to the Chief of Engineers a revised statement of the outlet into Lake Erie. Since the Corps of Engineers did not add this correction to my estimate of cost of the outlet into Lake Erie, it is necessary to correct their estimate of this item. If the work should be done at some time in the future, I would not want them to come across the erroneous estimate, due to their failure to include the correction of this item. The proper figure with this correction is not $7,000,000, but $15,000,000.

statement as to their limitations of time and money was conclusive to their inquiry in general, and applied to all elements of that study. I do not know whether TAMS told the Corps that it would need more time and money. However, the century-long record of the Corps in not making conclusive engineering analysis may have made it clear that such a request would be useless.

TAMS had definitely declined to explore the margins of the Conewango basin for the best outlet to Lake Erie. Therefore, as mentioned earlier in this chapter, I continued the search for alternatives after TAMS stopped. Several miles to the east I found a far superior outlet in a pre-glacial gorge 100-200 feet deep, a route costing only a minor fraction of that estimated by TAMS.

In length of channel, the two projects are not greatly different. In TAMS design there is a heavy excavation most of the way for about fifteen miles, with 20,000,000 cubic yards of excavation. In the Morgan design, the discharge from Conewango basin would be through a six mile channel into a pre-glacial branch and channel of the Allegheny River flowing into Lake Erie. For a considerable part of the distance this channel is a deep, narrow, rugged gorge, about 100 to 200 feet deep where the water can be turned loose, with little expense incurred. The total expense for the channel on the Morgan route would be only about a third of that on the TAMS route.

The discharge gates for the TAMS plan are in the Conewango basin, where there is no solid foundation, and which would require very heavy piling for support and a very heavy concrete structure to be stable in the basin. The piling alone for this structure is estimated to cost more than $1,500,000 and the estimate for concrete to make a stable foundation in the sand and clay of the basin is $3,000,000. In contrast the Morgan location is on solid rock, needing no piling and no artificial foundation. For the TAMS location only 3 feet of fall is possible through the gates. Therefore numerous and large gates are necessary to pass 100,000 cubic feet per second of water. With the Morgan design a fall of up to 50 feet is available, at a rock cliff. The water can be discharged at high velocity, and with only a fraction as many or as large gates as required by the TAMS design. The outlet works would cost probably less than a quarter as much. On the whole, because of these superior conditions, the cost of the outlet gates could be reduced by about $5,000,000. Rolled embankment at half a million dollars also would be entirely omitted from the Morgan setting, which would be an almost solid rock. About half a million dollars for steel reinforcement would not be needed. Such a structure as the diversion dam on Silver Creek near Lake Erie would be entirely unnecessary. There would be no place or need for that item of $1,250,000.

In short, the TAMS hydraulic design is strikingly inferior in the following respects: their channel calls for 20,000,000 cubic yards of excavation and only a third as much would be needed for the Morgan design; their gates provide only three feet of fall, and must be correspondingly larger for a given discharge, whereas 25 feet or more of head would be provided by the Morgan design gates; the TAMS diversion channel requires a diversion dam at a cost of $1,250,000, whereas the Morgan diversion channel requires no such dam.

The consultants had prematurely discontinued their study and had overlooked a vastly superior and less expensive solution, which would have saved more than $15,000,000. An honest and critical appraisal of my proposal would have been of value.

Another instance of the defensive attitude of the consultants and the Corps in the face of criticism is that of the Pennsylvania Railroad affair. I visited the offices of the consulting firm only once as I recall, and asked to see the report which was nearing completion, but was refused. I asked to see the plans for carrying the Pennsylvania Railroad across the southern tip of the diversion dam over the Allegheny River. The person in charge of designing this feature was a young man apparently in his twenties. He had settled on relocating the Pennsylvania Railroad for miles along the very irregular side of the mountain at a cost of between $9,000,000 and $10,000,000. The railroad grade was not quite as high as the top of the diversion dam, but well above the elevation of the "Project design flood," decided on by the Corps for Kinzua. It was clearly evident that the railroad should be carried through a shallow cut at the south extremity of the dam. In a maximum or "spillway design flood" which might occur once in a century or two, the water would be six or eight feet deep in the cut. The cut would be given very heavy concrete walls and bottom, with a diversion channel on the lower side, to carry water back to the adjacent river. This would cost only a few hundred thousand dollars, and would be completely safe.

When I asked the young man why he had not taken this more economical course, he replied, "I never thought of that!" Just then one of the partners of the firm came into the room. Overhearing what was said, he commented instantly to the young man in effect: "Oh, Morgan's plan is good engineering practice. We use that method."

There was no possibility of any technical question in this case. The shallow notch for the railroad would cost only a few hundred thousand dollars and would save more than $8,000,000. By that time, the TAMS report was in the process of printing. The change was not made, and the excess of between $8,000,000 and $9,000,000 remained in the estimate, along with some other wholly inexcusable items, aggregating millions of dollars, which added to TAMS' estimated cost of Conewango. When the Chief of Engineers made his required report to the Subcommittee on Public Works, the reporter had practice in plausibility, in justifying such items. These cases are typical of numerous others.

The Engineer Corps men did not ask to see our plans, but criticized what they imagined such plans might be. They pictured interrupted traffic and inefficient methods, and ended their criticism by declaring that "There is no reason to anticipate that such a scheme would even be entertained, let alone accepted." Of course with their imagined plan large extra costs would be involved.

When I found difficulty in getting a competent examination of my plans from the Corps, I described them briefly in a long letter to the Chief of Engineers, but received no acknowledgement from him. Then I received a letter from Mr. Dewey Short, Assistant Secretary of War, saying he had heard that I was having some difficulty with the Corps, and would I tell him about it. Yes, I would.

When we met in the office of the Assistant Secretary, the Chief of Engineers also was present, and entered briefly into the conversation.

As I was about to leave, the Chief of Engineers, General Itschner, who had been listening attentively, said as a courteous parting comment that he wished he knew more about my plans. This was such an opening as I had hoped for. I asked whether I might prepare and send to him a fairly full statement of one of the several alternatives provided by the Conewango project which I had developed when the TAMS organization had told me that they could not look into it. With this invitation from the Chief of Engineers I worked intensively for more than two months to prepare a 100 page statement of my plan.

When I took the plan to him in October, 1958, I had a most friendly greeting. The Chief knew of the difficulty I had with some of the top men of the Corps. He said he had a friend in the far west whose intelligence and independent judgment he greatly respected, to whom he would like to refer my plan. I thought that for him to refer the problem to such a person would take it outside the traditional commitments and turmoil of the situation, and he could get an unbiased judgment.

This was just what I had been hoping for. It was in mid-October. Congress would meet in early April and would be sure to deal soon afterwards with this issue. I had somewhat less than six months to talk to members of Congress and to the public through the press to tell my story. That was an important period. It might be my one chance to get a hearing of Congress before final decision would be made.

Yet what about the Chief of Engineers? Would it be

suitable for me to be talking to Congressmen and the public to get an understanding while the Chief of Engineers was making a good faith effort to get at the heart of the matter?

My communication with the Chief of Engineers had been brief, but I had been well impressed. I thought, "here is a man I can trust. He is holding himself apart and above the traditional stresses of the 'establishment' of the Corps. I will trust him, and he can trust me."

It seemed inappropriate that I should be campaigning with Congressmen while he was making a good faith effort to get at the facts. So I proposed to the Chief of Engineers that both sides of the controversy remain inactive until he should get the independent opinion of his friend. This decision was on the spur of the moment. General Itschner agreed to it. It did not occur to me until later to set a limit to the period of waiting. A short time should be enough to bring him an answer.

Not long after a letter from the Chief of Engineers informed me that the period of waiting might be somewhat longer than I might have expected. That letter troubled me. Might my own proposal be used to keep me quiet until Congress should meet? My decision was not to terminate my agreement.

The weeks passed quickly. Some of my friends thought that I had lost interest. Others thought I might have "sold out," for I did not explain.

So the weeks passed until about the first of April. The first indication to me that the judgment of the Chief of Engineers had been adverse was in the news I received that members of his staff were "briefing" critical congressmen on the issue. Then a letter was received from the Chief of Engineers to the effect that, after the correspondence with his distant friend his decision was against me. I wrote him of the effort and concern I had put into the situation, and asked whether I might see the opinion of the western friend, so that I might learn where I had been wrong. The Chief of Engineers replied that the House Appropriations Committee in "executive session" had directed his office to send information on the subject to it, and that under those circumstances that communication would be privileged, and he could not send it. I did not see why this should follow, but he did not let me see that letter.

I went to the Subcommittee on Public Works Appropriations of the House and was given a copy of the report referred to. The Subcommittee asked me to reply to it. Both the communications were handed by the Appropriations Subcommittee to its engineering advisory staff, which studied the documents, and recommended that no more appropriations be made to the Upper Allegheny project until an independent comparison had been made of the two plans. This was something else I had been hoping for.

As I examined the "privileged" statement presented by the Chief of Engineers to the Subcommittee I found an introductory statement from the Chief of Engineers, consisting only of the most abstract generalizations, such as:

> I have personally studied the report of Dr. Morgan, but find that his recommended Plan 6 does not supply a solution to the water resources development problem of the Allegheny River basin that compares favorably with the authorized plan. I find that his recommended plan gives insufficient treatment to some important engineering aspects and that the estimates he presents are not reconcilable with the scope of the work involved, or the conditions under which it must be performed, to construct a completely operating facility.[8]

The rest of this required, official report of the Chief of Engineers and of his staff to the Subcommittee on Public Works Appropriations apparently is a collection of comments by local or Washington members of the Corps.

What had the Corps been saying to those Congressmen? My period of self-imposed inactivity while waiting for the Chief of Engineers to hear from his western friend had prevented me from talking to members of Congress myself. Some time after I received the adverse judgment of the Chief, I attended a meeting of the Subcommittee on Indian Affairs, where Engineer Corps officers made an appearance.

Two or three Engineer Corps officers were conducting a small group of men to the committee meeting. The party included three persons: the head of the Department of Forests and Waters of the Pennsylvania State Government; one of the most powerful financial figures in the financial and business world of Pittsburgh—Adolph William Schmidt; and Senator Clark of Pennsylvania. The Corps officials introduced the members of their party to the members of the Subcommittee on Indian Affairs, and then asked to be heard. Their spokesman was Senator Clark. I had heard that the Senator had been briefed by the Corps. Two engineer officers of the Corps of Engineers stood near Senator Clark as he spoke.

Senator Clark stood at the railing surrounding the seats of the committee members. I sat about ten feet from him in the audience. Senator Clark, referring to my efforts, spoke with extreme indignation of the indignity which was being put upon the Corps and the public by the activity of an irresponsible publicity seeker in interfering with the soundly made plans of the U.S. Engineer Corps. The Senator was so deeply moved that he physically trembled as he held onto the post of the railing in front of him. He said that there were no responsible engineering or other technical plans presented by this irresponsible person. There were no legitimate plans involved but only nuisance-making by this personality.

When I wrote Senator Clark asking for the basis of his adverse opinion, he indicated that it was not from his personal knowledge, but from the Corps and from the head of the Department of Forests and Waters of Pennsylvania. When I wrote the head of the Department of Forests and Waters for the basis of his opinion, he replied that he had no personal knowledge on the engineering or other features, but based his opinion entirely on his reliance on the Corps of Engineers.

This incident gave me a hint as to what had been said to the Senator in briefing him. Some of the published remarks of the Corps members were of similar import but much more moderately stated. Quite frequently there was only suggestion of incompetence as in the case of mentioning the estimate of the cost of outlet works by TAMS at $28,000,000 and of my estimate of $7,000,000 with the inferred implication that approximately equivalent undertakings were involved, and that perhaps the great inadequacy of estimates was due to the incompetence and irresponsibility of an interfering engineer.[9] The art of plausibility is highly developed and is versatile.

As to Mr. Schmidt, representative of Pittsburgh financiers, I had been undertaking to reach this group, and to persuade them that the cost would be very small for them to select their own competent and wholly independent engineers to make a study of the two proposals. Pittsburgh had a large stake in this issue, and a little money spent in an independent appraisal might be good insurance.

There might be some temptation to a prudent financier to take that course. But now, in a committee room of Congress, Mr. Schmidt hears that I am a characterless, selfish, irresponsible publicity seeker. The Pittsburgh financial community let me know, in no uncertain terms, that the U.S. Engineer Corps was its final source of authority, and that the substantial industrialists of Pittsburgh would not look further for evidence.

This incident was perhaps unusual. I have been told by members of Congress that my proposals did not always meet with discourtesy and deprecation from Corps members. Perhaps the attitude in this case was to discourage the Pittsburgh Community from promoting an independent study.

When the young officers of the Pittsburgh Engineering Society suggested discussing the subject, I thought we might bring it to the attention of the city of Pittsburgh. But the Engineers Club officers told me that they were urged to give up the inquiry. They had a little activity to that end, and then it ceased.

I still seemed to have one chance to bring about a wholly independent comparison of the two plans. Because I believed that a change of plan would save more than $100,000,000 for our government, I thought I should leave no stone unturned. A large insurance company had financed the massive buildings on the low lands of West Pittsburgh which would be greatly damaged in case of flood. Being acquainted with a director of this insurance company, I suggested that the Insurance Company might make the very modest investment necessary to have the plans compared. I shortly heard from him to the effect that Pittsburgh finance disapproved of such an independent comparison.

Impartial Comparison of Plans Prevented

The Appropriations Committee of the House of Representatives has a subcommittee on public works which deals with appropriations for all public works agencies, most of which are constructed by the U.S. Corps of Engineers. This Subcommittee of Public Works has a bipartisan engineering staff, of Democrats and Republicans, to which it assigns all bills involving large public works, to get their opinions as to their engineering feasibility and value. When I prepared a hundred page analysis of the Kinzua project and my proposed alternative, a copy was given to the Subcommittee on Public Works Appropriations. That committee submitted it to their staff. The Public Works Appropriations Subcommittee directed the Corps of Engineers to make a statement appraising my proposal. When these statements were received, the subcommittee engineering staff examined the proposals for an alternative to Kinzua Reservoir. When the Committee's engineering staff had examined the Kinzua proposal of the Corps and also my proposal for an alternative—Conewango—and the Corps' criticism of it, the staff of the Public Works Committee advised the Public Works Appropriations Subcommittee that no further appropriations for Kinzua should be made until there had been an impartial engineering comparison of the two proposals.

The Public Works Subcommittee made that recommendation to the main Appropriation Committee of the House. The main Appropriation Committee, after discussing the report, drew up a provision in the Public Works Appropriations Bill to the effect that no more appropriations should be made for the Kinzua Project until the two proposals should be examined and compared by an impartial committee of engineers. That bill was presented on the floor of the House, and, after the provision for an impartial comparison of the two proposals had received more discussion than any other phase of the bill, the House passed it almost unanimously.

The Appropriations Committee, expecting that this course would be followed, asked me to suggest suitable members for such an impartial committee. It probably made a similar request of the Corps. I wrote to the American Society of Civil Engineers, asking for suggestions for such a committee, and when suggestions were received I sent the names to the Appropriations Committee staff member who had written me.

The situation in the Senate was very different than in the House. The Chairman of the Senate Committee on Appropriations Subcommittee was Senator Ellender of Louisiana. He was an unqualified supporter of the Corps of Engineers and a leading force in the Rivers and Harbors Congress. Often he would be the only member of the Committee present at hearings, or there might be one other member of the Committee present, who would take no part in the discussion. When, at a Senate Committee hearing, I criticized an action of the Corps, Senator Ellender responded, "We will find the truth about that, we will ask the Corps." He addressed Congress as a whole, as a member of the Rivers and Harbors Congress.

Senator Ellender took the position of the Corps in opposition to an impartial engineering comparison of the two plans. In reporting the House bill to the Senate, he omitted the provision for an impartial comparison of plans.

Probably few Senators were aware that this question of impartial comparison had been raised. This had been an item in a large bill, and the bill as a whole received little or no discussion, a marked contrast to the discussion it had received in the House. The Senate adopted the bill as the Corps and Senator Ellender wanted it.

Thereupon, when the two bills went to the Conference Committee for adjusting the differences, there was no discussion of impartial comparison of plans. The result was that the Senate version prevailed, by certain personal political arrangements.

The Rivers and Harbors Congress, which includes membership of the Corps of Engineers and their important contractors, and certain members of Congress, constitutes probably the most powerful lobby in America. As such, the Corps of Engineers, with the help of the Rivers and Harbors Congress, has been very effective as a determiner of legislation. Legislation has been passed that the building of public works by the Corps of Engineers takes place only where the Corps finds that the value of the proposed work is greater than the cost, the value and cost being estimated by the Corps. The Corps has in reserve hundreds of possible projects, with some in nearly every congressional district. These projects, especially the smaller ones, largely live or die at the decision of the Corps. There are many of these awaiting their turn. If a member of Congress is not on good terms with the Corps it is very easy to find that "with the calendar of work so full, we may not get to this for a few years." However, if it is time to do a congressman a favor, there may be a reexamination of the appraisal of costs and benefits which will make a project seem "feasible."

Chairman Clarence Cannon, long Chairman of the House Appropriations Committee, told me personally that the decision reached in the Conference Committee on impartial comparison of the two plans had nothing whatever to do with the merits of the case, that the decision was purely political. The strategy of the Corps was successful, and it prevented any impartial comparison of the two plans. The result of this victory is a great reduction of public benefits, and a financial loss of much more than $100,000,000 to our country.

The Corps manipulates appropriations in the control of individual Congressmen and profits by the exploitation of public eagerness for the gifts of the Corps to local projects, to be paid for by Federal rather than local funds. The incredible political power of the Corps, with the arrogance and stupidity of many of its projects, supported by its own misleading reports of its work, a program amounting to billions of dollars, constitutes a regime of favored dominance rarely paralleled in our government. The Rivers and Harbors Congress also includes groups seeking vast special privileges and supporting each other.

notes

1. Report of the Flood Commission of Pittsburgh, 1912, p. 47.

2. Pennsylvania Department of Forests and Water, and the U.S. Geological Survey, "The Floods of March, 1946, in Pennsylvania."

3. *Ibid.*

4. Colonel Smyser to the Public Works Sub-committee of the House Appropriations Committee of the 85th Congress, 2nd Session, part 2, p. 338.

5. Plate 7, TAMS Report, April 1958.

6. General E. C. Itschner, *op. cit.*, p. 26 (note 14, Chapter 10).

7. Arthur E. Morgan to TAMS, quoting from a letter of the late Barton Jones, 1957.

8. Major-General Itschner, Chief of Engineers, *op. cit.*, p. 26 (note 14, Chapter 10).

9. Itschner, *Ibid.*

part iii

chapter 12

insensitivity
to the
environment

Conclusive and inclusive engineering analysis must go beyond commonly recognized major objectives to consider all significant factors involved or disturbed. Especially in the case of large engineering undertakings it is important to get an adequate concept of the relations between obvious purposes and the less obvious social and ecological factors of the environment.

A steadily increasing part of the American population is coming to realize that the natural environment is one of our most precious possessions, and as such should not be unnecessarily destroyed, mutilated, or wasted.

When one is aware of the bare, uninspiring confinement of West Point cadets during four formative years, with a pattern rooted in the regime of Sylvanus Thayer and his Napoleon trained generals, and when we recognize the overwhelming concern of West Point with the destructive process of war, rather than the constructive process of peace, the lack of sensitiveness by the Corps to environmental values is not surprising. This lack of sensitivity, together with the lack of vision and imagination on the part of the Corps, has tended to preclude awareness of the need for ecological balance in their many projects across the country. An official announcement that the Corps will now give active attention to environmental factors will not suddenly dissipate the century-long insensitivity. Had there been sensitivity in the Corps of Engineers to environmental excellence, there would have been in the multitude of Corps projects many opportunities for the recognition and preservation of environmental values.

As an engineer I have found that the habit of considering environmental factors as an important aspect of inclusive engineering analysis can result in many opportunities for the preservation of the natural environment. As a direct result of projects of which I was chief engineer, or otherwise concerned, there are now preserved in several states more than a dozen areas of unspoiled nature, some embracing several square miles.

This, with some exceptions, is not the case with the Corps of Engineers. The lack of Engineer Corps' sensitivity to the environment is evidenced by the nationwide concern about present Corps programs. In many cases where the natural environment is destroyed or seriously mutilated by the work of the Corps the loss is substantially permanent. The impatient effort of the Corps to be active with projects, which may lead to the destruction of environmental values, demands public attention.

In this book I have not undertaken to adequately treat the nationwide destruction of the environment by the Corps of Engineers. I shall mention only two cases as examples.

The Florida Everglades

The Florida Everglades constitute a unique treasure of mankind. Nowhere else in the United States, or probably in North America, is there such a varied, unique, and precious expression of nature. Species are at home there which seldom or never are found anywhere else.

At the south tip of Florida just above sea level, great rock barriers tend to keep the fresh water in and the salt water out. A vast "river of grass" flows slowly southward a hundred miles from Lake Okeechobee to the Gulf. The lake provides large reservoir capacity which in its natural condition had largely preserved the balance of the Everglades between fresh and salt water during dry seasons. Taken altogether, this is no ordinary swamp, but something unique in the nation. All this nature teeming with life has been much disturbed by the ill-planned work of the U.S. Corps of Engineers.

Until well into the present century America in general was not aware of the remarkable variety of life in the Everglades. The great flat marsh lands of southern Florida were looked upon chiefly as waste acres waiting reclamation for agriculture. Especially irresponsible promoters looked on the area as a chance for exploitation and quick profits.

On two occasions during earlier years I contributed to preventing incompetent and totally inadequate treatment of the Florida Everglades area. The first occasion was in 1909 to 1912. A totally dishonest organization of exploiters had set up a nationwide sales organization and promotion program for selling small tracts of swamp land to persons of small means over the country with the promise that they could quickly be turned into orange groves. Thousands of school teachers, ministers, janitors, and craftsmen were committing their very small entire life savings to the purchase of ten-acre tracts, and dreamed of themselves as sitting under their orange trees.

The State of Florida government was sharing in this fraud by promising to reclaim this land, but the funds the state was committing to that purpose were not more than ten per cent of what would be necessary. It could no more than bungle and confuse the reclamation problem.

From 1907 until the end of 1909 I held an office of supervising drainage engineer in the U.S. Department of Agriculture, under C. G. Elliot, the head of the Office of Drainage Investigations. In 1909 when the Chief was away I partially undertook his responsibilities. One day there came to my desk a government bulletin on Florida drainage. It was sent for final approval before being distributed. On reading it I concluded that it was part of a conspiracy for selling worthless land to people of small means. On inquiry I found that three men related to the Department of Agriculture were in collusion with the real estate promotion mentioned above.

They had prepared the bulletin in high praise of the dishonest real estate promotion project, to be used to indicate government approval for the nationwide sales campaign. The leader of this government group was the chief legal officer of the Department of Agriculture. Another of the group, I was told, was the son of the Secretary of Agriculture. The third was an engineer with a rank like my own.

On reading the bulletin which was ready for distribution I withheld it from circulation, and wired my Chief, who was on the Pacific coast, about the circumstances. He replied that he had added warning paragraphs at the ends of some chapters, and directed me to release the bulletin for publication. Of course the salesman for the land sales concern would not quote the warning paragraphs, but only those in high praise of the land sale project. I wired the Chief again that I was continuing to hold the bulletin from publication, and that he had better come home. The Chief did return, and on reading the bulletin again, withdrew it from publication. Thereupon the chief legal officer found what he considered an impropriety in my Chief's record and the Secretary of Agriculture dismissed the Chief from his position. He was such a meticulously honest man that he kept his own private supply of pencils and paper for non-official use. The Department then issued the bulletin which my Chief had disapproved.

I tried to protest to the Secretary of Agriculture, but could not reach him. The Secretary commented to an inquiring congressman that the Department of Agriculture was not organized to protect foolish people who did not have the sense to protect themselves. Unable to reach the Secretary I publicized the fraud on a nationwide basis through the Associated Press. There was a strong reaction over the country. An honest member of Congress from Florida helped to bring about a congressional investigation. As the first witness for the investigation, I was questioned by the chief legal officer of the Department of Agriculture (who was the chief conspirator in preparing the questionable bulletin). He cross questioned me for two days. His office had meticulously gone over my correspondence and expense accounts for three years, searching for some impropriety, and he questioned me on that record. Finally the Chairman of the Investigation Committee told the legal officer that enough time had been spent on cross questioning me, and gave me opportunity to testify.

The outcome of the Congressional hearing was that the chief legal officer of the department was allowed to resign his position and the engineer gave up his position. My Chief was reinstated with an increase of salary. As a result of the widespread publicity the nationwide real estate racket crumbled and the entire land selling undertaking disappeared. I came to understand that about sixteen thousand people of small means had already been relieved of their savings. The totally inadequate drainage plans were abandoned. Thus the Florida Everglades got a temporary reprieve from mutilation. (My records for this period are in the archives of the Yonge Library of Florida History at the Florida State University.)

But the broad expanse of the Florida Everglades are a constant temptation to economic exploitation, as is evidenced by the second occasion for my temporarily preventing the mutilation of the Everglades. In 1926 to 1928 a Florida governor sought to make his place in history by draining the Everglades. With widespread and moving oratory he secured the legal power to effect a large bond issue, $20,000,000, for reclaiming the Everglades. The proposed plans were totally inadequate, and worse, they would have destroyed the quality of the Everglades which now gives its value to the Everglades Park.

A substantial body of private citizens and organizations united to prevent such action. This group asked for my counsel. I strongly opposed the Governor's plan because of the lack of anything like an inclusive analysis, and because of its obvious fatal design. When I pleaded with the Governor on the issue he commented: "When I want advice on my health I do not go to a blacksmith. When I want advice on public policy I do not call an engineer."

Having legislatively cleared the way, he undertook to sell

the bond issue for the work and the bonds were sold to a New York firm which dealt in such public securities. This could mean the eternal wreck of the unique ecology of the Everglades. However, my Florida clients were insistent, and showed the purchaser of the bonds my report. But what has an engineer to do with the sale of bonds? My clients secured the answer to that particular point. They made some inquiries among firms which dealt in bond issues. I quote here brief extracts from a few of the replies.

Horace Oakley of the Chicago law firm of Wood and Oakley was the number one authority in the United States on special assessment securities. He replied:

> From time to time for more than twenty years I have been counsel in flood control and drainage enterprises involving bond issues in which Mr. Arthur E. Morgan of the Morgan Engineering Company of Dayton and Memphis has been the hydraulic engineer and I have had occasion not only to consider legality and feasibility of his plans but frequently to discuss them with him personally so that I feel that I have first hand knowledge of Morgan both as man and as engineer. I consider him the sanest most competent most experienced and most conscientious hydraulic engineer with whom I have come into contact. Among financiers his opinion is highly respected. I know of no case in which his work has not accomplished its purpose and his achievement in the Miami River Case of which I had personal knowledge from its inception to its completion needs no comment. His judgement also in economic and financial questions is reliable and his character and integrity are the highest.[1]

At that time the National City Bank of New York was the largest bank in America. Its President, H. C. Sylvester, Jr., wired:

> Arthur E. Morgan in my opinion is the best authority on flood control in the country today. His reputation and standing are the best.[2]

The International Trust Company of Denver wired:

Referring to Mr. Arthur E. Morgan we believe him to be the foremost engineer in flood control matters in this country. He successfully planned among others the Miami Conservancy Project in Ohio, the Pueblo Conservancy Project and is now engineer for the Middle Rio Grande Conservancy District this institution participated in the financing of all three of these undertakings and our decision to participate was guided to a large extent by fact that the Dayton Morgan Engineering Company were retained to plan and guide the projects. Mr. Morgans general reputation and capability as hydraulic engineer expert in flood control laws and developments is in our opinion of the highest.[3]

James H. Pershing of the Denver financial law firm of Pershing, Nye, Tallmadge & Bosworth wired as follows:

This telegram concerning Arthur E. Morgan of Morgan Engineering Company Dayton Ohio sent by request Mr. Evans. My first acquaintance Mr. Morgan arose in connection with Ohio Conservancy Law and Miami Conservancy District. Engineering features Ohio law largely the product of Morgan receiving very highest commendation of New York and Chicago bankers and lawyers. Consequently Morgan employed to complete engineering work in connection with Pueblo Conservancy District to complete satisfaction of all interests. Recently I worked with Morgan in redraft of New Mexico Conservancy Law and reorganization of Middle Rio Grande Conservancy District. Morgans work and diplomatic influence invaluable. New York and Chicago banking interests regard Morgans approval of flood control and drainage enterprises as a guarantee of scientific and financial success.[4] *

*It is considered inappropriate for an author to quote expressions complimentary to himself. My reason for not observing that code relates to my earlier experience with the Corps of Engineers, especially in the case of the Upper Allegheny-Kinzua Dam project. The Corps took extreme care to insure that its plans and mine should not have independent, impartial comparison. A method not always, but frequently, used was to present my plans as those of a trivial publicity seeker whose proposals were inconsequential, and should not be allowed to disturb the solid work of the Corps. A prominent member of

Messages of similar import were received from Harris Forbes and Company; The Dayton Savings and Trust Company; Gordon S. Rentschler, Vice-president of the National City Bank of New York; E. J. B. Schubring, Madison, Wisconsin attorney; William R. Compton, investment banker of Chicago; and F. W. Chapman and Co., Inc., investment bankers of Chicago.

With such a report in its hands, the firm which had purchased the bonds felt misgivings. The head of the New York firm came out to Yellow Springs to see me and I gave him my view of the situation. The outcome was that the investment firm withdrew its bid on the large bond issue. The process of inquiry had made other possible purchasers of the bonds aware of the circumstances. The result was that the Governor of Florida never was able to find sale for the bonds and that the entire Everglades project died. Thus the Everglades had another temporary respite from destruction. (The records of this episode are included in the Morgan archives at Antioch College, Yellow Springs, Ohio.)

A book, *The Everglades: River of Grass*, by Marjory Stoneman Douglas, 1947, curiously verifies what I have written of this incident:

> Governor Martin, elected on a campaign of good roads, went also into the drainage question. . . . Governor Martin asked specifically for an Engineering Board of Control to build canals east and west and a great levee along the whole southern rim of the lake. He asked for a Bond Plan that would raise twenty million dollars for that project.
>
> There was a storm of opposition chiefly from Dade County, suffering from poverty and its own over-bonding. The Dayton Morgan Engineering Company reported that nothing practical could be accomplished in the

---

the Corps staff who later became Chief of Engineers commented concerning my proposals: "If the Ladies Society wishes to raise money to question the work of the Corps, it is their privilege to do so." The attitude of the Corps toward this book and its author will be somewhat less complimentary. The expressions quoted indicate that such a view is not universal.

Glades without a liquidation of past mismanagement and the elimination of politics, a sound study of facts and over-all administration.

Governor Martin and the Internal Improvement Fund trustees had to see all the drainage work slow down and stop. They had no more money.[5]

Again the Everglades is on the brink of active destruction. The environmental unit of Southern Florida which includes the Everglades is complex and presents many problems. It is doubtful whether any other natural environmental unit in the United States presents greater complexity. The Kissimmee River rises in the Lake region of south-central Florida and flows southerly for about a hundred miles to Lake Okeechobee, the second largest body of fresh water in the United States. This lake, thirty to forty miles across, in its natural condition constituted an immense reservoir which, prior to the intervention of the Corps, provided millions of acre feet of water storage for regulation of the flow of water for a hundred miles from Lake Okeechobee to the Gulf at the south tip of Florida. With a fall of only about three inches to the mile, this large flow did not dig itself a channel, but spread out over the surface of a broad belt of sawgrass, suggesting the name of "The River of Grass."

At times Lake Okeechobee would be filled beyond capacity and the excess water would damage profitable sugar plantations just to the east. Tropical hurricanes, such as that which swept across Lake Okeechobee drowning men and crops, have been a further source of danger. The Corps of Engineers, beginning in 1949, diverted excess water from Lake Okeechobee by a short route to the Gulf. The result was that the Everglades, lacking water in the low water season, largely dried up. After demands by conservationists and concerned people to supply water to the parched Everglades, the Corps opened only one of the four gates at Lake Okeechobee. But they only opened it one inch and for only one week. Yet at the same time the Corps was releasing 500 times that volume to flow to the sea, wasted, while a great part of the wildlife of the Everglades perished.[6] The marvelous ecological variety of the lower Glades, which made it a national treasure, suffered vast and varied loss. The great ocean of sawgrass dried up and caught fire, killing the wild life, and in many areas burning the grass roots down to bare rock.

Some cities of Florida, which had assumed that they had endless abundance of fresh water, discovered that they had been indirectly supplied by underground flow from Lake Okeechobee, and began to get salt water to drink, as ocean water moved in to replace the water lacking from Lake Okeechobee. The breeding grounds for Florida shrimp would be seriously damaged. An extract from an account by Peter Farb of the *Audubon* Magazine tells of the conditions:

> I visited Everglades National Park shortly after its dedication and there saw a truly unique water park—a living museum of soggy saw grass as far as the eye could see, majestic cypress forests, and coastal mangrove swamps interlaced by a network of winding streams.
>
> Thousands of wading and water birds—egrets and heron, ibis and spoonbills, cormorants and storks—filled the air over an area larger than the state of Delaware. It was the only place on the continent where I could see alligators in abundance, or any crocodiles at all; here also were sea cows, tree snails, tree orchids, and the only panthers east of the Mississippi.
>
> Last June I visited Everglades National Park again, . . . I found no Eden but rather a waterless hell under a blazing sun.
>
> Everywhere I saw Everglades drying up, the last drops of water evaporating from water holes, creeks and sloughs. . . . The saw grass was a brown and lifeless tinder; during my visit the sky was darkened by great pillars of smoke billowing from a rampaging, crackling fire.
>
> I revisited a place that had been a favorite on several previous trips: the Anhinga Trail, . . . The once-sparkling waters of the slough I now found a muddy soup in which floated the carcasses of gar and other fish. Alligators and turtles burrowed into the suncaked mud in a search for water. The anhingas, or water turkeys, for whom the trail

had been named, no longer could be seen swimming with their snakelike heads above the water; in fact, all except one forlorn bird had fled. Trees that should have been festooned with egrets and other birds were lifeless. Only the vultures seemed to be reaping a bonanza from the interminable drouth and the mass extermination of many kinds of animals to whom water is life.

Other national parks preserve geological or scenic features of our continent—but Everglades is the only national park created to perpetuate wildlife. This wildlife community, with its multiplicity of invisible strands that link all animals and plants, is considerably more delicate than a mountain or a canyon; it is easily thrown out of balance, and it can be destroyed so quickly that there is little opportunity to save it. Yet today this jewel in our chain of national parks is threatened by the folly of man, selfish interests and the shame of a water-control project that is proving a bottomless well for tax-payers' dollars.

. . . Because of unbelievable bungling, the managers of the flood-control project that borders the park dump more water into the sea in one season than the park could use in years. And because of engineering miscalculation, about two times as much water now escapes into the Atlantic Ocean through porous rock alone than is required to satisfy the park's entire water needs.

. . . The Corps' engineering studies at the time led them to assure the National Park Service that the project "would not damage or interfere with this great national park." In fact, the Corps stated confidently that the project would bring benefits to Everglades: "In dry periods it would be possible, because of the proposed conservation areas, to release water into the park area which would assist in reducing fire and other damage which accompanies periods of drought."

This plan provided for the biggest earth-moving job since the building of the Panama Canal. The Corps might have prevented future flood damage much less expensively—simply by buying up all of the flood-damaged property, at a total cost of no more than $12 million to $20 million, and letting it be flooded. Instead, it proposed a project with a cost of at least 20 times the value of the entire flooded area. This project, originally estimated to cost $200 million, has now soared to $381 million—and some knowledgeable observers believe that eventually it will cost more than half a billion dollars!

The explanation for these burgeoning costs is that the project was approved for flood control "and other purposes"-- and the other purposes have become much more important, and expensive, than simple flood control. In reality, the Central and Southern Florida Flood Control Project, as it is officially known, is concerned with floods only in a minor way; it is really a vast land reclamation project. It involves the reclamation of more land than all the irrigated acres in the famed Western big-dam projects.

The Corps of Engineers has gone into the water business in the biggest way ever seen on this continent. Yet, in these times of massive federal subsidies to farmers not to produce crops, through Soil Bank payments, this project aims to raise production on present farmland— and to bring an additional 735,000 acres of land into agricultural use. And 80 per cent of the cost of this project—for the benefit of a few large landowners and real-estate developers—comes out of the pockets of the nation's taxpayers.[7]

The sad disaster to the Park is directly and explicity a typical result of the century-long habit of the Corps of not making inclusive and conclusive engineering analysis. The Corps is proceeding with further actions, and is putting some of them into effect. Part of these new steps are contributing very seriously to limiting the future value of this wonderful Park. As one bit of patch work after another is done to correct one source of difficulty, other difficulties emerge.

Just as we go to press, the following description by Philip D. Carter of the *Los Angeles Times/Washington Post* Service is received concerning present conditions in the Everglades:

EVERGLADES NATIONAL PARK, Fla. — Florida's

worst natural drought on record and the unnatural works
of man have brought slow, choking death to the Everglades and threatened all south Florida with environmental disaster.

Within the 1.4 million-acre Everglades National Park at
the state's southern tip, vast sloughs and countless water-
holes, teaming with life in a normal May, are dry and
barren today. Alligators have vanished. Fish have disappeared. Birds and mammals have departed.

In the densely populated towns and cities of the state's
southern coasts, water rationing has been widely ordered
in the face of salt water contamination of local fresh-
water supplies.

In the once-thriving swamps and the fertile farmlands
outside the park, fires sweep out of control. By one
recent count, 7,366 fires have swept 560,518 acres of
South Florida this year in the course of the six-month
drought. In wide areas the earth itself is destroyed, and
the pungent smoke from the burning muck often black-
ens the skies of Miami.

Little more than 2 inches of rain have fallen across
south Florida in six months, compared with the previous
low of 6 inches recorded in 1947. Scattered showers have
recently brought some relief to limited areas. Drenching
rain fell yesterday. More rain is predicted—today, tomorrow, next week, next month—when the summer's wet
season is finally due to begin.

But the great dying off of the Everglades may never be
reversed. Shrunken and drained to fit the needs of
farmers and developers, its waters channeled to the cities
and the sea, the Everglades today are like a great,
crumbling sponge squeezed dry by man and nature. By
some measures, man's is the harsher hand.

Arthur R. Marshall, a University of Miami ecologist
who has studied the problems of the Everglades basin for
16 years, recently warned Gov. Reubin Askew (D) and
his cabinet that the region is approaching its "limits of
resiliency" as an ecological system.

"Should we continue on our past course of environmental insensitivity or indifference," he warned, "we

shall see a snowballing degeneration of major resources of the Everglades in this decade . . .

"The Everglades is not just stressed—it is distressed—a condition brought about to a major degree by past works of the flood control project."

The project he referred to is the work of the Central and South Florida Flood Control District, known locally as the FCD.

Since the project's inception in 1947, the FCD has spent more than a quarter billion dollars developing a complex network of canals, levees and water control systems aimed at controlling the natural annual flow of water through the region. The broadest effect of the project, which is controlled by the U.S. Army Corps of Engineers, has been the wholesale diversion of water away from the interior basin of the southern peninsula and into the sea.

In narrow, practical terms, the project has meant the "reclamation" of thousands of once-swampy acres for intensive agriculture and housing developments. In the broadest ecological terms, this "progress" has been bought at an unknowable but monumental price.

At the uppermost end of the region's "food chain," alligators and crocodiles presided. As recently as 1950, according to Dr. Frank Craighead, probably two million alligators survived. Today, he says, only 1 to 5% of that number survives. Crocodiles are virtually extinct.

John Ogden, a biologist for the U.S. Park Service stationed in the Everglades, observed that the "general deterioration and destruction of the food chains" has been particularly pronounced at the base, among the small fish, fresh-water shrimp and invertebrates and algae communities upon which "higher" life forms depend.

"As a consequence," he said, "some species that breed in the spring months just gave up this year."

In the meantime salt water is encroaching on the falling fresh water table in South Florida.

The dilemma is evident: the more people flock to south Florida, the more water they need: the more people in south Florida, the less water there can be.

> It may well turn out that the Everglades' present distress is a warning of human disasters yet to come. "The Everglades," said an ecologist, "is trying to tell us something."

This is absolutely the fault of the Corps of Engineers, due to the habitual total lack of adequate engineering analysis. For centuries, Lake Okeechobee had been an adequate total control of the Everglades situation.

A responsible study of the Kissimmee River, Lake Okeechobee, the grass river, Pay-hay-okee, the cypress swamp, Everglades Park complex, and its administration should be with a body or staff having maximum competence and sensitivity to the issues involved. For a century and a half, and up to the present, the Corps has never shown characteristics of thoroughness. For more than half a century the greatest project in its history, the control of the Mississippi River, was fumbled and bungled while the Corps was announcing to the Congress and the country that it was the leader of all the world in that field. Only when, under President Hoover, its whole pattern for the Mississippi River was shown to be profoundly in error, was a great change forced upon the Corps. The chapters on the Hydraulic Laboratory and on Shortening the Mississippi tell that story. Must such a sequence be repeated?

In pursuit of its long held purpose, to be the authority in any situation concerning the use of water, the Corps had placed itself in control of Lake Okeechobee. This lake is a rare controlling and regulating element and is the key to the entire Everglades situation. Before beginning digging, dyking, and diverting the water the Corps would have done well, through engineering analysis, to find out what it was doing. In such an analysis it would have omitted no element or condition in the entire watershed environmental unit from the source area in the group of small lakes in central Florida, then along the Kissimmee River to Lake Okeechobee, which is the control point, and then southward over the Everglades for a hundred miles to the Gulf at the South tip of Florida.

The entire area is very distinctly a clearly defined hydrographic unit.

In the legal creation of the boundaries of the Everglades National Park only the lower part of the broad expanse of the flat Everglades lands was included. As legally defined, the Everglades National Park does not constitute a natural or workable environmental unit. While it includes most of the remarkable ecological treasure of the area, it does not include Lake Okeechobee or the broad strip of Everglades character land between that lake and the legally defined Park boundary or the large cypress swamp along the way. It is by the management and administration of Lake Okeechobee and the intervening stretch of Everglades land and cypress swamp that the remarkable quality of the Park will be preserved or destroyed.

The Corps has tended to take the latter course. Not only was there failure to see the environmental unit as a whole, and to work it out as such, not overlooking any significant element, but along the way there has been continued failure to appraise and to guide the functions of the environmental unit. It seldom, if ever, consults the administration of the park in the carrying out of policy. If it should be assumed that the aim of the Corps is to ignore or to defeat the optimum aim for the Everglades Park, its course would support that assumption.

Today the future of the Everglades as a marvel of ecological value is threatened. The U.S. Corps of Engineers, with its concern for raising beans and tomatoes on land which should be added to the park as a vital element of its preservation, is sacrificing the promise of the Park. The Corps, being dominant in the control of Lake Okeechobee, is largely in the position of determining what course will be taken.

The south Florida environmental unit, like any large and complex engineering problem, should have critical study of every significant factor. But the U.S. Corps of Engineers never acquired a policy of that kind of inquiry. We can expect the Corps to express full intent to make such an analysis, as nothing is easier to the Corps than to make such promises. It has made similar promises many times.

It has been a common assertion of the U.S. Corps of Engineers that it is not a policy-making agency, but only the means for executing policies determined by the United States government, or by the state authority. This is pure fiction, useful to employ in avoiding an issue, or to prevent real purposes from being embarrassingly disclosed. The Corps of Engineers could have refused to participate in any violation of an optimum plan for the area, and could have been the agency for bringing about the fulfillment of such a plan. In the case of the Garrison Reservoir in North Dakota, the Corps was able to enter into policy-making and to radically change legislation. In the case of the Papagos, it went so far as to protest existing legislation and to call for new legislation which would fit its own wishes. There is no reticence in the Corps about interfering with and changing legislation of public policy. Here in Florida is a great national issue which the state may have assumed to be a local issue. The prospective expenditures are very great. With a sound ecological plan for the area, which is naturally and inevitably a unit, the Corps could, in its plans for Lake Okeechobee and other elements, have brought about the fulfillment of an optimum plan. It is only where the Corps wishes to prevent carrying through a program that it pleads its lack of power. With its control of Lake Okeechobee, no great reclamation project would be possible in this case without the approval or help of the Corps.

The Corps of Engineers has considerable power and influence over the destiny of the Florida Everglades. If they had made a complete objective analysis with ecological insight, the government would surely have accepted their solution, since they, not the Congressmen, are engineers. Such an analysis would have thrown light on the wisdom or non-wisdom of the great jetport, and of turning large areas of everglades near the park to raising beans and tomatoes.

To leave the destiny of that great ecological treasure in the hands of the Corps, which up to the present moment has ignored that need, is a tragic policy. Here is an issue of the century being decided by the interests of bean and tomato growers. Tomato growing has unlimited possibilities by advanced methods in our arid lands, and there are alternative locations for airports. There never will be another Everglades Park in all its ecological excellence and wonderful variety.

"Where no vision is, there the people perish." So also may perish man's best possessions of environmental excellence.

Allerton Park

A brief appraisal is presented here of the experience of the Corps of Engineers in the case of the Oakley Dam in Illinois less than five years ago. It is taken from the *Bulletin* of the Sierra Club for August, 1969. Since this project tended to greatly damage very important property of the University of Illinois, to the point of largely destroying it, the project received more persistent and more competent inquiry than is usual. This case is interesting for a number of reasons. It is concerned on a rather large scale with present important issues, including protection of a rare and precious environment, with values in the fine arts and recreation, and also includes the problem of pollution of waters. It is significant in another important respect. The project as a whole is not simple, involving a few clear factors. It is a complex project, calling for competence for each of several important and distinct elements. Each of its numerous parts and phases call for conclusive engineering analysis. The findings of the Corps are in error in a considerable variety of ways. It seems that in several of the various elements in which the Corps worked, it came to erroneous conclusions. The Oakley Dam is a case where there were inadequacies of engineering analysis in each element of the project, indicating such inadequacies to be an habitual characteristic. Such failures of the Corps are in considerable variety. There are numerous ways to be right and to be wrong. Here we observe the versatility of incompetence on the part of the Corps. It must be noted also that this case is concerned, not with the dark ages of the Corps fifty years ago but with live present issues. The discussion follows, from the *Bulletin* of the Sierra Club for August, 1969:

This confrontation was in the making years ago when settlers in Central Illinois first began plowing the nation's richest soil. In pre-pioneer days wide belts of trees flourished along Illinois rivers. As the years passed, the grain fields were pushed to the very edge of the river banks—except in a 1500-acre area along the Sangamon River. Here the primeval forest endured and a long forgotten ecology continued undisturbed.

The area is intact today through the farsightedness of a nineteenth-century Horatio Alger and his philanthropist son. The father, Samuel Allerton, built a fortune in the livestock market, and, as his fortune grew, he invested in land. By 1900 he owned 40,000 acres, including the 19,000 acres of land in Piatt County, Illinois, that he willed to his son, Robert.

Robert Allerton, in addition to administering the family properties, developed a deep interest in the fine arts. It was Robert who took the 1500 acres of black-soiled woodlands in the Sangamon Valley and fashioned one of the most beautiful estates in the Middle West. In the words of a University of Illinois publication: "Here, through the ministry of architecture, sculpture, and landscape design, he illustrated how art and nature may be blended for the delight and edification of man."

In developing the estate, Robert built a 20-room Georgian mansion, created a series of informal and formal gardens, and sowed the property with both originals and copies of some of the world's finest sculpture. In all his plans he considered the native Illinois landscape. His gardens, though some are based on foreign inspiration, feature native floral materials. And most of the 1500 acres, including the bottom lands that fringe the rambling Sangamon River, are covered by a forest that has been evolving undisturbed for 20,000 years.

In 1946 Robert Allerton donated the 1500-acre tract, including the mansion, to the University of Illinois to be used "as an educational and research center, as a forest and wildlife and plantlife reserve, as an example of landscape architecture, and as a public park." Along with the park, Allerton gave nearly 4000 acres of his farmland to provide a permanent income to care for the park.

The Corps finds a Damsite

As with a number of America's natural resources, this gift to the generations to come may not survive the present generation. The Army Corps of Engineers has proposed an Oakley Dam and Reservoir project that would flood more than 1000 acres of Allerton Park on the Sangamon River. Its main reservoir ("conservation" pool) would be 621 feet above sea level and during flood periods would reach 645 feet above sea level. The conservation pool would not inundate Allerton, but the flood pool periodically would cover about 700 acres of the park. The purposes of this dam were water supply for the nearby city of Decatur, flood control, and recreation. In 1962 Congress authorized the project.

During 1965 and 1966 the Corps instituted several changes. The dam was hiked to 60 feet—keep in mind that here on the Illinois prairie every foot added to the height of the dam means another mile of inundated land behind the dam. The conservation pool level was increased to 636 feet and the flood level to 654 feet.

The Corps sought to raise the dam to cover several mistakes made in the 1961 project proposal: siltation was greater than what they had figured and the maximum flood on record was not the one whose statistics they had used initially. By adding a fourth purpose, low flow augmentation (sewage dilution) for Decatur, these mistakes were covered up and the volume of water was increased enough to take care of the errors as well as the low flow.

The increased volume of water would also take care of Allerton Park. Instead of a dam that would trespass on Allerton during flood conditions, the revised project provided a dam that would permanently inundate over 40 per cent of the park.

In addition to the dam and reservoir, the Corps planned

100 miles of downstream channelization on the Sangamon River. The $18 million channel improvement would require that 2800 acres be cleared for flood releases from the Oakley project. Thus, a 100 foot wide spoil bank would dominate the cleared area for the entire 100 miles.

Then, in March of 1969, the Corps reported, that to meet Illinois' new water quality standard, the project had to be enlarged again. The conservation pool was set at an elevation of 641 feet, 20 feet higher than what was authorized by Congress, and the flood pool at 656 feet, 11 feet higher than originally planned. Allerton Park would be gradually split in two, as the waters of the Sangamon spilled over the lowlands. Finally, when the reservoir filled, flooding 650 acres of the park, only the higher fragments of the park on either side of the former river would be above water.

Conservationists Mobilize

In 1967, when the public learned that the revised Oakley project would require bulldozing about 650 acres of Allerton for the conservation pool and the periodic flooding of another 300 acres, the Committee on Allerton Park was formed. A technically diverse group of conservationists—economists, lawyers, engineers, biologists, botanists, zoologists, and artists, they decided to try a new approach in dealing with the Corps. Instead of harping at the Corps for its well known insensitivity to ecological and aesthetic values, the Committee on Allerton met the Corps head-on at a professional level. They out-thought and out-engineered the Corps, proving that an alternate, cheaper, and more aesthetic means existed to solve the same problems that the revised Oakley dam was proposed to solve.

The Committee on Allerton Park criticized the Corps on the following grounds:

(1) *The Corps was incredibly narrow in its exploration of alternatives.* The Committee presented a petition with 20,000 signatures (followed by one bearing 80,000) to Illinois Senators Dirksen and Percy and 22nd District Congressman Springer in December of 1967. The Illinois legislators responded by asking the Corps to restudy the

project. In March 1969 the Corps released 12 alternatives to Oakley, including proposals for an alternate water supply and advanced waste treatment for Decatur. While the Corps was doing its restudy, the Committee continued its investigations. The Committee found that the law states that storage and water releases are not to serve as a substitute for advance treatment or other means of controlling wastes at their sources. Yet the Corps had designated over 16 billion gallons (69 per cent of the initial lake volume) in the Oakley reservoir for low-flow augmentation. In fact, prior to its restudy the Corps had not considered a much cheaper advanced sewage treatment plant as an alternative to dilution storage at Oakley.

Another alternative the Corps neglected until it made its restudy was using the underground Teays Aquifer as an alternate water supply for Decatur. In 1954 Decatur installed two wells in this underground river. The wells have a capacity of five million gallons per day, one-fourth of the city's total current need, but they have never been used. This underground water is free of nitrate pollution, an increasingly dangerous pollutant common to surface water supplies.

The conservationists also found the Corps' plan for downstream channelization illogical. The Corps had calculated the costs of channelizing the 100 mile section of river at $18 million. The Committee for Allerton found that the entire 67,000 acres of bottom land along the same river section—much of which never floods—could be purchased at about the same cost.

(2) *The Corps overstated project benefits and frequently understated project costs.* The Committee on Allerton set its economists, engineers, and lawyers to work on each of the benefits claimed by the Corps for the Oakley project. The Committee's engineers reported that the Corps' claim of flood damage on the lower Sangamon was exaggerated by about 5 to 1, that crop losses occur about one year in 20, and that much of the flooded farmland is now in the federal idle-acres program. Flood damages on the Illinois River, relievable by a project at Oakley, were found to be exaggerated by about 2 to 1.

Recreation accounted for more than 30 per cent of the supposed benefits, so the Committee on Allerton pulled together statistics on recreation in the vicinity of the Oakley project. Within 65 miles of the proposed reservoir there is a population of 1,051,343. In the same area there are 26,838 surface acres of public lakes and only 3,505 acres of public woodlands. Allerton Park, the only large tract, represents one-third of this woodland acreage. However, the Corps of Engineers ignored the aesthetic and scientific values that would be lost, using instead the standard commercial price of bottom lands.

Almost half of the recreation benefit was to come from swimming in the reservoir. Lake Decatur, also a Sangamon river reservoir, was intended for swimming, too. However, Lake Decatur has been closed for several years because of silt and algae-ridden and often polluted water. Oakley, with its low-flow augmentation feature, would be particularly unattractive to swimmers because during the dry summer months the average drawdown would leave an extensive foul-odored mudflat throughout the Allerton Park bottomlands.

The Committee on Allerton discovered that the Corps' revised and expanded reservoir project would provide no additional water for Decatur. The original 621-foot conservation pool included 11,000-acre-feet of water for Decatur and the 636-foot conservation pool allotted Decatur the same number of acre-feet.

The Committee on Allerton also found that the Corps had overstated the benefits from low-flow augmentation. When the Corps decided to include dilution augmentation as a purpose in the multipurpose reservoir, they found it difficult to determine a benefit figure. Thus, they turned to the least-cost alternative concept. They calculated the cost of a single-purpose dam to hold the necessary dilution water and then claimed the cost of this fictitious dam as the benefit for dilution.

Thus the Corps calculated a $24 million low-flow benefit figure—the cost of a single-purpose dam, and they determined that the cost of dilution as a part of a multi-purpose dam is about $10 million. In this way the Corps claimed a benefit-cost ratio for dilution storage of

2.4 to 1. The Allerton Committee engineers calculated the cost of advanced sewage treatment, which would negate the sewage dilution feature of the dam, at about $5 million. The Committee claims that sewage dilution is the real least cost alternative, and that the actual benefit-cost ratio is about .5 to 1. However, the Corps does not customarily accept non-dam alternatives, because dam building is their business.

(3) *The dam is not economically justified at more realistic interest rates.* Congress recently set a new interest rate for computing costs on federally funded projects. Projects authorized before January 1, 1969, use the old 3¼ rate; those authorized after that date use the new 4-5/8 per cent interest rate, which is being raised. Despite the intensive 1969 project revisions, the Corps claims that the old 1962 authorization is still in effect. In this way the Corps is able to use the outdated rate, and they figure the revised project has a benefit-cost ratio of about 1.1. And if the actual rate on government borrowing, which approaches 5¾ per cent, is used, the project goes in the red.

The issue here is that, at a certain date Congress set the rate of interest on investment expenditures to be charged on such public works.

After January 28, 1969, the Corps very greatly enlarged its estimated expenditures, but claimed the old interest rate. At the rate of 3¼% the ratio between cost and value, according to the Corps' estimate of value, would be 1-1/10. After 1969 the Corps very largely increased the cost of its work. By claiming the old interest rate of 3¼% instead of the new rate of 4-5/8%, which made an extremely narrow margin between the cost and profit at the rate of money being paid by the government after 1969 at 5¾%, the entire project would be shown as costing more than it was worth. Many of the Corps projects cost 2 or more times the amount of the first estimates, so that at the official interest rate they would not be self-supporting. The Corps was very adept in juggling accounts of its estimates.

(4) *The Corps outstripped its initial authorization.* The Corps moved ahead—without additional authorization or public hearings—on the revised Oakley project. (These revisions required the purchase of 24,000 acres of land instead of the original 6,200 acres and an expenditure of $75 million instead of the original $29 million.) The Committee on Allerton repeatedly sought hearings on the revised project. But the Corps did not regard these changes as major, explaining that, "such advanced engineering and design almost always involves some refinement of the project."

The Committee on Allerton threatened the Corps with legal action if it would not make public the Army's regulations on public hearings. The Committee's lawyer contended these regulations are information in the public domain. After a year of requests for hearings, the regulations on how to apply for a hearing were finally released. A local governing body had to make the official request (one county and one city council then made such a request), and within three months hearings were held on 14 technical alternatives to the original project.

The Corps Retreats

For two years the Committee on Allerton has continued to check the Corps' data. The Committee's engineers, lawyers, and economists have scored against their Corps counterparts repeatedly. The Corps replaced three of its top people in an effort to meet this unusual challenge. But after two years of being severely drubbed on all its plans, the Corps turned the problem over to the State of Illinois. The state waterways engineers proposed a Waterway Alternative that was agreed to in May 1969 by the City of Decatur, the Board of Trustees of the University of Illinois, and the State of Illinois.

Key conservation victories in the Waterways Alternative are:

(1) Allerton Park is protected from permanent flooding by a return to the originally proposed 621-foot conservation pool and by the development of a major storage capability on a nearby tributary of the Sangamon. During periods of flood, the discharge rate from the reservoir is

to be adjusted to attain, as nearly as possible, the natural seasonal flooding conditions in the park.

(2) Decatur is denied the use of the Sangamon River for sewage dilution, which means the city must turn to advanced sewage treatment.

(3) A 22,500-acre recreational greenbelt is to be developed along the lower Sangamon River in lieu of the much more expensive and severely destructive proposed channel improvement.

The Waterways Alternative represents a defeat for the Corps, a defeat on technical grounds. To insure its gains the Committee on Allerton Park is urging that appropriations for Oakley in the nation's 1970 budget be made with the stipulation that capital expenditures be frozen until the Corps demonstrates the feasibility of and accepts the Waterways Alternative. The Committee considers the dam a compromise, and they have said, "If any larger or more destructive project is proposed, we shall be required to increase the already nation-wide opposition to the total project." A general and two colonels now in Asia know they can do it.[8]

The Corps of Engineers has been characteristically insensitive to the overall needs of the environment. This is due partly to the fact that they have consistently failed to account for all of the factors involved in building public works. The capacity for inclusive analysis is not easy to acquire and West Point has made its acquisition doubly difficult. Through many years up to the present day the patterned West Point training and regime has bred the curious uncreativeness and insensitivity of the Corps of Engineers.

From all parts of America there are cries of remonstrance from those who see destruction of priceless values under way at the hands of the Corps. With its position as almost a separate and independent department of government, and with no legal provision for appraisal of Corps projects, the Corps has great power.

Conclusive engineering analysis deals not only with construction plans, but with everything which pertains to human interest. The Corps' unrelieved absence of sensitivity to human values creates a serious national problem at the present moment. This is particularly true when the conservation of our national resources has become a clear and present need.

NOTES

1. Telegram from Horace S. Oakley to Senator John W. Watson, April 16, 1927.
2. Telegram from H. C. Sylvester, Jr., to Senator John W. Watson, April 16, 1927.
3. Telegram from the International Trust Co. to Senator John W. Watson, April 16, 1927.
4. Telegram from Pershing, Nye, Tallmadge & Bosworth, Denver, Colorado, to Senator John W. Watson, Tallahassee, Florida, April 16, 1927.
5. Marjory Stoneman Douglas, *The Everglades: River of Grass* (Coconut Grove, Florida: Hurricane House Publishers, Inc., 1947), p. 342.
6. Peter Farb, "Disaster Threatens the Everglades," *Audubon* Magazine, Sept.-Oct., 1965, p. 307.
7. *Ibid.*, pp. 302-306.
8. Bruce Hannon and Julie Cannon, "The Corps Out-Engineered," Sierra Club *Bulletin*, Vol. 54, No. 8, Aug. 1969, pp. 8-14.

epilogue

the corps
of engineers
as an
organization

In President F. D. Roosevelt's first administration he had a commission working on possible improvements of the water control laws of the United States. I was a member, and a young man, Gilbert White, served the Chairman somewhat as secretary. From seeing him in action there and from what I had heard I came to respect him. Later he became a part-time consultant of the Corps of Engineers in working out some phases of technology of water control. At present he is Professor of Behavioral Science at the University of Colorado.

Along the way he made critical reference to my work. Here was a man whom I respected and who doubtless had somewhat intimate and favorable relations with the Corps of Engineers. He wrote as follows:

"I disagree with Arthur Morgan on the ability of the Corps of Engineers. The recent self-examination and planning activities carried out by the Corps shows that great modifications are not only possible, but are now going forward.

It may be that there has been a somewhat uniform pattern of Corps of Engineers behavior for a century, but one must in all candor recognize that there has been a remarkable change since General Cassidy took over. When either an engineer or an organization has the courage or insight to radically change its course, it deserves recognition for it."[1]

In searching for evidence of new purpose in the Corps of Engineers, we have received the following from Professor Gilbert White, written June 4, 1971, from the Institute of Behavioral Science, University of Colorado:

"Dear Arthur Morgan:

With regard to your assessment of the Corps of Engineers, I can make a few suggestions that might be of some help to you as you consider a possible epilogue. At the outset, I suppose I should recognize that I am unwilling to write off any person or group of people as being entirely dishonest or unresponsive to human needs, and I don't think that the Corps of Engineers is an exception to this.

Perhaps the best evidence of there having been significant changes in the Corps of Engineers is that a number of important changes in policy were initiated when General Cassidy was Chief of Engineers and that his successor has carried them on and, in fact, extended them.

One clear evidence is contained in the enthusiastic participation by top Corps of Engineers officers in the new flood control policy which is embodied in House Document 465. That policy was initiated in 1966 with solid support from the Chief's office but with almost no understanding or support from the lower echelons. It now is being widely adopted, and I have just seen a report from Prairie du Chien, Wisconsin, in which the Corps of Engineers, instead of recommending large flood control works, proposes contributions of funds towards the cost of relocating unsuitable occupance and towards the cost of flood proofing remaining structures. The fact is that this change in policy is occurring, and that it has been advanced rather than cut off by a subsequent administrator to the man who helped initiate it.

A second concrete piece of evidence is in the framework study for the North Atlantic region which now is in its final stages and which presents for the first time in the United States a set of recommendations giving three alternative public aims (national economic efficiency, regional development, and environmental preservation) as a basis for public choice. This is a fundamental and highly significant shift in the mode of presenting recommendations to the public.

The third concrete case is the initiative taken by the Corps of Engineers in establishing five experimental projects in the use and re-use of solid waste in metropolitan areas around the country. This has been initiated with the support of John Shaeffer of the Office of the Secretary of the Army, who has been on leave from the University of Chicago during the current year, and descriptions of this could be obtained, if you wished, from the office of the Chief.

I do not believe that innovations of this sort and magnitude occurred during the previous administration since Lytle Brown.

Sincerely,

Gilbert White."

In a previous incident, under the direction of Lytle Brown, there was imposed upon the Corps some strikingly efficient work. In that case, however, the improvement of quality did not last beyond the regime set up by Herbert Hoover. Whether the present reported burst of quality has a longer future is not clear. The defects of skill and purpose in the Corps have been long-lasting and deep.

I will refer again to a comment quoted in the fourth chapter, concerning which I asked Gilbert White whether it was correct; he replied in April 1971: "That is entirely accurate." The comment is as follows:

"To expect the Corps of Engineers or Bureau of Reclamation to adopt a new *approach* as opposed to a new technique is like trying to set fire to soggy newspapers."[2]

It was General Cassidy who opposed further comparison of

the Conewango and Kinzua plans in the following contemptuous language:

"If the ladies' flower clubs of America want to contribute a quarter of a million dollars for such a study, we shall be glad to cooperate, but we could not justify the expenditure of *public* funds for such a purpose."

This was on the occasion that President Kennedy was undertaking to carry out his promise that there would be no violation of Indian treaties without competent examination. The treaty with the Senecas was prominent in that issue. Kennedy's request was denied and no examination was allowed. Cassidy expressed the opposition to Kennedy's request and an independent examination.

I shall try to define my position. No matter how powerfully the tradition of the Corps is exerted, occasionally a man will reject that enforced code and will be himself, holding to his personal standards. An example was Robert E. Lee. He planned his course bravely and carefully and never succumbed to the Corps pattern. Such persons should be recognized and respected. The members of the Engineer Corps, like those of the military corps, are graduates of West Point, and have been similarly conditioned. There is a spirit of the Corps and a "loyalty" to the Corps, to which most members conform. It is that spirit which largely rules the Corps. Also there is a body of Corps teaching which commonly comes to be accepted. A recent example of this solidarity: When women and children were assassinated in Viet Nam, that breach of law and of military rule was covered up by the loyalty of officials to each other. This common attitude spread through the ranks. When the Superintendent of West Point was allowed to resign because he was a party to it, the body of students at West Point gave him a rousing ovation.

I shall give a recent personal incident of Corps solidarity. When I took my plans for the Conewango Reservoir to the Chief of Engineers in October, 1958, I found him to be a straightforward appearing person whom I could trust. I said to myself, "I can trust him, and he can trust me." I laid aside my program of opposition for four or five months, while he was examining my plans.

In the meantime, the Subcommittee on Appropriations of the House of Representatives demanded of the Chief of Engineers that he submit to them a comparison of my plan for the Conewango Reservoir with that of the Engineer Corps for the Kinzua Reservoir. The Chief of Engineers submitted a comparison as demanded. He stated that he had personally studied the report carefully, and that it had his full approval. A chief question was whether the Kinzua plan of the Corps or the Conewango plan which I presented, was superior for its purpose. The Conewango plan which I had presented would have four or five times as great capacity for storing water to overcome pollution of the Ohio as would the Kinzua Reservoir. In his wholesale condemnation of my plan for the Conewango, the report of the Chief of Engineers made the following statement:

> "It is not practicable under present authorities to assess benefits for conjectural, possible, future water supply needs as a basis for justifying additional water supply storage.
> That additional investment (for Conewango) could not be justified on the basis of additional benefits that can now be evaluated."[3]

(Omitting some overestimation of the cost of Conewango by the Corps, its cost would not be larger than that of Kinzua.)

The above quotation is the Chief of Engineers speaking against Conewango. But notice what the same Chief of Engineers a few months from that date said of such additional storage when he was addressing the Ohio Valley Improvement Association:

> "The cost of acquiring land for reservoirs is rapidly becoming one of the most serious and expensive items of water resources development throughout the country. . .
> A third and highly important matter is that of combining provision for local and area water supply with Corps of Engineers reservoirs *built primarily for water supply.*"
> (Emphasis added.)[4]

As a matter of fact, the Ohio River is listed as the most polluted river in the United States,[5] and the information given by the Chief of Engineers in several public addresses was accurate. His statements to the Appropriations Subcommittee, made after studying my plans on the Conewango Reservoir, aimed at discrediting my proposals and saving the face of the Corps. This mis-statement was not an unimportant matter, but was of its very essence. The Conewango Reservoir would have caught four or five times as much flood water for the use of the Ohio River in low water, and would have been worth $200,000,000 more than the Kinzua. With building the Conewango Reservoir it would be all or none. With the Conewango Reservoir constructed, the Kinzua would be practically useless. This illustrates how far the Corps would go to save its face. I do not believe that the Chief of Engineers would have gone that far himself. He was, I think, under the very powerful compulsion of the Corps.

In the 1920's under President Hoover and Lytle Brown as Chief of Engineers, there appeared to be a far-reaching reform. The improvement was so striking that the Corps could not repudiate it, but absorbed it into its work and rewrote its history to claim as its own work. Yet when the stimulus of Hoover and Lytle Brown and two other men had passed, the Corps as a whole reverted to its ancient pattern.

Brigadier-General Groves, deputy director of Corps public works, said in March 1971:

> "I find it quite refreshing and reassuring that some of these people are coming to appreciate the position we are in and the measures we've taken."[6]

Currently, the General said, the Corps and most conservation organizations are in general agreement on a nationwide environmental program . . . but the squabbling will resume when it comes down to deciding which rivers will be primarily for naturalists and what streams will be developed for "pleasure seekers."[7]

Such an expression illustrates the need for change. The assumption of the Corps that there are notable differences between naturalists and pleasure seekers is characteristic Corps misrepresentation. Take, for instance, the case of the Oakley Reservoir. Three major elements are described in the chapter on "Insensitivity to Environment":

(1) The destruction for recreation purposes of a hundred miles of river margin.

(2) The creation of a reservoir to ruin Allerton Park, where mechanical disposal of waste would be far cheaper and better than a reservoir.

(3) The flooding of Allerton Park with its values for recreation and the arts and for natural environment.

There is no mention of the legal battle between the Corps and the University of Illinois:

> "1971—A suit to stop the entire Oakley Project is filed in Federal Court in Washington by the Environmental Defense Fund, the Committee on Allerton Park, the Piatt County Board of Supervisors, affected scientists, land-owners and others."[8]

Neither is there any suggestion of other issues which should be major, such as the yet-threatened complete destruction by the Corps of that finest of all natural American preserves, the Florida Everglades. Nor is there reference to the unnecessary, wanton and near-complete destruction of one of the nearest approaches to an ideal human community that has existed: The communities of the Three Affiliated Tribes in north-west North Dakota, where after centuries of searching for an ideal environment a group of people lived in a community with goodwill, economic independence and a large degree of safety from all except the Corps of Engineers, with adequate economy and a rare approach to communal fellowship.

The issue of human environment is one case. During the seventy years that the Corps of Engineers has had the control of river pollution in their hands, the Refuse Act of 1899 was a dead letter. Now, when public concern begins to enter this field of the Corps, they speak of "rediscovering the law." Under this Act the Corps of Engineers had the obligation to issue permits to industrial firms to dump waste into navigable rivers. This gave the Corps the authority and duty to control or to discontinue extreme pollution.

The Corps has become so powerful with the help of the Rivers and Harbors Congress, with Appropriations Committee chairmen appointed through its own influence, in favoring appointments to its friends and denying them to its opponents in Congress, and through its constantly repeated descriptions of wasteful and grossly mistaken and destructive work as the greatest in the world, that it has defeated or ignored President Hoover, President F. D. Roosevelt, President Truman and President Kennedy. As Secretary Ickes put it:

"One way to describe the Corps of Army Engineers is to say that it is the most powerful and most pervasive lobby in Washington. The aristocrats who compose it are our highest ruling class. Within the field they have elected to occupy, they are the law,—and therefore above the law. Senator Douglas of Illinois said on the floor of the Senate on March 29, 1950: 'They (the Army Engineers) have become the Congress of the United States.' "[9]

Such and much more Secretary Ickes quotes from Congressmen and from perhaps the only Appropriations Committee chairman in Congress, Clarence Cannon, who was free to criticize the Corps:

". . . despite their disingenuous, but purposeful, presentations to the contrary, the Engineers do, when they feel like it, make policy without even consulting the Congress or reporting to it. Nothing could be worse for the country than this willful and expensive Corps of Engineers, closely banded together as a self-serving clique in defiance of their superior officers and in contempt of public welfare."[10]

When Mr. Maass decided to write a book drastically criticizing the Corps of Engineers and their ignoring the President of the United States in order to help California capitalists carry through an enormous financial grab, he used as the introduction of the book the condemnations quoted above, and much more.

Under such circumstances what could the Corps do to quiet such criticism? The answer was not difficult. Put the author on the payroll. Let him work on engineering technicalities. There he could be doing perfectly honest work. So we find our very critical author doing honest chores for the Corps with Corps funds received through a university. There is no fundamental change in the Corps character or policies. During the intervening years since Maass' book was published, several of the most atrocious ecological tragedies in the history of America have been perpetrated by the Corps. Perhaps the most irreparable is the steady removal of any possible recovery of that incomparable national ecological treasure, the Florida Everglades, which had no comparison in America. Among others were the Cross-Florida Barge Canal, until it finally was stopped by President Nixon; the Sangamon River in Illinois with the destruction of the rare Allerton Park of which Illinois University is guardian for this state treasure; the Rappahannock River in Virginia; and the Red River Gorge in Kentucky.

The Corps scheme worked. In the Congressional Record, Mr. Maass now comes to the defense of the Corps. Naturally he gives the Corps a gentle slap on the wrist. To do less would be too obvious. He said he "is still critical of the Corps." He recommended one reform, which, incidentally, was already in effect, and then he proceeded to say he didn't think it was fair

> "to blame the Corps alone for doing what a great many Americans plainly wanted done at the time the Corps undertook its various assignments."[1]

(For instance, very many Americans wanted to raise beans and tomatoes around the edges of the Everglades, where the natural result would be the destruction of the Everglades. "Many men" want most everything.) Putting men on the payroll to do honest jobs of *technical* development is such an honorable way to bring quiet.

We mention this instance pointedly, because it may be that the Corps has in mind another process which may well serve its purpose. For more than seventy years the Corps has had the only legal authority for checking pollution in our rivers, and has done absolutely nothing about it. The trouble was not the state of technology. The Corps, with its billions of dollars, and with its habit of getting what funds it wanted for various purposes, could have created its own technology. For instance, for fifty years the Corps was opposed to the hydraulic laboratory, until a great engineer, John R. Freeman, committed his later years to bringing it about. In the 1920's Freeman had the active support of most leading private engineers in professional life. Yet the Corps was so strong in Congressional manipulation of appropriation chairmanships that it could ignore them. What changed the situation was the ability of President Hoover to refuse appointment to a whole galaxy of the elite of the Corps, to pass by ten successive nominations as Chief Engineer of the Corps, and to put in office as Chief a man in total rebellion to the Corps, and another as President of the Mississippi River Commission. These men, Lytle Brown and Ferguson, and a young rebel Corps member, Lieutenant Vogel, who had gone to Europe to see facts for himself, entirely discredited the whole vast structure of Corps theory for fifty years, as a result of careful research in the new hydraulic laboratory, which the Corps had fought stubbornly to prevent for half a century. But when President Hoover and these men were dead or retired, the Corps falsely claimed those enormous gains as its own work, and back to its old ways.

In the case of river pollution, until very lately, there has been no John R. Freeman to entirely depart from Corps practice and to discover for it the process of engineering research. In the matter of pollution the Corps, though having clear cut power, waited for the general public to wake up. The reason probably is that, as disclosed in the first chapter of this book, the Corps never has been pioneer and research-minded, nor has West Point given it the education to make it so.

Lieutenant-General Frederick J. Clarke, current Chief of Engineers, said:

". . . meeting . . . demands for water must inevitably have an impact on the landscape. But we of the Corps believe . . . we can plan to meet the needs in ways that will result in a balanced and harmonious treatment of resources and environment."[1] [2]

Its technique has been intrigue, lobbying, dictatorship and manipulation. Had Freeman and Hoover concerned themselves with research on pollution there might have been imposed upon the Corps half a century ago the not too technical research to create and direct public concern. In the immediate past, the Corps has been no further along in pollution control than it was seventy years ago. Had the Corps been what Thomas Jefferson dreamed of, and not in the tradition of Napoleonic advisors and officers and admirers in the "Napoleon Club" of West Point for a century, and of its carefully secluded and indoctrinated young men, the whole story probably would be very different.

Today a hope for a striking change is in prospect for America, but with the Corps holding a position from which it may return for greater power than ever.

That new hope is the recent creation of the E.P.A. (Environmental Protection Agency). The beginning of the new movement was a quiet taking over of some of the fundamental research so long avoided or overlooked by the Corps whose particular duty it was. At first it was Professor Warren Thornthwaite of New Jersey and Chicago who was one of the pioneers in sewage disposal. Others were Eugene T. Jensen, Senator Clifford Case of New Jersey, John R. Shaeffer, Richard Parizek, Robert Jordan, and Arthur Maass. The E.P.A. needed money—a few million dollars—barely a few days' funds for the powerful Corps. They got it from the O.M.B.—Office of Management and Budget.

In the negotiations between President Nixon, the E.P.A. and the Corps, an agreement has been (tentatively, perhaps) reached. President Nixon showed some muscle when he peremptorily cancelled the work of the Corps on the Cross-Florida Barge Canal. The Corps had the idle money, committed to research, which did not much interest the Corps.

The Corps was playing for great stakes. For fifty years the Corps had done nothing to study the problem of river pollution. Now, with the prospect of stopping pollution in all America, if the Corps should have a practical if not theoretical monopoly of that field, increase in function and power might be phenomenal. With its proven ability to retard or to enlarge operations by its present methods of political manipulation, its expenditures and its political influence might be very great. It might become the dominant political power in America, and its present great power might seem small in comparison. A reported solution was as follows:

The understanding between the E.P.A. and the Corps gave the E.P.A. clear control of what should be done and how:

> "The Corps assignment was to function as a 'consultant' to the E.P.A. in actual designing and building of projects—laying out specifications, drawing up contracts, and seeing that private contractors meet the specifications."[13]

Under such agreement probably eighty cents of every dollar would be spent by the Corps, as well as the real determination of what was to be spent.

The issues are being worked out. On the one side are the President, the E.P.A. and the O.M.B. A general sentiment seems to be: "If you can't lick them, join them." Looking back over the Corps' record for a hundred and fifty years and its feline qualities, I am reminded of the rhyme:

> "There was a young lady of Niger
> Who smiled as she rode on a tiger.
> They returned from the ride
> With the lady inside
> And the smile on the face of the tiger."

Is there enough realism in the people of America to face this issue?

What evidence is there that the work of the recent "progressive" Chief of Engineers would be more lasting? Has not the country suffered for over a century from a Corps-wide pattern of thought and action? Does it not seem that a change is necessary which will displace this lasting condition with a new type of control under radically different management? Such change is increasingly necessary. Yet the regime of indoctrination of young men in the West Point pattern of the Military Academy has the qualities, not of an individual man, but of an institution.

Just before going to press, we learn that the Corps and the Environmental Protection Agency have agreed to postpone the operation of the law prohibiting the discharge of industrial waste into streams. Is it possible that the E.P.A. has awakened to the enormous increase of Corps practice which would be involved? Is it possible that the E.P.A. is hesitating to enter into that fatal complex? May it be avoided? Or is that too much to hope?

SOURCES FOR EPILOGUE

1. Gilbert White, Letter to Arthur E. Morgan, April 21, 1971.
2. *Ibid.*
3. General E. C. Itschner, *Analysis of Allegheny Reservoir and Alternate Proposal of Dr. Arthur E. Morgan* to the Subcommittee on Public Works of the House Appropriations Committee, 1958.
4. General E. C. Itschner, Address to the Ohio Valley Improvement Association, Cincinnati, Ohio, Oct. 26, 1959, pp. 6, 7, 8.
5. Jack Shepherd, "Le Panorama 'Ecologique Fantastique': Where you won't swim this summer." *Look* Magazine, May 4, 1971, p. 25.
6. Brigadier-General Richard Groves, Interview with the Associated Press, reported in the *Christian Science Monitor*, March 17, 1971.
7. *Ibid.*
8. J. C. Marlin, editor, "The Battle for the Sangamon." Publication largely through the generosity of Champaign County Audubon Society, and landowners and scientists adversely affected by the Oakley Project, May, 1971, p. 13.

9. Harold Ickes, Foreword to *Muddy Waters* by Arthur Maass, Harvard University Press, Cambridge, Mass., 1951, p. ix.

10. *Ibid.*, p. xiv.

11. Arthur Maass, Letter in the Congressional Record, Extensions of Remarks, pages E-10680 to 10681, December 1970.

12. Lieut.-Gen. Frederick J. Clarke, Chief of Engineers, quoted in the *Wall Street Journal*, Jan. 6, 1970, p. 19, col. 1.

13. John Lear, Science Editor, "Environment Repair: The U.S. Army Engineers' New Assignment," *Saturday Review*, May 1, 1971.

index